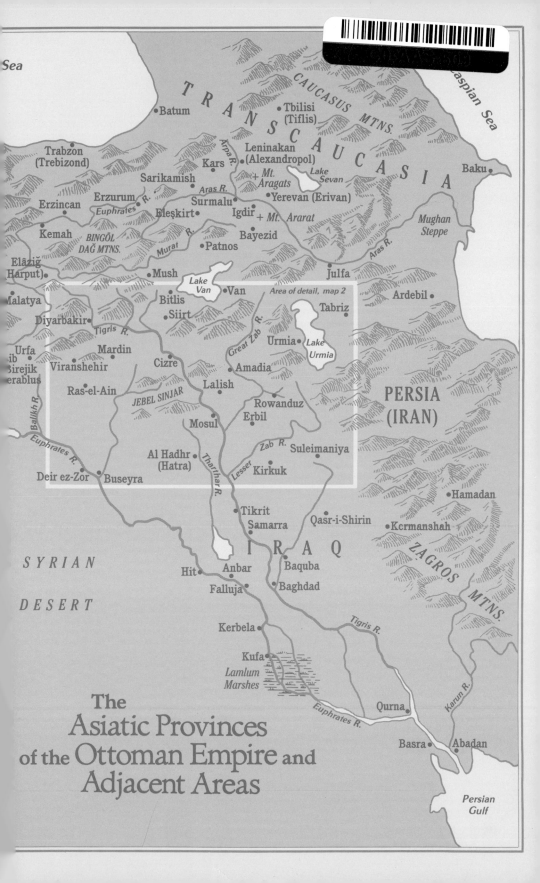

Sea

Caspian Sea

TRANSCAUCASIA

CAUCASUS MTNS.

•Batum

•Tbilisi (Tiflis)

Trabzon (Trebizond)

Kars

Leninakan (Alexandropol)

Baku•

Sarikamish

+ Mt. Aragats

Lake Sevan

Erzurum

Aras R.

•Yerevan (Erivan)

Euphrates R.

Surmalu

Igdir•

Mughan Steppe

Erzincan

Eleşkirt•

+ Mt. Ararat

Kemah

BINGÖL DAĞ MTNS.

Murat R.

Bayezid

•Patnos

Aras R.

Elâzığ (Harput)•

•Mush

Lake Van

•Van

Julfa•

Ardebil •

Malatya•

Bitlis

Area of detail, map 2

•Siirt

Tabriz•

Diyarbakir•

Tigris R.

Great Zab R.

Urmia•

Lake Urmia

Urfa•

Mardin•

Cizre•

•Amadia

PERSIA (IRAN)

Viranshehir•

ib

Birejik

Ras-el-Ain•

JEBEL SINJAR

Lalish•

erablus

Rowanduz•

Balikh R.

Mosul•

Erbil•

Euphrates R.

Al Hadhr (Hatra)•

Tharthar R.

Zab R.

Suleimaniya•

Lesser

Deir ez-Zor•

•Buseyra

Kirkuk•

•Hamadan

•Tikrit

Qasr-i-Shirin•

•Kermanshah

Samarra

I R A Q

ZAGROS MTNS.

S Y R I A N

•Hit

•Anbar

•Baquba

D E S E R T

Falluja•

•Baghdad

Tigris R.

•Kerbela

Kufa•

Lamlum Marshes

Qurna•

Karun R.

The Asiatic Provinces of the Ottoman Empire and Adjacent Areas

Basra•

•Abadan

Persian Gulf

The

Yezidis

The
Yezidis

A Study in Survival

John S. Guest

KPI

London and New York

First published in 1987 by KPI Limited
11 New Fetter Lane, London EC4P 4EE

Distributed by
Routledge & Kegan Paul, Associated Book Publishers (UK) Ltd.
11 New Fetter Lane, London EC4P 4EE

Methuen Inc., Routledge & Kegan Paul
29 West 35th Street
New York, NY 10001, USA

Produced by Worts-Power Associates

Set in Baskerville
by Illustrated Arts Ltd., 1 Lower Road, Sutton, Surrey SM1 4QJ
and printed in Great Britain
by Dotesios Printers Ltd, Bradford-on-Avon, Wiltshire.

ISBN 07103 0115-4

Contents

To
Margaret

List of Illustrations

Preface

A few years ago my family and I visited a village in Turkey inhabited by Yezidis. The Yezidis are a community of about 150,000 people who possess their own religion, quite distinct from their Moslem and Christian neighbours. They live in the northern parts of Iraq and Syria, in eastern Turkey and in the Armenian and Georgian republics of the USSR.

About half of the Yezidis live in northern Iraq, where the principal shrine of the community is located. Regrettably, I have not been able to visit the Yezidis in Iraq. My main contact has been with villagers in eastern Turkey, some of whom live and work in West Germany.

This book stems from a conversation with the Yezidi priest of the village where I stayed on my second visit. Pointing to the newly constructed schoolhouse, he remarked that now the children were learning to read and write they were asking him questions about the Yezidi scriptures and the history of the community. Lacking any written material, he could only repeat to them the oral traditions he had himself learned as a child.

Studies of the Yezidi religion have been written by Christians and Moslems from time to time. Perhaps only a Yezidi can write a definitive book about it. The third chapter of this book gives a general outline of the Yezidi religion; English translations of their two sacred books and their principal prayer are appended at the end of the book.

The history of this community, which goes back 900 years — even longer if its antecedents are taken into account — represents an extraordinary record of survival in a harsh environment. This narrative, pieced together from the testimony of those who knew or dealt with the Yezidis from their earliest days through 1957, is designed to fill a niche in Near Eastern history. I hope that it may be useful to my friend in Kurukavak.

The composition of this book has been eased and enriched by the help and advice I have received from many quarters.

I am most grateful for the access to official documents granted by the Public Record Office and the India Office Library and Records. Transcripts/translations of Crown-copyright records in the Public Record Office and unpublished Crown-copyright material in the India Office Records reproduced in this book appear by permission of the Controller of Her Majesty's Stationery Office. I am also grateful for similar permission from the French Ministère des Relations Extérieures, Division Historique des Archives Diplomatiques, and the Sacra Congregazione per l'Evangelizzazione dei Popoli o 'De Propaganda Fide'. In addition, Dr Ertuğrul Zekâi Ökte obtained for me copies of a number of relevant documents from the Ottoman archives in Istanbul.

Dr Abd el-Salam el-Awadly, General Inspector of Antiquities, and Dr Henri A. Arrad kindly accompanied me on my visit to the mausoleum of Sheikh Zein ed-Din Yusuf in Cairo at a time when it was not generally open to the public and enabled me to photograph the inscriptions.

I should also thank the following institutions for their kind permission to consult and, in the case of certain extracts, quote from documents in their archives: Church Missionary Society and the University of Birmingham Library, where the CMS archives are located; Presbyterian Historical Society, Philadelphia; Royal Geographical Society; The Society for Promoting Christian Knowledge (through the kind offices of the late Miss Teresa Child); United Church Board for World Ministries (successor to the American Board of Commissioners for Foreign Missions) and the Houghton Library; Harvard University, where the ABCFM archives are located; and the United Society for the Propagation of the Gospel. I am also obliged to the British Library, Department of Manuscripts, for permission to consult the Layard papers; to St. Antony's College, Middle East Centre, for permission to consult the C. J. Edmonds papers in their possession; and to the University of Newcastle upon Tyne, Department of Archaeology, for providing me with material from the Gertrude Bell Collection.

This book could not have been written if I had not been able to draw on the resources of some fifty public, private and university libraries in Britain, Continental Europe, the Middle East and North America which have allowed me to consult their collections or have sent me copies (often without charge) of material I had requested. In particular I should express my deep gratitude to the New York Public Library, especially to the staffs of the Oriental and Slavonic Divisions and to Mr Domenick Pilla and his colleagues in the Photographic Service of the library.

The author's venture into the Middle Eastern literary field owes much to the encouragement and advice received over the past six years from academic and lay friends (none of whom bears any responsibility for the contents of this book). Among them I am honoured to cite Dr Adriano Alpago-Novello; Fakhri N. Bakir and his brother Tahsin Bakr; Dr R. D. Barnett; Br Robert A. Bellows II OCD; Dr Erika S. Bleibtreu; Dr Sebastian Brock; Dr J. F. Coakley; Dr Dominique Collon; Dr Erica Cruikshank Dodd; Dr Nuri Eren; Dr Ahmet Evin; Prof F. M. Fales; David H. Finnie; Mrs Dorothea Seelye Franck; Prof Cyrus H. Gordon; my cousin Evan Guest; Chorepiscopus H. Aziz Günel; Dr Talat Halman; Prof R. Stephen Humphreys; Walter G. Korntheuer; Mrs Frances N. Lyman; Ms Eileen McIlvaine; Prof David MacKenzie; John MacPhee; Prof Dr Rudolf Macuch; Ali H. Neyzi; Edgar O'Ballance; Fethi Pirinçcoğlu; Clive Rassam; Dr Julian E. Reade; J. M. Rogers; Rodney Searight; A. Joshua Sherman; Rev William A. Taylor; David Townes; Gordon Waterfield; Victor Winstone; Dr M. J. L. Young and Prof Constantine K. Zurayk. I have also been kindly permitted to consult the unpublished manuscripts written by Mrs Franck (now at the Amherst College Library) and by Father Aziz Günel (in his possession).

I should like to acknowledge a specially heartfelt debt to two extraordinary men, Père J. M. Fiey OP., and the late Dr Henry Field; I wish that circumstances had permitted me to spend more time with each of them.

I need hardly state how pleased I was, at a critical point in my effort, when Prof Cunningham agreed to write a foreword to this book.

I have been exceptionally fortunate in having the opportunity to meet two living participants in twentieth-century Yezidi history — Major-General H. P. W. Hutson, RE, and Princess Wansa Ismail el-Amawy. I have been privileged to spend several hours with each of them and have reviewed with them the portions of my book that touch on their lives. In both cases, however, the author is solely responsible for the narrative of the events in which they took part.

I am grateful for the loan of photographs from General Hutson and his grandson Charles Walker; Princess Wansa and her brother Prince Mua'wia Ismail Al-Yazidi; Dr Dominique Collon; Rev. Dr Edwin C. Coon; Père J. M. Fiey, OP; John MacPhee and Major J. R. C. Riley. Two photographers, Tim Gidal and Elsie Trask Wheeler, kindly supplied prints for inclusion in this book.

I am immeasurably obliged to those kind friends who have enabled me to utilize source materials available only in Arabic, Turkish and other oriental languages — not only by translating for me certain key passages, but also by reviewing the contents of several major publications.

In first place I should acknowledge the contribution of Ms Rend al-Rahim, who led me through the principal Arabic source materials and has been a much-needed editorial assistant.

I should also thank my other Arabic translators, Prof Mona Mikhail, Prof Douglas Crow and an unnamed student of Prof Aptullah Kuran; my Turkish helpers, Ms Canan Usman, Günhan Demiralp, Dr Metin Kunt and Sefer Özdemir; my guide through Armenian sources, Dr James Russell; and Dr Sidney H. Griffith, who translated for me some puzzling Syriac texts.

Last but far from least I thank my typist, Ms Carol Wilson of New York City for her patience and endurance in converting a scissors and paste manuscript into publishable form.

Foreword

John Guest has chosen to write about one of those tantalisingly elusive communities, often small in numbers, which one finds here and there embedded colloidally in the main strata of Middle East societies; in this case, the Yezidis, a people whose very antiquity invites consideration of an associated mystery, the mechanics of survival for a small group when confronted with the constant challenge and threat of cultural assimilation. The very few European travellers who crossed the comfortless and unmapped wastes of northern Mesopotamia in the nineteenth century occasionally encountered the name, but only uncertainly the reality, of the Yezidis, a community usually dismissed by the Ottoman pashas of Mosul, in whose province they were largely to be found, as a worthless set of devil-worshipping trouble makers. They only worsened the nomadic turbulence of Ottoman Kurdistan, exchanging the life of sedentarists for that of marauders whenever a sequence of dry seasons occurred, or rival Kurdish tribal confederations closed in on their temporary success as farmers.

Unclassifiable with Muslims, Christians or Jews as *Ahl al-Kitab*, as people blessed with the divine revelation of a God-inspired book, the Yezidis found themselves consigned by their nominal rulers to the *Dahr ul-Harb*, that Domain of War where unguided mankind lived in theological darkness. Consequently, Yezidi land, lives and property were available to any pious folk able to prevail over them, and in effect they were outlaws, which was by no means the fate of most Kurds, however great their reputation for disloyalty at the Ottoman Porte. Extant eighteenth-century *firmans* admonish *vezirs* and pashas to be mindful of the Yezidis as an intractable law-and-order problem. While a few Europeans sensed that Ottoman knowledge of the Yezidi people and their religion was sketchy in the extreme, fewer still possessed the linguistic skills necessary to press more systematic enquiry to a fruitful conclusion. Just finding the Yezidis in their mountainous homelands was difficult enough. Thus for a long time they made only peripheral appearances in the scholarship of orientalists or the recollections of travellers.

In the eleventh edition of the *Encyclopaedia Britannica*, completed in 1911, the Yezidis are summarized as

> a sect of devil-worshippers...they regard the devil as creative agent of the Supreme God, a reinstated fallen angel who is the author of evil. They avoid mentioning his name and represent him by the peacock. They regard Christ as an angel in human form and recognize Mahomet as a prophet with Abraham and the patriarchs. They believe in a future life and practise both circumcision and baptism...Their sacred book is called *Al-Yalvah*, and its chief exponent was Shaikh Adi (*c.* 1200).

This was an agglomeration of truth, half-truth, and untruth, and it would have been nearer reality to perceive the Yezidis as angel-worshippers, certainly not as subscribers to a satanic cult. How they would have intrigued and astonished the author of *Paradise Lost*!

The trickle of Yezidi studies never quite dried up. To the *Britannica's* offering of Layard's *Nineveh and its Remains* (1850) and Menant's *Les Yézidiz* (1892), John Guest has been able to draw on the help of a fitful flow of occasionally quite noteworthy scholarship, not least in the translation and exegesis of Yezidi sacred texts. Over time, therefore, one might look for a more sustained and authoritative statement on this interesting people. The fifteenth edition of *Encyclopaedia Britannica*, completed in 1974, gives a brief, fairly accurate, description of the Yezidis. Fortunately, the now quite elderly *Encyclopaedia of Islam*, itself in process of revision, still offers over two columns of secondary references, and the last volume to appear will surely incorporate a good deal from the unusual diversity of primary materials on which Guest has drawn, as well as from his own, present contribution to the secondary sources.

The core community of the Yezidis has resided immemorially in what is today Kurdish Iraq. Its religious focus has been the Lalish valley, north of Mosul where the tomb of Sheikh Adi is surrounded by those of lesser holy men, and where for many generations past the valley has come to life in the autumn with lamps decorating the tombs, pilgrimages and processions, ritual ablutions, music and dancing. The physical centre of Yezidi survival in times of persecution, however, has long been the Jebel Sinjar, a great rock citadel west of Mosul in the fringes of the desert. From distant memories of conducting tribal reconnaissances in the area in a fabric-covered, vintage aircraft without a radio, the present writer can testify to the extraordinary isolation of this scorched plateau in the heat-haze of the northern Jazira. Small wonder the Ottomans lacked the will or means to subjugate the area, or that the Sinjar has been the Yezidis' guarantee of survival and separateness. Its meagre permanent population speaks Arabic as its second tongue, just as the scattered Yezidi pockets in eastern Anatolia use Turkish and the Yezidis in Transcaucasia use Russian, Armenian or Georgian in addition to their primary language, Kurdish.

Tradition as well as geography has isolated the Yezidis. According to some investigators, they believe they are descended miraculously from the seed of Adam after his death, and so must forever segregate themselves from the rest of mankind, the descendants of Eve. In Ottoman times monogamy, endogamy and emigration restrained their numbers, and in the Young Turk census of 1912 the Yezidi population in the province of Mosul is put at 18,000. Russian statistics show 24,500 Yezidis living in Transcaucasia in that year. Today John Guest estimates the Yezidi population at 150,000 – close to two thirds in Iraq, the rest in the Soviet Union, Turkey and Syria. The Yezidis are segmented by national borders, some of them closely guarded, and are vulnerable to governmental pressures in the countries where they live. This, nevertheless, is the context, tolerable rather than tolerant, in which the Yezidis have so long endured. If, despite their long record of survival, the community succumbs to the forces of nationalism or secularism, John Guest's tribute to the grand matriarch who governed the Yezidis for the first half of this century may prove, after all, to be the end of a very old song.

In Guest's account, the reader will find the continuum of religious practices as interesting as the shifting fortunes of the Yezidi communities. The clerical hierarchy, the sacred books, the brass or copper peacocks commemorative of Melek Taus and the other angels who assisted at the Creation, are all here. Melek Taus in particular is that fallen angel, restored through his repentance to God's favour, who ever afterward supervised the worldly affairs of mankind as the active agent of a passive God; far from inspiring worship of Satan, it was Melek's tears which extinguished the fires of Hell, a locality which has no place in Yezidi thought. At every turn in the narrative, the reader will find reasons for pondering the origins of Yezidi faith; shamanism shows in the burial procedures, the importance attached to visions and dreams, the use of dancing as exorcism; Nestorian Christian influences seem implicit in the practice of baptism, the use of wine in a eucharistic sense, and the willingness of Yezidis to attend church occasions like weddings; Islam may underlie the commitments to fasting, pilgrimage and circumcision, and Sufism the attachment to tomb-visiting, to secrecy and to revelation through ecstasy. Were the Yezidis once Nestorians, or Jacobite Christians, who came under Islamic dominance, as has been suggested? To speculate further back in time and argue a case for Zoroastrian origins seems to place a heavier burden of interpretation on the existing evidence than it can bear.

Allan Cunningham
Professor of History
Simon Fraser University
Burnaby, British Columbia

Chapter One

Antecedents

The people and events described in this book belong to a world, once known as the Near East, visited by few people nowadays. The cities are crowded, but the highways and rail lines carry only intermittent traffic and the rivers flow silently toward the sea. Most of the frontiers are closed.[1]

In the countryside life goes on as it has for thousands of years in these ancient lands. Shepherds tend flocks of sheep and goats, farmers raise crops from the fertile soil and camels aid man to subsist in the deserts to the south. But one element is missing — the immemorial movement of people and their animals — the traders, migrants, pilgrims and preachers who once frequented the traditional routes connecting the Mediterranean basin with the world east of Aleppo.

Before modern technology created air lines and motor highways across the desert, travellers were obliged to follow routes where they could find water and pasture for their livestock and could expect a reasonable degree of security from robber tribes. In those days three historic routes connected the trading cities of the Levant with Mesopotamia — the mellifluous name given by the Greeks to Iraq.[2]

The 'Great Desert Route', most direct of all, followed a series of water holes south of the Euphrates to Basra; but it was often endangered by tribal wars. The 'Little Desert Route' followed the Euphrates to a point level with Baghdad, making the final stages overland; the river itself was navigable most of the year.

But the preferred route was the one from Aleppo to Mosul and thence down the Tigris valley. At Mosul travellers could elect to transfer their families and goods to *keleks* — rafts supported by inflated sheepskins — for a swifter, less arduous passage downstream to Baghdad. Others crossed over the pontoon bridge to Mosul to follow the old 'Royal Road' by way of Erbil and Kirkuk to Baghdad.

Caravans, resembling modern convoys, were organized by important merchants at regular intervals, except during the hottest summer months. Other merchants, livestock dealers and ordinary travellers were welcome to join, thereby spreading the cost of the armed escort and the payments to the tribes whose pastures were crossed. A typical caravan of loaded camels, accompanied by thousands of horses, sheep and goats, would cover the 400 miles between Aleppo and Mosul in thirty to forty days.

Leaving Aleppo by the el-Hadid gate, the route crosses fifty miles of rolling country, dotted with beehive-shaped dwellings, to reach the great bend of the Euphrates, which flows from its sources in the Anatolian mountains south-westward to a point only 120 miles from the Mediterranean sea. The river, torrential in the Anatolian canyons, can be crossed at Birecik (the present Route E24 bridge), at Jerablus (the Baghdad railway bridge) and at other points downstream to Meskene (now submerged by the lake behind the Tabqa dam).[3] From this point the river turns to the southeast and runs through desert country until it reaches the lowlands of Iraq. Here, lined by date groves and tapped along its left bank by canals cut by Nebuchadnezzar and later kings, the Euphrates flows gently past the ruins of Babylon, Erech and Ur to join the Tigris at Qurna, the traditional site of the Garden of Eden. The united rivers flow past Basra to discharge into the gulf at Fao.

After crossing the Euphrates the caravan route runs along the foothills of the Anatolian plateau to Urfa — once known as Edessa or Callirhoe, the 'city of beautiful springs'. From Urfa the Balikh (Fish) river, much favoured by carp, flows south to the Euphrates past Harran, where the patriarch Abraham camped for several years with his flocks on the long journey from Ur to the lands of Melchizedek in Palestine and to remoter destinations in Egypt and Arabia. (In July 1911 the British archaeologist T. E. Lawrence walked from Harran to Jerablus in thirteen days.)[4]

At Urfa there was a choice between two routes. Camel caravans continued across the Khabur river basin to stage in the plain below Mardin. Hoofed animals generally followed another old trade route striking northeast from Urfa over the volcanic Karaca Dağ mountains to the walled city of Diyarbakir on the right bank of the Tigris. An extension of this route crossed the Tigris below Diyarbakir and two of its tributaries farther east, finally heading north up a third valley to the strategically located hill town of Bitlis. Once past Bitlis, this route followed the southern shore of Lake Van to the city of Van and thence eastward to Persia and Turkestan.

Below Diyarbakir the Tigris (traditionally known as 'the arrow') gathers speed, swollen by water from its northern tributaries and confined by rocky sides as it thrusts its way through the mountains to the Mesopotamian plain. Travellers who chose to travel by kelek from Diyarbakir never forgot the fearsome stretches where the river twisted and hurtled between sheer rock walls while passengers cast coins into the water to appease the dreaded whirlpools. The river flowed calmer as it approached Jezira b. Omar (now Cizre). But most merchants preferred to take the easy route south from Diyarbakir to the old fortress city of Mardin that overlooks the rich bottomlands of Mesopotamia.

On a clear day one can see from Mardin a range of hills stretching across the horizon to the south. The Jebel Sinjar, 60 miles long and 4914 ft high at its summit (snow-capped in winter), looms over the desert like an isolated plateau, recalling to a German observer the sheer cliffs of Heligoland in the North Sea.[5]

The northern slope of the Jebel Sinjar is a steep escarpment, indented by ravines, with manna-bearing oak forests and terraced gardens where grapes, figs and pomegranates grow. On the southern side clear mountain streams flow across a tableland past Beled Sinjar, capital of the district, down to the flat lands below. Sinjar water, channelled through underground conduits, once irrigated groves of date palms, orange and lemon trees and flowed into the Tharthar — the lost river of Mesopotamia — but for many centuries the plain south of the Jebel Sinjar has been a hot, thirsty desert where the streams of water evaporate or are lost. The Tharthar is now an arroyo that trickles past the deserted city of Hatra to vanish in a sink west of Baghdad (recently converted into a man-made lake fed by Tigris overflow).

Leaving the shelter of Mardin, the caravan route passes the ruined fortresses of Dara and Nisibin to cross the barren, salty watershed between the Euphrates and Tigris basins. Pinched between the Anatolian mountains and the Jebel Sinjar, this last most difficult stage of the long trail from Aleppo is plagued by dust devils and a scorching south wind that can single out a dehydrated man or beast for instant death.

The city of Mosul lies 80 miles east of Beled Sinjar on the right bank of the Tigris. Across the river lie the ruins of Nineveh and the foothills of the mountains of Kurdistan. The highest of these peaks, visible from Mosul and sometimes even from the Sinjar, is Jebel Judi, 6854 ft above sea level, where local tradition claims Noah brought his ark to rest.

Below Mosul three tributaries from the Zagros range bring fresh impetus to the current — the Great Zab, thrusting down from the Hakkari mountains; the Lesser Zab, with sources east and south of Rowanduz; and the broad valley of the Diyala, along which ran the old trade route from Baghdad to Hamadan, Kermanshah and the markets of the east.

The movement of travellers and merchandise between Syria and Mesopotamia has often been interrupted by war. The hieroglyphs of Egypt and the cuneiforms of Nineveh and Babylon record incessant struggles between the empires at each end of the trail, sometimes involving resettlement of entire peoples to provide labor to build pyramids, canals and other infrastructure.

In the eighth century BC the Assyrians removed ten Jewish tribes to Mesopotamia. But 100 years later the prophecies of Jonah, Nahum and other prophets were fulfilled. The city of Nineveh was destroyed by a Babylonian army allied with the Medes (a people believed by some to be the ancestors of the Kurdish race). A few years later Nebuchadnezzar took Jerusalem and carried the two remaining Jewish tribes back with him.

Babylon, too, was doomed to be conquered after a few decades by a coalition of Medes and Persians. Their leader Cyrus, styled 'great king' by the Greeks but known as 'shah' or *shahanshah* (king of kings) to his own people, permitted the Jews to return to Palestine. But many stayed in Mesopotamia, including Esther, wife of one of Cyrus' successors, the biblical Ahasuerus.

The Persians conquered the Anatolian plateau, but along the Mediterranean and Black Sea coasts the Greek people maintained their identity and their commercial skills. A new dimension was added in 401 BC, when another Cyrus, a grandson of Ahasuerus, enlisted an army of Greek mercenaries in a bold move to seize the Persian throne. Striking unopposed through Anatolia and down the Euphrates, the Greeks defeated the shah's army near Falluja, but in the battle the pretender was slain.

The Greek writer Xenophon has described the retreat up the Tigris to the point where theree were no more banks and the mercenaries had to fight their way through the mountains, harried by 'Karduchoi' — resembling the Kurds in name and behaviour — to reach the Black Sea at Trebizond.

Seventy years later another Greek army led by Alexander of Macedon, who had already conquered Anatolia, Syria and Egypt, marched eastward along the old caravan route to the Tigris and defeated the shah's last army near Erbil (Arbela). After Alexander died, his conquests were divided among his generals. Syria and Mesopotamia were awarded to Seleucus; the first new year's day of his reign fell on 1 October 312 BC — a date that commenced an era used by some communities to this day. Seleucus established a new capital, Seleucia, on the right bank of the Tigris and another new city, Antioch, west of Aleppo.

Over the next 1,000 years the Greeks — initially under Seleucus' dynasty and later as part of the Roman empire — expanded, maintained and gradually lost their dominion over the world east of Aleppo. Halfway through this millennium the contest between the two cultures was embittered by the rise of two new religions, each an offshoot of an older faith.

In Persia revival began in 226 AD. Ardeshir, a general who claimed descent from the old shahs, seized the throne and established Zoroastrianism as the state religion. A major element of this faith, founded 1,000 years earlier by Zoroaster and still practiced in some parts of Asia, is the battle for man's soul between his creator Ahura Mazda (also called Hormizd) and Ahriman, the spirit of evil.

Ardeshir's son Shahpur stamped the seal of victory on the new regime. At one point his army managed to trap the Roman emperor Valerian and his legions in the citadel of Urfa. Adamant in parleys, the shah forced the emperor to surrender with his entire army. Valerian, whose abject moment is carved in rock near the tombs of the ancient Persian shahs, died in captivity.

Three hundred and twelve years after the birth of Jesus, the emperor Constantine announced his conversion to Christianity, a religion that had survived years of persecution and inner conflict to emerge as a dedicated, disciplined church. The emperor established a new capital on the Bosporus at Byzantium, renamed Constantinople. His mother Helena made a pilgrimage to Jerusalem and unearthed a relic identified as the True Cross. (Manicheism, a third religion that combined Christian and Zoroastrian doctrines, especially the struggle between the powers of good and evil, gained many followers, including for a while Shahpur himself. But its prophet Mani was finally burned alive by the Persians and his followers were persecuted on both sides of the border.)

Constantine's pagan nephew Julian attempted to revive the glory of ancient Rome. The Christian church was disestablished, the administration of the empire reformed and legions were gathered from the western provinces for a decisive war against Persia, now ruled by Shahpur's great-grandson, Shahpur II.

In the spring of 363, escorted by a fleet of supply ships, the emperor and his army marched down the Euphrates valley, crossed Mesopotamia along Nebuchadnezzar's canal and challenged the shah outside the walls of his twin capitals of Seleucia and Ctesiphon. Shahpur shrewdly waited while the days grew longer and the weather hotter. Finally the emperor made the fateful decision to go back. The army crossed the Tigris, burning its boats and retreated northward along Xenophon's route toward the Kurdish hills.

The summer months in Mesopotamia are cruel. Harassed day and night by elusive Persian horsemen, the famished invaders plodded past fields of scorched crops until a stray javelin (perhaps thrown by a Roman auxiliary from the Tai tribe of Arabs) killed the emperor. His Christian successor Jovian negotiated a treaty with Shahpur, whereby the Jebel Sinjar and other territories were ceded to Persia as the price of an armistice that enabled the legions to re-cross the Tigris and limp back to the west.

Saturday, 1 October 589 opened the tenth century of the era of Seleucus. The events of the next 100 years are summarized in the following pages; many of them are engraved forever in the traditions of the communities who live today in Near Eastern lands.

For over 200 years Jovian's treaty, often breached but consistently renewed, had defined the frontier between the two empires. This strange coexistence, formalized by ambassadors bearing correspondence between the two monarchs, reflected a common fear of the Huns, a race of fierce, stirrupped horsemen from Central Asia who thrust incessantly against Persia's northern flank.

Blocked in Turkestan and by the Caucasus range, the Huns had moved westward, propelling an avalanche of other tribes who overran the old Roman provinces in the Balkans, West Germany, France, Britain, Italy and Spain.

The Roman empire, now governed from Constantinople, was reduced to the lands around the capital, the Anatolian glacis and a fringe along the Mediterranean coast that included the half-deserted cities of Athens, Antioch and Alexandria, Carthage and Cartagena, Genoa, Naples and Rome.

Amidst these catastrophes, Christianity — blamed by Gibbon as their cause but perceived by contemporaries as the best refuge — had become the established faith of the empire. From his palace beside the recently completed Santa Sophia cathedral, the emperor headed a hierarchy of patriarchs, metropolitans, bishops and lesser clergy. In the west the bishop of Rome (henceforth called 'the Pope') conducted missionary work in the conquered territories and over time converted their rulers to the faith.

There were many Christians in Mesopotamia. After years of persecution by the shahs, they finally organized a separate church, independent from the empire, with a patriarch who resided at Seleucia and became an important functionary at the Persian court. But despite official toleration of the new church — commonly called Nestorian because some of its tenets stemmed from the doctrines of Nestorius, a fifth-century patriarch of Constantinople — the state religion of Persia was Zoroastrianism. Conversion to Christianity was punishable by death. The construction of belfries was forbidden and worshippers were summoned to church by the sound of a wooden rattle.

On both sides of the frontier between the two empires the spiritual life of the Christian churches was invigorated by communities of monks and nuns who trained novices for the priesthood and copied and recopied the manuscripts of sacred books for future generations. Monasteries and convents stretched from Deir ez-Zafaran outside Mardin, through the highlands to the east known as the Tur Abdin — the mountain of the servants (of God) — to Mar* Behnam,

* The Syriac word 'Mar' means 'Lord'.

Mar Jonah (the prophet's reputed grave) and Mar Mattai on the left bank of the Tigris. Some monasteries were supported by the income from endowed farmlands, others by pilgrims' gifts. The less affluent assigned monks to carry their sacred relics, including mud pellets kneaded from the dust of departed saints, around the villages, collecting donations as they went.

In remoter spots hermits spent their lives in private contemplation and prayer — St Simeon Stylites atop a column in the hills northwest of Aleppo (later called the Jebel Seman in his memory), Ith Allaha in a cave in the Lalish valley north of Nineveh,[6] and many others.

Within the church, the need for a simpler faith was advocated by Jacob Baradeus ('the ragged one') who organized an underground church with cells throughout Anatolia, Mesopotamia, Syria and Egypt. His followers, condemned alike by the emperors and the Nestorians, were known as Monophysites or Jacobites. One of them, Gabriel of Sinjar, expelled by the Nestorians for bigamy, became personal physician (*drusbed*) to the shah's favourite wife.

The series of events that ended forever the long struggle between the Greeks and the Persians and brought into being the world east of Aleppo as we know it today, began in 590. A Persian general on the embattled northeastern border, now threatened by Turks, rebelled against the shah, whereupon a group of nobles in the capital deposed and blinded the shah, enthroning his son Khosrau. Unappeased, the rebel army advanced on Ctesiphon and scattered the palace guard. Giving orders to put his father out of his misery, Khosrau fled in disguise up the Euphrates to the Byzantine border post at Buseyra. Here, in the third watch of the night, the erstwhile king of kings requested shelter from his pursuers. Sanctuary was granted by the hospitable emperor Maurice, who provided him with a Greek wife and an army that defeated the usurper and restored Khosrau to his throne.

Twelve years later the tables were turned. Maurice was killed by mutinous troops, who proclaimed their ringleader emperor. Shah Khosrau, accompanied by an alleged son of Maurice, invaded the empire, captured Mardin, Urfa, Aleppo and Antioch and penetrated deep into Anatolia. (About this time a new fortress, later called Mosul, was established on the right bank of the Tigris opposite Nineveh, to serve as a staging point on the long road to Aleppo and the west.)

The years of Byzantium's ignominy marked the apogee of Khosrau's reign. Swearing never to set foot again in Ctesiphon, the shah built a new palace at Dastagerd in the foothills of the Zagros range. Here, surrounded by elephants, ostriches and peacocks, he accepted daily 1,000 pieces of gold from his tax-collector Yazdin, a well-born Nestorian from Kirkuk 'who was beloved by Khosrau even as was Joseph in the sight of Pharaoh, yea even more'.[7] Khosrau had two Christian wives, Maria the Greek and Shirin, the fabled beauty from Khuzistan whose doctor Gabriel of Sinjar bled her arm and enabled her to have a son.[8]

Meanwhile Maurice's killer had been overthrown by the Byzantine general Heraclius, who offered to negotiate with Persia. But for Khosrau, now surnamed 'Parviz' (the victorious), total victory seemed at hand. One army crossed Anatolia to camp along the Bosporus and plan a joint attack on Constantinople with barbarian allies from the north. Another army, led by the Persian general Shahrbaraz, headed south, capturing Damascus and Jerusalem, where the patriarch under torture revealed the hiding place of the True Cross, buried in a vegetable patch. The trophy was crated and shipped, along with other loot, to the collector of taxes.

Yazdin, known among Nestorians as 'the prince of believers', arranged a banquet — surely unique in the annals of entertainment — at which the True Cross was officially turned over to Khosrau, who graciously authorized the host to keep a piece for himself.[9]

Persian troops swept on to conquer Egypt. But ominous signs began to appear. Mogundat, a Persian officer in Palestine, deserted the army to join a Christian monastery where he stayed several years under the name of Anastasius until apprehended.[10] Farther south a shrewd observer in Mecca prophesied the ultimate victory of the Greeks and encouraged a friend to bet 100 camels that this would happen within 9 years.[11]

Indeed Heraclius — likened by Gibbon to the great Scipio and comparable to Churchill in our time — had not been idle. Gathering a war chest from the accumulated treasures of the church and leaving the capital well defended by its walls, the emperor slipped across the Bosporus into northern Anatolia, reformed his army and fought his way to the grassy Mughan steppes of Azerbaijan, whence he harassed the Persians around lakes Urmia and Van.

In September 627 Heraclius struck. Eluding the Persians massed east of Lake Urmia, he headed southwest over mountain passes and across the Great Zab river down to the open country east of the Tigris. It was strange weather; following eclipses of the sun and the moon earlier in the year, the sun remained behind the clouds from October onwards. On 12 December Heraclius defeated the Persians at the battle of Nineveh and advanced unopposed down the Tigris valley, celebrating Christmas at the deserted Yazdin estate outside Kirkuk. (By this time the prince of believers was dead and his family reduced to poverty.)

A few days later the shah, weakened by illness — the Sinjar healer long dead

— and sleepless from the fancied sound of Christian rattles, abandoned Dastagerd and withdrew to hateful Ctesiphon. Heraclius observed Twelfth Night in the smouldering ruins of the palace and pushed on south, freeing many captives of earlier years but too late to save Anastasius (martyred 22 January 628).

In February Heraclius decided to pull his troops back north over the mountains, just in time to escape the heaviest blizzard in memory. The passes were blocked by snow, but patrols brought fragmentary news of startling events in Mesopotamia. In April the sun reappeared and a Persian envoy confirmed that conspirators led by Yazdin's son Shamta had seized the shah, by now too feeble to escape, had killed all but one of his sons before his eyes, and had enthroned Maria's son, who now proposed peace with the empire. Armistice terms were soon agreed.

As the emperor moved slowly homewards, pausing to inspect Noah's landfall on Mount Judi, the days of reckoning came thick and fast in Ctesiphon. Khosrau Parviz was already gone, axed to death in prison by a conspirator while Shamta, loth to draw his sword, looked on. Shirin's end is unknown. Soon Shamta fell out with the new shah, who intercepted his flight to the west, cut off his right hand and put him in prison. In the spring the snow-swelled Tigris burst its levees to carve out a new channel that would last for centuries and irreparably flood the Great Swamp between the Tigris and the Euphrates. Plague claimed thousands, including the shah, who was succeeded by his young son.

Under the terms of the armistice the Persian armies evacuated the occupied provinces and in March 630 Heraclius entered the Church of the Resurrection in Jerusalem (burnt during the occupation but rebuilt at Yazdin's expense) to re-dedicate the True Cross. A spectator reported to Mohammed that his prophecy had been completely fulfilled.

A month later the Persian army of the Bosporus re-entered Ctesiphon, led by Shahrbaraz, who deposed and killed the child shah and ruled for forty days before himself being slain. Tormented by dysentery throughout his brief reign, Shahrbaraz found the strength to settle one old score. Shamta, who had once insulted the new shah's daughter, was dragged from prison and crucified at the gate of the principal Christian church in Seleucia.[12]

The memory of Yazdin and his son flickers faintly across the centuries that divide us from that twilight age. But the account of their deeds and misdeeds has been recorded for posterity in the chronicles of the Nestorian church.

Mohammed died in 632. During the next two decades the Arabs conquered the entire Middle East from Afghanistan to Mosul, Aleppo and the Nile. The last shah, Yezdegerd III, grandson of Khosrau and Shirin, died a fugitive in Turkestan. The Byzantines still held Anatolia but the court was moving to Sicily. Constantinople made ready for a siege.

The basic law of the new Arab empire was Islam, a new religion based on Mohammed's teachings as revealed in the Koran and the carefully preserved tradition of his sayings. He had enjoined respect for the Old Testament and its prophets and had recognized the virtues, but not the divinity, of Jesus. His successors, the caliphs, accordingly permitted the 'peoples of the book' — Jews, Christians and Sabaeans (a religion now believed extinct) — to practise their faiths and to pay a special head tax, collected from the religious leaders of each sect, in lieu of military service. In contrast the religion of Zoroaster withered away and Persia became a stronghold of Islam.

The Jacobite church, prescribed by the emperors, flourished anew, while the Nestorians, having sensed that the laws of the Medes and the Persians would soon be no more, collaborated with the Arab invaders and were confirmed in their privileges and possessions. Hormizd, a Nestorian priest from Khuzistan, established a new monastery in the hills above Alkosh, the birthplace of the prophet Nahum 30 miles north of Mosul.[13] Other Nestorian missionaries spread eastward to found churches in Central Asia, China and in South India along the coasts of Malabar and Coromandel.

Meanwhile the conquerors engaged in bloody feuds. Mohammed's first two successors — Abu Bekr, winner of the 100-camel wager, and the frugal Omar — had wielded the personal authority owed to close companions of the prophet. But the third caliph, Othman, although an early convert to Islam, was overthrown and slain by rebels, who chose Ali, cousin and son-in-law of Mohammed, to rule.

Civil war broke out between Ali, who had moved his capital from Medina to Kufa on the Euphrates, and the Omayyad clan to which Othman had belonged, now headed by two cousins — Moawiya b. Abu Sofian, the governor of Syria, and Merwan b. el-Hakam, who had been Othman's treasurer.* After a few years of turmoil Ali was murdered and his son Hasan recognized Moawiya as sole caliph.

Moawiya, a cool statesman, ruled without challenge for twenty years. From his palace in Damascus he directed the conquests of Libya, Tunis and Turkestan. But he missed the greatest prize of all — Constantinople.

The golden opportunity came in 668. The Greek emperor Constans was in Sicily, having left his son in charge of the capital. The commander of the Byzantine army in Anatolia — Sapor, of Persian extraction — revolted and

* The Arabic word 'Ibn', meaning 'son of', is often abbreviated to 'b.'. 'Abu' means 'father of'.

obtained from Moawiya the promise of an Arab contingent to support his bid for the throne.

The Arab force had reached Malatya when word arrived that Sapor was dead, thrown from his horse, and the rebellion was over.

Almost at the same time — the sequence and causation of these events is unclear to us, and perhaps was also then — the unloved emperor Constans paid a visit to the Daphne bathhouse in Syracuse. At a moment when his eyes were blinded by soap — a French variety blended on this occasion with marsh-mallow — the attendant killed him by hitting him on the head with the metal soap dish. The conspirators proclaimed the local army commander emperor. The capital stayed loyal to Constans' son.[14]

Somehow the Arabs in Anatolia made their way to Chalcedon (now Kadiköy) on the Asiatic shore of the Bosporus. Here the force wintered, decimated by hunger and disease, gazing at the great city that shimmered like a mirage across the cold, swift waters of the strait.

The caliph considered sending an army through undefended Anatolia to reinforce the Bosporus outpost. His son Yezid, twenty-six years old and recently married to a new wife, expressed his unconcern in a poem of strangely modern tone:

> Stretched softly upon rugs at Deir Morran, emptying the morning cup
> with Omm Kolthum beside me,
> What care I, forsooth, about the poxes and fevers that waste
> our troops at Chalcedon?[15]

But others cited Mohammed's promise of paradise for the first Moslems to attack Constantinople. The son of caliph Omar volunteered to fight, as did Abdallah Ibn Zobeir, grandson of caliph Abu Bekr and nephew of Mohammed. Even the aged Abu Ayyub, one of the last surviving companions of the prophet, insisted on joining the expedition.

In the spring of 669 the caliph's army, commanded by Yezid, reached Chalcedon. Arab historians, unconfirmed by Greek chroniclers, report that they crossed the straits without opposition and advanced upon Constantinople from the west. The Greeks were secure behind the city walls but unable to drive the invaders away. After weeks of stalemate, the Arabs withdrew, leaving behind the body of Abu Ayyub, who had died on the march and had asked Yezid to bury him at the farthest point of the Arab advance. Yezid and his army returned in glory to Damascus, bringing back spoils from Anatolian cities and tales of real and imaginary triumphs that still enrich the folklore of the east.

Moawiya died in 680, having designated Yezid his successor. In contrast to

11

his shrewd, calculating father, Yezid is described as 'extremely affable, quite devoid of conceit, loved by all those under his authority, hating the pomp of royalty, living like a private citizen'.[16] Dividing his time between Damascus and Howarin, 80 miles away on the edge of the desert, he enjoyed the pleasures of music and wine and the company of poets and artists, Christian as well as Moslem. (Yezid's mother Maisun, herself a poet, was a Christian Arab, as was one of his wives.) Skilled with horses, dogs, falcons and cheetahs, he loved to hunt gazelle, often accompanied by his pet monkey. But with all these qualities he lacked the stuff to rule; indeed Gibbon calls him 'a feeble and dissolute youth'.[17]

Two close relatives of Mohammed lived in Medina — Hussein, younger son of the caliph Ali by the prophet's daughter Fatima, and Abdallah Ibn Zobeir. Neither had sworn allegiance to Yezid as Moawiya's heir. Upon news of his accession, they refused to recognize him as caliph and fled by night to Mecca.

In Iraq (the Arab name for Mesopotamia) the supporters of Ali's family — known then and ever since as Shiites — urged Hussein to join them in Kufa. In August 680 Hussein and his household left Mecca by caravan to cross the 800 miles of desert, unaware that meanwhile the governor of Iraq had suppressed the rebellion and that they were riding slowly into a trap.

The end came for them on 10 October 680 in the desert near Kerbela. The official report to Yezid reads:

> Hussein the son of Ali came here with 17 members of his family and 60 supporters. We offered them the choice of battle or unconditional surrender to the governor Obeidallah. They chose to fight. We attacked them at dawn and surrounded them. When they felt our swords' point, they tried to escape to the hills and hollows. It did not take long. Just the time to slaughter a camel or to take a nap, and we overcame them. I send you their heads.[18]

Hussein's journey had come to nought. The surviving women and children were sent to Damascus, where Yezid expressed his regrets and allowed them to return home to Medina. But the memory of Hussein's death hardened the hearts of the Shiites and cleft Islam for all time.

Two years later Medina revolted. Mecca was already controlled by Ibn Zobeir. An expedition dispatched by the caliph stormed Medina and laid siege to Mecca, bombarding the Great Mosque with rocks. The Kaaba — the ancient sanctuary of the Arabs, reputedly built by Abraham and now the holiest shrine of Islam — caught fire, scorching the celebrated Black Stone mounted in its wall.

In the midst of these terrible events Yezid died suddenly at Howarin on 11

November 683. The circumstances of his death are unknown, nor — apart from his regrets about Kerbela — is there any record of how the caliph himself perceived the causes of his troubles or the effects of his officials' heavy-handed acts. The harsh verdict of Moslem historians places upon Yezid the guilt for the calamities of his reign and they have long considered him the Nero or the Pontius Pilate of Islam.

A few months after Yezid's death, his eldest son and designated successor, Moawiya II, died of the plague. He was succeeded by Merwan b. el-Hakam, head of the junior branch of the Omayyad clan, who married Yezid's widow. A younger son, Khalid b. Yezid, was named heir apparent but was soon set aside and retired to a life of scientific research. Another son, Abdallah, child of Omm Kolthum, was a noted archer.

Almost 1,000 years had passed since Seleucus entered the city of Babylon. In the space of three generations the ancient world had vanished forever. Constantinople still defied attackers, but elsewhere the armies of the caliphs who succeeded Merwan carried the torch of Islam westward to Toledo and eastward to Samarkand.

Internally the Omayyad caliphate was tainted by corruption and family disputes. Merwan II, grandson of Merwan b. el-Hakam, was a soldierly ruler known as 'the Ass'. He tried to restore order but was constantly engaged in fighting his own relatives as well as the Shiites and a new faction — the Abbasid clan, descended from Mohammed's uncle. In 750 an Abbasid army from Turkestan defeated Merwan on the left bank of the Great Zab river. The last Omayyad caliph fled to Egypt, where he was overtaken and slain. His head was sent to the Abbasid camp, where the victors remarked on his red hair and prominent blue eyes, legacies from his Kurdish mother.

The Abbasids applied themselves to the systematic extermination of the Omayyad clan. Even the graves of Caliph Yezid and many of his successors were desecrated. A few survivors escaped to the fringes of the Moslem world. One of them made his way to Spain, seized power and founded a dynasty that ruled for three hundred years. An old tradition relates that some of the last caliph's family took refuge in the mountains of Kurdistan.[19] But most of the Omayyads were hunted down, including Yezid's grandson Abu Mohammed, son of the archer, who was killed in Arabia.[20]

Despite their violent origins, the Abbasid caliphs presided over a period of consolidation, degenerating later into lethargy. A new capital was established in Baghdad, a few miles upstream from Ctesiphon. The wars of conquest ended, trade moved freely, arts and sciences flourished. Early in the ninth century a team of Arab astronomers determined the distance between two meridians of longitude, based on observations made in the desert of Sinjar.

In the course of time the caliphs lost effective control over many of the territories they claimed to rule. In the tenth century a Shiite dynasty tracing its descent from Fatima, the daughter of Mohammed, established a rival caliphate in North Africa and Egypt. Arabia was dominated for a while by a radical Shiite sect that condemned pilgrimages and actually removed the Black Stone from Mecca for twenty years. In Iraq a Shiite warlord dynasty from Persia descended on Baghdad and usurped the caliphs' power for 100 years.

Islam survived these imbroglios, just as Christianity outlived the Roman empire. Year after year, century after century, the faithful repeated five times daily the ritual prayers of the Moslem faith. Even in territories detached from the caliphate the rulers vied with each other in building mosques and endowing seminaries for the study and teaching of Islam. In the eleventh century a new revival movement swept across the politically divided, yet basically homogeneous, Moslem world.

Chapter Two

Sheikh Adi and His Order[1]

Adi b. Musafir, who is venerated as the prophet of the Yezidi religion, was born around 1075[2] in the Lebanese village of Beit Far (now Khirbet Qanafar) on the dry western slope of the Bekaa valley 37 miles south of Baalbek.[3]

His father, Musafir b. Ismail, was a Moslem holy man who traced his ancestry to the Omayyad caliph Merwan b. el-Hakam.[4] His mother's name was Yezda.[5] The graves of Adi's parents and of his sister lie beneath an ancient oak that looks down on the Bekaa valley.*[6]

For 100 years prior to Adi's birth the Bekaa valley had been ruled by the Shiite Fatimid caliphs of Egypt. But changes were in the wind.

For ages the Turks, a nation of shepherds and warriors, had tended their flocks in the plains of Central Asia and battled the rulers of Persia. At the beginning of the eleventh century the most warlike tribes, recently converted to Islam, broke through Persia's brittle northeastern border and swept westward to occupy Baghdad in 1055. The Abbasid caliph, confined in his palace by Shiite chieftains, welcomed the orthodox (Sunni) Turks who reaffirmed his position as the spitirual leader of Islam.

In Baghdad the schools of law and theology gained new vigour from a group of teachers led by Abu Hamid el-Ghazali, who preached that the higher truths of Islam could be revealed to initiates who followed the Sufi way of life — a mystic discipline that still enthralls devotees in the eastern and western worlds. Communities of disciples gathered in remote spots where Sufi masters — known as *sheikhs* (*pirs* in Persian) — instructed their followers. From these beginnings religious orders were formed, distinguished by their tattered woollen cloaks — ceremonially passed down from master to disciple — and dedicated to follow and preach their founders' precepts.

* See Plate 1.

15

The spread of Sufi mysticism was hastened by the westward advance of the Turkish armies, who broke into Anatolia in 1071 and captured the key cities of Malatya, Kaiseri and Konya. The Greek empire was pushed back to the coasts of Asia Minor, opening the way for a mass migration of Turkish tribesmen into the conquered territories. In northern Syria the Turks captured Aleppo and Damascus and drove the Egyptians from Baalbek in 1075.

As a young man Adi b. Musafir went to Baghdad, where he studied under el-Ghazali and other Sufi teachers. Among his fellow students was Abd el-Qadir el-Gilani, a Kurd who founded the Qadiriya order of Sufis (still in existence).[7]

Adi b. Musafir left Baghdad around the turn of the century and withdrew to Lalish, a remote valley 36 miles north-east of Mosul and 2,000 ft higher, where the Christian hermit Ith Allaha had once found solitude and peace. This mountainous region, inhabited by the Hakkari tribe of Kurds, had already sheltered other famed Sufis — the saintly Abu 'l-Hasan Ali, himself an Omayyad scion, who died in 1093; Okeil el-Mambiji, who gave Adi his first cloak; and the aged Abu 'l-Wafa el-Holwani, whose corpse Adi was chosen to wash.[8]

The valley of Lalish, only 2 miles long, lies in a fold of the mountains accessible at its eastern end through a narrow ravine. Travellers from the treeless plain of Nineveh make their way up the foothills to enter a world of mountain oaks, arbutus and mulberry, willows and terebinths, hawthorn and oleander. The first European to visit Lalish observed 'on a species of euphorbia, a yellow caterpillar with bright scarlet spots, and which attained from 3 to 4 inches in length, with a proportionate bulk of body'.[9] On the northern slope of the valley, where Adi's shrine now stands, clear spring water gushes out of the rock and irrigates a garden of plane, mulberry and fig trees. In the summer the air is filled with the fragrance of countless flowers, the songs of birds, the humming of bees and the gentle flight of butterflies. Winters are mild, with occasional snow.

Except for a pilgrimage to Mecca in 1116 in the company of el-Gilani, Adi b. Musafir spent the remainder of his life at his retreat in the Lalish valley.[10] As head of a religious community, he became known as Sheikh Adi — the name now commonly applied to Lalish — and his original identification as 'es-Sham'i' (the Syrian) changed to el-Hakkari (the man of Hakkari).

From time to time Sheikh Adi came down from Lalish to preach to the people of the plain. On one visit to Mosul around 1160, he was observed by Muzeffer-ed-Din, a boy who grew up to become governor of Erbil and later remembered the Sheikh as 'a man of middle size and tawny complexion'.[11] According to tradition Adi b. Musafir's eyes were soft and black, like those of a gazelle.[12]

Over the years Sheikh Adi became renowned for piety, austerity and miraculous powers. One disciple recalled that he recited the entire Koran twice each night. He lived on fruit he grew on the mountainside and made his clothes out of cotton from his own field. He was so emaciated by fasting that it was said that 'when he bowed his head in prayer, one could hear his brains knock against the inside of his skull, like pebbles in a calabash'.[13] A stream of pilgrims came to see him, some even from Morocco.

His friend and fellow pilgrim el-Gilani declared 'If one could attain the gift of prophecy through striving, Sheikh Adi b. Musafir would certainly have attained it'.[14] The great el-Ghazali was happy to oblige his friend by writing a letter of encouragement to a Sufi master recommended by Adi.[15]

The Sufi teachings of Sheikh Adi are embodied in four tracts and some psalms, all written in Arabic. The longer tracts, entitled 'The Creed of the [Sunni] Orthodox' (15 leaves)[16] and 'How to Improve the Soul' (3 leaves),[17] are followed by the brief 'Admonitions to the Caliph'[18] and 'Admonitions to Sheikh Qaid and the Other Disciples'.[19] All enjoin strict observance of the traditional faith of Islam, avoidance of innovative doctrines and a life of abstinence and prayer. In the last-named tract Adi cites Jesus' words to his followers:

> O ye disciples, let your bellies hunger and your livers thirst and
> cast away your raiment, that ye may see God on high; for fasting is
> the key to scorn of worldly things, and through fasting the soul and
> body are humbled and the heart becomes whole.

In contrast to the stern admonitions in Adi's prose tracts, his psalms are wild and exuberant in the tradition of Sufi poetry. The longest (twenty-eight verses)[20] conjures up visions inspired by a cup of mystical wine dispensed by God, through the medium of Mohammed, to the poet; one passage exclaims:

> God brought me near to him; and I attained
> closeness to him.
> He offered me to drink, poured life into me
> and became my boon companion.
> He became my comrade, the one whom I love in
> my cell.
> He granted me power over all the wine jugs
> and what they held within them.
> Then the hosts of love submitted to my will;
> And I became Sultan over all the servants of God.
> All the kings of the earth come to me humbly,

My horsemen speed in every land,
The drums roll in my honour in each quarter of
the heavens,
And the herald of my dominion calls out in
east and west.

The principal manuscript of Sheikh Adi's Sufi writings, copied in Damascus in 1509, is preserved in a small notebook (7 in. long x 5 in. wide), in the State Library in West Berlin. One of his psalms is contained in another Berlin manuscript; two others are in the British Library. In 1934 additional Sufi poems by Sheikh Adi were discovered by the American anthropologist Henry Field in the Jebel Sinjar; copies of these texts are now in the Library of Congress.[21]

In the thirteenth and fourteenth centuries Islamic commentators mentioned Sheikh Adi's teachings with approval. They were unaware of two other works, attributed to the sheikh and discussed in the next chapter, that constitute the holiest book of the Yezidi religion and the principal psalm of its devotees. (In later times Moslem attitudes changed to embarrassment; in one of the Berlin manuscripts Adi's name has been clumsily and incompletely altered to make it appear that the author was his contemporary Ahmed b. Ali er-Rifai, who founded an orthodox order of Sufis.)[22]

Adi b. Musafir died in January 1162; he was over ninety years old. He was buried at Lalish and his tomb soon became a shrine for pilgrims. According to one account the official deed authorizing the establishment of a religious foundation was signed by the atabeg Nur ed-Din, the head of the dynasty that governed Aleppo and Mosul.[23]

Obeying his deathbed wish, his followers chose as Adi's successor his nephew Abu 'l-Barakat b. Sahr, who had come to Lalish many years earlier from Beit Far and was respected for his scholarship and saintly deeds.

Abu 'l-Barakat is described as virtuous, gracious, dignified and shy. Under his leadership the order, now commonly known as Adawis, attracted new disciples and an increasing flow of pilgrims. He died at an advanced age and was buried near Sheikh Adi's tomb. His son and successor, the pious Adi b. Abu 'l-Barakat famed for his love of pilgrimages, was known as 'the father of benevolence'; he was also called 'Adi the Kurd' because he was the first sheikh to have been born in the Hakkari mountains.[24]

The contemplative community at Lalish was well sheltered from events in the outside world. At the turn of the century a crusading expedition from western Europe had conquered the coast of Palestine, restored Christian rule in Jerusalem and established for a while a fiefdom east of the Euphrates with its capital at Urfa.

But the Moslems held firmly the key cities of Aleppo, Baalbek and Damascus. In the mid-twelfth century they recovered Urfa and Birecik and the atabeg Nur ed-Din maintained a steady pressure on the crusaders.* In 1171 one of his generals — Saladin, a Kurd by birth — gained control of Egypt and put an end to the Fatimid caliphate. After Nur ed-Din's death Saladin united the Moslems of Egypt, Syria and Iraq and destroyed the crusader kingdom of Jerusalem. (Among his commanders was Muzeffer ed-Din Kökburi, the childhood admirer of Sheikh Adi; he later married Saladin's sister.)

At the end of the twelfth century the province of Mosul was governed by Nur ed-Din's family, loosely allied with Saladin and his successors to the west and with the Abbasid Caliph of Baghdad's shrunken patrimony in central Iraq. But from 1211 onward Mosul was effectively governed by Bedr ed-Din Lulu, the son of an Armenian slave, who acted as regent for a sickly atabeg and after his death for his sons, each of whom conveniently died before attaining his majority. In 1233 Lulu, a practising Moslem, received the title of atabeg from the caliph.

In Lalish the Adawi order acquired new life from Hasan b. Adi, born in 1195, who succeeded his pious father. Intelligent, dedicated and hardened by six years of solitary retreat (where he wrote a book called *The Revelation of the Skills of Solitude*, now lost), Hasan prescribed strict veneration of Sheikh Adi and absolute obedience from his disciples. A short tract by Hasan enjoining discipline, faith and austerity concludes the Berlin manuscript of Sheikh Adi's writings.[26]

In contrast to his contemplative forbears, Sheikh Hasan engaged actively in religious debate. On one occasion he was so moved by the words of another preacher that he sobbed and fainted, whereupon the Adawis, now largely Kurdish, killed the preacher for the crime of causing their Sheikh to lose his composure.[27]

The second of the two Yezidi sacred books — the Meshaf Resh (Kurdish for the 'black book'), which sets forth the rules of conduct — is traditionally ascribed to Sheikh Hasan. (A mysterious passage in this book, possibly of later date, ascribes the ancestry of the community's emirs to the Persian shahs Shahpur I and Shahpur II.)[28]

---

* One miracle attributed to Sheikh Adi credits him with the deliverance of forty Moslem prisoners from the crusader fortress of Tripoli and their magical transportation to Nisibin in one night.[25]

Meanwhile a great storm was brewing in the east. The Mongols, a spirit-worshipping people inspired by their leader Jengiz Khan's visions of world conquest and supported by the administrative skills of his Chinese vassals, rode down from their bleak homelands (known to Moslems as the land of Gog and Magog) across Turkestan into Persia. (Among the invaders was one tribe that had been converted to Christianity by Nestorian missionaries.)

In 1231, four years after Jengiz's death, the Mongols scattered the last army of Persia near Diyarbakir and swept westward to raid the rich Malatya plain before returning to their winter quarters — the grassy Mughan steppe northeast of Tabriz, where six centuries earlier the emperor Heraclius had rested his army before the decisive battle against Khosrau.

The forces of Islam, gathered along the Mediterranean shores to resist new crusades from Europe, were ill-prepared to face this new enemy. But Mongol strategy, formulated in faraway Karakorum (300 miles west of the present Ulan Bator) evolved slowly. For several years they limited themselves to cavalry raids into Iraq; one of these sacked Erbil while another crossed the Tigris and massacred an Aleppo-bound caravan near Sinjar.

Finally the main Mongol thrust was made clear. In 1236, bypassing Iraq and Anatolia, their armies moved west from Turkestan to conquer southern Russia and sweep on through Hungary to the Adriatic coast. At the end of the year they withdrew from central Europe to consolidate their conquests in Russia, where the inhabitants, then largely Turkish, found that they could only pay their taxes to the new rulers by selling their children to slave-traders for resale in the lucrative Egyptian market.

In 1243 the Mongol general Baiju invaded Anatolia and defeated the Turkish army near Erzincan. The sultan agreed to pay tribute to the Great Khan and allow his forces to use the fortresses and highways of Anatolia. Next year Mongol cavalry raided the outskirts of Aleppo. The lifeline from Syria to the Tigris valley was outflanked. Mosul and Baghdad were perilously exposed.

Throughout these ominous years Lulu reigned on in Mosul, devoting his time to embellishing his capital and adding to his possessions. But the Kurds, whose best soldiers were serving Saladin's heirs in Syria and Egypt, were restless. Lulu feared that the Adawis' ambitious new leader might give the signal to lay waste the whole province. In 1246 Hasan b. Adi was seized, imprisoned and strangled in the citadel of Mosul.[29]

The contrast between Lulu's unconcern toward the Mongol threat and his nervousness about the Kurds was shortly to be explained. In 1246 and 1247 two Dominican friars, bearing correspondence between Pope Innocent IV and the Mongols, passed through Mosul with safe-conducts from the local authorities. In 1249 one of them came back to Mosul with a Mongol escort, heading a mission to the Great Khan from Louis IX of France, who was then conducting a crusade against Egypt.

Lulu's collaboration with the Mongols, sealed by his son's marriage to a princess of their court, spelled doom for Baghdad. In 1253, the Mongol year of the ox, the Great Khan despatched a huge army, commanded by his brother Hulagu, with instructions to exterminate the Kurds and the Lurs (a related people) and proceed to the conquest of the Moslem world.[30]

At the same time the Great Khan's tax collector, travelling more swiftly than Hulagu, brought notice of increased assessments upon his tributaries. In 1254 Lulu found it necessary to send a punitive expedition against the Adawis, who had resented his harsh rule and heavy tax demands. A contemporary historian records that:

> after a bitter struggle, the Adawi Kurds were routed, some killed, others taken prisoner. Lulu crucified a hundred and executed a hundred more. He ordered their emir's arms and legs to be chopped off and displayed above the gates of Mosul. He also sent men to dig up Sheikh Adi's bones and burn them.[31]

A straw in the great conflagration that lay ahead, this short item, which does not even give the name of the slain Adawi leader, marks the end of a well-documented period of local history. Thereafter, only fragmentary glimpses of the community are found in the scanty chronicles of a darkening age.

While Hulagu's army marched inexorably to its goal, a tragi-comic sequence of events took place in Anatolia.[32] The Mongols' logistical plan called for Hulagu to reach the Mughan steppe late in 1256 and for Baiju to shift his winter quarters to western Anatolia. The Turkish authorities were to make appropriate arrangements.

In Konya, the Turkish capital, a dispute had raged for some years between two rival princes, Izz ed-Din Kaikaus II and his brother Rukn ed-Din Kilij Arslan IV, and a mission had been sent to Mongolia requesting the Great Khan to decide who should rule. Izz ed-Din was in charge when Baiju's orders reached Konya.

Izz ed-Din attempted to block the Mongols' move into Anatolia, but was defeated and took refuge with the Greek emperor. Baiju appointed Rukn ed-Din sultan, quartered his army as planned and left early in 1257 for Mughan to report to Hulagu. Rukn ed-Din likewise headed eastward to pay homage to the Great Khan's brother.

In a flash Izz ed-Din slipped back over the border and seized power in Konya. Baiju's army, leaderless and immobilized by winter conditions, saw its lines of communication severed as Izz ed-Din's henchmen took over the key fortresses of Malatya and Harput (now Elâzığ) on the upper Euphrates. Malatya was held by a chieftain of the Kurdish Hakkari tribe, while Harput was entrusted to Sheref ed-Din Mohammed, son of the Adawi Sheikh Hasan whom Lulu had slain ten years before.

Izz ed-Din's bold gamble failed. A Mongol force led by Hulagu's general Alighaq was on its way westward to install Rukn ed-Din as sultan. Sweeping aside Turkish resistance at Erzincan, the Mongols encountered Sheref ed-Din at the Kemah gorge 33 miles downstream, where the luckless Adawi was defeated and slain.[33]

Ironically, Izz ed-Din gained a reprieve when the Turkish delegation to Mongolia, three years on its way, arrived a few days after the Kemah battle, bearing the Great Khan's decree that Anatolia should be divided between the two brothers. Peace was arranged and in the spring Baiju's army moved eastward through Malatya and Harput according to plan.

Sheref ed-Din's brief moment in history had come and gone. No clues remain as to his earlier life or the reason for his presence in eastern Anatolia.

In the autumn of 1257 the Mongol strategic plan was set in motion. The main army under Hulagu advanced along the ancient road from Hamadan, past the ruins of Khosrau's palace at Dastagerd and his wife's mansion at Qasr-i-Shirin, down to the valley of the Tigris. In October Baiju's long march brought him to Mosul, where the inhabitants nervously watched the Mongol army cross over the bridge to Nineveh and head southward to join Hulagu. They were followed later by a small local contingent commanded by Lulu's son Ismail.

Baghdad fell quickly. Baiju's tireless troops forded the Tigris near Tikrit, using bridging equipment supplied by Lulu, and attacked the city from the west while Hulagu assaulted the city from the east. In February 1258 the caliph Mustasim, a keen pigeon-fancier but ineffective ruler, surrendered and was put to death. The heads of his commander-in-chief and two chief advisers were given to Ismail with instructions that his father should impale them on the walls of Mosul — a sad task for Lulu, for the general had been his friend.[34]

This grim reminder of Mongol power prompted Lulu, whose troops had not taken part in the battle for Baghdad, to assist more actively in the reduction of other points of resistance. Appeasement was consummated in August 1258, when the 93-year-old atabeg crossed the mountains of Kurdistan, laden with tribute, to pay homage to Hulagu at his summer encampment near Lake

Urmia. A contemporary writer records that after Lulu's initial terror had abated, the old sinner 'used such boldness and freedom of speech towards the King of Kings that he went up on the throne by his side, and took him by the ear, and with his own hands fastened therein an ear-ring made of pearls of great price.'*[35]

Lulu died in July 1259, full of years and infamy, and was succeeded as atabeg by Ismail. The Mongol armies swept irresistibly to the west, storming Aleppo in 1260 and occupying Syria without a blow. The great mosque at Damascus, once a cathedral, was restored to the Christians and the death-knell of Islam seemed to be at hand.

Fortitude and fortune stemmed the Mongol tide. For some years the Egyptian army, formerly recruited from Anatolia and Kurdistan, had formed regiments of Turkish slaves called Mamelukes imported from South Russia. In 1250 these soldiers, who 'had breathed in their infancy the keenness of a Scythian air',[†] seized power in Cairo. Ten years later, when Hulagu went home to attend the Great Khan's funeral, they wiped out the Mongol army of occupation in Syria and recaptured Damascus and Aleppo.

For a generation Hulagu and his successors battled the Mamelukes, but the Mongols never regained Syria. Neither did the Egyptians recover Iraq; their one attempt brought disaster to the house of Lulu.[37]

A younger son of Lulu had already fled from Iraq to join the Egyptians. In May 1261 the atabeg Ismail, suspected of treachery, escaped from Mosul to Syria, followed shortly by a third brother.

Another refugee reached Syria about this time — a dark-skinned individual named Mustansir who claimed to be the uncle of the last caliph. The sultan of Egypt enthroned him as caliph and treated the sons of Lulu as honoured guests. A bold project began to take shape.

In the autumn of 1261 Mustansir and the three brothers led a small force down the Euphrates, headed for Baghdad. At an early stage in the expedition Lulu's sons rode off; two of them made for the Jebel Sinjar, while Ismail went on to Mosul, where he was acclaimed by his former subjects. The 'black caliph' kept on, located another Abbasid survivor, Ahmed, who had been sheltered by desert Arabs, and got as far as Anbar. Here, only 70 miles from Baghdad but close to the battlefield where another pretender, Cyrus, had lost his life, Mustansir was defeated and killed by the Mongols. The atabeg's brothers and Ahmed[‡] hurried back to Cairo, leaving Ismail trapped in Mosul.

---

* At a subsequent audience the two Turkish sultans of Anatolia paid homage. Izz ed-Din received forgiveness for his offences after giving Hulagu a magnificent boot with his own portrait painted on the sole.[36]

† Gibbon, *Decline and Fall of the Roman Empire*, chapter LXIV.

‡ Ahmed survived to become the founder of a new line of caliphs in Cairo.

Seven months later, after an Egyptian relief force had been defeated near Sinjar, Ismail surrendered to the Mongols. Trusting in his father's panache, he approached the besiegers' camp with bands playing and acrobats tumbling. But the Mongols were in no mood for levity. Mosul was sacked, the inhabitants were massacred and the atabeg was taken away to a painful death at Hulagu's summer encampment.

Hulagu's successors owed allegiance to his cousin, the Great Khan Kublai in Peking, but in practice there was no more co-ordination among the Mongol leaders. The ruler of the Golden Horde in south Russia had embraced Islam and was allied with the Egyptians. The Mongol rulers of Persia and Iraq, called Ilkhans, relied increasingly on Christians and Jews to govern their predominantly Moslem lands. As the Mongol grip slackened, the Kurds emerged again to prey on the complacent Christians of Iraq.

In 1275, thirteen years after the sack of Mosul, a contemporary chronicler recorded news of the Adawi community. Two brothers belonging to Sheikh Adi's family were in dispute because the younger one had taken a Mongol wife. The elder brother utilized a brief lull in the Mongol-Mameluke war to move to Syria with four hundred followers and their horses, sheep and oxen. The following year the younger brother fled to Egypt with his wife.[38]

In those years the provincial government of Mosul was contested by Christian and Moslem factions. But the chronicler, a Jacobite, gives no reason for the emigration of the two brothers.

In 1281 the Adawi brother who had fled to Syria returned to Iraq. He asked pardon of the Ilkhan for his defection. But the time of his return was ill-chosen. The Mongols were once again at war with the Mamelukes. He was put to death.[39]

These sparse items in Bar Hebraeus' chronography terminate the contemporary reports on the community at Lalish.[40]

As the thirteenth century drew to its close the position of the Christians in Iraq began to deteriorate. Their Mongol patrons gradually lost touch with their old homelands and became assimilated to the Mesopotamian world. Some of the Ilkhan rulers became Moslems and turned a blind eye to attacks on Christians by urban Moslems and by raiding Kurds. In October 1295 Hulagu's great-grandson Ghazan declared Islam the official religion of the state and ordered churches and synagogues to be destroyed. The persecution ceased in the spring of 1296, but henceforth the Christians reverted to the inferior status prescribed by Islamic law.[41]

Meanwhile in Syria, protected by the Mameluke armies, the Adawi cult flourished anew. A biography of Sheikh Adi described many miracles ascribed to him. Parts of this work were summarized in a biography of el-Gilani and his contemporaries written by the Egyptian writer es-Shattanaufi toward the end of the thirteenth century.[42]

Zein ed-Din Yusuf, son of the slain Sheref ed-Din, settled in Damascus and later moved to the ancestral village of Beit Far. Here, sustained by gifts from Kurdish devotees — including one woman who gave him her entire fortune — the sheikh built a retreat famed for its sumptuous carpets, gold and silver vases, rich Chinese porcelain and wines of many colours. 'A generous host, high-principled and meek', Zein ed-Din established another community in Cairo, where he died in 1297.[43] His mausoleum, damaged by fire in 1907 but now restored, is one of the principal monuments of Islamic Cairo.[44]

In a period when their whole society was threatened, Moslem theologians were concerned by challenges to the strict Sunni interpretation of Islam. In the early years of the fourteenth century the Syrian theologian Ibn Taimiya published a lengthy epistle to the Adawis, urging them to moderate their veneration for Sheikh Adi and castigating Hasan b. Adi for exaggerating the cult of their founder. He also condemned another innovation ascribed to Hasan — the glorification of Caliph Yezid.[45]

Over the six centuries since Yezid's death theologians had debated his place in Moslem tradition. The Shiites detested him as the murderer of Hussein. But among the Sunnis his reputation had mellowed in the course of time. Occasional reports mention individuals or groups who spoke well of Yezid.[46] Sheikh Adi himself called Yezid 'an imam and the son of an imam, who battled the infidels' and declared that anyone who cursed him should be spurned.[47] Ibn Taimiya, while deploring the Adawis' partiality toward Yezid, counselled that the controversial caliph be neither worshipped nor cursed.[48]

Another contemporary theologian, answering an inquiry from some people in the Euphrates valley, denounced religious fanatics, citing certain Shiite sects as one extreme and 'the Adawis and Yezidis' as the other. The writer implies that the term 'Yezidi' applies to the Adawis of Iraq, for he cites Sheikh Hasan's despatch of preachers to Hit and other towns along the Euphrates, where they urged the inhabitants to kill anyone who defamed Caliph Yezid.[49]

In the midst of this turmoil, Zein ed-Din's son Izz ed-Din presided over the Adawis of Syria. In 1330/1 the sultan of Egypt, already disturbed by his popularity among the Kurds, learned that his followers were assembling horses, arms and equipment; under interrogation the Adawis in Cairo spoke of plans to conquer Egypt or the Yemen. Izz ed-Din disavowed all of these plans and suggested that, in order to calm things down, he be taken into custody. He died in prison.[50]

The Adawis continued for some time in Egypt and Syria as a Sufi religious order. But after Izz ed-Din there are no records of his branch of the Sheikh Adi family (though a manuscript from the Jebel Seman indicates that descendants of Izz ed-Din's brother lived there for at least five generations).[51]

A peace treaty was signed in 1322 between the Mongols and the mamelukes, setting the Euphrates as the border between the two states. The poems of Zein ed-Din spoke longingly of the valley of Lalish, but there are no fourteenth-century reports of its occupants. In 1327 the Moroccan traveller Ibn Battuta visited Mosul, Jezira b. Omar and Beled Sinjar (where he noted many Kurds).[52] The Egyptian encyclopaedist Ibn Fadlallah el-Omari, writing in 1338, knew about the Syrian Adawis and devoted eighteen pages to a survey of the tribes of Kurdistan.[53] But neither of these writers mentioned the community at Lalish.

Iraq never recovered from the Mongol conquest; in 1339 one third of the city of Mosul was still in ruins. Mid-century brought two more disasters — the Black Death and the break-up of the Mongol empire into an anarchy of warring principalities. Among those who suffered most were the Christians, originally favoured by the Mongols but later savagely persecuted. The Nestorian church, once pre-eminent along the trade routes of Asia, was constricted to the region bounded by Mosul, Urmia and Diyarbakir, with tenuous links to the faraway diocese of Malabar in southern India. The Jacobites survived in eastern Anatolia and the Tur Abdin.

The collapse of central authority provided opportunities for the Kurds. North of Mosul, in the mountains beyond Lalish, the Bahdinan clan established itself at Amadia, displacing the Hakkaris, who moved north to carve out a fiefdom southeast of Van. The Bohti clan took over the ruined city of Jezira b. Omar. Farther upstream, the citadel of Hisn Kaif and the great bridge across the Tigris were held by the heirs of Saladin, a last remnant of a once vast empire.

In 1393 the Kurdish chieftains hastened to kiss the carpet of Timur, a new world-conqueror from Turkestan, who swept through Iraq, leaving towers of skulls, many of them Christian, that glowed at night as an enduring relic of his passage. Eight years later, after conquering India, eastern Anatolia and the north of Syria, he descended again to wipe out a rebellion in Baghdad, leaving 100,000 civilians dead. The crippled conqueror (known in the west as Tamerlane) died in 1405, leaving Iraq to be fought over once more by old and new warlords.

Early in 1415 a surprising item of intelligence from Kuridstan became known in Cairo. The long-forgotten disciples of Sheikh Adi had become so powerful that Izz ed-Din, the emir of Jezira b. Omar, heeding the complaints of a Persian Sufi preacher, organized an expedition against them, assisted by el-Adil of Hisn Kaif, descendant and namesake of Saladin's brother, and two other chieftains. The combined force invaded the Hakkari mountains, killed great masses of Sheikh Adi's followers — then called *Sohbetiye* (the companions) by the Kurds — and took many prisoners. After the battle the invaders went to the village where Sheikh Adi was buried and levelled his tomb to the ground, burning his bones in front of the prisoners and taking much booty. The chronicler, Taqi ed-Din Maqrizi, records that 'the companions' re-gathered and rebuilt the tomb and adds that at the time of writing (some twenty years later) the cult was still thriving.[54]

Amazingly, the little community at Lalish had outlived the Abbasids, the Mongols, the Black Death and the visitations of Timur. But, apart from this brief entry in Magrizi's history, there is a gap of more than 200 years between the execution of Sheikh Adi's relative in 1281 and the next mention of his followers at the start of the sixteenth century.

By that time the obscure Yezidi cult had become a religion embracing many thousands of Kurds. But its doctrines had evolved far from the Sufi way of life. Mohammed, acclaimed five times daily as the true prophet by Moslems from the shores of the Atlantic ocean to the China sea, played no part in this new religion. The Koranic account of God's first actions after he created man, a tradition held in common with Christians and Jews, was rejected as untrue. A new intercessor was proclaimed for the faithful. His symbol was a peacock.

Chapter Three
The Yezidi Religion

The birth of a new religion is an awesome event in human affairs. Unlike the vain myths by which temporal rulers seek to sanctify their rule, religions have lives that endure for hundreds and thousands of years. The names of conquerors and kings sink into oblivion, but reverence is still paid to the memory of martyrs who gave their lives for a new faith, missionaries whose words touched the hearts and minds of listeners and, most of all, to those rare individuals whose inspirations changed the world.

The founder of the Yezidi religion[1] is unknown. Neither in their own traditions nor in the chronicles of their Christian and Moslem neighbours is there any mention of the person who first proclaimed their faith.

From this strange void some scholars have concluded that in the chaos of the thirteenth and fourteenth centuries Kurdish groups somehow patched together a religion out of ill-digested doctrines and ceremonials practised by Christian and Moslem sects.

Another hypothesis, favoured by many Yezidis, suggests that their religion is very old and that the historical details of its foundation are lost in the mists of antiquity. According to this theory, the faith was able to survive over the centuries because its devotees would allow themselves to be nominally converted to newer religions such as Christianity or Islam while retaining their ancient beliefs. The integrity of the religion was preserved through the transmigration of souls — a key Yezidi belief. From time to time some saintly personage would be imbued, consciously or unconsciously, with the spirit of a devout Yezidi, which he in turn would pass on to another. The most recent of these divine incarnations was Sheikh Adi b. Musafir.

The rapid expansion of the Yezidi religion in the fourteenth and early fifteenth centuries among a formerly Moslem and, to a lesser extent, Christian

28

population indicates that the message was heard by willing ears. But there are no records of the missionary work; nor is it known how or by whom it was organized, nor whether it was heralded as a new revelation or as the unveiling of older, still cherished, beliefs.

The earliest account of the Yezidis' beliefs, ceremonies and customs was written by a French Catholic missionary in Aleppo 300 years after their religion took hold among the Kurds.[2] Italian missionaries in Iraq described them briefly in 1769, 1781 and 1810.[3] These reports, as well as notes from travellers, stress the Yezidis' reluctance to discuss religious matters and their propensity to mislead a questioner by telling him what they thought he wanted to hear.

The science of Yezidology originated in 1850 with a paper read to the Prussian Academy of Science by Dr August Neander, Professor of Religion at the University of Berlin, shortly before his death.[4] Interest among orientalists was stimulated three decades later when the journal of the French Société Asiatique published a synopsis of the religion derived from Yezidi sources.[5] Over the past 100 years a flood of commentary has appeared in European, American and Oriental publications.* Two Yezidi princes have contributed to the literature about their faith.

The outline in the following pages makes no attempt to synthesize the work of generations of scholars. Rather, it is designed to provide a framework of generally accepted knowledge about the Yezidi religion within which the narrative of the community's history unfolds.

The Yezidis believe in one God, whom they address by the Kurdish name *Khuda* and worship as the First Cause and Prime Mover of the universe. The task of creation and the establishment of plant and animal life on earth was assigned to seven angels, of whom the greatest was Azaziel. God himself created man.

The story of the proud Azaziel's refusal to bow down before Adam and his banishment from the sight of God is an ancient tradition familiar to Jews, Christians and Moslems alike. But the sequel that identifies the fallen angel with the spirit of evil has no place in the Yezidi religion. The Yezidis believe that the act of disobedience has been forgiven by God and that those who recognize the angel as once again supreme will benefit from his special protection.

* See the Bibliography (pp. 251–282) for a list of the major books and articles about the Yezidi religion. Some of these studies are quite far-fetched, notably the 53-page article published in 1910 by the Scottish–Georgian orientalist N. Ya. Marr in a Russian periodical.[6] (In 1951, seventeen years after his death, Marr's entire approach to linguistics was criticized as un-Marxist by his compatriot and fellow academician J.V. Stalin.)

The name Azaziel is now little used. Satan, the term of abuse employed by the other faiths, is a forbidden word for Yezidis and, if used in their presence by others, is considered an insult requiring instant retribution. (Indeed, Yezidis have traditionally avoided using Kurdish or Arabic words combining the letters 'sh' and 't' because of the association with *Shaitan*.) The Yezidis employ the title 'Melek Taus' — Peacock Angel — and use representations of the peacock as the emblem of their faith. The most hallowed object they possess is a lifesize bronze figure called the *Anzal* (ancient) Peacock, also known as the Peacock of Mansur.

The Yezidi religion incorporates the universal principles of ethics and morality — right and wrong, justice, truth, loyalty, mercy and love. The Day of Judgment, when the Yezidis will be rewarded for their trust in Melek Taus, is quite remote; meanwhile souls live on through transmigration, sometimes an animal form. Evil, recognized as a fact of life, is not considered the work of any supernatural being. The story of Adam and Eve is part of the Yezidi tradition; but, far from encompassing Adam's fall, the angel is shown as a provider of practical advice on the biological functions of the body.

Another tradition traces the origin of the Yezidis to Adam alone (rather than Adam and Eve). Numerous legends, not always consistent, record memorable prehistorical events. Yezidis share with other communities in northern Iraq an indelible memory of the Flood — the construction of the ark (believed by the Yezidis to have been assembled at Ain Sifni, a village six miles south of Lalish), the perilous voyage across the flooded Tigris valley, perforation of the hull by the peak of Sinn el-Kilub in the Sinjar mountains — the vessel was saved by a snake which curled up to plug the hole — and the final happy landfall on the slopes of Mount Judi.

Historical names of uncertain provenance are found here and there among the traditions of the Yezidis. They preserve the memory of Ahab, the idolatrous king of Israel; Nebuchadnezzar of Babylon, who took the Jews into captivity; Ahasuerus, the Persian shah who favoured Esther; Shahpur I and his great-grandson Shahpur II, who defeated and killed two Roman emperors; and a mysterious Byzantine ruler named Aghriqalus, possibly a corruption of Heraclius.

The position of Caliph Yezid in the religion is unclear, perhaps deliberately so. His cult is strongest around Aleppo and in the Jebel Sinjar. In these districts, where the neighbouring Moslems follow the Sunni creed, Yezidi traditions commemorate the virtues and exploits of the caliph; a long panegyric recited by a Yezidi sheikh near Aleppo in 1936 narrates the miracles performed by Yezid during the first siege of Constantinople.[7]

East of the Tigris, where Yezidis live closer to the Shiite followers of the martyred Imam Hussein, the caliph's name occurs less frequently in their folklore. Nevertheless, Yezid is venerated as an incarnation of the divine spirit and his birthday is one of their most important feasts. Approriately, the divine permission for the Yezidis to drink wine and liquor is attributed to him.

The tenuous connection between the Omayyad caliph and the Yezidi religion has led scholars to seek a more rational origin for its name. A number of them have noted its similarity to the Persian word *yaz(a)d*, meaning 'supreme being'. Attempts to derive the name from other persons bearing the name 'Yezid' have met little acceptance. (One of the boldest theories, propounded in the first half of the nineteenth century, linked the Yezidis with Shah Khosrau's banker Yazdin, the Nestorian 'prince of believers', because his country house outside Kirkuk, identified in the Greek chronicles as the place where Emperor Heraclius celebrated Christmas 627, was fairly close to where the Yezidis lived in the sixteenth and seventeenth centuries.)[8]

It seems most probable that the name 'Yezidi' was employed by Moslems, particularly Shiites, as an insulting nickname for the members of this alien faith and that in the course of time it became their official designation.

The great prophet of the Yezidi religion, who links the aeons of faith and fable with the last 800 years of recorded history, is Sheikh Adi b. Musafir, whose tomb at Lalish is their most sacred shrine.

Yezidi traditions describe his miraculous birth to an elderly couple and his departure from home to seek his destiny at the age of fifteen. Five years later, while he was riding by moonlight across a plain, the summons came to him. In front of an old tomb an apparition rose out of the ground — two camels with legs 8 ft long, heads like water buffaloes, long bristly hair, big round ox-like eyes glowing green and a jet black skin, yet otherwise resembling a man. Meanwhile the tomb grew larger until it touched the clouds, taking the shape of a minaret which then began to shake. In his terror Adi knocked over a jug of water that stood nearby. The apparition now turned into a handsome boy with a peacock's tail, who said to him:

> Fear not; the minaret may well fall and destroy the world, but you and those that hearken to you will be unharmed and will rule over the ruins. I am Melek Taus and have chosen you to proclaim the religion of truth to the world.

Thereupon he took Adi's soul to heaven for seven years and God revealed the truth of everything while Adi's body slumbered by the tomb. When his soul came down from heaven to rejoin the body, the water from the overturned jug had not yet run out.[9]

The tradition describes how, armed with miracle-working powers, the prophet settled in Lalish and preached to the turbulent Hakkari Kurds.

Finally they agreed to become his followers and a great convocation was held, where Sheikh Adi set forth the rites of worship, the categories of believers and rules of conduct by which they all should live.

Among Sheikh Adi's precepts was a warning against written books. This injunction, together with the circumstances in which they lived, made the Yezidis a community of illiterates until a few decades ago. Conversely, they possess a rich lode of folklore, carried down by oral tradition, that researchers have barely started to mine.

A few Yezidi writings attributed to Sheikh Adi have survived.* The best-known is an inspiring hymn, first published in 1853; an English translation appears as Appendix I (iii).

The prophet's greatest bequest to his followers was the 'Kitab el-Jelwa' (Arabic for 'The Book of Revelation'), which he is believed to have dictated to his secretary, Fakhr ed-Din, shortly before he died. A brief work in Arabic containing slightly less than 500 words, the Jelwa is considered the most sacred book in the Yezidi religion. Extracts were published in 1891 and the full text in 1895.[10] An English translation appears as Appendix I (i).

The tomb of Sheikh Adi is in an inner room of the Lalish sanctuary, covered by silken cloths of many colours. A green curtain on the wall is embroidered with the words of the 'Ayat el-Kursi' (verse 256 of the second chapter of the Koran, a traditional valediction).

The first companions of Sheikh Adi are venerated by their descendants and by the whole Yezidi community. The greatest of these was Sheikh Shems ed-Din, whose tomb is near the main sanctuary. His descendants form one of the three main clans of Yezidi sheikhs.

The tomb of his brother Fakhr ed-Din is a short distance away. The chief religious official of the Yezidis, known as the 'Baba Sheikh', is chosen from the Fakhr ed-Din clan.

Abu Bekr, another companion of the prophet, related to his father Musafir and consequently an Omayyad like Yezid, is considered the ancestor of the present Chol dynasty of Yezidi princes. His tomb is in the Lalish sanctuary.

Sheikh Adi's great-grandnephew Hasan b. Adi, who set new directions for the Lalish community and fell victim to Atabeg Lulu's wrath, lies buried in a room adjoining the sepulchre of Sheikh Adi. (Since the advent of the Chol dynasty, who took over leadership of the Yezidis from Sheikh Hasan's descendants in the seventeenth century, he has been commemorated under the name of Hasan el-Basri, a precursor of the Sufis who died in 728.)

Sheikh Hasan is considered the author of the other sacred book of the Yezidi religion — the 'Meshaf Resh' (Kurdish words meaning 'The Black Book').

* None of the Sufi works written by Sheikh Adi (see pp 17–18) are considered canonical by the Yezidis.

This work, published in various versions between 1886 and 1909,[11] contains the Yezidi account of the creation of the world, the origin of man and the story of Adam and Eve; it also lists the major prohibitions of the faith. An English translation of the text appears as Appendix I (ii).

The third clan of sheikhs, traditionally devoted to maintaining the purity of the faith, trace their ancestry to Sheikh Hasan. One branch of the family, living at Bahzani, is responsible for training the *kawals* who circulate among the Yezidi villages, preaching and collecting alms. For years the sheikh who filled this position was the only Yezidi permitted to read and write. He was also the official custodian of the Jelwa. The office of *Peshimam*, the supervisor of weddings and marriage contracts, is always filled by a member of this clan.

Sheref ed-Din, the luckless son of Sheikh Hasan who lost his life fighting the Mongols for the Turks, achieved posthumous fame as the patron saint of the Sinjar. The local Yezidis regard him as the man who introduced their religion to the mountain. The tribesmen on the eastern slopes wear their hair hanging down in long braids in accordance with his command. There is a small shrine dedicated to Sheref ed-Din at the summit of Chilmeran, the highest peak of the mountain, and a larger shrine in a village lower down. The shrines are maintained out of one half of the alms collected in the name of Sheref ed-Din. The other half has for centuries been deposited in a cave somewhere on the mountain (reputedly at Deir Asi, 2 miles north of Beled Sinjar).

These semi-divine companions and successors of Sheikh Adi are identified in Yezidi mythology with the angels who assisted God and Melek Taus in the creation of the world. There are, in addition, a great number of saints whose shrines are of regional or local importance.

In the absence of historical records it is not possible to trace how the structure of the Yezidi religion evolved over the first centuries of its existence. The basic framework resembles that of a Sufi order, with some important differences. First described early in the nineteenth century,[12] the organization has changed little since that date.

There are a number of categories in the Yezidi hierarchy — in addition to the Mir, who embodies the secular arm of the community. The vicissitudes of the princes who have occupied this uneasy post are narrated in subsequent chapters.

The *sheikhs*, whose authority derives from the prophet's great convocation, are the active ministers of the faith. Their head, the 'Baba Sheikh', is appointed by the Mir. At present there are some 300 families of sheikhs whose members serve as pastors for the lay families assigned to their care. The sheikhs are responsible for arranging the religious festivals at Lalish and other shrines.

Ranking second in veneration are the *pirs* ('elders' in Persian). There are about 200 families of pirs belonging to four main clans descended from early Kurdish disciples of Sheikh Adi. The guardian of the Lalish sanctuary, called the 'Baba Chawush' (chief doorkeeper) is the most eminent of the pirs and must always remain unmarried. The pirs participate with the sheikhs in religious ceremonies, but they are generally unburdened by administrative duties and devote their time to meditation and prayer.

Subordinate to the sheikhs are the *kawals* (literally, reciters), drawn from two families living in the villages of Bashika and Bahzani. At Lalish they provide choirs for the festivals. But for over a century their main function has been to visit every Yezidi community, no matter how remote, carrying a peacock replica as proof of their identity. When the kawal comes to a village, the headman assigns him a room in his house, where the kawal fixes the peacock onto a stand and conducts a service accompanied by collection of alms on behalf of the 'sanjak'.* Each replica is named after its allotted territory — Syria, Zozan (a general term for the Anatolian highlands), Tabriz, Musquf (Muscovy), Sinjar and Sheikhan (both in northern Iraq). Kawals now also visit the Yezidi communities in West Germany, but the sanjaks of Tabriz and Muscovy perambulate no more. When not on circuit, the replicas are kept in the Mir's castle at Baadri.

The origin of this system of alms collection is unknown. According to one account, each sanjak used to be the property of a clan of sheikhs and its revenues were used to support their endowment. Around 1840 the Mir, pressed for funds to pay tribute, consolidated all collections into a single fund out of which all religious expenses were paid to the extent money was available.[13]

Next in importance is the category of *faqirs* (poor people), distinguished by the plain dress Sheikh Adi traditionally wore — a black smock, edged with red and caught up at the waist by a red and white braided girdle, and a black turban. Beneath their robes they wear a red and black cord necklace. Like the Sufi initiates of old, the faqirs achieve their status by penance and prayer. Theoretically open to any Yezidi, the rank of faqir tends to be carried down from father to son. In the Jebel Sinjar an entire tribe of *Faqiran* exists. The duties of a faqir are to minister to laymen in the absence of a sheikh. Some of them serve as acolytes at Lalish.

The most remarkable of all the grades in the Yezidi religion is that of *kochek* ('little one'). Most of these are pilgrims who left their homes to settle around

---

* The word 'sanjak' strictly means the stand, but is commonly used for the fully assembled image. It is also used generally to denote the right granted to a group of kawals to collect alms in a particular territory. (The same word was also used to designate minor administrative districts of the Ottoman empire.)

Lalish and work for the sanctuary as woodchoppers; during festivals they take care of the visitors' needs. But among them are individuals gifted with ecstatic powers who claim to communicate directly with Melek Taus himself. Around the middle of the eighteenth century a kochek declared to the 'Baba Sheikh' that in a vision during the night it was revealed to him that the indigo colour of the shirts then worn by Yezidis was unlucky and displeasing to Melek Taus. Orders at once went out that all blue clothes should be thrown away and henceforth only white clothes should be worn;[14] in many communities this rule is still observed.*

There is also an order of white-robed female attendants called *faqriyat* — a small number of widows and girls vowed to celibacy — who serve at the Lalish sanctuary under the direction of an abbess and weave wicks for the lamps.

Yezidi laymen are called *murids*, the traditional name given to Sufi novices. Each layman has his own sheikh and his own pir, to whom he makes offerings in money, in services or in kind. Despite their lowly position in the religious scheme of things, the murids — chiefs, landowners, shepherds, peasants and common workers — are the mainstay of Yezidi society and their labours support the religious superstructure.

The great staging points of human life are solemnized in Yezidi families with a blend of tribal customs and religious code.

At birth an infant is baptized by the sheikh and the pir, using water from Lalish or else local water into which dust from the shrine of Sheikh Adi has been sprinkled.

Circumcision is an important rite in the Yezidi religion. A peculiar custom known as *karif* prevails in northern Iraq, whereby a Yezidi boy may be circumcised on the knees of a Moslem man, thereby establishing a form of life-long blood-brotherhood between the two.

Another relationship, limited to Yezidis, is established at puberty, when each murid selects a 'brother/sister of the hereafter' from a family of sheikhs other than the one to which he is linked at birth. In addition, some Yezidis pick a 'tutor', generally from a non-affiliated family of pirs.

Marriage has customarily been arranged by the parents of the bride and groom; an important element is negotiation of a satisfactory bride-price to be paid by the groom to the bride's family (this payment is required even in cases of elopement). The wedding ceremony is performed by the sheikh and the pir, with the 'brother and sister of the hereafter' in attendance on the groom and bride. It is followed by feasting, dancing and the firing of rifles into the air.

* Other prohibitions forbid eating lettuce, fish or the meat of a gazelle.

35

Traditionally, Yezidis have not been permitted to marry outside their faith. This prohibition has recently been relaxed provided the spouse becomes a Yezidi.

Sheikhs and pirs are only permitted to marry within their own class; indeed, sheikhs are restricted to marriage within their particular clan. Faqirs tend to marry within their class. Kawals were recently permitted to marry murids because their class was beginning to die out.

Special marriage protocol was developed over the years for the Yezidi princely family, whose males could only marry relatives from their own family or members of one other family claimed to be of noble birth.

Although the Yezidi religion permits men to have more than one wife, this is uncommon. Divorce is permitted but is very rare.

Funerals are conducted by the sheikh and attended by the blood-brother and the 'brother of the hereafter'. After dust from Lalish has been sprinkled over the eyes, ears and mouth, the body is wrapped in a white shroud and lowered into the grave.

All of the foregoing ceremonies take place where the family lives. The Yezidis have no public places of worship in their villages. Daily prayers are said in private.

There are four official festivals in the Yezidi religious year, which begins on the first Wednesday in April in the Seleucid calendar (mid-April by the Gregorian calendar).

The feast of *Sarisal* (Persian for New Year's Day) is celebrated in every village where Yezidis live. Preparations for the feast include visiting family graves, where food is placed for passersby; gathering scarlet ranunculus to adorn their houses; and colourful decoration of eggs. At midnight, it is believed, angels pass.

The most elaborate celebration of this feast takes place at the Yezidi villages of Bashika and Bahzani east of Lalish. The Baba Sheikh, generally accompanied by the Mir and his family, conducts the ceremonies here, which include worship at the shrines of Sheikh Mohammed (the local saint), Melki Miran (a reputed ancestor of the princely family) and others. One of the sanjaks is unveiled on this occasion, which marks the start of its local spring circuit. The festival concludes with horse races, often attended by visitors from Mosul.

In the Jebel Sinjar the celebrations are held at the shrine of Sheref ed-Din on the peak of Mount Chilmeran with fireworks marking the start of a new year.

The second feast, celebrated only at Lalish, lasts for three days — from the evening of 18 July to the morning of 21 July (Seleucid), or 31 July–3 August (Gregorian). Known as the Feast of Sheikh Adi or the Feast of the Forty Days, it marks the end of the summer fast observed during daylight hours by the Baba Sheikh and the kocheks in memory of Sheikh Adi's similar fast.

The principal feast of the year is the seven-day Feast of the Assembly, held at Lalish to mark the anniversary of Sheikh Adi's original convocation. The feast lasts from the evening of 23 September to the morning of 30 September (Seleucid); these dates corresponded in the nineteenth century to 5–12 October and in this century to 6–13 October. The obligation to attend this festival is one of the articles of the Yezidi faith and delegations come from every tribe in the community when political and economic conditions permit.

For the pilgrims this festival combines the mystic experience of a revival with the joy of a carnival. The public ceremonies, witnessed by infrequent foreigners since 1846,* include ritual washing by arriving pilgrims; baptism of children at a shrine where the White Spring wells up into tanks inhabited by sacred newts; distribution of pellets formed by mixing dust from the sanctuary with water from the holiest spring of all beneath Sheikh Adi's tomb; visits to the many shrines and sacred spots; and participation in the prayers, processions, songs and dancing that continue throughout the week.

Shelter for the visitors is available in small dwellings scattered along the valley, maintained by each tribe for its members; some pilgrims pitch their tents on the slopes. Shops are set up in a courtyard of the sanctuary, where merchants sell haberdashery, jewellery, dried fruit and nuts. The pilgrims bring their own food, but the Mir provides certain ceremonial meals from kitchens near the shrine. At one of these functions pieces of meat are thrown into the crowd in memory of a meal once interrupted by the arrival of a long absent companion of Sheikh Adi. On another day groups of young men race up the mountainside, fire off their rifles and then pretend to steal a bull, which they parade around Sheikh Shems ed-Din's shrine before distributing the meal to the pilgrims.

For the leaders of the Yezidis the Feast of the Assembly is a solemn occasion at which the affairs of the community are discussed and the guidance of Melek Taus is sought. The nature of these ceremonies is a well-guarded secret. The great peacock is brought to Lalish for the feast and all of the sanjaks are due back from their circuits. Based on the results of these collections, expenditures are allocated for the coming year.

Throughout the week the Baba Sheikh, the Mir and other dignitaries mingle freely among the pilgrims. This is the only time when they can meet many of their followers; their usual channel of communication with the remoter Yezidi

---

* A vivid account by the first foreign beholder appears later on pp. 95–97.

settlements has been by means of the kawals.

The fourth official festival in the Yezidi calendar, preceded by three days of general fasting, occurs on the first Friday in December (Seleucid) or in mid-December (Gregorian). It commemorates the birthday of Yezid.

In addition to these official religious feasts, Yezidis commonly celebrate certain Moslem and Christian feasts such as the feast of Khidr Elias* in Turkish and Arab countries and the Armenian feast of St Sergius in Transcaucasia.

The transformation of Lalish from a retreat of the Adawi order into the headquarters of the Yezidi religion has brought about the development of a complex of buildings and open spaces enclosed on three sides by ashlar walls and on the north side by the live rock of the mountain. A stream runs down the valley in front of the sanctuary, joined by smaller streams from the northern mountain slope that run through the precincts. A big spring named Zemzem (the same name as the Moslems' sacred well near Mecca) issues from the mountain at the spot where Sheikh Adi's shrine is built; the water flows through the eastern end of the sanctuary to join the main stream lower down. (Plate 6 and the plan opposite show the general layout of the sanctuary and the principal buildings after the 1906/7 reconstruction.)

After crossing the stream the visitor arrives at the western end of the sanctuary. Passing beneath a large arched gateway, riders dismount in a courtyard lined to right and left by covered stalls used by merchants during the autumn festival and by visitors at other times. The courtyard is shaded by mulberry trees and contains several fountains and a trough.

From the outer courtyard, a place of common use, the visitor is led through a small doorway into an arched passage, where he removes his shoes before stepping into the sacred area. He then enters a walled inner courtyard, paved with flagstones and almost completely shaded by ancient mulberry trees. In the northwestern corner a low wall sets off a pergola where the Baba Sheikh receives his guests and oversees the distribution of pellets. During the festival ceremonial dances are conducted beneath the trees.

The eastern wall of this courtyard is decorated with carved symbols — a hatchet, a comb, staffs, birds, dogs and, most striking of all, a 6 ft high snake

---

* This feast is celebrated in the spring. El-Khidr ('the green man') is a mythical Arab saint, sometimes identified with the prophet Elijah, sometimes with the Christian St George and sometimes with the (Nestorian) Christian martyr Mar Behnam.[15]

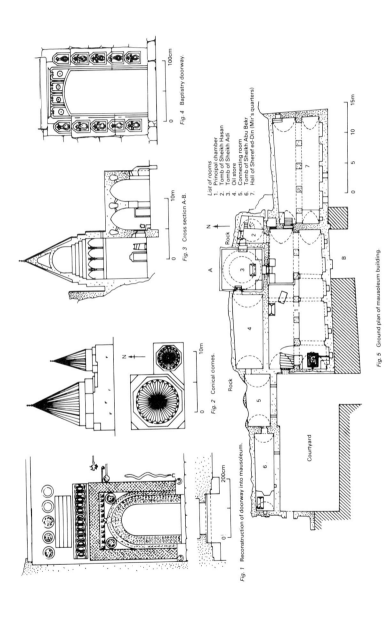

Fig. 4 Baptistry doorway.

Fig. 3 Cross section A-B.

Fig. 2 Conical comes.

Fig. 1 Reconstruction of doorway into mausoleum.

List of rooms
1. Principal chamber
2. Tomb of Sheikh Hasan
3. Tomb of Sheikh Adi
4. Oil store
5. Connecting room
6. Tomb of Sheikh Abu Bekr
7. Hall of Sheref ed-Din (Mir's quarters)

Rock

Rock

Courtyard

Fig. 5 Ground plan of mausoleum building.

Detailed plan of Lalish sanctuary in 1911
Source: Walter Bachmann, *Kirchen und Moscheen in Armenien und Kurdistan*, Leipzig, J. G. Hinrichs, 1913, Plate 15.
(Deutsche Orient-Gesellschaft, Wiss. Veröff., vol. 25. Photo: Orient Division, NYPL.)

carved in relief and blackened daily with shoe polish.* Immediately to the left is the doorway into the shrine; an Arabic inscription above the door records the most recent restoration.[16]

The first chamber in the shrine is 80 ft long and 36 ft wide, divided lengthwise by five stone pillars and a small step that makes the left side slightly higher than the right. To the right of the entrance is a cistern, 3 ft deep, through which flows water from the White Spring. A tomb at the centre of the left wall is believed to belong to Sheikh Abu 'l-Barakat, the first successor of Sheikh Adi.

At the end of the chamber a door leads into another room — the hall of Sheref ed-Din — connecting with the quarters occupied by the Mir for the festival. To the left of this door, another doorway leads into a small room containing the sarcophagus of Sheikh Hasan; a fluted conical dome rises 35 ft above the flat roof of this building.

To the west of this room but separated by a wall from the main chamber is a larger room, 25 ft x 25 ft, containing the tomb of Sheikh Adi. The tip of the conical dome that crowns his mausoleum is 40 ft above the roof of the building.

A long room to the west of Sheikh Adi's tomb chamber is used for storing jars of oil for the lamps; two more rooms extend farther westward. At the end of the last room is the tomb of Sheikh Abu Bekr, the companion of Sheikh Adi from whom the Yezidi princes descend; a conical dome rises above his tomb.

A spiral staircase leads from Sheikh Hasan's tomb chamber down to the basement of the shrine. A few steps down, a passage connects a series of rooms serving as a spillway carrying the waters of Zemzem to enclosed pools where ritual immersions of priests and pilgrims take place. The main source of the spring, believed to come out of the rock into a large chamber beneath Sheikh Adi's tomb chamber, has never been shown to anyone by the Yezidis.[17]

Another room not shown to visitors is the 'Treasury of the Merciful One', where the great peacock and the sanjaks are housed at the time of the Feast of the Assembly. (There is a similar room in the Mir's castle in Baadri, where the great peacock is kept under lock and key and where the sanjaks are placed when they come back from their circuits.)

The Lalish valley is dotted with smaller shrines — the Baptistry built above the White Spring; the Shrine of Sheikh Shems ed-Din with a fluted conical dome topped by a gilded ball that reflects the first rays of the morning sun; the shrine of Pir Hajjali; and many others. According to one account, there are also shrines dedicated to Sheikh Adi's friend Abd el-Qadir el-Gilani and to

* A recent renovation of the entrance to the shrine has plastered over many of these symbols. The snake is still there. (see Plate 15).

Hussein b. Mansur el-Hallaj, the Sufi mystic who first proclaimed the redemption of the fallen angel and was crucified as a heretic in the year 922 AD.[18]

A persistent tradition, stoutly maintained by the Chaldeans of northern Iraq, holds that the shrine of Sheikh Adi was once a Christian church, founded according to some accounts by two Nestorian monks named John and Jesusabran who lived in the seventh century AD.

The attribution to the two monks is based upon documents of dubious value; a leading expert on Nestorian church history believes that their monastery was located on Mount Maqlub overlooking Bashika and Bahzani, possibly on the site now occupied by the Yezidi village of Mohammed Resan.

The origin of the Lalish shrine remains a mystery. Some experts claim to recognize features typical of Nestorian architecture, while others consider the building to have been a mountain mosque.[19] The Yezidis themselves concede that it might once have been a Christian church; a modern inscription* above the doorway leading into the shrine proclaims the antiquity of their estate, reading:

> In the name of God the Almighty, the Merciful,
> Creator of Heaven and Earth
> Beneath this house [is]
> The place of Sheikh Adi el-Hakkari
> Sheikh of the Yezidis 695.[20]

AH 695 ran from 10 November 1295 to 29 October 1296. This was the year when the Mongol Ilkhan Ghazan became a Moslem and commenced a persecution of the Nestorian church.

---

* The doorway was completely reconstructed between 1911 and 1922. The former inscription above the door was remarked on by many travellers, but its text was not recorded, except for the date AH 133 (750/1 AD).[21] This was the year that followed the overthrow of the Omayyad caliph Merwan II, when some of his followers fled to Kurdistan.

Chapter Four

Early Encounters with the Outside World

Few chroniclers left records of the dark age that followed the break-up of the Mongol empire. Consequently, there are no contemporary accounts of the early spread of the Yezidi religion in the fourteenth century.

The earliest reference to the Yezidi religion appears in the Sheref-nameh ('The Book of Glory', sometimes called 'The Chronicles of the Kurds'), written in 1597 to memorialize the traditions of some thirty Kurdish tribes and the lineage of their ruling families. The author, Sheref ed-Din Khan, was the hereditary emir of Bitlis. His historical base goes back to the time of Tamerlane; earlier data blend fact with legend.

According to Sheref ed-Din seven of the principal Kurdish tribes were at one time or another wholly or partly Yezidi — a religion he describes as follows:

> They believe falsely that Sheikh Adi has taken upon himself their
> duties to fast and to pray, and that on the day of resurrection they
> will be carried to heaven without being exposed to any punishment
> or any reproach. These Kurds have sworn hatred and the most
> implacable enmity against the virtuous sages of Islam.[1]

The leading Yezidi tribe, then as now, are the Daseni, who occupy the foothills north and east of Mosul leading to Sheikh Adi's shrine at Lalish; for the last 200 years their territory has been known as the Sheikhan. Ibn Fadlallah's survey of Kurdistan had identified them as a branch of the Bohti, who lived in the mountains north of Mosul; he reported that the tribe disintegrated when their chief Bedr b. Kebanek departed in search of better pasture, leaving less than 1,000 men in the province of Mosul and some 500 men in the Akra district.[2]

42

The introduction to the Sheref-nameh lists among the book's contents a chapter on the Daseni. But in the original manuscript of the Sheref-nameh, signed by the author and now in the Bodleian Library at Oxford, the text of Book III Part 2 skips from the end of the sixth chapter to the beginning of the tenth chapter without a gap and with no explanation in the main body of the text or in the margin.[3] (Subsequent copyists of the Sheref-nameh called attention to the lacuna, blaming the manuscript from which they were copying.)[4] The three omitted chapters deal with the Tazra, the Ustuni (neither one identified by Sheref ed-Din as Yezidi) and the Daseni tribes.

At that time the Daseni territory extended to the southeast as far as Adiabene, the region between the Great and Lesser Zab rivers, when they feuded with their traditional enemies, the Soran.

Mosul remained a stronghold of Islam, but upstream the Yezidi religion found many adherents. Around Jezira b. Omar a significant portion of the Bohti tribe became Yezidis. For a while (presumably before 1410) their emirs observed 'the customs and principles...of the impious Yezidis' but were later reconciled to Islam.[5]

At Hisn Kaif the heirs of Saladin remained Moslem and took part in the 1410 expedition, but their territories north of the Tigris afforded summer pastures for nomadic Yezidi tribes — the Khaliti east of Batman and the Basian around Mayafariqin (now Silvan).[6]

Two other tribes, both mentioned in Ibn Fadlallah's report, originated from the Jezira b. Omar region and carried with them their belief in the Yezidi faith. The Mahmudi occupied the craggy fortress of Hosap, southeast of Van, while the Dunbeli moved to the mountains west of Lake Urmia.[7]

Far to the west the Sheref-nameh describes a group of Yezidis in northern Syria, with traditions going back to the Hakkari regiments that served under Saladin. Some time after the Crusaders had been expelled a Hakkari chieftain named Mend was granted their castle at Qoseir (west of Aleppo) and a fiefdom over the local Kurds, by then largely Yezidi.[8] The mountainous Jebel Seman region between Qoseir and Aleppo, once teeming with pilgrims visiting the shrine of St Simeon Stylites, still contains Yezidi villages.*

Sheref ed-Din's work occasionally mentions the Jebel Sinjar, but provides no historical information on its inhabitants.

The power vacuum that allowed the Kurdish principalities to flourish and the Yezidi religion to expand did not last long. After Tamerlane died at the height

* See p. 26.

of his power, new confederations arose to challenge his successors and one another in eastern Anatolia and Iraq. But at the close of the fifteenth century a new kind of warlord emerged.

Ismail Safawi, the first modern Shah of Persia, was hereditary master of a Sufi fraternity centred in Ardebil, a city in Azerbaijan. His teachings, based on the Shia form of Islam, gained a wide following among the Turks of eastern Anatolia and inspired a flow of fanatical recruits for his army. In 1501 the twenty-four-year-old Ismail, victorious over his enemies, was proclaimed Shahanshah — the first king of kings since Yezdegerd had fled the country over 800 years before. Within a few years Ismail had conquered Persia, Iraq and all of Anatolia east of the Euphrates. Diyarbakir was taken in 1507, Baghdad and Mosul in the following year.

Each in his fashion, the Kurdish chieftains bent with the wind. The Dunbelis and Mahmudis, closest to Persia, submitted to Ismail. The prince of Amadia rallied to the Shiite invader and seized the Yezidi fortress of Dohuk, 18 miles west of Lalish.[9] A delegation of thirteen other chiefs, anxious to be confirmed in their ancient fiefs, waited upon Ismail after the fall of Diyarbakir. The shah accepted two of them as vassals and imprisoned the others, including the princes of Jezira b. Omar, Hisn Kaif and Bitlis. After three years the prisoners were released and sent back to their tribes, with two exceptions. One of them was the prince of Hisn Kaif. The other was Sheref ed-Din's grand-father, the emir of Bitlis, who escaped, tried and failed to recapture his fortress and finally appealed to a western potentate for help.

In 1514, when the fugitive emir's message reached Sultan Selim, the Ottoman empire already covered central and western Anatolia, large parts of southern Russia and Romania, together with the entire Balkan peninsula. Its capital was the imperial city of Istanbul, where Julian, Heraclius and their successors had reigned. All of these conquests had been achieved in the space of 150 years after Ottoman Turk mercenaries had first crossed over into Europe to fight in a Greek civil war.

But in contrast to their string of victories over weak Christian states, the Ottomans had expanded with difficulty to the east. One of the sultans had been defeated and captured by Tamerlane and the Ottomans were fortunate to regain their independence when he died. The advent of Shah Ismail and his quasi-religious appeal to the Anatolian Turks was an even more lethal challenge to the empire.

After quelling an insurrection fomented by Ismail's followers, Sultan Selim — an orthodox Sunni justly named 'The Grim' — ordered the massacre of all

Shiites in Anatolia. Safe passage thus assured, the Ottoman army marched eastward to inflict a crushing defeat on the shah at Çaldiran (north of Lake Urmia) in August 1514. Within a few years Diyarbakir, Urfa, Mardin, Mosul and Sinjar came under Ottoman rule.

The new eastern provinces of the empire were given Ottoman governors, under whose authority the old Kurdish fiefdoms east of the Tigris were allowed to survive as autonomous border principalities.

In 1516 Selim invaded Syria, defeated the Egyptian army and captured Aleppo and Damascus. Qasim Beg, chief of the Kurds west of Aleppo, paid homage to the sultan; he had long been at odds with the Egyptians, who had sought to install a Yezidi, Sheikh Izz ed-Din, in his place. In the following year, after Selim had conquered Egypt, Qasim Beg accompanied the sultan on his triumphal return to Istanbul. Meanwhile Shiekh Izz ed-Din ingratiated himself with the new Ottoman governor of Aleppo and arranged for Qasim Beg to be executed on a charge of treason. The Yezidi leader was appointed emir of the Kurds, a post he retained until his death. He left no children and after some years the fiefdom was restored to the heirs of Qasim Beg.[10]

One of the spoils of Egypt was control of the pilgrimage to Mecca and Medina. After Selim had received the submission of the local authorities the Ottoman sultans assumed the title of 'caliph and servitor of the holy places' and terminated the line of Abbasid caliphs who had officiated in Cairo since the fall of Baghdad.

During the reign of Selim's successor, Sultan Suleiman the Magnificent, Ottoman expansion in Europe received its first decisive check at the hands of the Hapsburgs, an Austrian family that ruled over Germany, Italy, Spain and the newly discovered treasure houses of Mexico and Peru. A few years after his failure to take Vienna, the sultan signed a historic treaty with France, a rich and vigorous nation threatened by Hapsburg ambitions. The king of France was granted the right to establish trading posts, administered by consuls invested with extraterritorial rights, at various seaports and at Aleppo.

In the east the threat from Persia diminished after the battle of Çaldiran and Ismail's early death. In 1534 Suleiman undertook a campaign against his successor. Persian troops withdrew as the huge Ottoman army moved east from Diyarbakir to Van (where Suleiman accepted the submission of the Mahmudi tribe)[11] and Tabriz, thence southward through ice and snow to Hamadan, and finally southwest along Hulagu's old route to Baghdad, which surrendered in December.

Unlike the Mongols, Suleiman had not launched a second army from Mosul down the Tigris valley to Baghdad. The territory south of the Great Zab and the key fortresses of Erbil and Kirkuk along the road from Mosul to Baghdad were held by the Shiite tribe of Soran Kurds, allied to the shah. After capturing

Baghdad the sultan secured his communications with Mosul by executing the Soran emir and appointing a Yezidi, Hussein Beg of the Daseni tribe, to be governor of Erbil. Shortly thereafter, on the death of the slain chief's successor, Hussein Beg was granted the entire Soran fiefdom.

Yezidi rule over the Soran tribe, marked by persecution of the Shiite faith, was short-lived. A cousin of the Soran emirs who had fled to Persia managed to seize Erbil while Hussein Beg was absent. The Yezidi leader assembled a force to recapture Erbil but was defeated by the Soran with a loss of 500 men and much booty. After a second attempt was repulsed Hussein Beg was summoned to Istanbul and paid the price of failure with his life. (The Soran subsequently submitted to Ottoman rule.)[12]

Meanwhile, the sultan had returned to his capital by way of Lake Urmia and Tabriz, where he ordered the affairs of Kurdistan and executed a double-dealing Mahmudi chieftain.[13] In the course of his long reign Suleiman fought two more wars against Persia, but the frontier established by treaty in 1555 closely matches the present western boundary of Iran.

By the end of the sixteenth century the Dunbeli tribe was settled on the Persian side of the border; the chiefs and most of the tribesmen had become Sunni Moslems, but a minority clung to the Yezidi faith and some of them later migrated into Anatolia.[14] Their traditional enemies, the Mahmudi, lived on the Ottoman side of the border southeast of Van; this tribe had been largely converted to Islam on the orders of their chief.[15]

The Yezidi religion held its own along the Tigris valley between Diyarbakir and Mosul and in the Jebel Seman enclave west of Aleppo. About this time it began to flourish in a new setting — the isolated mountains of Sinjar, bypassed by history since the days of Atabeg Lulu but incorporated in the Ottoman empire since 1517. Early in the seventeenth century the Yezidis on the Jebel Sinjar inflicted a severe defeat on the Ottoman general Nasuh Pasha.[16]

In the seventeenth century the balance between the Ottoman empire, heavily involved in European wars, and Persia, ruled by the vigorous Shah Abbas, tilted toward the latter. A rebellious governor of Baghdad allowed the Persians to reoccupy the city in 1623. The Ottomans briefly lost but soon regained Kirkuk and Mosul.

At some point in this turbulent period the line of Daseni rulers descended from the martyred Sheikh Hasan was overthrown by a chieftain from the Soran mountains beyond the Great Zab who traced his ancestry to Sheikh Abu Bekr, a cousin of Sheikh Adi. After killing the Daseni Mir and eighty of his followers, Sheikh Mohammed — known as el-Kurdi (the Kurd), el-Erbili (the man from Erbil) and el-Batini (the revealer) — founded the dynasty of Mirs that still reigns over the Yezidis and guards the sanctuary at Lalish. The new Mir appointed henchmen from a related noble family, the Basmariya, to enforce his rule.[17]

Meanwhile the Ottoman sultan Murad IV, a worthy successor to Selim the Grim, led an army in person to recapture Baghdad. Leaving nothing to chance, he staged at Aleppo, Urfa, Diyarbakir, Mardin, Mosul and Kirkuk, reaching the walls of Baghdad on the 197th day of the march. At the end of December 1638 the city was taken by storm; contemporary accounts record the exploits of a Daseni contingent led by a chief named Mirza Beg.[18] In January 1639 Murad departed for Istanbul, where he died the following year. He was the second and last Ottoman sultan to visit Iraq.

For a number of years after Sultan Murad's death the direction of Ottoman policy was contested by rival factions. In 1649 the grand vizier Kara Murad Pasha appointed the Daseni Mirza Beg governor of Mosul with the rank of pasha. The following year the grand vizier was replaced and Mirza Pasha went to Istanbul to seek a new appointment.

Melek Ahmed Pasha, the new grand vizier, distrusted Yezidis. In 1640, when he was governor of Diyarbakir, he had led a punitive expedition against the Sacheli Kurds, a Yezidi tribe on the Jebel Sinjar, who plundered merchant and pilgrim caravans and raided villages in the plain below Mardin. The Ottoman army surrounded the mountain, stormed the Yezidi positions and after heavy casualties on both sides succeeded in recovering the stolen merchandise.[19]

After months of expensive and fruitless intrigue in Istanbul Mirza Pasha decided to return home. His rivals persuaded the grand vizier that he was going to stir up trouble. A body of troops, accompanied by the grand vizier's nephew Evliya Çelebi, intercepted the Daseni chieftain shortly after he had left the capital. He was executed on the way back and his head was sent to the palace to be displayed above the Topkapi gate.[20]

A few days later Melek Ahmed Pasha was dismissed. The former grand vizier was given an important post in the Balkans; in early 1655 he was appointed governor of Van. One of his first steps was to send Evliya Çelebi to Diyarbakir to collect an old debt from the local governor, Firari Mustafa Pasha.

Evliya Çelebi recorded his many travels in a monumental book, much of which has survived. He relates that upon reaching Diyarbakir he learned that the governor had set off on an expedition to collect taxes from the Sinjar Yezidis. He caught up with Mustafa Pasha in May 1655, encamped in the plain below Beled Sinjar. The mountaineers occupied the heights and the governor was uncertain how to proceed. Evliya recounted the story of his uncle's 1640 campaign. Finally the governor sent a delegation (including Evliya) to parley with the rebels and demand payment of taxes. The Kurds replied that 'if Melek Ahmed Pasha had come back to fight them, they would rub their faces in his footprints, but for Mustafa Pasha they would only give ten loads of silk.' Enraged, the pasha summoned reinforcements. At that point Evliya returned to his post and the outcome of the expedition is unknown.

Evliya spent one night on the mountain with the delegation. He describes an outlaw's paradise, watered by seventy springs and peopled by stocky, shaggy-haired men with round, black eyes, wearing multi-coloured woollen clothes, silk belts and turbans and heavy bamboo shoes, equipped with swords, scimitars, battleaxes and guns 'capable of hitting a flea in the eye'. Their women wore their hair ankle-length. Dogs, plentiful and mostly black, were cherished. The daily diet was millet bread, supplemented by mutton and occasionally quail. They also raised manna, honey, grapes, raisins and silk, all highly esteemed by merchants in Mardin and Baghdad.

He did not inquire into the religion of the Sinjar Yezidis, whom he describes as 'godless'. He noted that, in addition to Yezidis, the population of the mountain included Moslem Kurds and Arabs. The desert lands to the west were grazed, as in Julian's day, by the Tai tribe of Arabs.[21]

Evliya's next mission that year took him to Tabriz, once again in Persian hands, where he negotiated the release of the Ottoman governor of Baghdad, who had been kidnapped by Dunbeli marauders. After touring western Persia he reached Baghdad in January 1656. A few weeks later he departed for Mosul on the long road back to Van.

But after leaving Mosul he made a lengthy detour, first going south to Barqana at the confluence of the Tigris and Great Zab rivers, thence north into the Daseni country, northward again to Amadia and finally westward to Jezira b. Omar.

Evliya's account of his visit to the Daseni is tantalizingly brief. After leaving Barqana his first stop was at Manar, a village of 500 houses belonging to the district of Akra and administered from Mosul. It was populated by Yezidis, all armed with muskets and capable of hitting a sparrow in the eye. Any Moslem who cursed Satan, Yezid or 'the black dog' risked instant death; the same penalty was imposed for stepping on an onion or striking a black dog.

The next day Evliya's party reached the headquarters of the chief of the Daseni, identified as 'one of the great tribal chiefs in the Dohuk district governed from Mosul'. Upon seeing Evliya's letter of recommendation from the governor of Mosul, he showed the utmost hospitality to the travellers. Evliya describes him as 'a spirited man, yet with perfect manners', noting that he commanded 10,000 musketeers and that the Yezidis hated Shiites.

Evliya reported that the sanctuary of Sheikh Adi was located in the centre of the Yezidi territory. It was 'a large convent beside a high-domed tomb; among the hundreds of thousands of Sunni Kurdish shrines none can match the sumptuous gold decorations of this edifice'.

The Yezidis tried to persuade Evliya that Shiekh Adi had been one of the Imam Hussein's followers at Kerbela, who had left him to join his enemies. In the account of his journey Evliya scoffed at this clever piece of disinformation, preferring to believe that Sheikh Adi was a companion of the Prophet Mohammed who died of wounds suffered when the Arabs took Mosul.[22]

In 1672, Père Jean-Marie de Jésus, a Carmelite priest, encountered near Nisibin one of the migrant tribes that formed an important element in seventeenth-century Yezidi life. His diary notes that:

> we met the 'king' or 'prince' of the Yazidis or Kurds; who from the
> desert was going to pass the summer in the coolness of the
> mountains, with an innumerable number of people, all very poor
> and miserable, who were driving numberless sheep and cows, on
> which they support themselves for a living. In front of this 'prince'
> — if so he can be called — was borne a standard, red bordered with
> yellow, with Muhammadan emblems, because on it was depicted
> a half-moon and seven medallions, and on the other side a sword
> split up like a compass. Some seven persons followed on horseback,
> armed with arrows and cleavers: last there came the king garbed
> in a fur coat lined outside with green cloth, and a white *Turkish*
> turban, also mounted on a horse, which was rather poor... . We
> saw all this as close as half a stone's throw.[23]

The reappearance of Christian missionaries in the Near East was no act of chance. The balance of power in Europe had changed. The Hapsburgs, weakened by civil war in Germany and bankruptcy in Spain, no longer over-shadowed the continent. France was now the leading power in the west and in the first half of the seventeenth century its chief ministers were cardinals in the Catholic church.

In 1622 Pope Gregory XV established the Sacred Congregation for the Pro-pagation of the Faith, an institution generally known as 'Propaganda Fide'. Its objects were to convert the heathen and bring back into the church the Protes-tants of northern Europe and the ancient Christian communities of the Orient.

Although the Ottoman empire maintained the traditional system of the caliphs, whereby Christian communities were governed and taxed by their own patriarchs, the condition of the churches was deplorable.

The Nestorian church, oldest of them all, still survived under a hereditary patriarch living at Alkosh. But its days of glory were long past; in the sixteenth century the northern dioceses, stretching from Diyarbakir and Mardin to the Hakkari mountains and Lake Urmia, had split off under a rival patriarch affiliated with Rome. (Toward the end of the seventeenth century this patriarchate, which had moved to the Urmia district, severed its ties with the Pope.) In faraway South India the Nestorians, persecuted as heretics by the Portuguese, transferred their allegiance to the Jacobite church in 1665. A few years earlier the last Nestorian metropolitan of Sinjar had died. No successor was appointed and after a while the congregation became Yezidis.[24]

The Jacobite patriarch still lived at the Deir ez-Zafaran monastery outside Mardin, governing a much diminished community in the Tur Abdin. His deputy in Iraq, styled the 'maphrian', resided in Mosul.

Catholic missionary work in the Near East was assigned by Propaganda to the French provinces of the Capuchin, Carmelite and Jesuit orders. (A Franciscan mission, now mainly recruited from Italy and Spain, had long guarded the Christian holy places in Jerusalem, Bethlehem and Nazareth and attended to pilgrims' wants.) The French consuls in Aleppo and other towns provided a degree of diplomatic protection for the missionaries. By the middle of the seventeenth century the Capuchin province of Touraine supported missions in Egypt, Cyprus, Syria, Mesopotamia, Persia and India, supervised by a 'custos' in Aleppo.

Père Jean-Baptiste de Saint-Aignan, born in a small village on the river Cher east of Tours, had been a missionary for sixteen years when he came to Aleppo in 1661. After learning Arabic he was assigned to Mesopotamia. The archives of his order record that he was a man of unusual determination and drive (according to one account he once walked from Mosul to Aleppo in thirty-two days) who spread the gospel throughout Syria, Anatolia and Iraq. Père Jean-Baptiste even made some death-bed conversions, when he would produce a phial of holy water (in the guise of precious essences), rub two or three drops on the patient's stomach and pour some more on his head, softly reciting the words of the sacrament.[25]

In the spring of 1667 Père Jean-Baptiste was summoned from Mosul to the mission headquarters in Aleppo. On the way he was detained in Diyarbakir for many months to heal the pasha and his brother, both gravely ill. (As a reward he was granted permission to start a mission in that city to work with the local Nestorians, whose bishop later became Catholic and founded a new line of 'Chaldean' patriarchs). When he finally reached Aleppo in 1668 Père Jean-Baptiste was placed in charge of the local mission; a year later he was appointed custos of all the Capuchin missions in the Near East.

Among the handful of Capuchins in Aleppo was Père Justinien de Neuvy-sur-Loire, a missionary with five years' experience among the local Armenians who was also fluent in Arabic and knew some Kurdish. At the beginning of

1668 his Armenian contacts brought him interesting news about the nearby Yezidis of the Jebel Seman, with whom they had some business dealings.[26]

Somehow two of the Yezidi chiefs had recently met the Protestant chaplain of the English community in Aleppo. They told him that for forty years the Yezidis had asked God to show them the right road to salvation and that strong urges and inner lights had convinced them they should embrace Christianity. The chaplain had received them kindly and was now giving them guidance. The Armenians had failed to tell the Yezidis that the English themselves had strayed from the true church.

Père Jean-Baptiste and Père Justinien went promptly to the Armenians with whom the Yezidis were staying. After several days of discussion the missionaries determined that the Yezidis were sincere, persuaded them that the Pope was the true father of all Christians and arranged that Père Justinien should pay a visit to the community the following week.

His report, forwarded in its entirety to Propaganda, describes his departure from Aleppo on foot, accompanied by Yezidi guides. Half a league from the city they made him change into plain clothes, mounted him on a horse and pressed on through Yezidi territory; his escort told inquirers that he was visiting Christian shrines. In the morning they reached the foot of the mountains, where one of the sheikhs, named Adi, saluted the missionary with deep bows, a hearty embrace and a drink of brandy. The other sheikh was expected to arrive shortly from Kilis, a town some eleven hours away.

When Père Justinien arrived at the Yezidi encampment, they brought sheep to be slaughtered before him to the music of flutes, tambourines, kettledrums and lutes. The women, dressed in their finest clothes, emerged from black tents with shrill cries of joy. The celebration lasted several days, with ceremonial dances in honour of the Pope, the king of France, the French consul and the Capuchin mission. Vast quantities of brandy were consumed 'like milk'. Yet the tribesmen and their elders conducted themselves with dignity and throughout his stay the missionary did not hear a single light or dissolute remark. He described the Yezidis as 'reserved, modest and straightforward'.

Everyone — the two sheikhs, the black-robed priests and the tribesmen, dressed in white cloth cut round at the neck — desired to learn about Christianity. Plans were made to hold a mass with kettledrums and tambourines in the ruined basilica of St Simeon Stylites and there was talk of convening delegates from all the Yezidis in Persia and the Ottoman empire to send envoys to the Pope. The Yezidis satisfied Père Justinien that they did not worship the devil and that their refusal to curse him was part of a general rule that none of God's creatures should be cursed. 'When I saw their eagerness to draw to the bosom of the church, their tears and their affection', the missionary wrote, 'I thought I was seeing a dream rather than reality'.

Encouraged by Père Justinien's report, Père Jean-Baptiste came out from Aleppo and celebrated his name-day by holding a mass at daybreak on 24 June 1668 in the Jebel Seman. A reading of the first chapter of Jeremiah had allayed his concern that the Yezidis might not understand the Latin service, which was conducted by the two Capuchins and three Armenian lay brothers, one of whom wore a surplice. The mass commenced fittingly with the singing of the hymn *Veni Creator Spiritus* (Come, Holy Ghost, Creator Blest) and concluded with the baptism of the two sheikhs under the new names of Peter and Paul. A large crowd of Yezidis gathered to greet the missionaries; one tribesman recalled a tradition that his people were descended from some of the old crusaders who fled to the mountains after the fall of Antioch. The only jarring note came from the Armenians, who persisted in fishing despite the Yezidis' plea to spare hallowed animal lives.

When Père Jean-Baptiste returned to Aleppo, Père Justinien carried on the missionary work. Altogether he spent seven months in the mountains and baptized thirteen more Yezidis. In November 1669 he was in Aleppo, awaiting a guide assigned to take him to a gathering of Yezidi chiefs 'four or five days away'. At this point reality took over from the dream.

The Armenians who had originally introduced Père Justinien to the Yezidis now turned against him. They prevailed upon his prospective guide to complain that the missionary had usurped the functions of their chief and that the tribesmen would prefer to deal with one of the other orders. The Carmelites rejected the proposal but the Jesuits, who had targeted the Yezidis as prospects eighteen years before,[27] offered to help. Two other Yezidis — a chief named Dervish Sowar and an important sheikh named Barakat Bac — visited the Jesuits and were favourably impressed by the similarities of name and garb. The Armenians hinted that a subsidy to their Yezidi friends would be very acceptable.

The ensuing dispute was finally resolved by the French consul, who ruled that any missionary endeavour involving actual or potential money payments should be approved by all three missions — thereby suspending all further work among the local Yezidis.[28]

Père Jean-Baptiste de Saint-Aignan was not a man who gave up easily. In April 1670 he advised Colbert, the French minister of finance, that he was still in touch with the Yezidis and mentioned that they had offered to field 30,000 men whenever the king of France decided to attack their common enemy. He also wrote to the superior of his order in France; later that year he received authority from Propaganda to resume the Yezidi mission quietly and without notifying the other missions.[29]

Early in 1671 a new French consul, Joseph Dupont, arrived in Aleppo. In his first letter to Propaganda he raised the question of the mission to the

Yezidis; unaware of the secret instructions from Rome, he suggested that the territory be divided between the Capuchins and the Jesuits and pointed out that the larger part of the Yezidi community was still accessible to the Capuchin missions in Diyarbakir and Mosul. Following standard procedures, he sent a second copy a month later, with a postscript adding some details he had forgotten to mention.[30]

He reported that the spiritual leaders of the Yezidis, despatched from distant lands by a high priest named Chersouar, had been assembled for several months near St Simeon Stylites' monastery, patiently awaiting word from the Christian missionaries. Two of them had recently been to see the Jesuits.

Dupont's second letter sought to allay any concern in Rome that Yezidi territories might be unsafe. In a brief overview — the first such study since the incomplete Sheref-nameh — he described the condition of the communities east of Aleppo and unwittingly revealed the close communications that existed among them.

On the Jebel Sinjar three years of fighting between the Sacheli tribe and the armies of the neighbouring pashas had ended in a victory for the mountaineers, who took over 4,000 prisoners. The road to Jebel Sinjar was now open.

The Enidi (Dennedi) tribesmen living in twenty villages in the plain below Mardin were more vulnerable. They sent annual gifts to the sultan and a few cattle to the pasha of Mardin.

The Daseni, living near Mosul beside the river Zab, had their own prince and had allegedly declared 'that if the Christians would put the sign of the cross on their foreheads, they would raise it over their heads'.

Last but not least were the Khaliti, a robber tribe living along the Batman river near Bitlis (encountered in 1600 by John Cartwright, an English traveller).[31] They owed direct allegiance to the high priest Chersouar and to his delegates now assembled on the Jebel Seman.

The approval from Propaganda came too late. In June 1671 Père Jean-Baptiste and the heads of the Carmelite and Franciscan missions in Aleppo tersely reported that 'having learned by experience that there was little chance of achieving anything with the devil-worshipping Yezidis, they had decided to stop trying to convert them'. The Jesuits continued on their own.[32]

A history of the Ottoman empire published in 1680 by Sir Paul Rycaut, an Englishman long resident in Istanbul and Izmir, relates a story about the Yezidis 'from such of our Country-men, as have lately entertained Society with them'. He reported that:

> the chief Country and City of those near Aleppo is called Jeumee
> [the Kurdish name for the Afrin valley], where they have a

53

Convent of twelve Priests with a Superiour over them, and another
of the like Sort near Mosul, or Nineveth. The two Chiefs of these
Monasteries meet at fixed times to consult for the good of the
Common-weal. Their Devotions are private in a Cave; they tell us
of but one Book, which contains both their Law and their Rituals.

Rycaut does not mention the abortive English missionary effort, but he
claims to have heard that:

a Capuchin Fryer was once invited amongst them, with promise to
give him a sight of their Book of Rituals, and being come to Jeumee,
was detained a Day or two in a Cave, on pretence that the other
Superiour of Mosul was then amongst them, who being a severe
person, if he knew of his being there, would certainly put him to
Death, as one who came to alter their Religion; upon which
suspicion the Capuchin forgetting his Curiosity, fled for safety,
with all speed possible.[33]

Some years earlier, in 1674, a book was published in Rome entitled
Specchio, o vero descrizione della Turchia, dedicated to the Catholic ex-
Queen Christina of Sweden by the author, 'R. P. F. Michele Febvre de Novi'.
A French edition, published the following year in Paris, was dedicated to King
Louis XIV. (An expanded version, entitled *Teatro della Turchia* and dedi-
cated to Pope Innocent XI was published in 1681 and later translated into
several languages.) Both works contained an extensive description of the Otto-
man empire and its non-Moslem minorities, including the Yezidis.

The author, whose identity has been much debated,* gave a detailed
account of the Yezidi community, based on the Capuchins' experiences in the
Jebel Seman.[34] (Beyond stating that the Yezidis numbered 200,000, mostly in
the Ottoman empire but some in Persia, 'Febvre' did not refer to those living
east of Aleppo.) His description of their religion differs little from the outline
in the previous chapter of this book, though resemblances to Christianity were
stressed. The Peacock Angel was correctly identified; Sheikh Adi was mentioned as a saint, with no further details. The Yezidis' respect for animals was
related to their belief in the transmigration of souls. The author did not
mention the black dog cult reported by Evliya (and also by Rycaut).[36]

Meanwhile the French consul Joseph Dupont maintained his contact with
the Jebel Seman Yezidis through the Jesuit mission. When the French

* Some scholars credit Père Jean-Baptiste de Saint-Aignan, others Père Justinien de
Neuvy.[35]

ambassador, Marquis de Nointel, visited Aleppo in 1674 a secret nocturnal meeting was arranged with the chief of the Yezidis, 'a wise and cunning man' who inquired about Louis XIV and his intentions and offered the ambassador 50,000 soldiers to help the French king conquer Palestine and Syria. On their way back from St Simeon's monastery to the coast the ambassador's party encountered the Yezidi chief and his escort of well-mounted, strangely dressed men, armed with spears, bows and arrows, bidding *au revoir* to the French.[37]

A few months later Nointel received word that the 'Sachelié' in the Jebel Sinjar, allied with the Yezidi 'Chelekié' and a Moslem tribe, had inflicted a severe defeat on the Ottoman general Kaplan Pasha.[38]

Père Joseph Besson, the stubborn Jesuit superior, persevered with the Yezidis. In 1679, the year Joseph Dupont retired, news came from Paris that a M. Pierre Dupont, described as a priest and a doctor of theology, had established a charity yielding 600 livres (£42.10.0) a year to fund a Jesuit mission to the Yezidis.[39] But Père Besson too had to admit defeat; a biographer records that the missionaries he sent out 'did not take long to perceive that the hour for the conversion of this unhappy people was not yet come... They returned, shaking the dust off their shoes.'[40] In the winter of 1681–2 a last futile effort was made in the Mardin district by another Jesuit, Père Michel Nau.[41] (Around this time one of the Aleppo Jesuits wrote an anonymous account of the Yezidis that repeated many of the details in Dupont's letter and mentioned the writer's six years of acquaintance with Dello, emir of the Joumé mountain Yezidis, and 'their spiritual leader Sheikh Souard'.)[42] Nau died in 1683, Besson eight years later. The Capuchin custos, Père Jean-Baptiste de Saint-Aignan died in 1685.

The records of the Yezidis' first encounters with the Christian world, plentiful but too often self-serving, leave much unexplained. But a curious incident that occurred some years earlier in Mardin casts a harsh light on the status of unrecognized minorities in the Ottoman empire and their eagerness to be included in an officially tolerated community.

When Sultan Murad IV passed through Mardin on his return from Baghdad, it came to his attention that there were 100 families in the city called Shemsiehs, who still adhered to a prehistoric sun-worshipping cult. They possessed no religious books and consequently were doomed by Islamic law to choose exile or death. Their dilemma was finally resolved by the Jacobite patriarch, who overlooked their pagan usages and agreed to admit them into his community. Two centuries later this special group of Jacobites still survived in Mardin.[43]

Between 1680 and 1720 the balance of power between the Ottoman empire and the western world registered a decisive shift, obliging the sultans to give back to the Hapsburgs territories their ancestors had conquered 200 years before. France, their traditional ally, was engaged in costly wars by land and sea that continued intermittently throughout the eighteenth century and enabled Britain to acquire large parts of India.

In the east the Ottoman armies faced Persia, at most times a weaker foe; indeed, at one point the Ottomans agreed to a partition of the shah's territories in eastern Transcaucasia with the Russian czar Peter the Great. But in Iraq the sultan's rule was eroded by his own lieutenants; from 1704 onward Baghdad was ruled by self-perpetuating military chieftains, while the province of Mosul was governed by a local family, the Jalilis. Appointments, decided on the spot and often by force of arms, were routinely confirmed in Istanbul.

In contrast with earlier times, first-hand accounts of the Yezidis in the eighteenth century are scarce. The Ottoman geographer Kâtib Çelebi's *Cosmorama*, written around 1655 and published in 1732, confirmed the locations of the Yezidi tribes identified by Sheref ed-Din. European travellers, some of them Catholic missionaries, others servants of the British 'Honourable East India Company' who preferred the short overland route by way of Basra and Aleppo to the longer sea voyage by the Cape of Good Hope, dutifully mentioned the Yezidis, well known in Europe since publication of the *Teatro della Turchia*. The Yezidi community in northern Syria also received passing mention in travellers' reports. In 1704 the thieving Khalitis of Diyarbakir province found their first, condemnatory mention in the Ottoman archives.[44]

In the second quarter of the eighteenth century the somnolence of Iraq was disturbed for some years by a new world-conqueror of Turkish birth who seized power in Persia and became known as Nadir Shah. After reconquering Transcaucasia, he laid siege to Baghdad (saved by a relieving force from Anatolia) and later ravaged India and Turkestan.

Nadir Shah invaded Iraq again in 1743, aiming this time for Mosul. After capturing Kirkuk and Altun Köprü he detached a force to subdue the Yezidi chieftain As, who had often raided the western provinces of Persia from his base in the mountains around Koi Sanjak. The Persians outmanoeuvered and routed an army of several thousand Yezidis, killing their leader Yezid. The resourceful As escaped, enlisted allies and laid siege to a ruined fort where Persian outriders had imprisoned the Yezidi womenfolk. The defenders were at their last gasp when the shah's nephew brought reinforcements and raised the siege. Abandoned by his allies, As considered suicide, but finally submitted to Nadir Shah and was appointed governor of the district.[45]

Nadir Shah went on to besiege Mosul, but withdrew after forty days and was murdered in 1747.

After this time few Yezidis are reported south of the Great Zab, though for over a century they operated the principal ferry across the river at a point appropriately called Kelek.[46]

In the course of the eighteenth century the Yezidi Mirs of Sheikhan became subject to the Kurdish principality of Amadia, one of the semi-autonomous mountain fiefdoms that guarded the Ottoman frontiers in the east. The princely family, strict Sunni Moslems reputedly descended from the Abbasids, had ruled Amadia since the days of Tamerlane. They enjoyed the hereditary rank of pashas, granted by the Ottoman sultan. According to one account, the prince's dignity required him always to eat alone.[47]

Amadia was home to an important community of Jews. The district also included Nestorians, actively proselytized by a Dominican mission that operated there from 1759 to 1779. One of the missionaries, Padre Maurizio Garzoni, wrote some brief notes about the Yezidis and reported that the princes of Amadia always gave the post of executioner to a Yezidi, never loath to shed Moslem blood.[48]

In 1770–71 Bedagh Beg, Mir of the Sheikhan, joined a rebellion against Ismail Pasha, prince of Amadia, but was captured and fined. Sixteen years later his son Jolo Beg was involved in another revolt and had to flee to the hills. Jolo was still Mir in 1789–90, when he battled Tai Arabs who were raiding the Shiekhan, but in the following year he and his brother were put to death by Ismail Pasha, who appointed a new Mir, Khanjar Beg, from the second-ranking Basmariya family. In 1791–92 the old dynasty was restored when Ismail Beg quarrelled with Khanjar and replaced him with Jolo's son Hasan Beg.[49]

Whoever controlled the Sheikhan derived material benefits from the pilgrim traffic to Lalish. Votive inscriptions at the sanctuary dating back to 1779 and 1781 attest to the piety and affluence of the pilgrims.[50] Many of them came from the Jebel Sinjar.

The eighteenth century marked the heyday of the marauding Yezidis of the Sinjar, the terror of every caravan passing between Mosul and Mardin. (Even the 'Little Desert Route' was not immune; in 1782 one band attacked a caravan on its way from Ana on the Euphrates toward Baghdad, seizing thirty donkey-loads of cotton goods.) Caravans escorted by well-armed, reliable guards could fight off the raiders; the fate of others was ransom or total loss. The choicest targets were the lightly armed official couriers, who rode without an escort, relying on speed to reach the next stage point with their packets of official and private mail. On one memorable occasion a captured courier was found to be carrying 40,000 carats of high grade pearls.[51]

Such misdeeds did not go unpunished, but the Sinjar Yezidis benefited significantly from an administrative decision of the central government that transferred the Mardin district from the province of Diyarbakir to the province of Baghdad. The first punitive expedition from Baghdad, launched in 1715, inflicted heavy casualties, as did a later attack in 1753. But subsequent expeditions against the Sinjar from Baghdad and Mosul — at least eight are recorded between 1767 and 1809 — were less intensive and could be considered by the brigands as a cost of doing business. Military action and enslavement of prisoners were legitimized by Moslem theologians who denounced the Yezidis as heretics.[52]

A curious incident occurred in 1785, when Abd el-Baqi Pasha, the governor of Mosul, led a raid on the Dennedi tribe of Yezidis living east of the Tigris. While his troops were looting the villages, the pasha and his brother were ambushed and killed. The soldiers fled panic-stricken to Mosul.[53] The sequel to this episode is not reported.

Toward the end of the eighteenth century the Catholic missions in Iraq began to wither. A revolution had taken place in France; the king and queen were executed and the religious orders dispossessed. General war broke out in Europe, from which France emerged victorious under a new leader, Napoleon Bonaparte. In 1798 he led a seaborne expedition to Egypt and Syria that ended three years later in the surrender of the French invaders to an Ottoman–British force. But on the continent of Europe Napoleon, crowned emperor in 1804, was all-powerful. The Hapsburg monarchy was humbled and the Pope led off in captivity to France.

After many battles Napoleon was brought down in 1814, returned briefly to power the next year and was finally defeated at Waterloo. The former administrations in France and elsewhere were restored.

Two countries emerged stronger from the Napoleonic wars. Russia, whose armies had battled the French from Moscow to the gates of Paris, was poised to resume its southward thrust along the Balkan and Caucasian shores of the Black Sea. Britain, protected by geography and a vigilant navy, pre-eminent in trade, led the world in new methods of manufacture and navigation by steam; its material progress was matched by the spread of education and the rise of new religious movements that inspired fresh missionary endeavours in the Near East.

A combination of events involving Britain, Russia and the Ottoman empire was soon to shatter and remake the life of the Yezidi community.

Chapter Five

Prisoners on a Sinking Ship

The Ottoman empire emerged outwardly intact after the Napoleonic wars. But its inner strength had waned. In the capital the sultan's authority was challenged by a mutinous army. In the Balkans and Greece rebel chieftains emerged. In the Moslem provinces the central government received only token allegiance from the rulers of North Africa, including Mehemet Ali, the ambitious governor of Egypt, and from the self-perpetuating pashas of Baghdad. The old Ottoman regime was falling apart and was about to undergo a near-fatal crisis, from which it would emerge as 'the sick man of Europe', domineered and despoiled by friends and enemies alike.

The autonomous status of Iraq owed much to the territory's commerce with India. In 1808 the East India Company appointed as its Resident in Baghdad a twenty-one-year-old Irishman named Claudius James Rich, who represented it until his premature death from cholera in 1821.

En route to England in 1813, Rich and his wife stayed in Mosul with Padre Raffaello Campanile, a good-natured Neapolitan who served at the Dominican mission from 1803 to 1815 and was the first European to give a first-hand account of the Sinjar Yezidis. In his book, published in 1818,[1] Padre Raffaello describes a community of 16,000 souls, enumerates their thirteen villages and praises their oak-galls, walnuts, hazelnuts, rice, raisins, honey, beeswax and fruit — especially their large dried figs from which they made 'a liquor like honey of an exquisite taste'. He reported that the bracing mountain air enabled almost everyone to live to be 100 years old and women to bear children up to the age of sixty. Their main source of income was robbing caravans, located by Yezidi spies. The neighbouring Tai Arabs, employed by the Ottomans to protect the caravans, also received 1,000 piastres (£50) a year from the

59

Yezidis. One-tenth of the Yezidi loot was thrown into a deep well inside a cave.*

Only two Ottoman expeditions to the Sinjar are recorded in the early years of the nineteenth century — a large-scale attack by Ali Pasha of Baghdad in 1803 that resulted in the destruction of three or four villages and the enslavement of a few families; and a raid in 1809 by his successor Suleiman Pasha. During that period the Sinjar Yezidis were led by Hussein Dublein (probably a member of the Dunbeli tribe, some of whom still live on the Jebel Sinjar and in the Sheikhan).[2]

When Rich passed through Mosul again in 1816, he met four Sinjar chiefs, 'square, stout-built men dressed like Kurds, with white vests and mantles, red fezes and cloaks of the same colour, [who] never shaved or cut their hair and had a very wild appearance'.† They informed him that:

> a treaty had just been sworn between them and the Pasha, and the oath which was binding to them was made in a curious way. A khanjar or dagger was stuck in the ground, a white handkerchief was thrown over it and, placing their right hand on it, they swore to maintain the treaty.[3]

In the Sheikhan, the Yezidis prospered under Hasan Beg, who rebuilt the Lalish sanctuary in 1806 but was treacherously murdered a few years later by a prince of Amadia.[4] His death was long remembered. In 1820 the Riches, spending the night at a Yezidi village, heard a lament for the slain Mir sung by a blind guitar-player named Lasso.‡ Fifty years later a German orientalist transcribed a poem that told of a battle between two Bahdinan princes in which Sheikhan and Dennedi tribesmen avenged the death of Hasan Beg.[5]

Hasan was succeeded as Mir by Salih Beg, who is said to have been highly respected by his people but was murdered by an ill-wisher in Mosul. There followed a confused period of dynastic strife, ending with the accession of Ali Beg 'the Great', a son of Mir Hasan Beg.[6]

The Yezidis had long lived in amity with their Christian neighbours. One group had coexisted with the Nestorian community in the Hakkari mountains north of Amadia until the beginning of the nineteenth century, when they moved to the Sheikhan and the Jebel Sinjar. One of the Yezidis' principal burying grounds, the Sheikhan village of Bozan, was only a few miles from Alkosh, the ancient patriarchal residence, and the ruined monastery of Rabban Hormuzd, which had been reoccupied since 1808 by an austere order

* See p. 33.
† See Plate 45.
‡ See Plate 17.

of Chaldean* monks founded by Gabriel Dambo, a native of Mardin. The Sinjar Yezidis were traditionally friendly to the Christians; according to one account (written prior to the 1830 reconciliation between the patriarchate and Rome), their chief sheikh would each year pay a ceremonial visit to Alkosh.[7]

Another example of friendship between Yezidis and Christians was reported from Redwan, a village east of Diyarbakir on the left bank of the Garzan (a tributary of the Tigris long known as the Yezidhane river), where the once-dreaded Khaliti tribesmen now lived peaceably with their Christian neighbours. The Yezidi chief, Mirza Aga, built a church for the Armenians and housed their archimandrite, Ghazar Ter Ghevondian, who taught his children Turkish and Armenian. (Unfortunately, as the priest later related, 'the pupils found the name "Satan" in the textbook and all hell broke loose.')[8]

In the first quarter of the nineteenth century Mirza Aga headed an autonomous fiefdom, constantly at war with other Kurdish chieftains and with the sultan's tax-collectors. The exploits of his warriors, many of them Armenians led by an earlier priest named Pogos, are still commemorated in Kurdish folklore.[9]

Farther to the east a new menace began to take shape. Russia, unconquered by Napoleon, now threatened the Ottomans, not only in the Balkans, but also in Anatolia. The Christian kingdom of Georgia, a long-time recruiting ground for Ottoman regiments and harems, had merged into Russia in 1801. The Russians fought several wars with Persia along the shores of the Caspian Sea, culminating in General Count Paskievitch's victorious 1827–28 campaign, in which they captured Ardebil, removing from the state library one of the earliest Sheref-nameh manuscripts, and forced the shah to cede the province of Erivan.

In April 1828 war broke out between Russia and the Ottoman empire. In the Balkans the Ottomans, led by the Georgian Reshid Pasha, a brave warrior but no strategist, held the line of the Danube despite the loss of Varna on the Black Sea. But in the summer of 1829 he was outmanoeuvred by the Russians, who swept down the Black Sea coast and captured Edirne, only 150 miles from Istanbul.

Meanwhile in the east Paskievitch had stormed the fortress of Kars and captured Erzurum. His left wing, led by a Georgian general, Prince Alexander Chavchavadze, took Bayezid.

In June 1829 the Russian poet Alexander Pushkin visited his brother, an officer in the Nizhegorodsky Dragoons, and took part in the decisive envelopment of the Ottoman position on the fir-covered Soganli mountains that

---

* Nestorian converts to Catholicism were known as 'Chaldeans'.

barred the way to Erzurum. Among those reporting to General Rayevsky, the Russian cavalry commander, he noticed 'a tall monster of a man in a red tunic and black cap', the leader of a Yezidi detachment serving with the Russian army. The poet, who carried with him a copy of Garzoni's *Notice sur les Yézidis*, inquired about his religion and was relieved to learn that the Yezidis worshipped God, not Satan.[10]

Pushkin's informant was Hasan Aga, sixty-year-old chief of the Hasanli tribe, who lived in Ottoman territory near Bayezid — one of many Kurdish tribes who sensed that a new wind was blowing in eastern Anatolia. His scarlet coat, lined in fox fur, was a present from General Chavchavadze in recognition of his service with the Russians in the capture of Eleşkirt, west of Bayezid.[11]

A peace treaty signed in August 1829 gave Russia minor territorial gains in the Caucasus. In the spring of 1830 Paskievitch's army withdrew from Anatolia, accompanied by thousands of Armenians to whom the czar offered a new home in the province of Erivan. The Hasanli tribe moved to Surmalu on the northern slope of Mount Ararat just inside the Russian border, where their chief would proudly display his coat to visitors, even in the warmest weather.[12]

The Russian archives record a curious postscript to Paskievitch's campaign. In December 1830 a man named Petros, described as 'a Christian', came to the Russian headquarters in Tiflis with a letter addressed to the viceroy from Mirza Aga of Redwan. The Yezidi chieftain stated that this was his third attempt to get in touch with the Russians. In 1829, when he heard that they had reached the Lake Van region, he had sent off two messengers, presumed killed. (One messenger actually reached the Russians at Bayezid, although Mirza Aga's letter had been impounded en route by the Ottomans.) Later that year he had dispatched an Armenian named Kirakos, who had reached Erzurum and returned with a letter in Russian that no one in the village could read. On his third try, unaware that the war was over, he sent Kirakos and Petros with an offer to field 1,500 horsemen and 5,000 infantry to join the Russians once they reached Bitlis. When the messengers discovered that Paskievitch had left Erzurum, they followed his trail to Tiflis, where Kirakos died of cholera, leaving Petros to deliver the letter. The file closes with a notation that in February 1831 Petros was sent back with a red brocaded cloth coat valued at 75 roubles (£11.17.6) for Mirza Aga and some medicine for his son's eyes.[13]

Russia's easy triumphs in Anatolia were perceived in Britain as a potential threat to its courier communications with India, maintained since 1800 by a dromedary post between Aleppo and Basra, connecting with Bombay by sea. Colonel Robert Taylor, Rich's successor as Resident in Baghdad, supplied arms to the provincial governor Daud Pasha and urged him to acquire a potent new weapon — armed river steamers to keep order along the Tigris and the

Euphrates. The Resident's brother, James Taylor, was on his way from Mosul to start surveying the Euphrates, when his party was ambushed near Tel Kochek (the present frontier station between Syria and Iraq) by Sinjar Yezidis and Turks from Tel Afar (a community that thrived by fencing Yezidi loot). In an exchange of fire one Yezidi was killed, whereupon Taylor and two of his British companions were cut to pieces — a rare instance of conflict between Yezidis and westerners.[14]

The Ottoman sultan Mahmud II also drew some conclusions from the war with Russia, which had weakened the allegiance of the governors of his two richest provinces, Egypt and Iraq. Mehemet Ali, who had ruled Egypt for twenty-five years, commanded a modern army trained by Napoleonic veterans and was too powerful to punish. Daud Pasha, the devout, corrupt and indecisive governor of Baghdad, appeared more vulnerable.

In 1830 the sultan ordered Ali Riza Pasha, governor of Aleppo, to turn over his post to Mohammed Pasha Ince Bairaktar (a veteran of the siege of Varna, recently released from Russian captivity) and proceed with an army of loyal troops to take over the province of Baghdad. After an eight-month siege, aggravated by plague, flooding and civil strife, Daud Pasha surrendered and a new administration of appointive governors was installed in Iraq.

A few weeks after Daud's surrender, Mehemet Ali made his move. A well-equipped Egyptian army, led by his son Ibrahim and a French chief of staff, invaded Palestine and Syria. In July 1832 the Ottoman army was defeated in a decisive battle outside Homs, known as 'the defeat of the pashas' because the Ottoman army included nine pashas, three of whom were named Osman and three others Mohammed. Among the latter were two veterans of the Balkan campaign — Mohammed Kiritli Oğlu (son of a Cretan), governor of Silistria, who led the last vain cavalry charge against the Egyptian guns; and Mohammed Ince Bairaktar (little cornet), the new governor of Aleppo, whose irregulars fled so fast from the Homs battlefield that the pasha was deprived of his command.[15]

During the summer of 1832 Ibrahim occupied Damascus, Aleppo, Adana and Urfa. The historic routes from Aleppo to Mosul and from Damascus to Mecca, held by the Ottomans for three centuries, were severed. The empire and the dynasty were at risk.

Reshid Pasha, now Grand Vizier, moved to Konya, the historic city where Izz ed-Din and Rukn ed-Din had once toyed with the Mongols. Here, sheltered by the Taurus mountains, he formed a new army out of reinforcements from Anatolia and Europe. But Ibrahim's army crossed the 3500 ft Cilician Gates over the Taurus and destroyed Reshid's army outside Konya in December 1832. The grand vizier was taken prisoner. The capital was only fifteen days' march away.

Mehemet Ali, like the old caliph Moawiya, was a cautious man. Ibrahim was instructed to press on with deliberate speed through snowy Anatolia. By February 1833 his advance guards were only 50 miles from the Sea of Marmara.

But, unlike Yezid, Ibrahim was fated not to reach the water. A Russian army, invited by the desperate sultan, had landed on the Asiatic shore of the Bosporus to block the way.

Peace was soon arranged, enabling Mehemet Ali and his son to keep Palestine, Syria and Cilicia. The Russians departed. But new troubles were brewing in the east.

The chaos in Iraq had provided an opportunity for the Soran Kurds of Rowanduz, long-time enemies of the Daseni Yezidis, to take over the key points of Erbil and Altun Köprü on the Baghdad–Mosul highway and establish a virtually independent state, grudgingly recognized by the new governor of Baghdad.

The chief of the Sorans, Kör (Blind) Mohammed, bey of Rowanduz was described by an eyewitness in 1833 as:

> a benevolent pleasing-looking man of about forty-five years of age; fair, marked with the small-pox, and blind of an eye, which was depressed and opake. His beard was about twelve inches long, of a light brown colour, the lower half being uncombed and quite felted together: in other respects, he was rather tidy in dress. He was lame of one leg from the kick of a horse, and spoke with a weak voice.

His campaign tent was plainly furnished with a wooden bed, a few carpets, an old English double-barrelled gun, a rifle, a sword, a telescope and an umbrella. He was a strict Sunni Moslem who had a deep respect for mullahs.[16]

Early in 1832 the bey of Rowanduz raided the plains east of Mosul belonging to the principality of Amadia. The pretext was provided by an unwise act committed by the Yezidi Mir of Sheikhan. Ali Beg had long feuded with a nearby Kurdish chieftain named Ali Aga. Finally he sent him a conciliatory message, inviting him to come to Baadri and be *karif* for the Yezidi leader's son. Ali Aga, a devout Moslem, was flattered by this offer and arrived with only a few attendants, who were unable to save their master when the Yezidi Mir Ali Beg's bodyguard slaughtered his unsuspecting guest. The Mir may have had some misgivings after the deed was done, for he called in forty Yezidi notables and made each of them stab the corpse.

The prince of Amadia, suzerain of both tribes, was thought to have had a hand in the affair because he refused to allow Ali Aga's tribe to take revenge. But the dead chieftain was related to an eminent Kurdish mullah, who complained initially and without result to Ali Riza Pasha in Baghdad, but subsequently appealed to Kör Mohammed for redress. Kör Mohammed responded promptly and in force.[17]

A Kurdish poem describes how Ali Beg, learning of his enemy's approach, mounted his dark bay horse, loosened the long sleeves of his shirt to grip the hilt of his gilded lance and rode unescorted to meet the one-eyed Soran chief. Kör Mohammed summoned him to abjure his faith and become a Moslem. Ali Beg refused and was sent captive to Rowanduz accompanied by a single follower. After vain efforts to convert the Mir, Kör Mohammed struck off his head and ordered his follower to hold out his hands, which he cut off, saying 'Go back and tell your people what you have seen'.[18]

Kör Mohammed's army swept on, killing all the Yezidis they could find. At Alkosh they set upon Christians, Jews and Yezidis alike, despoiling the tomb of Nahum and killing three Rabban Hormuzd monks, including the superior Gabriel Dambo, recently returned from an audience with Pope Gregory XVI in Rome.[19]

The Yezidis soon rebelled against their Soran masters and killed the bey's representative. There are no contemporary accounts of the holocaust that ensued, but an Englishman who later befriended the Yezidis was told that:

> the inhabitants of Sheikhan fled to Mosul. It was in spring; the
> river had overflowed its banks, and the bridge of boats had been
> removed. A few succeeded in crossing the stream; but a vast crowd
> of men, women, and children were left upon the opposite side, and
> congregated on the great mound of Kouyounjik. The Bey of
> Rowandiz followed them. An indiscriminate slaughter ensued; and
> the people of Mosul beheld, from their terraces, the murder of these
> unfortunate fugitives, who cried to them in vain for help.[20]

This tragedy, still recalled as 'the Soran massacre', marks the low point of Yezidi history. Ali Beg's young son Hussein Beg was carried into hiding in the Sinjar. Jasim Beg, who belonged to the senior branch of the Chol family, took over as Mir of Sheikhan.[21]

But a chain of events that would bring deliverance to the Yezidis was already in motion. In March 1837 their villages near Rabban Hormuzd were visited by two persons in British government service. They belonged to the Euphrates Expedition and were prospecting for coal.

The Euphrates Expedition ranks with Columbus' first voyage and the Soviet sputnik among the boldest enterprises undertaken by any government.[22]

After Napoleon's brief occupation of Egypt and Syria, Britain was acutely aware of the importance of rapid, secure communications with India. The principal route, by way of Egypt, was unusable between June and September, when the southwest monsoon prevented ships from sailing from Bombay to the Red Sea. This was exactly the season when another waterway, the river Euphrates, was believed to be navigable in both directions between Birecik and Basra by a modern but widely used vessel — the flat-bottomed paddle steamer. Such were the concusions reached in 1834 by the Steam Committee of the British House of Commons,* based on expert technical advice (which found steamships too unreliable for ocean voyages) and on a survey of the lower Euphrates secretly conducted in 1831 and 1832 by a British artillery officer, Captain Francis Chesney. (The committee was satisfied from studying the accounts of the emperor Julian and various sixteenth-century travellers that the unsurveyed upper portion of the river was navigable downstream from Birecik.)

Thereupon an expedition was authorized with instructions to sail from England to the coast of Syria, carrying sections and components of two newly built iron steamers — the *Euphrates* (108 ft long, 19 ft beam, two 25 hp engines) and the *Tigris* (68 ft long, 15 ft beam, two 10 hp engines), both drawing less than three ft of water — which were to be hauled overland to a point opposite Birecik where the vessels would be put together and would steam 1117 miles to Basra. They would bring with them 137 tons of coal, to be placed at suitable points along the river.

Command of the expedition was entrusted to Francis Chesney (appointed temporary colonel), an Irishman of immense courage and determination, fired by a fanatical enthusiasm for the project. Fifty naval and military officers and men joined the expedition, along with a few civilians, including William F. Ainsworth, aged twenty-eight, engaged as surgeon and geologist.

Six months after the start of the project, all was ready. Sultan Mahmud had approved the enterprise and it was believed that Mehemet Ali would not object. In February 1835 King William IV and the Duke of Wellington (then foreign secretary) sent parting messages to the expedition, which reached Malta, a British colony acquired during the Napoleonic wars, on 12 March 1835. During the week they stayed at Malta Colonel Chesney engaged an Arabic-speaking interpreter recommended by a local banker with whom Chesney had gone to school.[23] The interpreter signed on as C. A. Rassam.

* The author's great-grandfather, Josiah John Guest, MP for Merthyr Tydfil (South Wales) served on this committee.

Isa Antun Rassam, the man who brought the Yezidis into the nineteenth century, was born in 1808. His father, Antun Rassam, was an archdeacon in the Chaldean church. His mother, named Theresa, was the granddaughter of Ishak Halabi of Aleppo. It is uncertain whether their son was born in Aleppo or in Mosul, but he always considered himself a citizen of the latter town.[24]

There is more than one account of the origin of the Rassam family, members of which are still among the leading Christian families in Iraq. (In Arabic the name Rassam means 'designer of patterns for textiles'.) In 1832 Isa stated that his father 'was originally an English Subject and came as a young man from the East Indies to Mosul'.[25] Colonel Chesney's account of the expedition states that it was Isa's great-grandfather who had migrated to Mosul from the coast of Malabar.[26] In 1837 Rassam stated that his great-grandfather:

> was a Spaniard of wealth who was sent by the Pope to attempt to reconcile the Nestorians. He died at Aleppo, having first married a woman of that place and leaving a family. His grandfather, with his sisters, removed to Mosul or Nineveh, and married into the first Christian family there, and was the means of reconciling twenty-five bishoprics in *the plain* to Rome.[27]

In 1827 Isa's father sent him to Rome to study theology in the company of two priests. Near Aleppo their caravan was attacked by desert Arabs, who killed the priests and robbed Isa of all his possessions except for a little money that enabled him to reach Cairo, where he found shelter and employment with a cousin.[28]

In Cairo he became acquainted with the missionaries of the Church Missionary Society, a British institution which had recently started a school for local Christian children. Teaching material was supplied from Malta, where the society had a printing press with Arabic type. For some time the Malta mission had been looking for a qualified translator. Finally, in 1829 the Cairo missionaries decided to educate a translator there and prepare him for Malta. Their choice fell on 'Isa of Baghdad', whom they recommended as 'a clever, capable and moral youth'. In addition to his teaching chores, he studied hard to learn English and literary Arabic and was commended for his 'indefatigable zeal for Philology'. His salary was $10, later raised to $15, a month.[29]

Isa made good progress. By the time he left for Malta in 1832, he had joined the Church of England and had translated Isaac Watts' *Historical Catechisms* into Arabic. The head of the Cairo mission praised his 'noble character', reporting that 'he was always serviceable, diligent, and never have we observed in him the Arabic love of money, he is content with the necessary food and raiment; it is not at all his propensity to gather a treasure of money.'[30]

In Malta he impressed the missionaries as a 'sober & obliging' youth who 'studies the Scriptures diligently & seems eager to embrace every opportunity for his further improvement'.[31] A few years later another writer noted that 'his striking height, his dark complexion, and the child-like, kindly expression of his face formed a singular whole. He was, in fact, a child in artlessness and amiable ignorance of the world'.[32] On New Year's Day 1835 he married Matilda Badger, whose father, a sergeant and regimental schoolmaster, had died leaving a pious widow, a daughter and a son, Percy, who was employed locally as a printer.[33]

The recruitment of Rassam, married only ten weeks before the Euphrates Expedition reached Malta, was not easy. Subsequently Chesney wrote that 'he enthusiastically quitted his position' and Rassam is said to have 'expressed his satisfaction at being set free from the strict rule of the pious folk at Malta'.[34] But at the time the acting head of the CMS mission reported that Rassam:

> yielded only with the greatest reluctance to the most urgent and persevering entreaties of Col. Chesney and some other gentlemen of the expedition, who deemed his acquaintance with those countries, the people, and their language, of such great value for their object, that they really seemed to think they could not proceed without him; and it was not till after the Governor himself had promised to him in my presence and of some of those gentlemen, to satisfy our Society on his behalf, that he made up his mind to follow them.

Although Rassam joined the expedition on a volunteer status, arrangements were made to provide for the support of his wife during his absence (assumed to be five or six months) and 'a pension promised in case he should meet with his death during the Expedition'.[35]

A member of the expedition noted later that 'he was an excellent chess player, there was no match for him on board'.[36]

The expedition proceeded eastward after this brief but well-documented pause. Early in April, welcomed by flamingos but by no Egyptian officials, their ship unloaded the steamer parts on the shores of the Bay of Antioch. They named the spot Amelia Depot in honour of William IV's sister, who had died much lamented at the age of twenty-seven, and planned to move onward to an assembly site named Port William on the right bank of the Euphrates, 140 miles to the east.

Twelve months of frustration were to elapse before the two vessels steamed down the great river. A road, strong enough to bear weights up to 5 tons, had to be built from Antioch to the Euphrates. The Arabic interpreter Rassam impressed his superiors with his skill in procuring and managing wagons, oxen and labourers. (Strangely, although the road followed the lower Afrin valley, there are no reports of Yezidi sightings.) In large part the delays could be attributed to human, technical and medical problems incident to the introduction of nineteenth-century progress into a traditional society. But underlying these inconveniences was the basic political incompatibility between the regime of Mehemet Ali, the successful rebel, and his nominal suzerain, Sultan Mahmud, who had sanctioned the expedition.

After the humiliating 1833 treaty, the sultan's main concern was to regain control of Anatolia and utilize its sturdy manpower to build a new army and regain Syria. Reshid Pasha, released from captivity, was placed in charge. His first move was to build a 400-mile military road from the Black Sea to Diyarbakir capable of transporting guns. In 1834 and 1835 he subdued the Kurds of central and northeastern Anatolia; among those who submitted was the Yezidi chief Mirza Aga of Redwan. At the same time Ottoman troops reoccupied Urfa and suppressed a revolt in Mardin.

At this point communications between Anatolia and the newly reconquered province of Iraq, impeded by Mehemet Ali's occupation of Aleppo, were further endangered by the westward expansion of Kör Mohammed of Rowanduz, who captured Amadia in 1834 and dominated the Tigris crossing at Jezira b. Omar through alliance with another Kurd, Bedr Khan Beg, the emir of Bohtan.

In the spring of 1836 Reshid's army marched east from Diyarbakir, well equipped with cannon. Jezira b. Omar was shelled for several months and left a heap of ruins; the population, largely Yezidis, was massacred or enslaved.[37] Bedr Khan Beg was besieged in his mountain castle for forty days, then surrendered and joined the pasha. Kör Mohammed, outnumbered and outgunned, pulled back toward Rowanduz and finally surrendered to the Ottomans in August of that year. He was sent into captivity in Istanbul. After a few months he was pardoned by the sultan and reappointed governor of Rowanduz, but on the way back his escort was overtaken by a messenger from the sultan with fresh instructions and he died suddenly at Amasya after drinking a cup of coffee.[38]

On his way back from northern Iraq, Reshid Pasha mounted an attack on the Yezidis of Sinjar and inflicted many casualties.[39]

In January 1837 Reshid Pasha died of cholera. He was succeeded by Hafiz Pasha, a lean, energetic Circassian renowned for his courage, swordsmanship and trust in Koranic interpretations and soothsayers' advice.

In mid-March 1836 the *Euphrates* left Port William, to be followed shortly by the *Tigris*. As they steamed down the broad, meandering river they were often grounded on uncharted shoals and sandbanks. But by the beginning of May both vessels were ready to depart from Meskene, where the Euphrates makes its great bend to the southeast.

The next 160 miles of river were navigated without trouble. The little *Tigris*, on which Chesney made his quarters, acted as pilot ship for the *Euphrates*, which carried Ainsworth, Rassam and most of the expedition. At Buseyra, where the Khabur enters the main stream and where Khosrau Parviz had once sought sanctuary, the *Tigris* steamed 10 miles up the tributary, but turned back when the Arabs who lined the shore 'did not report favourably as to the possibility of reaching Sinjar'.

Two days later, a few miles downstream from Buseyra, disaster struck in the form of a brief but violent sandstorm that sank the *Tigris* with the loss of twenty lives. Chesney and a few others swam to shore. The *Euphrates* was saved by mooring to the river bank.

Undaunted by this tragedy — and by a dispatch from London ordering the expedition to be broken up by the end of July — Chesney completed the voyage with the *Euphrates*, reaching Basra on 19 June. The British government authorized a six-month extension, enabling the *Euphrates* to steam up the Tigris to Baghdad and back and to set forth on its return voyage upstream in October. But while attempting to get through the treacherous Lamlum marshes, a vital engine part broke and the vessel had to go back to Basra. The expedition was over and its uniformed members returned to their duties.

For two civilians adventure still beckoned. Ainsworth received authority to go home by way of Mosul and Aleppo, accompanied by Christian Rassam (the name he assumed henceforth), with instructions to report on any coal and other mineral deposits they might find. They left Baghdad in February 1837 and arrived in Mosul at the end of the month — Rassam's first sight of his home town in ten years.[40]

From Mosul the two prospectors headed north, spending the first night at the Yezidi village of Deleb, where Ainsworth noted that 'the inhabitants were very unwilling to receive us'.[41] They pushed onward, noting that 'this seemed to be the festive season of the land tortoises, for they assembled in groups, and kept knocking their shells together in a noisy manner'.[42] After passing Jezira b. Omar they attempted to go directly to Diyarbakir along the Tigris gorges, but were turned back by rebel Kurdish horsemen and obliged to go by way of Mardin (aptly described by Ainsworth as 'the Quito of Mesopotamia').[43]

In Diyarbakir, reached at the beginning of April, Ainsworth and Rassam met Hafiz Pasha and learned the reason for the Yezidis' lack of warmth. The pasha, still smarting from the loss of a consignment of military uniforms to the robbers of Sinjar, was preparing a campaign to subdue, once and for all, this last and most troublesome threat to the newly re-established line of communication between Diyarbakir and Mosul.[44]

A few weeks later Hafiz Pasha's army advanced on Jebel Sinjar from the west, while troops from Mosul stormed Tel Afar and approached the mountain from the east. Unsure of the terrain but encouraged by a dream in which a heavenly being had appeared to one of his aides and predicted a Yezidi defeat, Hafiz encircled the mountain and called on the Yezidis to submit. One tribe, the Mihirkan, defied the pasha's order and opened fire after sending their non-combatants to safety in caves. Fighting lasted for three months, with heavy casualties on both sides, including Hafiz Pasha himself, who was painfully stung by a centipede.[45]

Finally the Yezidis' ammunition ran short and their leader, Lalu, surrendered unconditionally. As they emerged from their hiding places, no less than 516 persons were counted coming out of one cave. Among the booty were the stolen uniforms, twenty saddles stolen from government couriers, 30,000 sheep and a number of female captives, who fetched between $4.50 and $30 in the Mardin slave market. One report states that the Yezidis surrendered their buried treasure to Hafiz, but according to another account they showed him a cave where they had placed a few valuables and kept the secret of their real cache.[46]

After considering deportation of the tribesmen to the plains, Hafiz Pasha allowed them to stay on the mountain. They were permitted to keep their religion, laws and customs, but were inscribed on the tax rolls of the empire and a garrison was established on the main highway at Nisibin.[47]

The following year an English traveller obtained permission to visit the mountain, accompanied by a Yezidi sheikh from Bashika. In his account, thirty pages long, Dr Forbes mentions a visit to Kirsi, a miserable village on the north slope of the mountain. When the traveller asked why the inhabitants were not working, his guide answered:

> Do you see that hill opposite the village? Before Háfiz Páshá came here, the whole employment of the people of Kirsí was to sit on the top of it all day, looking out for travellers and caravans, in order to plunder them; now that is at an end, they have nothing to do.[48]

About this time Hafiz Pasha put an end to the autonomy enjoyed by Mirza Aga of Redwan, east of Diyarbakir. In Reshid Pasha's time an Ottoman governor had been installed in the castle, but he abducted Mirza Aga's wife and was killed by the Yezidis in revenge. Mirza Aga was pardoned and reinstated as

71

governor, but after Reshid's death he was invited to the headquarters of the new Ottoman commander, where he was put to death.[49] His descendants lived on for many years in Redwan as private citizens.[50]

In 1838 Hafiz Pasha renewed his campaign to bring recalcitrant Kurds under Ottoman rule and raise levies for his new army. The sultan sent him two advisers on loan from Prussia — the thirty-eight-year-old Captain Baron Helmuth von Moltke of the general staff and an engineer officer, Captain Heinrich von Mühlbach, who brought with him his draughtsman, Corporal O'Flaherty.[51]

Moltke's first tactical assignment was to help one of Hafiz's commanders reduce a Kurdish fortress near Mount Judi. The Ottoman force included a detachment of Kurdish irregulars under Bedr Khan Beg, the emir of Bohtan. On one cold night in early May the baron was glad to share the emir's fur blanket as they slept on a rock ledge under the stars.[52]

In June Hafiz's operations northeast of Diyarbakir were interrupted by an order from the sultan to concentrate his army at Malatya and prepare to move south. Mahmud II was getting ready to recover the provinces he had lost to the Egyptians.

Chapter Six

English-speaking Missionaries and Explorers

In the year 1800 the population of the seven northeastern states of the United States of America comprising New York and New England was 2,635,000. This small, highly literate community supported a number of colleges and schools of divinity.

The religious revival that swept over Britain in the eighteenth century had left its mark on the American colonies. At the start of the next century only a fraction of the Protestant population of New York and New England belonged to the Episcopal Church (affiliated with the Church of England) while most belonged to the Congregational, Presbyterian and other 'dissenting' churches.

The missionary impulses inspired by this revival were felt strongly across the ocean, reinforced by a concern that time was running out for conversion of the heathen and regeneration of Christian faith. In 1798 the President of Yale College, a Congregational minister, surveying the state of Europe and Asia, concluded that the old Bible prophecies were being fulfilled and that 'the advent of Christ is at least at our doors'.[1]

In 1810 the General Associations of Congregational Ministers of Massachusetts and Connecticut established the American Board of Commissioners for Foreign Missions,[2] which was joined within a few years by the Presbyterian and Dutch Reformed Churches. Twenty years later the American Board operated missions in the American Indian territories and in Hawaii, the eastern Mediterranean, India and Ceylon.

The Board's missionaries in Syria and Palestine, western Anatolia and Greece sought to improve the local Christians' understanding of their faith by preaching and education. Literature was supplied by a printing press in Malta. Among those employed there was a young Englishman named Percy Badger, whose sister married Isa, later Christian, Rassam. At the end of 1834 the Arabic section of the press was moved to Beirut, followed by Badger, who wrote to the CMS mission that his brother-in-law was 'much valued and respected by the officers' (of the Euphrates expedition) and that he might be detained by Colonel Chesney after his six months of service had expired.[3]

Meanwhile, new horizons had been opened for the American Board by the treaty that ended the 1828–29 war between the Ottoman empire and Russia. The Black Sea, re-opened to foreign ships, gave direct access to northeastern Anatolia and the old trade route from Trebizond across the Persian border to Tabriz. In 1830 two American missionaries set forth from Malta to report on the prospects for work among the Armenians and also to investigate the condition of the Nestorians who lived under Persian rule in the fertile plains west of Lake Urmia. Their patriarch Simon XVII Abraham (commonly known as Mar Shimun), who lived in Ottoman territory in the Hakkari mountains, headed the branch of the Nestorian Church once briefly united with Rome but separated since 1672.*

The trip to Persia was productive.[4] The shah authorized establishment of an American Board mission and school. The first head of the mission was Justin Perkins, an upright, determined minister from Springfield, Massachusetts. In 1837, en route from Urmia to Erzurum, Perkins met a group of Sipkis, a Yezidi tribe, moving along the upper Euphrates south of Mount Ararat — the first recorded Yezidi encounter with an American. Their spokesman was friendly, but refused to discuss their religion.[5]

The experience of Père Jean-Baptiste de Saint-Aignan and many others had proved that medical skills enabled missionaries to gain the confidence of the people and sometimes a degree of tolerance from their rulers when they needed help from Western doctors. In line with this tradition, the American Board appointed as a lay member of the Urmia mission Dr Asahel Grant, a graduate of the Pittsfield, Mass. Medical Institution who had been practising in Utica, New York.[6]

Born in 1807 on a farm in remote Allegany County, New York, Asahel Grant was already a widower, with two boys left in the care of relatives, when he set forth with his new wife for Urmia in 1835. A contemporary described him as medium in build, with a dark complexion and bright black eyes; 'his aspect [was] friendly, with a dash of enterprise and enthusiasm'.[7] The secretary of the American Board who hired him was especially impressed with 'his commanding form and mien, joined with calm decision and courage'.[8] These measured judgements fall short by far in conveying the impact upon contemporaries of Asahel Grant's indomitable personality.

The Urmia mission filled a real need; within a few years a dozen village schools were operating, while Grant attended to an endless stream of patients.

* See p. 50.

But the doctor yearned to get away from the 'familiar sycophancy'[9] of the peasants in the plains and start a mission in the mountains to the west. After much deliberation the American Board authorized Grant to discuss the mountain mission project with Mar Shimun, but directed him to make his way to the Hakkari district by a roundabout route through Erzurum, Diyarbakir, Mardin and Mosul. He left Urmia in April 1839, only a few weeks after his wife died of malaria, leaving three children to be cared for by other mission families.

The success of the American Board mission among the Urmia Nestorians attracted the notice of other denominations. The Protestant Episcopal Church in the United States sent a missionary, Rev Horatio Southgate, to explore possibilities in Persia, Iraq and Anatolia in 1837 and 1838. A French Catholic layman, Eugène Boré, covered the same ground between 1838 and 1842 and convinced the Lazarist order to establish a mission to the Chaldeans in the Urmia plain; he also started a new Catholic school in Mosul.[10]

Britain, glowing with the wealth and vigour of the early Victorian age, was quick to make use of an unforeseen dividend from its £40,000 investment in the Euphrates Expedition — the presence in London of a personable, cultured, shrewd Nestorian who was a Protestant, experienced in missionary work and familiar with Oriental languages and peoples.

Christian Rassam was warmly welcomed by Chesney when he reached England in mid-1837 and shared the acclaim that that generous nation bestows on failed endeavours. He made a good impression in church, university and political circles and was awarded a gold chronometer by the Honourable Board of the East India Company.[11]

Within a few months the Royal Geographical Society and the Society for Promoting Christian Knowledge jointly approved a two-year 'Expedition for the Exploration of Kurdistan' consisting of Ainsworth, Rassam and a surveyor qualified to operate the expedition's three-footed telescope and other scientific equipment. The primary objects of the expedition were to explore central and eastern Anatolia, northern Iraq and the Sinjar and to report on the condition and needs of the Nestorian and Jacobite churches. The instructions added that:

the political and moral state of the tribes of Mohammedan Kurds throughout this district, their languages, superstitions, and other peculiarities, will also, of course, not escape your observation; and it would be desirable to verify the reports concerning the Yezídís, or Fire Worshippers, or *Shaïtan perest*, or Devil Worshippers.[12]

The new expedition assembled in Istanbul in September 1838, after Rassam had spent some time in Malta revisiting his wife and settling accounts with the mission, where his brother-in-law Percy Badger, back from Syria well schooled in Arabic, was now in charge of the CMS printing press. Matilda Rassam accompanied her husband to Istanbul, but was dissuaded from joining the expedition.[13]

The travellers headed into the interior of Anatolia, were held snow-bound in Ankara for several weeks and arrived in Malatya at the end of May 1839.

Here they faced a choice between taking the direct eastward route to Mosul trodden six centuries earlier by Baiju and his Mongols, or making a southerly detour to Birecik, where Hafiz Pasha had just set up his headquarters after an arduous march across the mountains, accompanied by his Prussian technical advisers and mullahs versed in Islamic lore. Remembrance of the pasha's friendship two years earlier, a desire to revisit the site of Port William and the smell of history in the making combined to persuade Ainsworth to go south.

The 21 June 1839, the longest day of the year, saw the three travellers ensconced as honoured guests in Hafiz Pasha's camp at Nisib, 10 miles west of the Euphrates. Ainsworth reports that the centre of their tent, which was close to Hafiz Pasha's, 'was lined with a pretty pattern of red print, on the floor were carpets, and in front a double row of cushions, with variegated yellow and red silks, on which flowers of gold were exquisitely wrought'.[14] The pasha discouraged their idea of proceeding to Sinjar, where the Yezidis were proving troublesome, and urged them to stay and watch his 34,000-man army in action against the Egyptian forces assembling immediately to the south.

That same night the smaller but better equipped Egyptian army, commanded by Ibrahim Pasha and his French chief of staff, a Napoleonic veteran, began moving cautiously around the Ottoman flank to occupy unguarded ground in Hafiz's rear. The next morning the threat was clear; Hafiz had only two options — to attack the Egyptians on the move, or to pull back to a fortified position along the Euphrates. But the pasha remained passive, engrossed in the study of old prophecies and the interpretation of dreams.

Ainsworth has described the tense scene in Hafiz's tent in the afternoon of 22 June, when Moltke and Mühlbach, using Rassam as interpreter, insisted on a retreat before the army was cut off from its base. The pasha hesitated; at first he seemed to agree, but the mullahs persuaded him to stand and fight.[15]

The next day the two armies prepared for battle. The Ottomans were encouraged by the arrival of reinforcements, including 750 irregulars commanded by Bedr Khan Beg, the emir of Bohtan, who were assigned to hold a key position on the flank.[16] The Prussians dutifully supervised the deployment of Hafiz's troops. Ainsworth and his companions packed their bags.

The battle of Nisib on 24 June 1839 lasted only two hours. The Ottoman soldiers, mostly conscripted Kurds, were not trained to face sustained artillery fire. Panic ensued; soldiers became looters and headed into the mountains despite efforts by Hafiz and the Prussians to stem the flight. Ainsworth and the surveyor got separated from Rassam; their baggage and instruments were lost.

Contemporaries recognized Nisib as a landmark in Ottoman history. Sultan Mahmud II, whose carefully laid plans were shattered in a single morning, died before hearing the news. The ministers who advised his youthful successor appealed for help to the empire's old enemies, Russia and the Hapsburg empire, and to its two more recent friends — Britain and Prussia. Under diplomatic and military pressure from these powers, Mehemet Ali finally agreed to withdraw his troops from Syria and Palestine in exchange for a grant of Egypt in perpetuity to him and his heirs.

Throughout Anatolia Hafiz's Kurdish conscripts, keeping their arms and ammunition, streamed eastward to their homes. Bedr Khan Beg, who had disengaged his forces early in the battle,* rode back to his Bohtan fiefdom reconsidering his oath of allegiance to the sultan.

Other careers were altered by the battle of Nisib. Hafiz Pasha was court-martialled, acquitted and appointed governor of Erzurum. Moltke and his colleagues returned to the Prussian army. The members of the Kurdistan expedition, reunited but destitute, made their way to Istanbul, whence Ainsworth and Rassam set forth again later in the year.

Dr Grant, en route towards Mosul with another missionary, Rev Henry Homes, was in Diyarbakir when the news of Nisib arrived. They pushed on to Mardin, but were delayed there for two months by Grant's illness and the general anarchy that culminated in a riot in which a mob murdered the governor and other notables and pursued the missionaries to the Deir ez-Zafaran monastery outside the town, where the Jacobite patriarch gave them timely shelter. A week later troops headed by the governor of Mosul restored order. Homes, who had spent his time gathering material for an article about the Yezidis, decided to return to Istanbul. But, as Grant wrote later, 'while Providence called him back to Constantinople, to me it seemed to cry "Onward to the mountains!".'[18]

The governor of Mosul, Mohammed Pasha Ince Bairaktar, was in his late fifties at the time of Grant's arrival in the city.[19] A Turk by origin, who started life as a groom and never learned to read or write, he stands out among his con-

---

* In 1886, forty-seven years after the battle of Nisib, Moltke did not recollect that Bedr Khan Beg had even been there.[17]

temporaries as a soft-spoken, pitiless man of action — a type familiar to those living in troubled times such as the third-century Roman empire or the later years of the twentieth century.

Ince Bairaktar's beard had already turned white when he was transferred from Syria to assist Ali Riza's new administration in Iraq. At first the British Resident, Colonel Taylor, was favourably impressed, reporting that 'this nobleman, in spite of his failure before the troops of Egypt, . . . seems to me to be a man superior in talent to any of the Turkish Officers now here'.[20]

Two years later the same observer recognized a darker side to the pasha's character, calling him 'a most unfit and unworthy tyrant'.[21] The diary of an anonymous Ottoman engineer officer describes the horrors of a punitive expedition to Mardin led by Ince Bairaktar, who is depicted as a cruel and arbitrary commander, addicted in his leisure hours to drinking and the company of dancing boys.[22]

In 1835 Ince Bairaktar was appointed governor of Mosul, a once prosperous city ruined by plague, cholera, famine and civil disorders. He quickly erased the stain of his flight from Homs by helping Reshid Pasha defeat the bey of Rowanduz. His collaboration with Hafiz Pasha in the Sinjar campaign was even more fruitful; the capture of Tel Afar yielded a huge treasure representing two centuries of ill-gotten gains.[23]

In Mosul he restored order by selective executions and confiscations and avoided assassination by making his headquarters outside the city walls, where he built a barracks (with a water supply designed by Moltke), a foundry to make guns and caissons and an ammunition factory supplied with locally mined sulphur. It was his practice to charge the central government for these improvements, while retaining the bulk of provincial tax revenues and remitting only minimal amounts needed to keep his tax farming concession in force. At one time he stated that the sultan's treasury owed him £150,000.[24]

In the summer of 1839, after the Ottoman defeat at Nisib, the governor of Baghdad transferred to Ince Bairaktar jurisdiction over the Kurdish principality of Amadia, which still had among its tributaries the Yezidis of Sheikhan.[25]

The prince of Amadia, Ismail Pasha, sometimes known as 'the last of the Abbasids', challenged his new suzerain, but was defeated at Akra and interned at Mosul. A relative, Mohammed Said Pasha, was named his successor at Akra but forbidden to enter Amadia, where an Ottoman garrison was installed.[26]

North of Amadia, the Nestorian tribes owed allegiance to Nurallah Bey, the emir of Hakkari, another reputed Abbasid, described as 'a man of noble mien, [whose] figure is commanding, and his countenance manly, when not darkened by suspicion'.[27] The patriarch Mar Shimun, foreseeing the end of Kurdish autonomy within the Ottoman empire, aspired to become the civil as well as the religious leader of his mountain community. Although aware of the

American mission's work at Urmia, the patriarch had only once met a foreigner. In 1829 he was visited by Friedrich Schulz, a German archaeologist, who was murdered shortly afterwards by order of Nurallah Bey.

Between Hakkari and Lake Van another chieftain, Khan Mahmud, called 'the Rob Roy of Kurdistan',[28] dominated the territory south of the lake, while Sherif Bey, descended from the author of the Sheref-nameh, governed Bitlis.

All of these chieftains benefited from the weakening of Ottoman authority after the disaster at Nisib. But the most powerful of them all was the bold and bigoted Bedr Khan Beg of the Azizan clan, who governed Jezira b. Omar and the mountains to the north and west, inhabited by Moslem, Yezidi and Christian Jacobite villagers. In 1844 a visitor recalls a 'fine powerful looking man 35 years old, nearly six feet high, slightly marked with small pox, with light mustachios, but no beard'.[29] Another, more impressionable traveller who encountered him riding with his escort along the highway describes 'the stern, mysterious figure, swathed in a cashmere shawl, with dyed black beard and brows, a grecian nose and fiery, challenging black eyes'.[30] Although exercizing absolute authority, Bedr Khan Beg took pains to make it clear that he ruled in the name of his brother Saif ed-Din, the legitimate chief, who was kept under close guard.[31]

Such was the political cauldron that awaited Asahel Grant as he set forth from Mosul in October 1839 on the first of his five journeys to the mountain Nestorians. Ince Bairaktar, who assured him that 'to the borders of their country, my head for yours; carry gold on it, and fear not!', arranged for him to proceed by way of Akra to obtain an escort from the prince of Amadia, who welcomed him warmly and asked him to feel his pulse. Grant also prescribed for the Ottoman troop commander, afflicted with delirium tremens. Stopping briefly in Amadia, he rode into the Hakkari mountains and reached the patriarch's residence at the end of the month.[32]

After an encouraging five weeks' stay with Mar Shimun, Grant paid a visit to the dreaded emir of Hakkari, who required immediate treatment for 'a violent cold, attended with fever and inflammation'. In the middle of the night Grant was awakened with news that Nurallah Bey was worse. Conducted to the emir's room, where swords, pistols, guns and daggers hung on the walls, the doctor prescribed an emetic, which the patient swallowed after first making his attendants taste it. Nurallah rapidly recovered and gave Grant a horse for his onward trip to Urmia, where the missionary arrived in December.[33] A month later he suffered two more bereavements when his twin daughters, aged seventeen months, died.

In May 1840 Asahel Grant left Urmia again, bound for Boston to report in person to the American Board. Holding in his arms his four-year-old son Henry and often sleeping with him in the snow, the tireless missionary retraced his way back into the mountains along trails once traversed by the legions of Heraclius, arriving a week later at the headwaters of the river Zab.[34]

The patriarch and the Hakkari emir's deputy (the actual murderer of Schulz) reaffirmed their approval of the mission project. The doctor rode off with his small companion to Van, Trebizond and the United States, earning a compliment from one observer that 'a good soldier was spoiled when that man became a missionary'.[35]

Three weeks after Grant's departure, Mar Shimun was visited by the Expedition to Explore Kurdistan. Despite the loss of their surveyor, invalided back to England, the two societies had agreed to finance a new two-man project consisting of Ainsworth and Rassam. (Unbeknownst to his sponsors, Ainsworth added a third member to the party – a young girl he had married during the summer in Istanbul). They left the capital again in November 1839 and travelled uneventfully across western Anatolia to Aleppo and thence past the Nisib battlefield to Urfa and Mardin, reaching Mosul in January 1840. Shortly after their arrival Rassam went to Baghdad to confer with Colonel Taylor. Upon his return, Ainsworth and Rassam made a side trip to the ruins of Hatra accompanied by two young English travellers, Henry Layard and Edward Mitford, who were on their way to Ceylon. It was thus early June before they undertook the SPCK assignment to contact the Nestorian patriarch.[36]

Avoiding the main road to Amadia, filled by one of Ince Bairaktar's punitive expeditions, Ainsworth and Rassam took a secondary route that enabled them to accomplish a task set by the Royal Geographical Society. On their second day out from Mosul — 8 June 1840 — they ascended the ravine north of Ain Sifni and saw before them a narrow, wooded valley; 'and out of a dense and beautiful grove at the head of this rose the conical spires of the temple or tomb of Sheikh Adi, at once a secluded and beautiful site'. After tethering their mules in an adjoining valley, Ainsworth and Rassam made their way to the Yezidi sanctuary. A guardian, hesitant and slightly dubious, led them through the sacred buildings. Damage from two visits by Kör Mohammed's troops had been promptly repaired; the sanctuary was spotlessly clean, cool and intact.

The guide politely evaded questions about the Yezidi religion. Pleased and refreshed by a parting gift of mulberries, the travellers continued to Amadia and onward to Mar Shimun's residence in the mountains of Hakkari.[37]

Ainsworth and Rassam met the Nestorian patriarch on 20 June and conversed with him for eight hours. Mar Shimun had heard of England but knew nothing about its church and needed time to comprehend the difference between its doctrines and those of the Roman Catholics and the American missionaries. He accepted the expedition's presents of calico, boots, olives, pipe-tops, frankincense, soap and snuff, but intimated that he would also like a watch.[38]

They did not see the bey of Hakkari or his deputy. Nor, when they reached Urmia, did they call on the American missionaries. (Ainsworth later excused this discourtesy by pleading lack of proper clothes, the pressure of time and his preference for sleeping outdoors.)[39]

Ainsworth and Rassam came back from Urmia via Rowanduz, now peaceably governed by the deceased bey's brother, and reached Mosul in July 1840.

The finances of the Kurdistan expedition obliged the travellers to remain in Mosul for the next six weeks. New instruments had finally arrived to replace those lost at Nisib, but the crate had been loaded in Syria on camel-back, so that 'every single object in it was broken into fragments'.[40]

The party left Mosul at the end of August 1840, taking the Tigris valley route barred to them three years before. They made their way past Redwan, Siirt, Bitlis and Mush, but on the last chilly stretch over the Bingöl Dağ range to Erzurum attacks of malaria brought them to a halt. Rassam, who had just been notified officially of his appointment as British vice-consul in Mosul,* pushed ahead with some other travellers to Erzurum. James Brant, the local British representative who had aided many distressed travellers, advised the embassy of Rassam's arrival, adding that 'a few days after Dr and Mrs Ainsworth arrived, both in a bad state of health, Mrs Ainsworth unhappily died yesterday in consequence'. Described by Ainsworth as 'good, kind and piously disposed'[41], her identity is unknown.

Bereaved and embittered, Ainsworth finally returned to England in mid-1841 to face an audit by the expedition sponsors. By that time Christian and Matilda Rassam had installed themselves in Mosul. A traveller who visited them in June 1841 was told that:

> when the flag of England was first raised upon the consulate at Mossoul, the whole city were gathered upon their roofs to witness the sight, and remained there most of the day gazing upon the novel spectacle. The Christians were filled with wonder and admiration at the appearance of the cross floating in mid air, while the Mussulmans, enraged at the sight, went to the Pasha and complained that it was soaring above the crescent on a mosque that was close by.[42]

---

* Ainsworth had hoped to obtain this post and claimed that this was the reason he had brought his wife with him to Mosul.

Chapter Seven

Rassam and Layard

A few years before Rassam's arrival in Mosul Prince de Talleyrand, the veteran French diplomat, had outlined the characteristics of an ideal consul assigned to a post in the Ottoman empire:

> [The duties of a consul] call for a mass of practical knowledge for which specialized training is normally required. Within the scope of their jurisdiction they must act as judges, arbiters and conciliators among their countrymen; often they act as civil servants or notaries, sometimes as maritime officials; they inspect and check on public health conditions; and through their usual contacts they are able to provide an accurate, complete picture of the state of commerce, navigation and industry in the country where they reside.

The British government had recognized all these qualities in Rassam, some of them native to a product of the Mosul trading community, others acquired in the hard school of the Euphrates expedition.[1]

As a young, newly appointed representative of a powerful but faraway employer in a city governed by a rapacious tyrant, the new vice-consul started on a cautious note. The French consul in Baghdad reported to Paris in April 1841 that 'Mohammed Pasha treats him with indifference'.[2]

But as time went on the governor became aware of a growing number of transactions, undertaken by consular protégés or in the name of the consul himself and thereby entitled to exemption from the multitude of permits and fines that augmented the provincial tax revenues. Ince Bairaktar began to recognize in the former translator of Bible tracts a commercial instinct as keen as his own.

The first year of Rassam's service was marred by the tragic start of the American mission to the mountain Nestorians. (At that time the United States had limited diplomatic relations with oriental countries; in the Ottoman empire American missionaries operated under British protection, in Persia sometimes under British, sometimes under Russian, protection.)

The Prudential Committee of the American Board, impressed by Grant's achievements and prospects, assigned two missionaries to proceed with their wives from the United States to Mosul, which would serve as the year-round base for mission work in the mountains. In the summer of 1841 Grant was back in Hakkari on his third visit, paving the way for his new colleagues, when his work was cut short by the news that one missionary had died en route, his wife had died on arrival in Mosul and that the other couple, Rev Abel Hinsdale and his wife, were gravely ill. Grant hastened back to join the survivors in Mosul and nurse them back to health.[3]

In November of that year Grant and Hinsdale made a tour of the Nestorian villages in the foothills northeast of Mosul — an unpromising field already proselytized by Catholic priests. As they travelled through Yezidi villages, Grant was intrigued by what he learned about their religion and also by the possibility that the Yezidis and the Nestorians might be descended from the lost tribes of Israel.[4]

On their way back to Mosul the two missionaries visited Lalish and spent the night in the village of Baadri, the traditional residence of the Mir of Sheikhan. In the morning they received an invitation to join him for breakfast. (Their account does not give the Mir's name, but it appears probable that the person they met was the shadowy Jasim Beg.)

The published account of the first meeting between a Mir of Sheikhan and western visitors is brief. They found him:

> seated on a rug in one corner of the room, richly attired in silks of
> purple and scarlet. The house, which contained but one
> apartment, was made of small stones laid in mud, and plastered on
> the inside with clay; the walls about six feet in height, with
> thatched roof and clay floor, the clay broken.

The conversation, carried on over a meal of chicken, rice, raisins, almonds, onions and peas with side dishes of honey and watermelon, is reported to have covered general topics.

The complete journal of the missionaries, written by Hinsdale and preserved in the archives of the American Board, fills out a scenario that would have been familiar to the Capuchins of Louis XIV. On the evening of the missionaries' arrival in Baadri the journal records that:

we received a visit from the Emeer with whom we had an interesting conversation. He is an intelligent, fine-looking gentlemanly man, & has the bearing of a prince in every look & movement. He was evidently much gratified, that we had been to their sacred place, & also to find that we knew so much about their own history, customs &c. He made many inquiries of Dr. G. relating to his visit to Mar Shimoon, and to the mountain Nestorians, for whom he professed to entertain great regard; said that they were formerly *one*, and were now as brethren; that Mar Shimoon had invited him to come to the mountains telling him that he would be welcome to spend five years with him as his guest.

This account continues the following morning, when before breakfast, the Mir:

beckoned us to seats on a rug by his side, & entered into conversation in a very affable, easy manner, regarding his people &c. He has the reputation of being a very brave man, & says that he once headed 3000 of the Tiyary Nestorians, whom he represented as a bold, spirited race. His people, he said, were formerly of the same faith with the Nestorians, & still believe in Christ. It is generally believed that their religion prohibits education, but this he denied, & added 'we have been so much addicted to robbing and fighting, as to care but little for anything else; & now we have but little use for learning. Moreover were I to employ a Moolah to instruct my children, he would whip them, & this I would not allow.*

At this point breakfast was served, 'of which the Emeer, his son six or eight years old, & two or three of his great men partook with us'.[5]

To the end of his life Asahel Grant was fascinated by the Yezidi enigma. But his first concern was to press ahead with the mission to the mountain Nestorians.

The fateful year 1842 commenced with the escape of Ismail Pasha, the ex-prince of Amadia, from his honourable captivity in Mosul. He headed first for Jezira b. Omar, where Bedr Khan Beg sheltered him and enabled him to raise a small army. In April he raided the Chaldean monastery of Rabban Hormuzd, searched in vain for hidden treasure and moved on to seize Amadia, dragging with him as hostages the superior and twelve monks, shackled together with chains.[6]

* A few months earlier, when Grant was in the United States, one of the Urmia missionaries reported that 'the Yezidees have petitioned Mar Shimoon for a school'. The Prudential Committee took no action on the request.

This overt challenge to Ince Bairaktar, whose jurisdiction had recently been extended to Jezira b. Omar, evoked a vigorous response. The governor was too shrewd to attack Bedr Khan Beg, but he strengthened his grip on the fortress of Zakho, where he had already placed a garrison after arranging the assassination of its Kurdish ruler and confiscating his wealth. In the east he assumed direct control of Akra, deposing the puppet prince and requisitioning stores of grain, rice and cotton. The main Ottoman force laid siege to Amadia.

Inconvenienced but undeterred by these military operations, Grant set out again at the beginning of June on his fourth journey to the mountains. On this occasion he took the roundabout route through Rowanduz and Urmia by which Ainsworth and Rassam had returned two years before. At his first stop, the Yezidi village of Bahzani, Grant and Hinsdale had the rare fortune to encounter one of the sanjaks on a tour of the district. Hinsdale returned to his ailing wife at Mosul and Grant went on alone.[7]

The Hakkari mountains were astir with rumours, conspiracies and deceit. At the emir's summer camp Grant encountered Ismail Pasha of Amadia, plotting with his kinsmen to raise a force to relieve his beleaguered capital. The Nestorians were called on for contingents, but Mar Shimun, engaged in secret correspondence with Ince Bairaktar, urged his followers to hold off.

The relief expedition failed. Amadia surrendered to the Ottomans in September, releasing those monks who had survived captivity and torture. The ex-prince remained at large, while the British vice-consul provided shelter and support for the family he had left in Mosul.

Extinguishment of the autonomous principality of Amadia made the Yezidis of Sheikhan directly subject to the governor of Mosul. Ince Bairaktar was accustomed to having his taxes paid punctually and in full. At the end of 1842 the Sinjar Yezidis, delinquent in their payments, were visited by a punitive expedition. The Yezidi delegation bearing peace offerings and excuses was massacred and the head of the chief and sixty pairs of ears were hung above the river gate at Mosul.[8]

The winter of 1842–43 marked the turning point when the luck of Asahel Grant, pressed so hard and so long against a host of adversities, started to run out.

At the time he left the mountains in December 1842 construction had already started on the new mission house. But Nurallah Bey, plotting with Bedr Khan Beg and Ismail to punish Mar Shimun for his disobedience, suspected that it was designed to serve as a fortress and that the windows (a novelty in Hakkari) were really loopholes. Ince Bairaktar claimed to believe that the four-room building designed for three mission families was in fact a 250-room building 900 ft x 900 ft square, financed by British gold. At one point the pasha gave orders for Grant to be ambushed at a lonely spot, but the missionary had left by another route to attend the critically ill Hinsdale, who died a week after he arrived. A new missionary couple had arrived from Boston; but at year end, as the little band of Americans faced the future, they could only hope and pray.[9]

No such doubts troubled the members of an Anglican mission to the Nestorians, sponsored by the Gospel Propagation and Christian Knowledge Societies, that reached Mosul in November 1842 after a seven-month journey, bearing greetings from the Archbishop of Canterbury and the Bishop of London. This new delegation, a sequel to the Ainsworth–Rassam expedition, was headed by a newly ordained clergyman, twenty-seven years old but fluent in Arabic — Rev George Percy Badger, brother-in-law to Christian Rassam. He was accompanied by his wife, a former CMS missionary, and a lay assistant, James Fletcher. Their instructions were to offer help to Mar Shimun and warn him against the pernicious doctrines of American dissenters.[10]

Delivery of these exalted tidings was delayed by a fever that kept Badger in bed for three months; his wife was ill even longer. (In his book, published ten years later, Badger recorded 'with gratitude the kind professional services which Dr Grant spontaneously offered us during our sickness'.[11] His religious principles required him to eschew any social contact.) Finally in February 1843 Badger left for the mountains, carrying with him as a present to the patriarch:

> two pair of red boots, one canister of snuff, 20 lbs. of soap, 20 lbs. of coffee, 20 lbs. of incense, two large scarlet cloaks, several muslin kerchiefs, a quantity of ginger, 50 pipe-bowls, 50 flints, paper, pencils, a telescope, and other small articles.

Needles, pins, cottons and tapes were also brought along for the patriarch's womenfolk.[12]

Mar Shimun greeted Badger cordially and invited him to attend a meeting of the tribal elders. By ill chance their discussions were interrupted by a knock on the door. Two messengers were outside, bearing an ultimatum from Nurallah Bey to Mar Shimun, summoning him to report at once in person to the emir. There are different versions of what Badger said, or what the patriarch thought he said. In any case, Mar Shimun's reply was negative.[13] Badger returned to Mosul, pausing for a shady noonday rest at Lalish,[14] satisfied that everything was for the best.

In April 1843 Grant left Mosul on his fifth and last journey to the mountains, accompanied by his new colleague, Rev Thomas Laurie (who took a quick look at the Lalish sanctuary on the way).[15] The mission building was near completion but the atmosphere was charged with alarm. The pasha of Erzurum (a successor to Hafiz) had authorized Bedr Khan Beg and Nurallah to chastise the Nestorians. Ince Bairaktar moved troops up to Amadia to keep trouble away from his province.

In June Grant took a long trip westward to answer a strange request.[16] Bedr Khan Beg, whose troops were hovering like vultures around the doomed Nestorians, sent word that he desired a professional visit from the doctor. Faithful to the New Testament and the Hippocratic oath, Grant made his way across the mountains to the emir's castle at Derguleh, northeast of Jezira b. Omar.

Bedr Khan Beg received Grant with formality. He was wearing a richly embroidered turban and a Damascus silk robe with an ivory-handled dagger protruding from his belt. Beside him were Nurallah Bey of Hakkari, Ismail Pasha and even Khan Mahmud from the province of Van. All of them discussed freely the impending attack on the Nestorians. After a few days Grant departed, leaving some suggestions for Bedr Khan Beg's personal health care and carrying his promise that the mission house would suffer no harm. After warning the Nestorians to prepare for the worst, Grant rode sorrowfully back to Mosul.

The Kurdish onslaught was brutally swift. The Nestorians, disorganized and distraught, offered little resistance; some tribes collaborated with the Kurds. Villagers loyal to Mar Shimun were massacred or enslaved; mutilated corpses, including the patriarch's mother, floated down the Zab. The Ottoman forces at Amadia made no move to intervene. Homeless, bereaved refugees sought safety in Mosul, comforted by sympathetic Yezidis on their way. One of the first to escape was Mar Shimun, who reached Mosul two weeks after Grant. Fletcher recalls the arrival of the tall, muscular figure with long scarlet pantaloons and a short jacket, and noted that his hair was prematurely grey.[17] With Ince Bairaktar's approval he was accorded British protection by the vice-consul.

During the winter a typhus epidemic raged in the city and on 24 April 1844 the name of Dr Asahel Grant of Marshall, New York, was numbered among the twelve Americans and thousands of Nestorians whose lives were cut short between 1835 and 1844 by their commitment to the cause of Christianity in Kurdistan.

One of Grant's last house calls was to the deathbed of Ince Bairaktar, who suffered a heart attack following a drinking bout and died five days later on

18 January 1844. His survivors, according to Fletcher, included his wife, a Greek whom he had married in his youth and esteemed for her constancy and sound advice, and two Georgian concubines 'who enjoyed little consideration from a man who had outlived the attractions of lust'.[18]

Official seals were immediately placed on Ince Bairaktar's treasure chests. Consequently some time elapsed before the government auditors came across a document that indicated that in June 1843 the little cornet had delivered to Rassam a draft on an Istanbul banker in the amount of 1,000,000 piastres — an amount worth £10,000 sterling and equal to a quarter of the entire annual revenue of the province of Mosul.

Many years were to come and go before this transaction would be even partially explained.[19]

In 1841 the French government appointed its first consular agent in Mosul, an Italian-born career official named Paul-Émile Botta who had served as a doctor with Ibrahim Pasha in Syria in 1832. Besides the duties enumerated by Talleyrand, the new envoy was instructed to protect the local Chaldean church and in his spare time to excavate the ruins of Nineveh, believed to be buried under the vast man-made mounds on the east bank of the Tigris across from Mosul. Botta arrived at his post in May 1842.

His first archaeological target was Kuyunjik, the prominent mound opposite Mosul where ten years earlier the bey of Rowanduz had massacred the fleeing Yezidis. By mid-June he had started test diggings there, when he received a visit from Henry Layard, the young Englishman who had accompanied Ainsworth and Rassam on their trip to Hatra.

Austen Henry Layard, the emancipator of the Yezidis, was born in Paris on 5 March 1817, the son of a retired Ceylon civil servant.[20] Raised in England, he left at the age of 22 with Edward Mitford, another bold contemporary, on a land journey to Ceylon, where he hoped to find employment as a lawyer. After many adventures they reached Aleppo in March 1840 and made plans to ride unescorted to Mosul.

On their first day out they lost their way in a rainstorm and took shelter in a cave used by Yezidi peasants as a stable for their oxen.[21] Their onward trip by way of Urfa, Mardin and Jezira b. Omar was marked by more usual incidents of travel and they reached Mosul at the beginning of April, in time to join the Hatra trip with Ainsworth and Rassam. When they arrived in Baghdad, they decided to approach India by way of Persia, where their paths diverged. Mitford continued eastward, but his companion never went on to Ceylon.

After sojourning for a year among the Bakhtiyari tribesmen in southern Persia, Layard returned to Baghdad, where he learned about archaeology from books in Colonel Taylor's library and field trips in southern Iraq. His visit to Mosul in 1842 was occasioned by an assignment to carry despatches from the East India Company to the British ambassador in Istanbul — the redoubtable Stratford Canning, one of the giants of Victorian diplomacy, whose haughty demeanour to his opponents was balanced by a keen sympathy for the minorities in the Ottoman empire.

In March 1843, nine months after Layard's visit, Botta shifted his work from Kuyunjik to the village of Khorsabad, 10 miles north of Mosul, where a local dyer was reported to be using inscribed bricks to line his oven. On the third day of excavation the workmen uncovered huge limestone slabs sculptured with bas-reliefs of battling men and beasts. Fletcher, who happened to be visiting the nearby Yezidi village of Bashika, hurried over in time to witness the historic moment when Botta realized that he had unearthed a palace of the Assyrian kings. The French government sent Botta additional funds to finance a proper digging programme, thereby exciting the cupidity and suspicions of Ince Bairaktar. Work was in fact suspended from October 1843 until after the pasha's death.[22]

In September 1843 Percy Badger, with his wife and a group of friends, took a quick look at Botta's excavations. They were passing through Khorsabad on a two-day expedition to Lalish. The notes taken on this visit provide the first detailed description of the Yezidi shrine.[23]

The first night of their trip was spent at Ain Sifni, where the travellers' ignorance of Kurdish hampered communication with their hosts. At Lalish, however, they were able to transcribe the Arabic votive tablets on the walls and learn something about the Yezidi religion. Badger and the guide sparred for a while on theological matters. When asked to explain the meaning of the combs sculptured on the walls of the temple courtyard, the guide stated that they were tokens of respect for the long beard of Mir Hasan Beg.

Badger was pleased to be recognized from his previous visit on his way back from the mountains. In his book he claims that only one European had previously visited the temple — an artfully phrased concession to Ainsworth which by definition ignored the Asiatic member of the Kurdistan expedition (his own brother-in-law, Christian Rassam) and the American missionaries (two visits by Grant, one by Hinsdale and one by Laurie). The temple guardians allowed Badger's group to remain overnight in the temple courtyard — a favour no other foreigners had received.

On their way back they spent the night as guests of the chief sheikh of the Yezidis at Baadri. One of the visitors describes:

his very attractive, good-natured face, small eyes, straight nose and magnificent black beard. He was dressed mostly in the Arab style — a white burnoose with crimson strings worn over a long red Arab robe with yellow stripes, girt with a red and green belt; white trousers, yellow Arab slippers; on his head he wore a red and green turban. In his belt he wore a dagger; and in his hands he held a string of beads.[24]

Strangely, Badger's account of his group's enjoyable visit to the Yezidi country omits the name of one exotic participant — Ilya Nikolayevitch Berezin, a 24-year-old instructor at the University of Kazan, who spent twelve days in the Mosul area in the course of a three-year journey devoted to linguistic and general research in the Near East and sponsored by the Russian Ministry of Public Education.[25]

Berezin's report on his visit to Lalish, published in a Moscow periodical in 1854, two years after Badger's book, provides a fuller, more factual account of the trip, enlivened by colourful impressions of the chief sheikh (cited above) and of Badger himself *, described as 'a kindly Maltese, a man of frank and gay temperament'.[26] Berezin was a prolific writer — in another article he related the story that Botta had tried to convert Badger's sister Matilda Rassam to Catholicism[28] — but the account of his visit to the Yezidis earned one imperishable distinction — a laudatory review by the revolutionary critic N. G. Chernyshevsky, a precursor of V. I. Lenin.[29]

The chief sheikh, whose name is not given in the account, was particularly attentive to Berezin (who noted that a Russian traveller was an unusual sight in Kurdistan, especially for Yezidi women) and called his attention to the state of affairs on the Russian border, where the four clans living in Transcaucasia were forbidden to make their pilgrimage to Lalish, while some nomadic Yezidis still under Ottoman rule were prevented from crossing the frontier into Transcausia.

In the early years of his vice-consulate Christian Rassam's despatches dealt mainly with commercial matters. He volunteered no information on his dealings with Ince Bairaktar nor on another matter, certainly known to him but

---

* A photograph of Badger taken in 1873, when he was fifty-eight, shows a strikingly handsome man with greying hair. While in Mosul, according to one account, he 'went about in a long maroon coloured silk robe with a red shawl wound round his waist, and a red fez on his head'.[27]

more rightly judged to be of no concern to his employer — the change in the leadership of the Yezidi community, first mentioned in an 1875 traveller's report and historically confirmed in 1949.[30]

At some point in the early 1840s, most probably between Grant's visit in December 1841 and the Badger/Berezin visit in the autumn of 1843, Mir Jasim Beg's reign came to a violent end. Hussein Beg, the young son of Ali Beg the Great, made his way from the Jebel Sinjar to Esiyan, a village near Baadri, where he killed his cousin. He was then himself elected Mir under the tutelage of Sheikh Nasr, the Baba Sheikh, who resided at Esiyan.

In the spring of 1844 Badger and Fletcher served as guides for another member of the Kazan faculty — Vil'yam Franzevitch Dittel. This traveller, twenty-six years old and sized up by Fletcher as 'an agreeable compagnon de voyage', was on a similar mission to Berezin. He came well equipped 'with two small pocket pistols hung suspended by a silver chain from his belt, in which were deposited two others of larger size, while by his side swung a heavy cavalry sword'.[31]

The party rode first to the mound of Nimrud at the confluence of the Tigris and the Zab, where they set about digging with Dittel's sabre and some swords and spears borrowed from nearby villagers. Three hours later they uncovered a stone slab with cuneiform inscriptions. Badger deduced correctly that Nimrud, like Khorsabad, was a part of greater Nineveh and wrote to Stratford Canning that Britain should do something about it.[32]

Badger returned to Mosul, while his two companions went on to Lalish and Rabban Hormuzd. Dittel died a few years later before he could publish this portion of his notes. Fletcher does not report in his book how the Yezidis reacted to Dittel.*[33]

The next visitors to Lalish were tepidly received. Toward the end of July 1844, a few days before the Feast of Sheikh Adi, a group of four Americans — the forlorn remnant of the mission to the mountain Nestorians — arrived at the sanctuary and were grudgingly given accommodation in the outer court. Sending their horses back to Mosul, they announced their desire to escape the torrid heat of the Tigris valley by spending a week at Lalish. The horses returned to bear them away just as the first pilgrims were arriving, but

---

* In his *Notes from Nineveh*, published in 1850, Fletcher's description of his visit to Lalish implies that he first went there in the spring of 1843. His claim is weakened by Badger's vigorous assertion of priority and by the inconsistencies in Fletcher's own chronology; but it would explain the lack of detail about his visit with Dittel in 1844.

throughout their stay the visitors — Dr and Mrs Azariah Smith, Thomas Laurie and Mrs Hinsdale (the two latter recently widowed) — were made to understand that their presence was inopportune — most notably by Sheikh Nasr, described as 'quite young, and neither impressive nor reverend in his appearance and demeanor', who displeased the missionaries by his 'foppish-ness' and his unrequited hints that they might like to give him their old Britannia teapot.[34]

Soon after their return to Mosul, the missionaries were reassigned. The Prudential Committee in Boston had decided to conduct future work among the mountain Nestorians out of Urmia.

Meanwhile in Europe and America the reports of Nestorian massacres and deportations caused widespread concern. Badger's role in the affair was criticized (though Grant before he died wrote a letter to a New York news-paper absolving him of blame)[35] and the SPCK recalled him and Fletcher in May 1844. Rassam was instructed by Canning to procure the release of the captive women and children — some of whom had been fraudulently labelled as Yezidis in the slave market.[36]

Bedr Khan Beg was in his heyday, acclaimed by his courtiers as the scourge of infidels and the greatest Kurd since Saladin. A Jacobite bishop was waylaid by his henchmen, who sent his heart as a trophy to the emir. The Yezidis, bereft of civil rights under Islamic law, were special objects of his zeal. Rassam reported that at the feast of Bairam, when Moslems celebrate Abraham's ritual sacrifice of Isaac by slaughtering a sheep, Bedr Khan Beg would round up Yezidis for a grisly ceremony where those who refused to embrace Islam were sacrificed by his own hand. Others, too frightened to answer, were charit-ably deemed to have assented and were placed in the emir's household.* A medical missionary from Urmia who visited Derguleh in 1846 saw forty or fifty Yezidi converts in Bedr Khan Beg's castle, enjoying his special attention and exciting jealousy among his less favoured attendants.[37]

The province of Mosul relapsed quickly into the disorder from which it had been dragooned by Ince Bairaktar. His successor lasted only a year and was replaced in 1845 by one of the little cornet's comrades-in-arms — Mohammed Pasha Kiritli Oğlu. Only 4 ft tall, with a harsh voice and uncouth gestures, the new governor had been decorated by the sultan for his military prowess, evi-

---

* One of these is said to have been a Chol princess who became one of the emir's wives and ancestress of Jeladet and Kamuran Bedr Khan, noted twentieth-century Kurdologists.[38]

denced by battle scars that included the loss of one eye and one ear. But the stalwart of Homs was now fat, bent and lame and his character had been warped by monetary greed.[39]

Recent legislation abolishing the tax farming system had somewhat circumscribed provincial governors' scope for enrichment. But Kiritli Oğlu showed ingenuity in reviving ancient imposts such as Tooth Money, levied on villages that entertained transient officials as indemnity for wear and tear on their teeth. In Mosul he once spread a false report of his death, then fined the citizens for the unseemly celebrations that ensued.[40]

A punitive expedition to the Sinjar at the start of his administration managed to lure a number of Mihirkan tribesmen into the Ottoman camp, where the men were beheaded and the women and children enslaved. In addition, according to Rassam, the pasha's forces returned with 'about 400 Donkeys, 10,000 Sheep, some Cattle, a great number of Tents and old Copper'. The vice-consul estimated that there were now only eleven villages left on the mountain, with about 1,500 men capable of bearing arms.[41]

In mid-1845 Kiritli Oğlu determined that the Sheikhan Yezidis owed more taxes. As security for the pasha's claim, his soldiers seized Sheikh Nasr — or so they thought. Actually his deputy, a pir named Sino, allowed himself to be imprisoned and tortured in his place without revealing the deception.

Rassam ransomed the hostage by paying the pasha 'a considerable sum' and arranged to be reimbursed by the Yezidis over a period of time from the yield of their crops.[42]

At the end of October 1845 Henry Layard returned to Mosul with an allowance from Canning and the promise of a mandate to dig anywhere in the province of Mosul. He had the field to himself, as Botta had returned in triumph to France.

Despite obstruction by Kiritli Oğlu (replaced at year-end by a milder governor and a team of auditors), Layard started excavations at Nimrud, assisted by the vice-consul's younger brother Hormuzd Rassam and a crew of Nestorian refugee workmen. On the very first day they unearthed foundations of a palace and early in 1846 the diggers were rewarded by the discovery of a winged human-headed lion 12 ft high — the first of the great series of Assyrian sculptures that were to make him famous by the age of thirty.

At the end of August 1846 Layard and Hormuzd Rassam set off on a trip to the Hakkari mountains with letters of recommendation from Mar Shimun, still interned in the consulate. They spent a night at Lalish and were shown around the sanctuary, then headed on past Amadia to shattered villages where the memory of Asahel Grant still lived on. All was quiet, despite rumours of an impending new attack by Bedr Khan Beg and the emir of Hakkari upon the Nestorians east of the Zab. At the farthest point on their journey they passed a mounted troop of Kurds led by Nurallah's deputy, who scowled at them from beneath his huge turban and sent back a warning that spies should remember the fate of Schulz. Layard was eager to push on to Nurallah's castle, but Hormuzd Rassam persuaded him to turn back. A week after they left the mountains Bedr Khan Beg struck again and added one more chapter to the litany of Nestorian woes.[43]

Meanwhile a new governor had arrived in Mosul, the fifth in three years. Tayyar Pasha is described by Layard as 'a venerable old man, bland and polished in his manners, courteous to Europeans, and well informed on subjects connected with the literature and history of his country'.[44]

The prospect of better times under Tayyar Pasha and the benevolent interest of the British vice-consul encouraged the Sheikhan Yezidis to resume their annual Feast of the Assembly, which had not been celebrated for several years. Sheikh Nasr and Hussein Beg invited Christian Rassam and Layard to be their honoured guests. The vice-consul was unable to attend, but Layard was happy to accept.[45]

Toward the end of September 1846 Layard left Mosul in the company of the consular dragoman and a Yezidi guide. Upon arrival at Baadri next morning, they were greeted by a delegation led by Hussein Beg, clad in 'an ample white cloak of fine texture, thrown over his rich jacket and robes'. He sought to kiss Layard's hand and lead his horse, but Layard courteously objected, embraced the Mir 'after the fashion of the country' and walked together with him to his home.

Hussein Beg, as described by Layard, was:

> about eighteen years of age, and one of the handsomest young men I ever saw. His features were regular and delicate, his eye lustrous, and the long curls, which fell from under his variegated turban, of the deepest black.

Layard stated that after his escape to the Sinjar Hussein 'was carefully brought up by the Yezidis, and from his infancy had been regarded as their chief.' There is no mention of how he came to power.

Resting after breakfast in the Mir's house, Layard was awakened by a shrill but joyous female shriek. A few minutes later Hussein Beg announced with pride the birth of his first son and invited the auspicious guest to name the child. Well coached in Yezidi history, Layard suggested the name Ali in memory of the Mir's father, martyred at Rowanduz.

Later in the day came more good news. Two mounted kawals, worn and weather-beaten, arrived from a journey to the Yezidis in faraway Transcaucasia, more fortunate than a previous mission intercepted and killed by the emir of Bitlis. Throwing down their guns, the messengers kissed Hussein's hand and reported that the Yezidis in Transcaucasia were flourishing and had given them a substantial offering to the Mir's treasury.

The next morning the Mir and Layard led a procession from Baadri over the pass to Lalish. Upon first sight of the fluted domes, the entire party fired off a salute that echoed along the valley and was answered by welcoming salvoes from the sanctuary. As later groups caught sight of the shrine, they fired off their guns and shouted the cry of their tribe. Each pilgrim carefully washed himself and his clothes in a stream before entering the valley.

Sheikh Nasr and the principal sheikhs, dressed in white linen, welcomed the Mir and Layard as they approached the sanctuary. Layard describes Sheikh Nasr as a man of 'most mild and pleasing manners', whose age could scarcely have exceeded forty.

In his writings Layard skilfully combines details of archaeological finds with scenes of contemporary oriental life. His first book, published in 1849 and reprinted in many editions, provides the earliest and most colourful account of the opening day of the week-long Feast of the Assembly.

Sheikh Nasr led the Mir and Layard ceremoniously through the outer court, filled with pilgrims and lined with booths and shelters, toward the inner courtyard. Leaving their shoes at the entrance, they seated themselves on carpets spread beneath a shady vine, facing the sheikhs and kawals on the other sides of the court. In the centre was a plaster case filled with balls of clay mixed with dust from the shrine, used as talismans by pilgrims. On one side of the courtyard was the doorway into the sanctuary, ornamented with carvings of a snake, a lion, a hatchet, a man and a comb. Sheikh Nasr told Layard that these had been cut recently by a Christian mason who had repaired the tomb and that they were just ornaments suggested by his fancy.

After a while Sheikh Nasr, the Mir and Layard went back through the outer courtyard and sat by a fountain at the end of an avenue of trees, watching dancers accompanied by flute and tambourine and greeting the arriving pilgrims — swarthy, long-haired, white-robed mountaineers from the Sinjar; poor peasants from the Mosul plain; and colourfully dressed nomadic tribesmen like those encountered by Père Jean-Marie de Jésus, accompanied by their women:

> richly clad in silk antaris [bodices]; their hair, braided in many
> tresses, falling down their backs, and adorned with wild flowers;
> their foreheads almost concealed by gold and silver coins; and huge

95

strings of glass beads, coins, and engraved stones hanging round their necks.

Toward the end of the afternoon Layard returned to his assigned resting place on the roof of a building near the shrine of Sheikh Shems ed-Din. After paying a call on Sheikh Nasr's wife, who entertained him 'with a long account of her domestic employments', he returned to the shrine, where at sunset he observed white oxen being led into an adjoining pen. Asking to whom the animals belonged, he was told that they were dedicated to Sheikh Shems and slaughtered only on great festivals, when their meat was distributed to the poor. In Layard's words 'this unexpected answer gave rise to an agreeable musing; and I sat almost unconscious of the scene around me, until darkness stole over the valley'.

As the twilight faded he could see faqirs in brown robes and black turbans hurrying out of the sanctuary, bearing lamps and oil-soaked wicks, with which they trimmed smaller lamps placed in walls, rock crevices and trunks of trees. As the faqirs went by, a pilgrim would pass his right hand through the flame, touch his right eyebrow and then his lips. Platters of roast meat, rice and fruit were distributed. The darkened valley came alive with the hum of 5,000 voices while countless dots of light from their torches and from the sacred lamps twinkled through the trees.

All at once there was silence:

> A strain, solemn and melancholy, arose from the valley. It
> resembled some majestic chant which years before I had listened to
> in the cathedral of a distant land. Music so pathetic and so sweet I
> had never before heard in the East. The voices of men and women
> were blended in harmony with the soft notes of many flutes. At
> measured intervals the song was broken by the loud clash of
> cymbals and tambourines; and those who were without the
> precincts of the tomb then joined in the melody.

Hastening to join Sheikh Nasr in the inner court, Layard watched the sheikhs, kawals and nuns singing this hymn — an Arabic chant, unintelligible to the Kurdish-speaking pilgrims, that included a song to Jesus — and was told that it marked the close of a secret ceremony where the image of Melek Taus had been displayed to the sheikhs. The singing continued for about an hour in the same slow and solemn strain. Then the tempo quickened:

The chant gradually gave way to a lively melody, which, increasing in measure, was finally lost in a confusion of sounds. The tambourines were beaten with extraordinary energy; the flutes poured forth a rapid flood of notes; the voices were raised to their highest pitch; the men outside joined in the cry; whilst the women made the rocks resound with their shrill *tahlehl* [trilling]. The musicians, giving way to the excitement, threw their instruments into the air, and strained their limbs into every contortion, until they fell exhausted to the ground. I never heard a more frightful yell than that which rose in the valley. It was midnight.

Layard carefully notes that this climax was not followed by the orgies attributed to the Yezidis by their detractors and writes that 'the various groups resumed their previous cheerfulness, and again wandered through the valley, or seated themselves under the trees'. Sheikh Nasr, the Mir and Layard went back to their seat by the fountain and listened to flute and tambourine music until the night was almost done.

The second day followed the pattern of the first, and after three days Layard departed, bearing with him a letter of recommendation from Sheikh Nasr addressed in the name of Sheikh Adi, 'the greatest of all Sheikhs, and of all Khasseens [initiates]' to the chieftains of the Jebel Sinjar, where Layard planned to go in the following month.[46]

Layard's trip to the Jebel Sinjar, as the guest of Tayyar Pasha, was a sorry contract to his euphoric visit to Lalish. The governor and his entourage left Mosul at three o'clock in the afternoon of 8 October 1846 — the point in time declared by mullahs to be most auspicious — escorted by a regiment of infantry, several squadrons of irregular cavalry and a battery of guns. The stated purpose of the expedition was to examine the state of the country and consider petitions for abatement of taxes.[47]

Six days after leaving Mosul the expedition camped beneath the eastern tip of the Jebel Sinjar. A delegation from all the Yezidi tribes except the Mihirkan welcomed the pasha, who informed them that their tax assessment had been halved and that one-half of the new taxes might be deferred. A reconnaissance party, including Layard, rode up the slope to reassure the Mihirkan tribesmen, whose chief Isa Aga[48] still remembered the previous year's entrapment. They were greeted with a volley of fire that killed two troopers and mooted Layard's prospects of presenting Sheikh Nasr's letter of introduction to the villagers of Mihirkan.

The pasha ordered his troops to storm the village, already emptied of its able-bodied inhabitants, who withdrew to 'some caverns situated on a sharp aclivity [sic] difficult of access'. Killing an old man and woman too infirm to get away, the soldiers set fire to the houses; Layard noted that 'even the old pasha, with his grey hair and tottering step, hurried to and fro amongst the smoking ruins, and helped to add the torch where the fire was not doing its work'.

For three days the Ottoman force was pinned down by rifle fire, despite the brave example set by Tayyar, who directed their attacks from a conspicuous rock, where he calmly spread his carpet, smoked his pipe and chatted over coffee with the nervous Layard while bullets whistled past, spattering their faces with dirt. On the fourth day the Yezidi position was overrun without a fight; its defenders had slipped away to another part of the mountain. The only trophies of the costly battle were 'a few rude figures of men and goats, formed of dried figs fastened upon sticks', which were sent by the puzzled pasha to Istanbul.

After a brief visit to Beled Sinjar, Layard returned to Mosul. The pasha moved onwards with his ill-starred expedition, despoiling Yezidi and Arab villages on the way to Mardin. Here Tayyar Pasha committed a grave bureaucratic blunder, allowing his unruly troops to seize 14,000 sheep and 400 young camels from the nearby Milli Kurds, in those days a peaceful tribe under the jurisdiction of the governor of Aleppo. The old pasha, muttering '*Evim yiktiniz* [you have ruined me]' to the guilty officers, fell ill, was bled by a physician and was found dead in his bed after his bandages became loose in the night.

In 1847, while Layard was winding up his work at Nimrud before leaving Mosul in June of that year, the sultan's government struck a decisive blow against Bedr Khan Beg. An army commanded by the Croat general Osman Pasha moved down from Anatolia to Jezira b. Omar, which was surrendered without a blow by Yezdanshir, the son of Bedr Khan Beg's deposed brother. The emir, rejecting Rassam's offer to mediate, retreated to Derguleh.

One by one, Bedr Khan Beg's allies fell away. Ottoman forces, aided by a Yezidi contingent, defeated and captured Khan Mahmud at Tilleh on the Tigris south of Siirt. Nurallah Bey of Hakkari fled to Persia. Ismail Pasha, the last of the Abbasids, accepted a fitting place of retirement in Baghdad. Finally, in July 1847 Bedr Khan Beg negotiated a surrender with full pardon for his crimes and honourable exile in Crete.[49]

A campaign medal was struck to commemorate the defeat of the rebel chief.[50] At a firework display held in Diyarbakir in October 1847 to celebrate the circumcision of the heir to the throne the populace cheered and groaned at the blazing apparition and extinguishment of a gigantic, well-remembered figure in military garb with an enormous turban on his head.[51]

The defeat of the Kurdish chieftains (the last of them, Sherif Bey of Bitlis, was deposed in 1849) ushered in a period when orderly government became the norm, rather than the exception, in eastern Anatolia and northern Iraq. The administrative reach of the sultan's authority, historically dependent on his courier service, was soon to be enlarged by a new invention — the electric telegraph, which linked Istanbul with western Europe in 1858 and was extended by way of Diyarbakir and Mosul to Baghdad in 1861. The powers of provincial governors were gradually restricted to civil affairs, while the army developed its own chain of command and recruiting system.

The advent of law and order found the Yezidis in an anomalous position. The new regulations now applicable to Iraq subjected them to taxes and military service; yet under Islamic law they possessed no civil status — not even the limited rights accorded by Mohammed to Christians and Jews as 'peoples of the book'. Military conscription created particular problems for the Yezidis on account of their dietary laws and their religious objections to wearing blue clothing and to bathing together with Moslems.

At that time British policy, as applied by Stratford Canning, encouraged modernization and strengthening of the Ottoman empire; intervention was limited to commercial matters and cases of injustice to non-Catholic Christian minorities. However, Rassam managed to enlist Canning's interest in the Yezidis' plight by pointing out that they, like the Nestorians and the Jacobites, had been persecuted and enslaved by Bedr Khan Beg and trusted Britain to procure release of all his former slaves.

Early in 1849 Rassam arranged for Yusuf, the chief kawal of the Yezidis, to go to Istanbul with four chiefs from the province of Diyarbakir, bearing a petition to the grand vizier seeking justice, toleration and the right to commute their military service obligations on the same basis as Christians.[52] Upon arrival at the British embassy, the delegates found an old friend and ally — Henry Layard, who had returned from England at the end of 1848 and was preparing to resume digging in Iraq on behalf of the British Museum.

Kawal Yusuf was a picturesque envoy. His dark face, brilliant black eyes and jet-black beard were shaded by a large black turban. A striped *aba* [cloak] of coarse texture was thrown loosely over a robe of red silk. One British observer noted that 'he was in countenance and figure a handsome Asiatic, with an intelligent, pleasing expression, and most obliging manners'. Another, more romantic diarist remarked that Yusuf's 'large features were set in the regular antique model of the old Assyrian monarchs', imagined at another time that he saw traits of 'the gallant Kurd Saladin' and summed him up as 'altogether a fine fellow'.[53]

After months of waiting and many interventions by Canning and Layard, an edict was finally issued in mid-1849. The text lies buried in the Ottoman and British archives, but according to Layard it freed the Yezidis:

> from all illegal impositions, forbade the sale of their children as
> slaves, secured to them the full enjoyment of their religion, and
> placed them on the same footing as other sects of the empire. It was
> further promised that arrangements should be made to release
> them from such military regulations as rendered their service in the
> army incompatible with the strict observance of their religious
> duties.[54]

Meanwhile, the publication of Layard's book had stimulated widespread interest in Nineveh. The British Museum authorized a full-scale archaeological expedition consisting of Layard, an assistant (Hormuzd Rassam), a doctor (Humphry Sandwith) and an artist (Frederick Cooper).* The group left Istanbul on 28 August 1849 on a Black Sea steamer to Trebizond, taking with them Kawal Yusuf. The other Yezidis stayed behind in the capital to obtain further official documents.[55]

From Trebizond the party headed south through Erzurum to Bitlis, now under direct Ottoman rule. Here, armed with an order from the grand vizier, Layard succeeded in recovering out of Sherif Bey's forfeited wealth the money stolen some years earlier from the Yezidi kawals — relatives of Yusuf — who had been murdered by order of the Kurdish emir.

Layard's journey through the Yezidi country south of Bitlis was a triumphal progress, escorted and feasted by amazed villagers who had heard that Yusuf had been put to death, the petition rejected and that new persecutions were in store. As they approached Redwan, the party was joined by three kawals on their annual visit to the district and was greeted by a multitude of Yezidis, many of them mounted, wearing flowers and leaves in their turbans, followed by Armenians, Jacobites and Chaldeans. Layard recalls that:

> women and children lined the entrance to the place and thronged
> the housetops. I alighted amidst the din of music and the 'tahlel' at
> the house of Nazi [Mirza Aga's nephew, now chief of the district],
> two sheep being slain before me as I took my feet from the stirrups.

The travellers rested in the courtyard of the Armenian church, sheltering at sunset from a 15-minute windstorm that 'swept from the housetops the beds and carpets already spread for the night's repose'. After it had passed, the air

---

* See Plates 4, 8, 9, 30 and 31.

was particularly calm and Layard joined Nazi — described as 'a pretty good-natured fellow — apparently not of very warlike propensities' — to watch white-robed Yezidis dancing by moonlight far into the night.

The next morning Kawal Yusuf took Layard and Hormuzd Rassam into a dark inner room of Nazi's house and removed a large red coverlet to reveal a copper bird on a stand — one of the sacred sanjaks carried by the kawals on their travels as the emblem of the Yezidi faith. A copper offertory bowl and the bag that held the sanjak when disassembled, both of them objects of reverence, lay beside. Upon leaving, Yusuf and the other kawals replaced the coverlet over the sanjak and kissed the corner of the cloth. (Layard's sketch of the sanjak is shown on Plate 16.)*

Layard's trip down the Tigris valley continued in the same style until they passed Findik, a village still governed by Resul, one of Bedr Khan Beg's most fanatical supporters. A few miles beyond the village they were forcibly brought back by savage, weather-beaten Kurds. After some confusion, Layard learned that in the 1847 battle when the Ottomans defeated Khan Mahmud, Resul had been captured by Yezidis and that one of their leaders had saved him from being pitched into the Tigris, consequently and despite their religious differences becoming his blood-brother. The Kurdish chief, wearing a red and yellow turban three feet wide and claret coloured trousers, entertained them abundantly and satisfied Layard's 'curiosity upon many points of revenue, internal administration, tribe-history, and local curiosities'.

Thirty miles north of Mosul they were welcomed by a group of horsemen led by Sheikh Nasr (described by Dr Sandwith as 'a man of about forty, with a mild, intelligent countenance') and Hussein Beg. The Mir, according to the doctor, was 'a pale, sickly youth of nineteen, a beardless boy' — no longer the Adonis Layard saw in 1846; but some of the former charisma is evoked in Sandwith's description of his light-coloured turban and his:

> crimson jacket gorgeously worked in gold, which glittered like a
> lizard in the sun. Over this he wore a very light gauze-like white
> cloak, which scarcely clouded the splendour of the gold
> embroidery. A heavy silver sheath enclosed a bright curved
> scimitar, his late father's.

Soon after their arrival in Mosul, Layard and his party, together with Christian Rassam, attended the 1849 autumn festival at Lalish.[56] Attendance was lighter than three years earlier, due to Arab raids on several Yezidi settle-

---

* A fountain built in 1982 in the nearby village of Kurukavak commemorates Layard's visit to Redwan (Plate 50).

ments; only a few well-armed pilgrims came from the Sinjar. But the ceremonies, conducted on this occasion by Sheikh Jindi, a black-bearded priest with a severe countenance of the deepest brown, who had never been known to smile, were no less moving. After the dances were concluded, Layard and the Rassam brothers joined the tribal elders in a discussion of the new edict and its likely application. He urged the Yezidis to trust the central government and to send letters of appreciation to the grand vizier and the British ambassador.* On the whole Layard was satisfied with the result of his endeavours, but he noted that:

> Hussein Beg is too young to think much on public matters and is chiefly occupied in paying attention to the prettiest of his female subjects — who rather aim at being the objects of the admiration of their young chief.

During his stay at Lalish Layard inquired about the sacred book of the Yezidi religion. Sir Paul Rycaut had spoken of 'one Book' and Forbes had heard in the Jebel Sinjar that a book called 'Aswad' (the Arabic word for 'black') contained their laws and precepts. Asahel Grant had been told by Yezidis in Bashika that they had a sacred book called the 'Fourkal'; his colleague Homes had been told by a learned Moslem in Mardin that 'they have a book called Jelu, which they pretend was written by Sheikh Adi, who was not guilty of it'.[57]

Layard was informed that before the great massacre by the bey of Rowanduz the Yezidis had possessed many books, which were lost in the general panic or destroyed by the Kurds. Kawal Yusuf and Sheikh Nasr's secretary brought to Layard a volume of 'a few tattered leaves, of no ancient date' which contained the hymn of Sheikh Adi. They admitted that this was not 'the book of glad tidings' or 'the book that comforteth the oppressed' mentioned in the hymn and hinted that this book still existed. Layard was led to believe that a copy of the book might exist at Bashika or Baazani. (Many years later an article in a Russian journal quoted a story told by a resident of Mosul named Abu Jezirawi, an employee at the French consulate. He alleged that Layard had once hired him to steal a Yezidi sacred book, but that the enterprise had failed. There is no confirmation of this story.)[58]

---

* See Appendix II, pp. 207–210 for the text of these letters, the oldest official documents of the Yezidis known to exist.

Chapter Eight

The Tribulations of Mir Hussein Beg

The middle years of the nineteenth century marked the zenith of British influence in the Ottoman empire. Represented for many years (1841–58) by Stratford Canning, Britain vigorously supported the sultan's ministers against Russian expansion and urged them with some success to improve the state administration and tolerate non-Moslem minorities.

Among the beneficiaries of these reforms were the small Protestant groups in the empire, still legally obliged to pay taxes through the churches from which they had been expelled. Through the efforts of the British ambassador, decrees were issued between 1846 and 1854 recognizing separate Protestant communities and directing them to pay their taxes through elected financial agents.

The status of the Yezidis, settled in principle in 1849, was complicated by the question of their liability to military service, from which Christians had been exempt (and indeed ineligible) since the days of the caliphs. The October 1849 letter of thanks addressed to the Grand Vizier by Hussein Beg, Sheikh Nasr and twenty-eight other Yezidi chiefs affirmed their loyalty to the sultan and their readiness to serve, just as their forbears had once served in Murad IV's army.* They requested, however, that in view of their depleted manpower resulting from previous massacres they might be permitted for the next five years to pay a tax in lieu of providing recruits for the army. Thereafter they would accept liability to military service, though they requested that the Yezidis be formed into separate units or serve with Christian soldiers rather than be merged among Moslem troops.[1]

Early in 1850 Stratford Canning informed Rassam that things had been

* See p. 47.

103

arranged. The despatch containing the terms is missing from the archives, but the Yezidi leaders declared themselves satisfied and were warned by Rassam to keep secret the fact that Canning had intervened on their behalf. The recent separation of civil and military authority in the Ottoman state administration delayed implementation of the new arrangements; recruiting notices still were issued and at one point Hussein Beg was held hostage until the Yezidi contingent should arrive.[2] After a while matters were worked out, much to Rassam's relief, since a shortage of field labour would have reduced the Yezidis' harvest and delayed repayment of his loan.

By this time Christian Rassam had developed into 'a very portly influential Vice-Consul'[3] and had become the leading merchant of Mosul, dealing in hides, wool, gall-nuts and grain. He had no children, but his wife was greatly attached to her green parrot. Their house provided an oasis of hospitality and comfort for a series of visitors — one of whom recalled the oval ceiling of the drawing-room, 'beautifully painted in blue, and ornamented with gilt vines, flowers, and stars', while another noted approvingly that *Punch* magazine, then in its ninth year of publication, had found its way to Mosul.[4]

Layard continued excavating at Nimrud and at Kuyunjik, where he discovered the celebrated Royal Library of the Assyrian kings that contained thousands of cylinders and tablets. In the course of an archaeological trip to the Khabur valley in the spring of 1850 he revisited the Jebel Sinjar, accompanied by Kawal Yusuf and three other Yezidis. He found the Ottoman commander at Beled Sinjar 'almost shut up within the walls of his wretched fort, in company with a garrison of a score of half-starved Albanians'. The tribal chiefs had resumed their lawless ways and were fighting one another. Isa, the Mihirkan chieftain, was persuaded by Layard to settle a feud with a neighbouring tribe, who gave a lavish love-feast and offered their visitors gifts of 'dried figs, strung in rows and made up into grotesque figures' — the same curious artifacts that had baffled Tayyar Pasha in 1846.[5]

In July 1850 Layard visited Mar Shimun, recently restored to his position after a vexatious exile at the American mission in Urmia. The patriarch blamed all his troubles on the Americans and praised the Church of England. After spending the winter months surveying the ruins of Babylon, Layard left Mosul for England in April 1851.

During his eighteen-month stay at Urmia Mar Shimun became convinced that the American missionaries were undermining the local Nestorians' loyalty to their patriarch. The missionaries, whose churches had no bishops, were displeased by his autocratic behaviour. After his departure Rev Justin Perkins, founder and head of the mission, made a trip across the mountains to Mosul in the spring of 1849. Although many Nestorian villages had become Catholic, he felt there was enough prospect among the remainder and among the Jacobites to warrant establishing an 'Assyria Mission' to cover the provinces of Mosul, Mardin and Diyarbakir. The Prudential Committee agreed and in March 1850 the first missionary, Rev Dwight Marsh, arrived in Mosul.[6]

A few months earlier a more controversial visitor came to Mosul with his wife for an extended stay. Percy Badger, the vice-consul's brother-in-law, had been posted since 1846 as chaplain to the British governor of newly acquired Aden in south western Arabia. He had just been granted a medical leave of absence, during which he planned to complete a two-volume work entitled *The Nestorians and their Rituals* that combined liturgical analysis with a justification of his conduct in 1842–44.

The relationship between Badger and Layard was cool. Badger's claims to have discovered Nimrud on his March 1844 excursion with Fletcher and Dittel had been overshadowed by Layard's well-publicized results.[7] Layard, in turn, had offended Badger by reporting to the London press that Badger was to blame for the Nestorian massacres.[8]

In the spring of 1850 the Badgers moved from Mosul to a house rented by Rassam in the Yezidi village of Bashika. But before settling down to work Percy Badger went back to the Hakkari mountains to revisit Mar Shimun and to inspect some ancient church manuscripts in his possession. An affecting reunion took place between Badger, still resilient in his mid-thirties, and the Nestorian patriarch, at forty-nine years old a broken man.[9]

Badger did not revisit Lalish on this occasion. The Yezidi leaders were away, attending the New Year festival in the Sheikhan plain. On 18 April Sheikh Nasr and the Mir's younger brother came to Bashika, where the entrances to many of the houses were decorated with 'wild scarlet anemonies'. After ceremonial dancing and feasting, the Yezidi leaders called on the vice-consul; Mrs Badger's diary noted that Sheikh Nasr 'appeared a very quiet humble man, with a benevolent but sorrowful countenance'. The following day was filled with more celebrations and in the evening Hussein Beg called on the Rassams. Mrs Badger noticed that there was much jealousy between him and Sheikh Nasr and that he 'is but a stripling, and has three wives already'.

The next day a solemn procession, accompanied by pipes and tambourines, escorted the Sheikhan sanjak from Bahzani to Bashika. The sacred object was preceded by two pirs, waving incense-burning censers. On the last day of its stay in Bashika, Mrs Rassam and Mrs Badger were permitted to view the sanjak and to make a sketch of it.[10]

Badger rejoined the family group at Bashika at the end of April. One evening, while watching a Yezidi celebration, he was approached by 'a common looking man...[who] had evidently drunk too much arrack, which made him remarkably loquacious'. The man told Badger that he was Sheikh Nasr's scribe and, when bantered about his people's illiteracy, declared 'that he possessed a written Poem, the only relic of many learned volumes now left to the Yezidees'. After much prodding, he agreed to lend the manuscript to Badger, who took it to the Mar Mattai monastery, where the family moved in June to escape the heat of the plain. The text was none other than the Sheikh Adi hymn which Layard had seen in October 1849. Humphry Sandwith, Layard's doctor, was staying at Mar Mattai and wanted to transcribe the manuscript; Badger subsequently sent him a copy. Before returning the manuscript to the Yezidis, Badger made a translation 'with the assistance of the most learned natives at Mosul', which was incorporated in his book (completed in August 1850 and published in 1852). Subsequently, after Layard's *Nineveh and Babylon*, published in 1853, included a translation of the poem attributed to Hormuzd Rassam, Badger wrote an indignant letter to the London *Athenaeum*, reciting the events at Bashika, including the despatch of a copy of the text to Sandwith, and observing that Hormuzd Rassam was not a classical Arabic scholar. He was careful to state that he was not accusing Layard of plagiarism, but noted that 'nevertheless, with the exception of a few lines, there is a remarkable resemblance in the two versions'. There is no record of any reply by Layard.[11]

In May 1850 Christian Rassam, whose consular aegis already protected Badger, the new American mission and occasional representatives of the London Society for Promoting Christianity amongst the Jews, was visited by two delegates from his old employers, the Church Missionary Society — Rev John Bowen, an eager clergyman who had given up farming in Ontario to join the church, and his Bavarian lay assistant, the voluminous diarist Carl Sandreczki. Their trip was part of a survey, funded by Bowen, assessing the Middle Eastern prospects for the CMS, to whom Mar Shimun had sent appeals for help. Soon after their arrival, Bowen headed north for Erzurum and Urmia, while Sandreczki whiled away the summer in Mosul, recording trivia about Rassam and his wife, Layard, the Badgers, Marsh and miscellaneous transients. In July he left Mosul to join Bowen in Urmia.[12]

In September the two missionaries called on Mar Shimun. Aged and embittered by adversity, the patriarch lived in poverty and was grateful for Bowen's gift of a horse, since he did not have one of his own. Mar Shimun showed them the simple patriarchal church, where Sandreczki was amazed to see a candlestick shaped like a Yezidi sanjak but forbore inquiring of their guide.[13]

On their way back to Mosul, Bowen and Sandreczki visited Lalish and spent the night with Sheikh Nasr at Esiyan. Layard's fellow-traveller, Kawal Yusuf, acted as interpreter. In response to one of their questions, they understood Sheikh Nasr to say that the Sheikh Adi mausoleum was 1,803 years old. Sandreczki had earlier been impressed by the high standards of cleanliness and industry at the Yezidi village of Bashika and confided to his diary that he would enjoy preaching the Gospel to them.[14]

His wish was not fulfilled. Sandreczki spent the rest of his working life in Palestine, where Bowen persuaded the CMS to start a mission, leaving the Nestorian field to the Americans.[15] Mar Shimun, disappointed by English-speaking churchmen, began to develop contacts with the Russians.[16]

The new American mission started to work in Mosul among the Jacobites. This community had been initially reserved for the Episcopalians; Southgate and Badger had conferred lengthily with their maphrian, but little was achieved. In 1843 Grant and his colleagues, wintering in Mosul after the collapse of their mountain mission, had started work among the Jacobites, but a few months later the surviving missionaries were withdrawn. Six years later Perkins learned that their converts — about sixty men, mostly Jacobites with some ex-Catholics — met regularly to read the scriptures. One of them, 'a very interesting, intelligent' young man, so impressed Perkins during his ten-day stay in Mosul that he took him back to Urmia for missionary training.[17]

Jeremiah Shamir, whose long life touched many facets of Yezidi history, was born on 13 July 1821 in the village of Karaimlais, 15 miles east of Mosul, where his mother had taken her children to escape the plague in their native village of Ainkawa (near Erbil). When his father Isaac, who was studying at Rabban Hormuzd to become a Catholic priest, learned of the child's birth, Gabriel Dambo, founder and superior of the monastery, asked Isaac to name the boy Gabriel and to promise him to the church.

Orphaned in his infancy, he learned to read and write at the Ainkawa church school. At the age of fourteen he was accepted as a novice at Rabban Hormuzd. The monks were still in mourning for Gabriel Dambo, murdered the previous year by the Soran Kurds,* and it was decided to change the boy's name from Gabriel to Jeremiah. Already fluent in Turkish and Kurdish, he learned Syriac, Arabic and some Italian. After eight years he was appointed *Shammas* [deacon] in charge of the sacred ornaments and collection of offerings.

In 1846 a spiritual crisis shattered Jeremiah's sheltered life and promising vocation. The monastery had sent him to Mosul to teach in the Catholic school

* See p. 65.

established by Eugène Boré.* While in the city he met people who had attended meetings held by Asahel Grant and his colleagues. Back at Rabban Hormuzd, he secretly compared the Biblical texts distributed by the missionaries against those used by the monks. Belief gave way to doubt and he informed the superior that he had decided not to become a priest. Unmoved by three months of strict penance, he fled the monastery and made his way to Mosul, where he sought assistance from the British vice-consul. Rassam, himself once headed for a Catholic church career, befriended Jeremiah and arranged for him to teach at the Jacobite school in Mosul.[18]

In a curious replay of Rassam's own life story, Jeremiah Shamir had been married for just three months when opportunity beckoned in the form of Justin Perkins.

The journey to Urmia started on an embarrassing note. Perkins had arranged to visit the Rabban Hormuzd monastery; but as they approached the mountain, a messenger from the superior, who had recognized Jeremiah, told them that he must be left behind. Subsequently, however, Jeremiah proved a useful diplomat in dealing with the Hakkari mountaineers.[19]

Jeremiah stayed for a year in Urmia, where he learned some English and Hebrew and was spiritually regenerated at one of the mission's revival meetings. In 1850 he returned to Mosul, where it was remarked that 'the great change in his whole character made a striking impression on all who had previously known him'. He was assigned to preach under the direction of the newly arrived Dwight Marsh, who was joined by a colleague, Rev Frederic Williams, in 1851.[20]

A third missionary reached Mosul in May 1852. Henry Lobdell, a graduate of Amherst College, Auburn Theological Seminary and Yale Medical School, was twenty-five years old when he arrived with his wife and one-year-old daughter. Physically he was tall, slightly stooped and as a student had been very pale and thin, but his energy was tireless; Marsh noted that 'he commonly rode at a gallop'. Born poor — his father was a comb-maker in Danbury, Connecticut — he worked his way through school and college, where he read Gibbon, Goethe and Shakespeare and contributed an essay on Chaucer to a New York magazine. His decision to join the church followed months of inner anguish, but as a missionary and a doctor he radiated enthusiasm, confidence and warmth.[21]

The dynamic Lobdell recognized a kindred soul in Jeremiah Shamir, with whom he visited villages in the Nineveh plain. In 1854, when the Mosul Protestants received official recognition as an independent community, the ex-deacon was appointed to be their fiscal agent.[22]

In October 1852 Rassam invited the missionary families to visit the Yezidis'

* See p. 75.

autumn festival. The group, led by the vice-consul and Matilda Rassam, included Lobdell, his wife and child and Williams's wife and baby daughter.

As they approached Baadri, Christian Rassan went on ahead to arrange accommodation for the party in his new barn. Mir Hussein Beg greeted them when they arrived and introduced them to Kawal Sivok, who had accompanied his colleague Yusuf on the 1849 delegation to Istanbul. He entertained the party with accounts of life at the British embassy, where he had stayed for nearly a year and had attended several balls and receptions. The kawal recalled that at one of these functions his wife had worn a silk dress given to her by Lady Canning, remodelled at the neck to conform to the Yezidis' traditional circular style.

The next morning Hussein Beg and the kawal joined Rassam and Lobdell on a trip to the Rabban Hormuzd monastery. The Mir was escorted by ten attendants with 'long spears, girdles full of daggers, gay kerchiefs, and white shawls...The heads and breasts of the horses were hung with gaudy trappings'. On the road they greeted 'bands of pilgrims on their way to [Lalish], all decked out in their whitest robes — some mounted on donkeys, with *tanjeras* [pots] or cooking vessels slung on their shoulders or over their heads; others trudging gaily along on foot, with their arms full of guns, pistols and babies'.

The superior of the monastery, a survivor of the Amadia captivity, showed them the monks' cells, the tombs of the patriarchs and the chapel, where Henry Lobdell carved his name on the wall alongside those of Claudius Rich, Henry Layard and Justin Perkins. The superior winked slyly as a monk granted Hussein Beg's request for some earth from the ground over Rabban Hormuzd's tomb, reputed to have febrifuge properties. Then he led his visitors — Lobdell noted that their group comprised a Chaldean, two Yezidis, an ex-Catholic Anglican and a Congregationalist — to a cell where they were served a dinner of chicken, rice, grapes, cucumbers and figs, washed down by a rich wine. Lobdell, who had belonged to the Amherst Antivenenian Society, a group of total abstainers from 'ardent spirits, wine, opium and tobacco',[23] did not take any wine. But he noticed that 'Hussein Bey poured down several tumblers of it, and Sivok said the red color of it reminded him of the brandy, two bottles of which the English Ambassador furnished him daily at Stambul!'[24]

The cultural diversity savoured by Lobdell at Rabban Hormuzd carried through the next day (a Sunday) at Baadri, commencing with an Episcopal church service and a sermon:

> About sunset the French Consul [the archaeologist Victor Place] arrived from Mosul with his party, and did not hesitate to partake largely of the *arrack* of our host.... The timbrel and dance of the

natives preceded some Anglo-American hymns, and we retired to
our mud floors for the night.

Lobdell reported that the procession next morning from Baadri to the
Sheikh Adi sanctuary was dignified by 'the *cuirasses* of the two Consuls, with
their silver-hilted daggers and swords, their tight red breeches and tasseled
fezes, their gold embroidered vests and black moustaches'.

The visitors watched the ceremonies at Lalish from start to finish and
attested to the veracity of Layard's account. While Rassam, whom 'the people
all treat with as much reverence as the holiest of the Sheiks', conferred with the
Yezidi chiefs, the Lobdells called on Sheikh Nasr and were introduced to 'his
three broad faced wives'. The sheikh, whose 'face was remarkably mild and
pleasant', told them that he had 'the only books belonging to the tribe, in his
possession'.

Another personage was pointed out to Lobdell — 'the man in black'
(presumably a kochek), who was said to be the means of direct communication
between Sheikh Nasr and Melek Taus.

Later they paid a visit to the harem of Hussein Beg and noticed that each of
his four wives had:

> her peculiar temperament — the sanguine, the lymphatic, the
> nervous and the bilious, were all represented. All wore immense
> silver bracelets, their eyes were tinged black with *kohl*, their heads
> decked with pieces of gold and silver and becoming veils, which
> they drew aside in honor of our presence.

A fifth wife was expected from Diyarbakir.

At the end of the week the group returned to Mosul. Lobdell conceded that
'it was a week not mis-spent. It was well for us to breathe the invigorating air
of the mountains and to see a tinge of heathendom' in order to pursue more
strongly the missionary work.

Four months later, in February 1853, the popular Mir Hussein Beg was
abruptly deposed by Helmy Pasha, the governor of Mosul.[25] The pretext was
a dispute regarding the provision of substitute recruits owed by the Yezidis,
but the real reason was said to be the pasha's anger at Sheikh Nasr's rejection
of his offer of 200 piastres (£1.16.0) for a horse he coveted which was valued by
the sheikh at 2,000 piastres.

The new Mir of the Yezidis appointed by Helmy Pasha was Hussein Beg's
brother-in-law Jasim Beg, a youth described by Rassam as 'abhored [sic] and
excommunicated by the Kawals and Sheikh of their sect'.[26] His reign was
short.

1   Khirbet Qanafar (formerly Beit Far), Lebanon: the birthplace of Sheikh Adi. Tomb and ruined house of his father Musafir.

2   Diyarbakir, eastern Turkey: passengers boarding kelek for passage down Tigris in 1903.

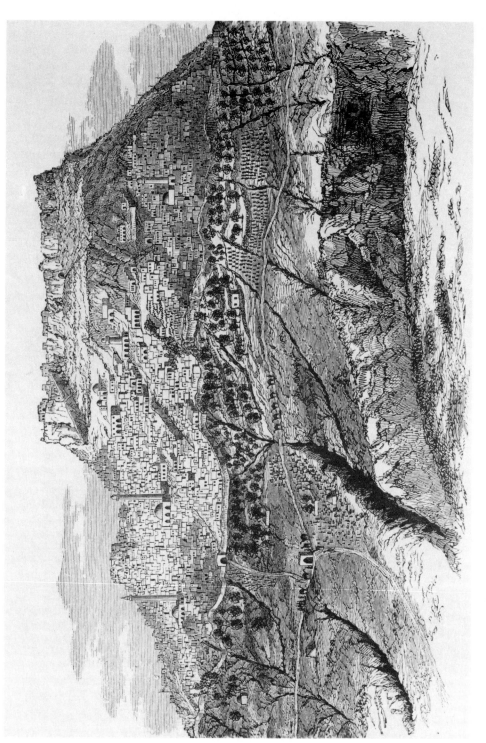

3 *Mardin, southeastern Turkey, in 1889. American Board mission house at extreme left, identified by (1).*

b. French Consulate   a. English Vice Consulate.

4   Mosul, Iraq, around 1850.

5   General view of the Yezidi Sanctuary at Lalish in 1850.

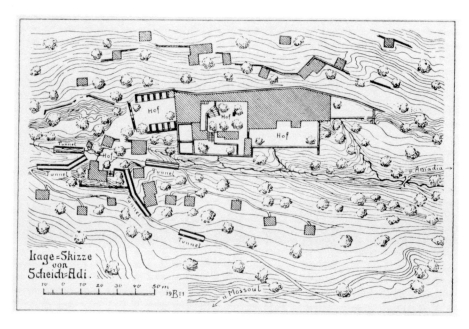

6   Site plan of Lalish sanctuary in 1911.

7   Lalish sanctuary: Yezidi pilgrims at west wall of inner courtyard in 1981.

FC Cooper. lith.

Printed by C.Grof.1 Great Castle St

FRONT OF ENCLOSURE FACING THE TEMPLE OF SHEIKH ADI.

A. Nazir's Seat.

8 *Lalish sanctuary: west wall of inner courtyard in 1849.*

9 *Lalish sanctuary: east wall of inner courtyard with door leading to mausoleum of Sheikh Adi in 1849.*

10   *Lalish sanctuary: east wall of inner courtyard, photographed by Athelstan Riley in 1886.*

11   *Lalish sanctuary: east wall of inner courtyard, photographed by Gertrude Bell in 1909.*

12 *Lalish sanctuary: doorway into mausoleum of Sheikh Adi in 1978.*

13 *Lalish sanctuary: Tomb of Sheikh Adi in 1943.*

14   Lalish sanctuary: doorway into mausoleum of Sheikh Adi in 1981.

15   Lalish sanctuary: detail of doorway into mausoleum of Sheikh Adi in 1981.

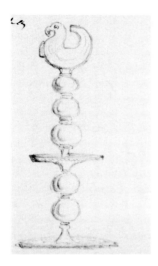

16 *Sanjak sketched by Layard in Redwan, eastern Turkey, in 1849.*

17 *Lasso, a blind Yezidi musician, sketched by C.J. Rich in 1820.*

18 Yezidi kawals, drawn by Henry Layard in 1849.

19 Yezidi kawals at Bashika in 1981.

20　The sanjak of Sheikhan, sketched by
Mrs Badger in Bashika, Iraq, in 1850.

21 Alleged sanjak owned by a Baghdad family in 1911.

DRAWN BY S. BEGG, OUR SPECIAL ARTIST IN INDIA FOR THE DURBAR.

MUCH INTERESTED IN THE STEEL PEACOCK OF MESOPOTAMIAN LUCIFER-WORSHIPPERS: THE QUEEN-EMPRESS VISITING
MR. SCHWAIGER'S COLLECTION AT THE KASHMIR GATE ON DURBAR DAY.

22   *Another alleged sanjak, Delhi, 1911.*

23   The horses of Hondaghsag, Soviet Armenia.

24   *Mausoleum of Zein ed-Din Yusuf, Cairo: portal with inscription.*

25 *Henry Layard in the 1830s.*

26 *Christian Rassam in 1838.*

27 *Asahel Grant, MD: a daguerrotype taken in 1841, with autograph from his last letter to his son written 5 April 1844.*

28 *Rev. Henry Lobdell, MD, around 1850.*

THE FRERE MISSION
Cairo, December 22, 1873

29   Rev. George Percy Badger (back row, right).

F. C. Cooper, lith.

Printed by C. Graf, 1, G't Castle St.

30 *Sheikh Nasr in 1849.*

31   *Mir Hussein Beg and his brother Abdi Beg in 1849.*

32   Mir Hussein Beg around 1870.

33　*Mir Ali Beg in 1909, photographed by Gertrude Bell. A kawal stands to the right of the Mir and the Chaldean
secretary to the left. Gertrude Bell's Armenian servant stands behind the Mir.*

*Rev. Alpheus N. Andrus, American Board mission-
ary in Mardin, Turkey, 1869–1915.*

35　*Isya Joseph, BA, Columbia College, New York
City, 1906.*

36 *Capt. H.W. Hutson, R.E., reviewing plans for Jebel Sinjar reconnaissance with an Arab chief, July 1918*

37   Ismail Beg inspecting an R.A.F. R.E.8 ('Harry Tate') reconnaissance bomber in 1918.

38   Mayan Khatun and Mir Said Beg, around 1930.

39   Ismail Beg around 1930. (Note R.A.F. and Iraq Levies badges.)

40   Wansa and Mayan Khatun around 1935.

41 *A recent picture of Princess Wansa.*

12 Mir Said Beg (on extreme right) at doorway to the mausoleum of Sheikh Adi, photographed by Rosita Forbes in 1929.

43 Mir Tahsin Beg and his grandmother, Mayan Khatun, around 1945.

44 Mir Tahsin Beg (second from left) and his mother, Khokhe Khatun, in 1981.

A YEZID MAN & WOMAN FROM SINJAH.

45   Yezidis from Sinjar around 1820.

46   A Yezidi aga from the Jebel Sinjar.

47 Hammu Shiru, Yezidi leader in the Jebel
Sinjar 1890–1932, photographed around 1930.

48 Henry Field, anthropologist and explorer, in 1928.

49 Prince Mua'wia Ismail Al-Yazidi, son of Ismail Beg, around 1980.

50 *Author and Yezidi villagers at Layard Fountain, Kurukavak (formerly Hemduna), eastern Turkey, in 198*

An Ottoman official, escorted by a troop of cavalry, conducted Jasim Beg to his new domain. Their first stop was at Sheikh Nasr's house at Esiyan, where Hussein Beg was summoned to appear in person, 'which he did, though reluctantly and sat down on his arrival below the rest'. The ex-Mir stated 'that he was much obliged to H.E. [the governor] for appointing another Emeer' and commented ruefully that his post 'had immersed him in debt'. (Rassam estimated that his debts amounted to 122,000 piastres, or £1100.) In the course of a dispute over surrendering the residence in Baadri to the new Mir, Jasim Beg 'spoke in a very disrespectful manner to Hussein Bey, which so exasperated the Yezedees that stood by that they shot him instantaniously [sic]'. One of Jasim Beg's followers drew his sword and Hussein Beg struck him a severe blow with his sword in return.

Hussein Beg rode back to Baadri, gathered his family and fled to the Jebel Sinjar. Sheikh Nasr agreed to go back with the official to Mosul, but on the way he was rescued by a large body of mounted Yezidis. In fear of retribution the Sheikhan villagers abandoned their homes, leaving the fields untilled.

Rassam's seven-page despatch to the British embassy concluded with the news that 'Sheikh Nasir has just arrived in town, and I hear the Pasha has requested him to do all in his power to restore tranquility among the people of his persuasion'. The vice-consul blamed the governor for the consequences of his imprudence and accused him of conniving with the notables of Mosul, 'who are deeply implicated in this sad affair' and were planning to send a report to the capital exculpating his conduct.

Vested interests were indeed at stake. Rassam had recently signed a crop-sharing agreement with Hussein Beg and had put up a new barn at Baadri.[27] The Mir's flight and the exodus of field labourers from the villages jeopardized this investment, just at a time when grain prices were rising in anticipation of war with Russia.

The vice-consul's anxiety was relieved in April 1853, when the governor granted him a lien on the Yezidi crop.[28] Hussein Beg's redemption took more time. In June Helmy Pasha disregarded his government's appeal for troops to guard the borders and mounted an expedition of 600 musketeers, 300 irregular horse and 150 artillerymen with three field guns to go to the Sinjar, with instructions to collect back taxes and capture Hussein Beg.[29] The financial outcome of this effort is unknown, but on June 15 Dr Lobdell, staging on the right bank of the Zab en route from Mosul to Urmia with Jeremiah Shamir, watched his erstwhile host escape across the river and head south to find shelter among the Tai Arabs of Adiabene.[30]

Eventually Hussein Beg was restored to his position, but the details of his rehabilitation are not reported.

The joint appearance of Christian Rassam and Victor Place at the Yezidis' festival — one representing Queen Victoria, niece of Chesney's sponsor, the other accredited by Napoleon III, nephew of the great emperor — was not fortuitous. The governments of the two age-long rival powers had recently been brought together by a Russian threat to their commercial and strategic interests in the Mediterranean and the Middle East. Allies of convenience, Britain and France encouraged the Sultan to reject Russian demands for a protectorate over the Greek population of his empire. At the end of 1853 they supported the Ottoman declaration of war against Russia by moving their battle fleets into the Black Sea.

In September 1854 an allied force landed in the Crimea, a peninsula once part of the Ottoman empire but now defended stoutly by the Russians, whose main naval base was at Sevastopol. In Transcaucasia the Russians defeated the Ottomans east of Kars but withdrew behind the border as winter set in.

The Ottoman army's resources were strained by the need to man three fronts — the Balkans, the Caucasus, and later the Crimea. The army's other function — maintenance of internal security — suffered. In April and May 1854 a contingent of 2,000 Kurds, recruited in the districts of Akra and Rowanduz by the blind Mir's brother Resul and headed for Kars, terrorized the citizens of Mosul for several days. Lobdell's biographer records that they threatened the missionary 'crying "Ho, Franjee, [Frank] let us kill him".' Rassam finally prevailed upon Helmy Pasha to order their commander to bastinado the principal looters and move the contingent on its way.[31]

The fearful summer heat of Mosul persuaded the American missionaries that they should plan a mountain retreat for their families. In October 1854 the Lobdells and Jeremiah set off for the chosen spot near Amadia, accompanied part of the way by Dwight Marsh and his wife. Lobdell's journal notes that on 5 October they all visited Lalish, where they took daguerrotypes of Sheikh Nasr and Hussein Beg, presiding as usual at the Yezidis' autumn festival. Marsh recalled that on the way back:

> the Doctor had ridden on. As we followed, creeping along a
> precipice overhanging a torrent, we caught sight of him down
> under an eternal wall of rock, sitting upon a boulder, and
> breaking up minerals. His favorite horse was standing content in
> mid-stream.[32]

A month later more serious trouble broke out among the Kurds.[33] Helmy Pasha received orders to advance funds to Yezdanshir Beg, nephew and betrayer of Bedr Khan Beg, who proposed to enlist 800 horsemen and 700 infantry to serve the sultan on the Caucasian front. Yezdanshir, a handsome man with a military demeanour and a small black moustache,[34] had been replaced at Jezira b. Omar by an Ottoman official and was living in Mosul, where he frequented the British vice-consulate and was noted for his bigoted views. Lobdell once heard him say 'that he would like to drink the blood of every Yezidee, Jew, and Christian, excepting his particular friends, such as myself'.[35]

In November 1854 Yezdanshir and his force reached Jezira b. Omar, seized the town and killed the local Ottoman administrators. The governor of Mardin attempted to recapture the place, but was driven off with the loss of several guns.[36] Zakho, 35 miles to the east, submitted to Yezdanshir, while his brother Mansur raided Midyat and the Tur Abdin.

Yezdanshir's next move was to the upper Tigris valley. He captured Siirt, defeated a weak Ottoman force sent against him, and despatched messengers to the Russians proposing a junction at Bitlis or Van. He then moved on to Redwan, where he implemented his boast to Lobdell; one informant told the British vice-consul in Diyarbakir that:

> he was eye witness to the murder, by the Bey's own hand, at
> different times, of between twenty five and thirty Yezidees, whom
> this fanatic considered it most meritorious to slaughter. He even
> offered five hundred piastres [£4.10.0] to whomsoever would
> bring him a live Yezid, simply for the pleasure of cutting the poor
> wretch's throat.[37]

Immobilized by snow, the Ottoman field army and its British adviser, General Fenwick Williams, could do little against this threat to the rear of its thinly held right flank. (The Russians, poorly informed about events in Kurdistan, remained in their winter quarters). But at the moment of his triumph Yezdanshir had to hurry south to face a new attack from the governors of Baghdad and Mosul.

One column of troops led by Reshid Pasha, the bespectacled governor of Baghdad who claimed to have personally accepted Bedr Khan Beg's surrender, reached Jezira b. Omar in February 1855. Another force, organized by Helmy Pasha, comprised 2,000 Yezidi horsemen led by Mir Hussein Beg, who recognized in Yezdanshir a worse enemy than the governor. Rassam reported with satisfaction that the Yezidis defeated the rebels outside Zakho, entered the town without resistance and that Hussein Beg 'had taken the town in the name of His Majesty the Sultan'. On the west bank of the Tigris the troops from Baghdad captured Jezira b. Omar after heavy fighting. Yezdanshir and his brother fled to a mountain fortress.

Reshid Pasha's forces prepared for a final assault, but the rebellion ended in an unexpected way. Early in March 1855 Matilda Rassam sent the consular dragoman down to the riverfront at Mosul, where a group of men had just ferried their way across the swollen Tigris. The party consisted of Yezdanshir Beg, his brother and fifteen followers, escorted by an Ottoman army officer bearing a safe-conduct issued by General Williams in the name of the British and French governments. Helmy Pasha's soldiers attempted to take them into custody, but after four hours of bickering the dragoman was allowed to take the Kurds to the British vice-consulate. Yezdanshir stayed there five months, until the embassy sent instructions for him to be turned over to the governor, who had been ordered to send him to Istanbul.

Responsibility for Yezdanshir's surrender and sequestration was generally ascribed to the crafty vice-consul, who happened to be in Jezira b. Omar around that time. Mar Shimun told his Russian correspondent, Colonel Khreshchatitsky, that the Kurdish leader had been tricked by Rassam.[38] A Berlin professor passing through Mosul heard that Rassam and Yezdanshir had done business together in the past; another report claimed that he had procured the surrender with a bribe of 200,000 piastres (£1,800).[39] Rassam had indeed been involved in the negotiation with Yezdanshir, but the real credit belongs to a Polish officer on General Williams' staff, who brought the safe-conduct offer, accepted Yezdanshir's surrender and escorted him to Mosul. The Kurds had already found sanctuary at the vice-consulate by the time Rassam returned to the city.*

In the Crimea, the main theatre of war, the armies of the sultan and his European allies endured a hard winter and finally gained the upper hand. The turning point occurred in February 1855, when a Russian attack on the invasion base at Eupatoria was beaten off; among those killed in that engagement was Mohammed Pasha Kiritli Oğlu, sometime governor of Mosul.[40] Sevastopol fell in September. The war ended in March 1856; the peace treaty did not change the boundaries in eastern Anatolia.

The twenty years that followed the Crimean war, a relatively uneventful period in Yezidi history, brought a heroic age to its close.

One by one, the personages of the first half-century left the stage. Stratford Canning retired from the diplomatic service in 1858. One of his last acts as ambassador was to rebuke Rassam for his tardiness in complying with a decision of a commercial court that the heirs of Ince Bairaktar should be paid the

---

* In Kurdish folklore the Yezdanshir saga is embellished with a romance between him and Matilda Rassam.[41]

proceeds of the 1,000,000 piastre draft the pasha had given the vice-consul in 1843.[42]

Christian Rassam, widowed in 1867[43] and unhappily remarried, retained his post at Mosul until his death on 30 May 1872. He was distressed that in the Ince Bairaktar litigation the court had refused to consider his counter-claims for damages resulting from military requisitions at Akra and Zakho;* but by private negotiation he was able to settle the case by paying the heirs 750,000 piastres (£6,750), one-third in cash and the balance in installments.[43] A claim by Rassam against the Ottoman government for 417,508 piastres in respect of exactions by Kiritli Oğlu, ably presented by Percy Badger (now retired from church duties), was settled in 1866 for 1,000,000 piastres.[44]

As he grew older, Rassam's youthful enthusiasm for church affairs and philology flourished anew. On a visit to England in 1868 he submitted an appeal from the Nestorian clergy to the Archbishop of Canterbury. Two years earlier a British visitor to Mosul found the vice-consul:

> actively engaged in translating portions of the Old Testament,
> especially the Prophet Isaiah, from the original into English,
> giving each word in Syriac, with his authorities for his
> interpretation of colloquial Arabic phrases [sic].[45]

Layard, only thirty-four when he returned to England in 1851, found a new avocation in politics and diplomacy. He came back to Istanbul in 1877 to serve for three years as British ambassador, but he never revisited Mosul. His friend and forerunner Paul Botta died in obscurity in 1870. The ebullient Victor Place, implicated in a New York contractor's swindle, died in Romania in 1875.[46] Bedr Khan Beg ended his days peacefully in Damascus in 1868, mourned by sixty-five sons and many daughters.

Among the missionaries, Justin Perkins completed thirty-six years of service at Urmia in 1869 and retired to die later that year in Massachusetts. Dwight Marsh returned to the United States in 1860. His colleague Frederic Williams, whose first and second wives died in Iraq, moved the mission headquarters to the cooler climate of Mardin in 1858 and lived there until his death in 1871. The brief, eager life of Henry Lobdell was terminated by fever in March 1855, shortly after he returned to Mosul from a trip to Baghdad with Jeremiah Shamir.

Jeremiah worked on at the mission as long as it remained in Mosul. In 1858, five years before Mar Shimun's death, he was appointed business agent for the Nestorians as well as for the Protestant community.[47] But by 1864 he was

*See p. 85.

living in Diyarbakir, employed as dragoman at the British consulate.[48] In 1868 and 1870 he was the Nestorian agent in Van, where he made sure that the British knew that the new patriarch (Simon XVIII Reuben) was also seeking aid from the Grand Duke Michael Nikolayevitch, viceroy of the Caucasus and brother of the czar.[49]

The status of the Yezidi community within the Ottoman empire was acknowledged by the sultan, who received Mir Hussein Beg and awarded him the title of *kapi çuhadari* (keeper of the official gate).[50]

But two decades of active political and matrimonial life — Hussein was married seven times[51] — had sapped the character of the Mir. Already in 1860 a British traveller[52] who spent a night at Ain Sifni armed with a letter from Rassam had been told of Hussein Beg's 'unfortunate propensity to indulge largely in strong waters'. He describes the Mir, who visited him the next morning with a group of white-robed kawals, as 'quite a young man, with a countenance indicative of cunning and acuteness', but with a 'sleepy, heavy, and louring look'. It later transpired that his 'very sullen and sulky' manner registered the receipt earlier that morning of 'a very pressing demand for the payment of a debt' owed to Rassam.

Rassam's long friendship with the Yezidis had indeed begun to sour. In 1860 he reported that Hussein Beg was taxing his people at a higher rate than he was remitting to the authorities in Mosul.[53] In 1866 a French traveller[54] was told that the sanjak revenues had been farmed out to the Italian consular agent for 40,000 piastres (£360) a year. (The same author relates that during the Ramadan fast Hussein Beg had shocked pious Moslems by riding through the streets dead drunk, finally falling off his mule and injuring himself.)

The Sinjar Yezidis had never enjoyed the vice-consul's sympathy, particularly after his failure to recover camels worth 165,000 piastres (£1,485) stolen from Rassam by Arab raiders who had quartered them with the Yezidis during a tribal war. In 1859 Yezidis raided an Arab camp; among those killed was an Iraqi agent of a British wool-buying firm, all of whose funds were taken. Eight years later the Arabs managed to steal 30,000 sheep; anticipating reprisals, the German botanist Carl Haussknecht's timid Arab guides obliged him to find his way alone to the Jebel Sinjar (where he was cordially received and collected many specimens).[55]

In 1869 Midhat Pasha, a vigorous, progressive administrator, passed through Mosul on his way to take up the post of governor of the province of Baghdad, which at that time included most of Iraq. Rassam reported with satisfaction that one of his first steps had been to send a punitive expedition to the Sinjar and that this 'lawless, refractory, fearless set' of tribesmen had paid up their back taxes and agreed to provide twelve recruits annually to the army.[56]

Mir Hussein Beg came to Mosul to pay his respects to the new governor and was urged to prepare his sons for their future responsibilities by giving them a proper education. But when Hussein brought a professor to teach them to read and write, the community was scandalized and the sheikhs persuaded the youths to refuse to attend any more classes.[57]

In 1872 Midhat Pasha decided that the time had come to put an end to the anomaly whereby the Sheikhan Yezidis were exempt from military service. Colonel Mohammed Tahir Bey, chief of staff of the Baghdad army corps, was promoted to the temporary rank of field-marshal and sent to Mosul to take a census of eligible males.

Rassam was too ill to help the Yezidis, even if he had been so inclined. But confrontation with the authorities was avoided by the recall of Midhat Pasha. His successor, Rauf Pasha, suggested that the Yezidis prepare a statement setting forth their religious objections to personal service in the Ottoman army.

Sheikh Nasr dictated an 'exposé', written in Arabic, Turkish and French, that for the first time revealed the code of conduct prescribed by the Yezidi religion.[58] This document, generally known as 'the 1872 Petition', was signed by Mir Hussein Beg, Sheikh Nasr and fifteen Sheikhan headmen and submitted to Rauf Pasha in March 1873. Moslem sages in Mosul declared that the Yezidi doctrines were false, but the 'exposé' served its purpose. Around 1875 the Ottoman government confirmed that Yezidis were exempt from military service (though four years later the implementing decree had still not been issued and the amount of commutation tax was still unsettled).[59]

The Jebel Sinjar, detached from some years from the province of Mosul and placed under Deir ez-Zor, suffered under the harsh rule of Ahmed Bey, a local official who appointed the pliable Sofuk Aga of the Musqora tribe to be 'head of the mountain'. Tribes fought one another; in 1875 Ahmed Bey was killed while trying to suppress one dispute. In revenge the governor of Deir ez-Zor executed a number of chiefs including Layard's friend Isa Aga, the Mihirkan leader who had battled Tayyar Pasha.[60]

About this time Mir Hussein Beg was arrested and interned in Mosul on grounds that he had been stirring up unrest in the Sheikhan. During his detention his younger brother Abdi Beg acted as chief of the Yezidis. Two of Hussein's sons, Hadi and Hasan, saw a chance to seize the sanjaks and appropriate the princely revenues. Two other sons, Mirza and Ali, supported their uncle Abdi. After a year the two rebels were defeated and killed; their mother came in disguise to Hussein's place of confinement to tell him what had happened. He replied 'I would rather they had seized the emirate than lost their lives'.[61]

A last glimpse of Hussein Beg comes from the diary of a German traveller who was taken to see him in Mosul in December 1875. Entering an old, dark house, the visitors found the Mir lying on a sickbed in a large, unheated room. There is no record of any conversation, but the haunting expression in his eyes convinced the diarist that there was truth in the reports that Hussein Beg, embittered by the disloyalty of his family and his community, was devoting his dreary existence to drink and sensuality in a vain effort to banish his fear of being killed by his enemies.[62]

After three years of internment Hussein Beg was released, but his authority was reduced. The power of life and death was taken away from the Mir; in his place an Ottoman administrator was installed at Baadri and criminal cases were adjudicated in the regular court system. Broken down by too much drinking, Hussein Beg died in 1879 at the age of fifty.[63]

Ali Beg, the eldest son, yielded the succession to the third son, Mirza Beg. The second son was less accommodating and after much discussion the two brothers, fully armed, rode up the hill above Ain Sifni and disappeared behind the crest. After a while Mirza Beg returned alone and was acclaimed Mir. Fearful as to the Ottoman government's view of these proceedings, Mirza Beg withdrew to the Sinjar but eventually, after payment of a suitable indemnity, he was confirmed as Mir.[64]

Throughout this interregnum Abdi Beg governed the Yezidis, assisted by the faithful Sheikh Nasr.[65]

Chapter Nine

Abdul Hamid and the Yezidis

In August 1876 Abdul Hamid II, aged thirty-three, was proclaimed sultan of the Ottoman empire. Known chiefly for piety and abstemious conduct befitting his second title — caliph and servitor of the holy cities of Mecca, Medina and Jerusalem — carried down from his ancestor Selim the Grim, the slight, reserved monarch inherited an empty treasury, revolt in the Balkan provinces and, even more menacing, the lengthening shadows of the Great Powers of Europe.

The last quarter of the nineteenth century was dominated by five super-powers representing the greatest concentrations of wealth and arrogance the world had ever seen. Foremost was Britain, paramount in finance and trade, with ships and colonies girdling the globe. France, a republic since 1870, was almost as rich; its investors and engineers had built the Suez Canal. Russia's vast land masses were being unified by a spreading railway network. The venerable Hapsburg empire, now styled Austria-Hungary, still challenged Russian expansion in the Balkans. Newest to reach the first rank was the German Empire, created after three swift, victorious wars waged by Helmuth von Moltke, the Prussian chief of staff.

Like majestic beasts in the jungle, the rulers of these five states observed each other constantly, ever ready to pounce on a weaker denizen or dispute another's spoil.

In 1877 the Russian government saw an opportunity in the Balkans. After a ritual declaration of war, the czar's armies marched through Romania and Bulgaria, overcame stiff Ottoman resistance and halted on the shores of the Sea of Marmara ten miles from the walls of Istanbul. In the east the Russians took Kars and laid siege to Erzurum. The sultan's ministers quickly made peace on Russian terms. But the other powers, moving belatedly to assert their interests, convened a conference at Berlin to settle the 'Eastern Question'.

The settlement was costly for the sultan. Several Balkan provinces were detached to form independent states; two others were placed under Hapsburg rule. Cyprus was granted to Britain, while in Anatolia the provinces of Kars, Ardahan and Batum were ceded to Russia. Within a few years Britain occupied Egypt and the French took Tunis.

The treatment of Armenian and other Christians in the Ottoman empire was declared to be a matter of international concern. Consulates and vice-consulates proliferated in the Asiatic provinces to monitor the condition of the Christian communities, to protect missionaries and to watch one another.

After Rassam's death the British vice-consular post at Mosul was filled by salaried officials of the Levant Consular Service, reporting to the consul at Baghdad. But life was quiet; Mosul had been bypassed by progress. The Suez Canal, opened in 1869, provided a fast, convenient means of passage between Europe and India. A few years earlier the Ottoman telegraph line had been extended from Baghdad to the Persian Gulf, connecting there with the Indian cable system, and offering a swifter, more reliable service than the dromedary post. Indeed, in 1885 the vice-consul told a French traveller that for six years no Englishman had passed through Mosul.[1] In 1886 the vice-consulate was abolished.

In January 1880 a German orientalist, Eduard Sachau, arrived from Syria, having travelled by way of the Sinjar (once again ruled from Mosul), where he noted the Yezidis' surly attitude toward the Ottoman authorities. In Mosul the professor was impressed by the soup kitchen set up at the British vice-consulate for famine sufferers. He also became acquainted with Jeremiah Shamir, now back in Mosul dealing in books and manuscripts and in his spare time teaching a half-dozen children to read and write.[2]

The American Board mission in Mardin, headed since 1871 by Rev Alpheus Andrus, paid occasional visits to the small Protestant community in Mosul and subsequently stationed a missionary there for the winter months. The first of these, Rev Caleb Gates from Chicago, conducted a thorough survey of the field and paid a visit to Mirza Beg in Baadri in February 1883. In his report, which brings to mind the Capuchin and Jesuit missions to the Yezidis two centuries earlier, he concluded that 'the time has not yet come for work among them'.[3]

The French vice-consul, Nicolas Siouffi, was a man of unusual attainments. Born in 1829 of Christian Arab parents in Damascus, he worked as a dragoman in various French consulates in Syria. He later became interpreter and advisor to Emir Abd el-Kader, an Algerian chieftain who fought the French for several years and after surrendering was exiled to Damascus. In 1865 Abd el-Kader, accompanied by Siouffi, visited Paris to receive thanks from the government for saving French lives during a local insurrection. Siouffi was granted French citizenship and joined the consular corps, becoming vice-consul at Mosul in October 1878.

In the course of his career Siouffi acquired a collection of coins and medals and became known as an expert in numismatics and early Arabian inscriptions. He was interested in lesser-known Oriental religions and wrote a book on the Mandaeans of southern Iraq. His wife, also from Damascus, earned many compliments from travellers for her charm and her hospitality *en véritable française.*[4]

Eager to learn about the Yezidis, the vice-consul was pleased to receive a visit in October 1879 from Sheikh Nasr, who had come to Mosul to see the governor about disputed commutation tax claims. Siouffi describes him as 'a man close to sixty, with a friendly, intelligent expression, who seems to have a gentle, modest disposition and friendly, dignified manners'. He was wearing a long robe and a fur jacket, covered by a black woollen cloak. On his head he wore a white turban wrapped around a black cap, rather like a tiara.

After informing the vice-consul that Mirza Beg was still awaiting government recognition as Mir, Sheikh Nasr disclosed for the first time the sources of the princely revenues. For many years, kawals had visited the scattered Yezidi communities to collect alms, carrying the sanjaks as objects of veneration and proofs of their authority. There used to be seven or eight sanjaks, but now there were only five. One was held by a Christian in Mosul as security for a debt owed by Hussein Beg.* Another was actually in Siouffi's possession, having been purchased shortly after he arrived in Mosul. The vice-consul's report supplied no details as to its provenance — according to one account it had been stolen from a kawal and sold to Siouffi for five Turkish pounds (£4.10.0)[5] — nor as to his plans for its disposition.

According to Sheikh Nasr, the remaining sanjaks were allocated as follows: the first was taken to the Jebel Sinjar in summer and winter and to the Jezira b. Omar area in spring and autumn; the second would make an annual tour of the communities to the west, including the Aleppo district; the third covered the Siirt region once a year. The fourth sanjak would make an annual visit to the districts of Mush, Van and Bayezid and to the communities across the border under Russian rule. The fifth would cover the Sheikhan three times a year. In some cases the Mir would auction the canvassing right to the highest-

* See p. 116.

bidding kawal against an amount certain; in other cases the kawal would act as agent for the Mir on a commission basis.

Sheikh Nasr confirmed the report, long current but never established, that the truths of the Yezidi religion were contained in two sacred books, written in Arabic, which no stranger might see. Remembering that a Moslem commentary on the Yezidis' 1872 petition had mentioned a book called 'Jiloun', Siouffi was told that this was 'the old book', called 'Jalaou' [Jelwa]. The second book, called 'Mashafi Rache'[Meshaf Resh], the 'Black Book', was a commentary on the Jelwa which had been given by Sheikh Adi to his followers when he came from Syria with the words 'I was the one who existed in the past and now I am come to you'.* Siouffi asked what this meant, but the sheikh would say no more.

In the course of time Siouffi also became friendly with Mulla Haider, a Yezidi resident of Bashika, who provided valuable information for the vice-consul's description of the community which was published in 1882 and 1885, with a cautionary note from the editor, in the journal of the Société Asiatique in Paris.[6]

Despite several invitations, Siouffi never visited Lalish. In 1883 he asked the Ministry of Foreign Affairs for a special grant of 400 francs (£16) for presents to be taken to the Yezidi chiefs and the Rabban Hormuzd monks, but the request was turned down.(Two years later the Ministry granted Siouffi a week's leave to visit Sinjar as the guest of the Ottoman administrator. The vice-consul reported 8,360 Yezidis, 540 Moslems and no Christians living in the eighteen villages on the mountain; the administrative district, which then included Tel Afar, annually produced 50,000 bushels of wheat and barley and yielded 500,000 piastres, £4,500, in taxes).[7]

In 1883 Russia established a vice-consulate in Mosul headed by Yuri Sergeyevitch Kartsov,[8] thirty-five years old, ambitious, intensely patriotic and well connected in governmental and ultra-nationalist political circles. For the previous four years he had served in the Russian embassy in Istanbul, where he was considered a keen but maladroit intriguer. He was briefed on his new assignment in St. Petersburg and also in Tiflis, where he urged the viceroy's staff to include in their war plans the option of a surprise seaborne attack on Istanbul. Travelling by way of Erzurum, Bitlis and Siirt, he arrived in Mosul at the beginning of December 1883.

* Misunderstanding his informant, the vice-consul attributed the opening words in the Jelwa (pp. 200 below) to the Meshaf Resh and ascribed the authorship of the latter book to Sheikh Adi.

After an initial skirmish with the governor of Mosul regarding the proper attire for ceremonial occasions — Kartsov insisted on uniform, while the governor preferred civilian clothes — the new vice-consul settled down to the humdrum life of a provincial city, little suited to a young, energetic bachelor. His staff consisted of two Russian assistants and a locally engaged dragoman named Nasir, a son of Jeremiah Shamir.

Kartsov had no use for his opposite numbers in the Mosul consular corps. W. S. Richards, the British vice-consul, he rated as an all-around nonentity. Siouffi and his wife were 'old, deep-rooted Levantines, even less interesting'. More congenial were two central European doctors serving in the Ottoman army — Dr Bronislaw Hempel, a blonde, carefree Polish exile, and the Austrian Dr L. E. Browski, 'an enigmatic character, dark-haired, with a literary style of speech, genteel manners and a steely, hostile gaze'.

A primary function of the new Russian post at Mosul was to develop relations with the local Jacobites, readily accessible, and also with the mountain Nestorians, now more commonly called 'Assyrians', among whom the dragoman had spent several years. Not pressed for time like Badger, Kartsov decided to await the spring thaw before calling upon the patriarch.

As an interim relief from boredom Kartsov accepted an invitation to visit Mirza Beg, whose acquaintance he had made soon after arriving in Mosul. Long interested in Yezidi beliefs and customs, the vice-consul had obtained from the dragoman's father Jeremiah a copy of an Arabic manuscript about the Yezidi doctrines written by a Rabban Hormuzd monk.*

The party, consisting of the three Russians, Dr Browski, the dragoman, two servants and some muleteers, left Mosul around the turn of the year. At Baadri they were joined by Mirza Beg, who escorted them to the sanctuary. As they entered the Lalish valley Dr Browski shouted 'Wild romantisch!', lowering his head to ride beneath the stone portals of the shrine.

Sheikh Nasr was their host during the Russians' two-day stay at Lalish. In his travel notes Kartsov remembers him as 'a tall, thin old man, extremely haughty' whom the visitors almost wore out with questions. The sardonic Browski found him 'an ignorant, uncultured fellow who manages to impress people with his long white beard and unctuous chatter'.[9]

They were taken into the sanctuary and were shown Sheikh Adi's tomb. In an adjoining room they saw the sacred bronze images – the Great Peacock, judged by Browski to weigh 678 lb, and five much smaller replicas. They were told how much the annual collection brought in — 6,000 Turkish pounds

---

* Jeremiah Shamir's relations with the Chaldean church appear to have mellowed over time. In the winter of 1881–82 he borrowed a Syriac manuscript from Patriarch Elias XIV to make a copy for Sachau. But he remained a staunch Protestant.[10]

(£5,400) according to Kartsov, 8,000 Turkish pounds according to Browski.

They inquired about the sacred book of the religion and were told that it was kept in the custody of Mulla Haider, a descendant of Sheikh Hasan who was the only person authorized to read and write. Browski learned that this book was at that moment in Lalish and claims that 'by a most extraordinary accident' he got hold of it and was able to keep it long enough to copy it. Kartsov does not mention this incident.

After exploring the nearby foothills and spending a night in a cave with a Kurdish outlaw, the Russians moved on to Rabban Hormuzd, where the monks showed them the original of their manuscript dealing with the Yezidis and allowed the vice-consul and Dr Browski to take notes.

The last night of the trip was spent at Baadri. Kartsov describes the Mir's residence as 'a plain country house with a courtyard, surrounded by an earthen wall'. Browski was offended by the piles of manure in the yard and the draught blowing through the unpaned windows in the hall; he noted without comment a wicker table covered by a green cloth beneath a huge coloured Bohemian glass chandelier. Both visitors remarked on the peacocks strutting around the premises.

As dusk fell servants brought in lamps and the Mir emerged from his quarters to greet his guests. Kartsov describes Mirza Beg as 'a young man, unassuming in appearance, exploited by everyone, who could not remember how old he was'. But the weary travellers were glad to accept his hospitality and soothe their aches with water-pipes, raki and the seductive songs of dancing boys. Twenty years later Kartsov still recalled the atmosphere of that evening as 'undefinable, strange, rather relaxing, rather entrancing'. Browski merely noted that Mirza Beg was 'a mighty tippler in the sight of the Lord' and usually had to be put to bed by his servants.

The party returned to Mosul the next day after an absence of two weeks.

In March 1884 Kartsov and the dragoman took off into the desert west of Mosul to inspect some horses owned by an Arab chieftain. On the second day of the trip they sighted a wild boar and gave chase. As he came close to the boar Kartsov drew his revolver and shot himself in the leg. Friendly Arabs applied first aid, wrapping the skin of a freshly slaughtered lamb around the wound. The vice-consul was carried back to Mosul, where Browski and his colleagues were unable to locate the bullet. Kartsov was finally evacuated to Aleppo, where he was operated upon. He survived, but was disabled for life.

An article by Dr Browski, published by a German magazine in 1886, gave the first account of the Russian visit to the Yezidis. Kartsov's fuller account, written in 1884 and printed for official use in 1886, was not published until 1891 and his memoirs did not appear until 1906. He was the first and last representative of Imperial Russia in Mosul. His end is unknown.

The next visitors to Lalish were representatives of the Archbishop of Canterbury. The Assyrian petition forwarded by Rassam in 1868 had led eight years later to an exploratory trip by an Anglican clergyman and the subsequent despatch of another cleric who stayed in the Hakkari mountains for several years. Finally, after a further reconnaissance by Athelstan Riley, a prominent layman close to the primate, the Archbishop's Mission to the Assyrian Christians was launched in 1886. Escorted by Riley, the first two missionaries, both Cambridge graduates, arrived in Urmia and hastened to pay their respects to the patriarch.

In September 1886, after completing arrangements with the Assyrians, Riley rode south to Mosul. On the way he spent two days (11–12 September 1886) at Lalish and was shown around the sanctuary by the guardians. His published account and his recently located journal add little to the reports from Kartsov and Browski, except that Riley had a camera and was allowed to photograph the inner court of the sanctuary. The guardians threatened to destroy his plates when they saw him washing the negatives in a sacred fountain and drying them on a hallowed stone. But they were mollified by the astute churchman, whose travel album consequently contains the earliest photographs of the Lalish mausoleum.*

Regrettably Riley found Mirza Beg absent from his residence at Baadri and never had a chance to savour the hospitality of the Mir.[11]

In the following year one of the missionaries, Canon A. J. Maclean, also visited the Yezidis, remarking that 'the spire of [the] temple of Sheikh Adai rises in a picturesque valley like that of an English village church'. At Ain Sifni he encountered Sheikh Nasr — 'a dear old man, the same who was Sheikh in Layard's and Badger's time, and he knew them well'. In Mosul he noted in his diary 'Shamasha Eremia is the head of the [Protestant] community; I liked him very much'.[12]

Sheikh Nasr died in the autumn of 1889.[13] A half-century of comparative peace and quiet had elapsed since the grim days of Ince Bairaktar and Kiritli Oğlu. But now the Yezidi community was about to face the gravest threat to its existence since the reign of Atabeg Bedr ed-Din Lulu.

Contemporary and modern students of history and psychology have long sought to understand the personality and policies of Sultan Abdul Hamid,

* See Plate 10.

who early in his reign dismissed the politicians to whom he owed his throne and thereafter single-handedly ruled the Ottoman empire from the well-guarded Yildiz palace outside Istanbul.

Intelligent and hard-working — Layard described him as 'one of the most amiable men he ever knew; with nothing but good impulses'[14] — the sultan quickly perceived that the strength of his empire lay in the untapped resources and manpower of Anatolia. The examples of Russia and North America had shown how railroads facilitated political unity, economic development and the movement of troops. Concessions were granted to the German-owned Anatolian Railway Company, which completed a line from the Bosporus to Ankara in 1892 and began work on a line to the southeast that reached Konya in 1896. Plans were started on still greater projects: an extension of the railway beyond Konya to Aleppo, Mosul, Baghdad and the Persian Gulf; and a railway along the old pilgrim route from Damascus to Medina and Mecca.

The other side of Abdul Hamid's nature was obsessed with conspiracies and plots. Although the Anatolia heartland was mainly inhabited by Turks, the outlying provinces were peopled by Christians (largely Armenian) of uncertain loyalty, undisciplined Kurds and marauding Arab tribes.

One of Abdul Hamid's priorities was the reorganization and re-equipment of the Ottoman army. He was aided by a German military mission despatched in 1882 by Field-marshal von Moltke. But no foreign advisors could remedy the basic problem of inadequate manpower resulting from loss of territory, exemption of non-Moslems from military service and uneven application of the conscription law.

Except for the brief, disastrous period when Reshid Pasha and Hafiz Pasha dragooned the Kurds like criminals into the Ottoman army, little effort had been made to utilize their military zeal in peacetime. In 1891, however, the sultan announced the formation of the Hamidieh, a new Kurdish corps of irregular cavalry modelled after the Russian cossacks and assigned a similar mission — defence of the frontiers and maintenance of government authority in the interior. Among the prominent Kurds appointed to command Hamidieh regiments was Brigadier-General Ibrahim Pasha, chief of the Milli tribe, who built up a fiefdom in the Viranshehir district and inspired terror among Arab raiders and local inhabitants alike.[15]

The Yezidis — Kurds but not Moslems, entitled to commute military service obligation by paying 50 Turkish pounds (£45) per draftee — represented an anomaly in the eyes of military planners and a heresy in the mind of the pious sultan. In 1885 the government decided to place them on the same conscription basis as Moslems and to require a minimum period of service in addition to collecting the 50 Turkish pounds.[16] The new regulations were applied without trouble to the Yezidi communities in the provinces of

Aleppo, Diyarbakir and Van. But enforcement was more difficult in Iraq; in November 1890 the British archaeologist Wallis Budge saw and heard evidence of atrocities committed in the Sinjar by a special detachment headed by Ayub Beg, a central government official who was also trying to force the Yezidis to become Moslems.[17]

The origin of the scheme to convert the Yezidis to Islam is hard to trace. Siouffi attributes it to 'certain staff officers in Mosul'. Andrus reported that 'this movement originated in Mosul & was brought to the attention of the Sultan who seems to have been attracted by it.' A British vice-consul at Diyarbakir, writing a few years later, blames Surri Pasha, the governor of Diyarbakir.[18] Whatever the authorship, the idea was viewed by its sponsors as a clever administrative step that would find favour with the sultan.

In the spring of 1891 a new commission arrived from Istanbul, composed of an army officer and two mullahs. They carried a message from the sultan to the Yezidis pointing out that they had originally been Moslems and urging them to return to their ancient fold. According to a contemporary account, Mirza Beg and the sheikhs replied that this was not so, saying:

> How is it possible that we were originally Moslems when our reli-
> gion antedates yours by so many thousands of years? For was not
> Nebuchadnezzar a Yezidee? Rather have you strayed away from
> us than we from you!

At this point the Yezidis were reminded that their commutation taxes were two years in arrears. If they chose to keep their religion, these taxes must be paid immediately and the quota of recruits must be provided. If they embraced Islam the sultan might be disposed to relieve them from military service for the present. In order to expedite matters, the Yezidi chiefs were put in prison, but were later released on bail.

In their perplexity the Yezidis turned to American missionaries for help.

The American mission in Urmia, operated since 1871 by the Presbyterian Board of Foreign Missions, had been stimulated by the arrival of the Anglican missionaries to renew their work in the Hakkari mountains. Rev Edmund W. McDowell, a native of Highland Park, Illinois who joined the Urmia mission in 1887, set off in November 1888, stopping first in Mosul to rally the local Protestants before moving on to the mountains. McDowell, like Grant and Lobdell, dreamed of converting the Yezidis to Christianity; with this object he sent Keena, a local Protestant pastor, to Alkosh to get acquainted with the Yezidis in that district, but the emissary became embroiled in disputes with Chaldean factions and was expelled from the village early in 1889 with a rope around his neck. Later that year McDowell sent two lay assistants to live with the Yezidis in the Sheikhan as 'artisans'. They reported that the 'lower classes' were open to religious conversation, but that 'the rulers, who are very suspicious would fight [mission work] to the death'. They recommended that personal work done by Christian masons would be productive of much good.[19]

Alpheus Andrus, the American Board missionary in Mardin, also became interested in the Yezidis after an unnamed English lady 'sent a small sum for a tentative effort among them'. After sending a lay preacher to contact the local tribesmen, Andrus considered starting schools for them in the Viranshehir region.[20]

Edmund McDowell had reported to the Board of Foreign Missions that missionary prospects among the Yezidis were poor. He and Andrus (who was engaged in transferring the Mosul parish to the Presbyterians) were therefore quite startled in May 1891 when Jurjis, one of the Mosul Protestants, brought a message from the Yezidi leaders that they would be interested in learning how the Yezidi community might be received into the Protestant church.

Two hundred years after Père Jean-Baptiste had listened to the enticing pleas from the Jebel Seman, the Christian Church had a second chance to convert the heathen. But Alpheus Andrus, a shrewd New Yorker, had lived thirty years in Mardin and remembered the story of the persecuted Shemsiehs who had secretly retained their cult after acceptance into the Jacobite church.* After discussion with other members of the mission, Andrus sent back to Mosul a ten-point questionnaire to be answered in written form. Among the items raised was the question whether, if the Yezidis joined the Protestant church, the latter would be liable for the Yezidis' tax arrears.

After some delay caused by Jurjis' fear of being discovered in communication with the dangerous sect, Andrus reported that the Yezidis 'promised to submit a formal paper to us, after that they should have perfected their consultations, and become entirely united upon the step to be taken'.

In July 1891 Mirza Beg, his brother Ali Beg and the chief sheikh were summoned to Mosul, along with the principal chiefs of the Sheikhan villages, to learn the government's decision about the Yezidis. The governor, attended by officers and troops of the garrison, ordered them to accept the obligation of military service on behalf of their community. After protesting in vain that they could not impose conscription upon unwilling subjects, the chiefs were themselves made to draw lots. Out of thirty-eight Yezidis present twenty-two were picked, including Mirza Beg and his brother and several persons over fifty years old, all of whom were conducted to the barracks and forced to put on the hated blue uniform. The Mir sent a messenger to his old friend Siouffi (now the only foreign consular representative in Mosul) and was advised to

* See p. 55.

keep calm while the vice-consul tried to help.

In fact, the government changed its tactics. Masud Effendi, an Ottoman official from Diyarbakir, arrived on a new mission with instructions 'to convert the Yezidis through advice and kindness'. But after a while he became exasperated by his lack of success and recommended that they send an army officer, vested with extraordinary powers 'to teach a lesson to these arrogant, thievish sinners and straighten out whatever needed to be straightened out'.[21]

At the beginning of July 1892, during an interregnum between the departure of the last governor and the arrival of the next one, a Tigris kelek brought a new functionary from Istanbul — Lieutenant-General Omar Wehbi Pasha, an energetic officer reputed to be close to the Grand Vizier, a fellow Damascene, and to the Minister of War, a classmate at the military college who had arranged for his rapid promotion. Typical in an autocratic state, the new-comer's powers were broad and undefined.[22]

The general's first actions in Mosul were to improve the living conditions of the garrison troops, to enforce law and order and to punish corrupt council-lors. The bastinado, long disused, was brought back, along with the custom of parading a convicted criminal through the streets preceded by a town crier proclaiming his guilt. At the end of fifty days Siouffi reported to Paris that 'of the hundreds of Ottoman officials I have known in the forty-two years of my career, I have never seen one to match Omar Pasha in integrity and rectitude'. He predicted that, if the general could curb a tendency to impetuous action, he could render immense service to the government in this backward corner of the Ottoman empire.

No time was lost in addressing the Yezidi problem. An expedition was despatched to the Sinjar. Its commander, a police colonel, reported a success-ful engagement, with ten Yezidis killed and thirty-five wounded at a cost of two soldiers killed and four wounded. One hundred and twenty prisoners were brought back to Mosul.

The general was no less forceful in dealing with a prominent Yezidi chief in the Sheikhan who repeatedly evaded a summons to Mosul. A detachment of soldiers was sent to kill everyone in the village and bring back their heads to the city.

Intimidated by these events, Mirza Beg brought a delegation of some forty Yezidi chiefs from the Sheikhan to Mosul. They were greeted at the Tigris bridge by Omar Wehbi Pasha and a number of Moslem dignitaries. A crowd of spectators followed their progress to the barracks, where they were quartered for the night.

The next day (19 August 1892) the general convened the council of the province (a body that included Christians as well as Moslems) and formally called on the Yezidi leaders to embrace Islam. About a quarter of the chiefs refused and were beaten; one of them later died from his injuries. The remainder, headed by the Mir, pronounced the irrevocable words of the Mohammedan profession of faith.

The exuberant general telegraphed to the capital that several thousand Yezidi families had become Moslems — a premature announcement he hoped to back up by sending religious teachers, administrators and soldiers into every village in the Sheikhan.

Mirza Beg, his brother Badi Beg and another prince were rewarded for their conversion with the title of pasha; each of them was granted a salary of 2,000 piastres (£18) a month. At the general's request they sent a fulsome letter of thanks to the sultan, 'under whose auspices their entire sect, composing 1,100,000 Yezidis, had left the path of error and ignorance to enter the way of perfection'. (A postscript in Omar Wehbi Pasha's handwriting suggested that a copy be sent to an Istanbul newspaper.) But another brother, Ali Beg (the one who had received his name from Layard), refused to change his religion and was imprisoned.

Meanwhile a petition bearing more than 100 names, including one of the Yezidi princes, was brought to Sioufﬁ by an envoy who stated that the community was ready to become Christian. The vice-consul answered that he could not accept such an ill-timed proposal but promised to do his best to help them. He urged the general, with whom he had become quite friendly, to employ persuasion rather than force and warned him that otherwise he would bring his conduct to the attention of the French government. (He soon learned that this was a hollow threat; within a fortnight Siouﬁi was ordered by his ambassador in Istanbul to keep out of the Yezidi affair.)

About this time the new governor, Osman Pasha, arrived in Mosul. The city notables, Moslem and Christian alike, were becoming alarmed by Omar Wehbi Pasha's arbitrary methods and feared that trouble in the Sheikhan would hurt the supply of foodstuffs. But the governor, who had been unemployed for six years and needed time to pay off his debts, feared to challenge the influential general.

In mid-September, without troubling to notify the governor, Omar Wehbi Pasha sent off a punitive expedition to the Sheikhan. Its commanders, described by Siouﬁi as inexperienced and hot-blooded, were the general's son Assem Bey, aged twenty-five, and Reshid Eﬁendi Omari, a few years older, the black sheep of an old Mosul family. The force consisted of several hundred regular army soldiers.

Unlike the Jebel Sinjar mountaineers, the Sheikhan Yezidis, mostly field labourers, were defenceless against a military attack. Accounts vary as to the number of villages destroyed and associated murders, robberies and rapes. One poignant incident, reported by several sources, involved a group of young village girls who hid from the soldiers in a wheatfield but perished when the soldiers set fire to the crop. A few weeks later Omar Wehbi Pasha, accusing Siouffi and others for inciting the Yezidis, blamed them for causing 300–400 deaths. The survivors fled from their homes; some sought refuge in the mountains to the north, while another group, led by a kochek named Mirza, made their way to the Sinjar.[23]

But the key objective of the expedition was the sanctuary at Lalish. An Ottoman writer who had access to the official documents itemizes the objects removed:

> Five bronze peacock images (Hazret Daud, Sheikh Shems ed-Din, Yezid b. Moawiya, Sheikh Adi and Hasan el-Basri).

> Khalil er-Rahman Kotchy, a bronze image in the shape of a ram.

> The bronze rod of Moses.

> A cast bronze snake.

> The Shahrur, a cast bronze nightingale.

> The cummerbund of Seyyid Ahmed er-Rifai.[*]

> A rosary of Seyyid Ahmed el-Bedewi (called Sheikh Ahmed el-Kebir by the Yezidis).

> A comb of el-Junayd of Baghdad [a ninth-century Sufi master, teacher of el-Hallaj].

> A wooden staff of Sheikh Abd el-Qadir el-Gilani.

> A bronze cup connected with the glory of Solomon.

Not included in the loot were the great peacock and the two sacred books, which Assem Bey's soldiers were unable to find. The other relics were taken to the barracks at Mosul and afterwards allegedly removed to army corps headquarters in Baghdad. (According to one account, the hiding-place of the great

* See p. 18.

peacock was betrayed to the Ottomans and this too was confiscated.)

Later in the month the expedition swept through Bashika and Bahzani, destroying many hallowed shrines. The villagers' shirts were torn open to conform to the Arab style. The word 'Yezidi' was forbidden to be uttered. But one observer noted that, when commanded to curse Satan, many of them mumbled the like-sounding word 'Sultan'. Another reported that the villagers assembled as ordered for the Friday prayer, but that after the preacher had completed his 15 minutes of devotion, his congregation had melted away.

Estranged from Siouffi, hated by the Mosul merchants and fearful that the central government would catch up with him, the general sought to banish his frustrations by continuous playing of military music. Ali Beg, along with other recalcitrants, was kept in prison and tortured; after two months' confinement orders arrived from Istanbul that he should be exiled to Kastamuni in northern Anatolia.

By this time word of Omar Wehbi's excesses had reached Istanbul through various channels. The British Foreign Office had been alerted in September 1892 by Hormuzd Rassam, now retired, who forwarded a report from Andrus. But the sender was reminded that 'interference between the Sultan and his Majesty's subjects is apt to be detrimental to the interests of the latter, unless in cases where H.M. Gvt can allege a definite right to intervene'. Tactfully, the reply omitted the Permanent Under-Secretary's jesting note to his minister:

> I really do not see what claim we have to interfere on behalf of the devil worshippers, and if they are correctly described it is suicidal to claim a locus standi.

The last act of the drama opened at the beginning of October 1892, when the general's son Assem Bey headed for the Sinjar with five battalions of regular troops.

A few days later an Anglican clergyman, Rev. Oswald H. Parry, arrived in Mosul with one of Andrus' assistants. Parry was engaged on an inspection trip for the Syrian Patriarchate Education Society and had spent six months with the Jacobite patriarch Ignatius XXXIV Peter IV at the Deir ez-Zafaran monastery outside Mardin. He was on good terms with Alpheus Andrus, who gave him a letter of introduction to Jeremiah Shamir; he was consequently well acquainted with Yezidi affairs.

On the evening of 4 November 1892 the music ceased to play outside the government compound. Jeremiah told Parry that bad news had arrived from the Sinjar. In Parry's words:

The soldiers of the Fariq [general] had been sent to the Yazidi
villages on the lower slopes of the Sinjar mountains, and were
preparing to loot the houses, from which the inhabitants had not
had time to carry their property into security among the rocks,
when some of the chiefs came with an avowal of Islam, and with a
promise, if their villages were spared, to conduct the soldiers by
night and surprise the villages higher up. This was readily agreed
to, and soon after nightfall a start was made. What was the surprise
of the soldiers when, on entering a gorge halfway to the summit,
they were received by a rapid succession of volleys, while their
treacherous guides hurried on to join their friends, between whom,
stationed in two companies on each side of the gorge, they had led
the soldiers. To make matters worse, the soldiers found that very
few of their own shots took effect, the gunpowder in the cartridges
having been secretly replaced by dust. It may seem incredible, but
it is said that not infrequently peculating officials take these means
to enrich themselves. At any rate the unlucky soldiers, unlucky,
too, that this persecution of the Yazidis was little to their taste,
made the best retreat they could, but found by this time the villages
deserted and little left to eat. The belief that a hundred were killed
was confirmed by a soldier brought in wounded to Mosul a few
days later.

That same evening there was a total eclipse of the moon. Parry and his
companions, startled by the indignant citizens' trumpets and kettle-drums,
went up to the roof of their house, where 'the perfectly clear air and immense
space of horizon, with all the subtle beauty of an eastern night, combined to
form one of the most lovely sights imaginable'.

Four days later the governor received a telegram from Istanbul repeating a
previous demand for a report on the general's activities which Osman Pasha
had failed to send. Stubborn to the last, Omar Wehbi Pasha set off from Mosul
on 18 November to join his troops, accompanied by the hapless Mir Mirza
Beg. En route he conscripted a thousand villagers and Arab tent-dwellers to
serve as auxiliaries. (A telegram from Istanbul ordered him to send them back
to their homes.)

A few days later the general sent word to Mosul that he had won a great
victory over the Yezidis, inflicting 100 casualties at the cost of one officer and
four soldiers wounded. Rumours that the army had in fact suffered another defeat were supported by the general's demands for reinforcements, ammunition

and medical supplies, as well as by the moderation of his offer to the Sinjar Yezidis, whereby they could keep their religious freedom provided they paid their
back taxes and returned the rifles they had captured from his soldiers. (The
capture of the rifles was the work of Hammu Shiru, a member of the
Faqiran tribe, newcomers to the Jebel Sinjar.)[24]

On 9 December 1892 a telegram arrived from Sultan Abdul Hamid himself,
dismissing Omar Wehbi Pasha from his post and ordering him to remain in
Mosul pending arrival of a commission of inquiry and to be prepared to answer charges that he had used Ottoman troops in combat without permission
from the Ministry of War. Four months later the general returned to the capital in disgrace. (Ironically, one of the major charges against him was a
disrespectful remark he made about the Imam Hussein, grandson of
Mohammed, when he learned that the tomb of one of Hussein's descendants
had been destroyed by Assem Bey in mistake for a Yezidi shrine.)

The situation in the Jebel Sinjar continued tense throughout 1893. The
Shammar Arabs refused to release livestock escrowed in their care during the
previous year's fighting, so that the Yezidis could not pay back taxes. The
kochek Mirza stirred up the tribesmen by predicting the imminent collapse of
Islam, to be followed by the reign of justice when Yezidis would rule the earth.
In July Siouffi, shortly due to retire, reported that Brigadier-General Bekir
Pasha, commander of the Mosul garrison, had moved several battalions to the
Sinjar.

Fighting was renewed in October 1893, in which each side suffered about
100 casualties. Finally, Sofuk Aga, the Yezidi leader, agreed to negotiate. The
kochek was sent off to the Sheikhan with 1,000,000 piastres (£9,000) he had re-
portedly collected from his followers. (He built a castle for himself and urged
the Yezidis to send him their alms rather than to Lalish. After a while he was
killed, allegedly by order of Mir Mirza Beg.) Peace was restored on the mountain, but the Ottomans kept a strong force at Beled Sinjar.[25]

The Yezidis had won a reprieve from extinction, but the community had been
badly shaken by these convulsions.

In the Tur Abdin foothills west of the Sinjar, one Yezidi chieftain, Hasan
Kanjo, accepted Islam and joined the Hamidieh with his tribesmen. He soon
became the right hand man of Ibrahim Pasha, the powerful Milli leader highly
regarded by Sultan Abdul Hamid and, according to one report, the person
who advised him to recall Omar Wehbi Pasha.

Hasan Kanjo, described by a visitor as 'a tall apparition, with a face framed by a long flowing beard, who walked with a measured pace', built a fortress on a bare slope at Haleli (east of Viranshehir) to serve as a base for fighting the Shammar and other desert Arab tribes.[26] His followers and their families, who appear to have been allowed to keep their Yezidi faith, were camped around the fort.

The small Yezidi community in the Jebel Seman hills west of Aleppo maintained its identity and was occasionally visited by travellers. But the villages were obliged to provide recruits for the army, most of whom were sent to garrison the Yemen and never returned.[27]

In the upper Tigris and Euphrates valleys the Yezidi communites were steadily eroded by persecution, Kurdish raids and emigration to the Sinjar and, to a lesser extent, to Transcaucasia.

In Mosul the timid Osman Pasha had been replaced by a new governor, Aziz Pasha, who arranged the peace settlement in the Jebel Sinjar and allowed the Yezidis in the Sheikhan to practice their religion once again. Mirza Beg and the other prominent converts to Islam resumed their old faith (though Ali Beg remained in exile). The price for these concessions was enforcement of military service, continuance of the Islamic schools in the villages on a voluntary basis and surrender of the Lalish sanctuary to Moslem dervishes, who established a retreat there and operated a religious school. The sanjaks and other religious objects remained in custody.[28]

In the spring of 1894 Saturnino Ximenez, a Spanish journalist from Istanbul, was authorized by Aziz Pasha to visit the Sheikhan. The trip started in Nineveh with an open air banquet in a ruined Assyrian palace, attended by government officials, army officers, Arab chiefs, Chaldean notables, Dominican monks and Mirza Beg himself with his brother Badi Beg. The next day Ximenez moved on to Baadri escorted by Mirza Beg, his brother, his sons and fifty Yezidi horsemen armed with long bamboo lances. At one point the Mir's youngest son, aged fifteen, showed off his horsemanship by galloping away at full speed, then suddenly vanished, to return later pale and silent with a fractured shinbone from a fall.[29]

At the Mir's residence Ximenez was shown into an enormous room with couches and Persian carpets, where dinner was served. The next morning he talked lengthily with the Mir in a ground floor room with two sofas while water from a fountain trickled into the garden through an open door. Afterwards, accompanied by a now idled kochek, he strolled through an orchard and sat down by a little pond, where they talked in the shade of a pomegranate tree and noticed that its fallen petals made the surface of the water look dark red, like blood.

Mirza Beg was taken aback when the journalist asked him if he would like to come with him to see the Sheikh Adi sanctuary. After two days of conference with hastily summoned elders, he agreed to the trip, prearranged by Ximenez with the pasha. When the Mir left his house the next morning with his brother and sons, Baadri teemed with Yezidis, hundreds of them mounted, others on foot bearing Martini–Henry rifles. The handful of policemen serving as Ximenez's escort nervously went along.

The sun rose as the long procession climbed up the narrow path in complete silence. Finally, catching sight of the fluted spires among the trees, the leading Yezidi raised his lance above his head with a shrill cry and intoned the first bars of a hymn, picked up by those behind until the whole gorge was filled with song.

The dervishes did not attempt to block the flood of pilgrims, who scattered among the well-remembered shrines and holy places, embracing the door frames and reverently kissing the spring water. After much discussion the sheikh of the dervishes consented to open the sanctuary, now a mosque. Ximenez saw only a gloomy chamber with smoke-blackened walls. But the Yezidis could see everything — the empty spot where the great peacock used to be kept, the nails from which amulets once hung down, the bare sarcophagus of Sheikh Adi and much more besides.

Ximenez's servants brought him a light lunch, which he invited the Mir to share; but the offer was courteously declined. They left Sheikh Adi around four o'clock in the afternoon and reached Baadri at nightfall. Dismounting at the entrance to his residence, Mirza Beg kissed the Spaniard's hand.[30]

In 1897 Lord Warkworth, a young, adventurous member of Parliament, undertook a personal inspection of the eastern provinces of the Ottoman empire. On his way from Amadia to Mosul he passed the forlorn sanctuary at Lalish. The courtyards and surrounding dwellings were ruined and of the main building only the outer shell and roof survived. The mullah who kept the key of Sheikh Adi's mausoleum was away. The traveller rode on to Mosul.[31]

Mirza Beg died in 1899. The last years of his reign were clouded by fresh humiliations, including a demand that he reaffirm his allegiance to Islam or risk losing his salary. In May 1899 a German traveller was told that the governor of Mosul had ordered the Mir and his two brothers to go in person to the Sinjar to collect the taxes.[32]

The exiled brother Ali Beg, who had stubbornly refused to become a Moslem, had been allowed to return home in 1898 through the good offices of the British embassy. After Mirza Beg's death he was elected Mir at the age of fifty-three; the Ottomans limited his authority to religious affairs. Aided by his wife Mayan, a daughter of Abdi Beg, who had shared his exile, the new ruler carefully set about healing the material and spiritual wounds of the past ten years.[33]

In the Sinjar resentment still smouldered from the devastation wrought by Omar Wehbi Pasha. In April 1906 a British traveller — the young Mark Sykes, honorary attaché at the Istanbul embassy, adventurous like Layard but less tolerant — travelled along the old Aleppo–Mosul caravan route, where German engineers were already starting work on the railway line to Baghdad. After stopping at Viranshehir to visit Ibrahim Pasha and his ex-Yezidi lieutenant, Sykes crossed the desert and reached a Yezidi encampment on the western slopes of the Jebel Sinjar. Writing in the facetious style then fashionable among explorers, he describes how the chieftain, 'a man with a strange and evil countenance, received us with a chilling reserve', while 'scores of his white-robed henchmen came in, and glared at us in grim silence'. He noted that:

> their clothing is strange in the extreme – on the head, a tall brown
> conical cap, around which is wound a black or red turban; the body
> is swathed in a long flowing shirt of white, cut square at the neck,
> and a short cloak of brown leather; and pointed, curled-over shoes
> complete the costume. When I saw these curious figures around
> me, it seemed as if four thousand years had slipped back, and I was
> sitting among some forgotten primaeval people, such as those who
> carved their barbarous monuments upon the rocks at Ivriz [a
> Hittite inscription west of Konya].

When Sykes returned to his camp, he found 'a crowd of silent men, slowly and deliberately examining all my furniture'. But he was reassured later by the arrival of 'Shaykh Hamo' (Hammu Shiru), whom Sykes found:

> of more cheerful aspect than the others ... . He came into my tent,
> and I entertained him to the best of my ability. He said that if war
> broke out between Persia and Turkey [then considered possible],
> the men of Sinjar would kill every Moslem within reach, a
> sentiment loudly applauded by the rest; indeed, the solitary
> yapping cry by which they marked their approbation of their
> pastor's speech was the only sign of animation which I noticed
> among them all that day.

The next morning he went on to Beled Sinjar, where he found a kindred soul in the Ottoman administrator;

by birth an Arab of Mosul, of good family, he is well off, and does
government work rather for an amusement than for a livelihood.
... The people are loud in his praise, and for good reason — he does
not 'eat' money, keeps the peace, and punishes evil-doers.[34]

The dervishes were still at Lalish in 1904. In May of that year Rev W. A.
Wigram of the Archbishop's Mission, travelling through the Hakkari mountains, decided to make a side trip to Nineveh and Mosul. On his way back he
stopped at the Sheikh Adi shrine, abandoned except for a Kurdish caretaker.
The stone buildings were intact but overgrown with nettles and undergrowth;
in places the roofs had fallen in. The dome above Sheikh Adi's mausoleum had
been smashed, allowing the daylight to come in. Wigram went down to the
basement (an area previous visitors were never shown) but could see little
owing to 'a scanty supply of wax vestas'.[35] Later that year the sanctuary was
restored to the Yezidis by a new governor of Mosul, Mustafa Nuri Pasha.[36]

In the summer of 1906 a British missionary from Mosul,* invited by the
Yezidis to visit Lalish, noted that the shrine of Sheikh Adi was 'in a church-like
building with a newly-built steeple' and that the snake beside the entrance
porch 'is kept blackened daily with charcoal by the two or three old monks who
live in the shrine'. However the inside of the shrine contained only 'a pool of
water, said by them to be used as a baptistery, and little else but bare walls'.[37]

The fall of Abdul Hamid was the work of a secret society — the Committee of
Union and Progress, commonly known as the Young Turks — that had infil-
trated the civil and military branches of the Ottoman establishment. In July
1908 a group of army officers in Macedonia defied the sultan and threatened
to march on Istanbul. Within a few days their demands were conceded and a
parliamentary regime came into being, with Abdul Hamid occupying the role
of a constitutional monarch after three decades of absolute rule.

The thirty-second anniversary of Abdul Hamid's accession was signaled by
the opening of the Hejaz Railway. A special train carried a party of officials the
full 814 miles from Damascus to Medina; at all the principal stations they were
welcomed by military bands playing the Hamidieh march.

Among the army units present for the celebrations at Damascus were 800
cavalrymen commanded by Ibrahim Pasha. The Milli chieftain had reluc-

* In 1901 the Church Missionary Society took over the Mosul mission from the
American Presbyterians, thereby fulfilling Christian Rassam's long-cherished desire.

tantly agreed to supply a contingent for guard duty on the railroad, while retaining the bulk of his forces to consolidate his influence in south eastern Anatolia.

Sensing a chance to remove a pillar of the old regime, the government in Istanbul sent orders to Damascus that Ibrahim's troopers should turn in their rifles and be sent home; their commander was ordered to proceed to the capital. Replying that he would turn in the rifles at Aleppo, Ibrahim marched north, then swiftly led his force over the desert to Viranshehir, eluding Ottoman pursuers.

In October 1908 regular army troops laid siege to Viranshehir. After a while Ibrahim agreed to surrender; but after half of his men had laid down their arms the sound of shooting was heard. Fearing a trap, Ibrahim fled from Viranshehir with his family and the rest of his horsemen; the aged chieftain, suffering from dysentery, was strapped to a camel because he was too weak to ride.

The rebels found shelter with Hasan Kanjo at Haleli. But the Ottomans besieged the fortress and Hasan Kanjo surrendered without a fight. Ibrahim escaped again with his family and a few followers, heading for the Jebel Sinjar. But his strength gave out and he died before reaching the mountain. The survivors gave themselves up in Nisibin.[38]

After Hasan Kanjo was led off to captivity, Ottoman soldiers burned the tents around the fortress. Alpheus Andrus provided food and shelter for many Yezidi refugees who reached Mardin, and reported to the American Board that out of 4,500–5,000 Yezidi followers of Ibrahim Pasha 400 had been killed and some 300 women and children were missing; the totals included almost 300 persons classified as 'died from fright'.[39]

In April 1909 the Istanbul garrison overthrew the new government, but was subdued within a few days by troops from Macedonia. Abdul Hamid was forced to abdicate and died nine years later in a palace on the Asiatic shore of the Bosporus. The ex-sultan's library at Yildiz is believed to have contained an anonymous Arabic manuscript, now located at Istanbul University, which described the religion and customs of the Yezidis and included the texts of their sacred books. The origins of this document, which was compiled in 1907, are discussed in the following chapter.[40]

The events of 1908–9 marked the last milestone in the decline and fall of the Ottoman empire. The Great Powers of Europe sharpened their knives, while within the crumbling society each community prepared to look out for itself. The few remaining giants from earlier times died during the reign of Abdul Hamid. Stratford Canning died in 1880 at the age of ninety-three. Moltke, who had served the sultan's grandfather and lived to see German influence once more ascendant in Istanbul, died in 1891. Layard, retired since 1881, died in 1894, outliving his old adversary Percy Badger by six years. Finally in 1896 William Ainsworth, the last survivor of the Euphrates and Kurdistan expeditions, died in his ninetieth year, taking his secret with him to the grave.

Jeremiah Shamir died in 1906, aged 85.[41] A minor player in the dramas of his time, he left behind him fuel for a literary controversy that simmers to this day.

Chapter Ten

The Publication of the Sacred Books

There is an old man, well-known to the few Englishmen who have visited Mosul, once an East-Syrian monk of the Monastery of Rabban Hormuzd, now a deacon of the Presbyterian community. He has a history which would be worth writing, especially if he wrote it himself; for he has been a traveller with the manners of an Englishman and the heart of a Syrian; and he has seen many troubles among his own people, and changes in the country from Erzingan to Mosul. But before all things he is a gossip; if there is news from Stamboul, Shammas is the first to retail it; for is not his wife's third cousin third-division clerk in the telegraph office? Has the Mufti run off with a Mulla's wife? Shammas was at the bottom of it, and probably supplied from his own stud (for he is a bit of a dealer in horse-flesh) the requisite barb. He deals, too, in manuscripts and ancient books, Persian, Arabic, Syriac; and once on a time over-reached himself in this pursuit. Among some books, which I was examining, he showed me one more especially commendable. Its actual personality so shamelessly belied its decent age and virtue as described by Shammas, that he drew forth a request that even if he loved gold, he should spare my folly. But with a candour, quite disarming rebuke, he drew out a letter, which he regarded as a high testimonial to his integrity as a dealer in palimpsests, but, in fact, containing so sound a rating of a rascal, that it seemed to bear more on the subject than perhaps the old man would have cared to acknowledge. Yet he reads and understands English well; truly these people have a strangely twisted sense of straightness, or more dullness than they get credit for.[1]

This classic description of Jeremiah Shamir by Oswald Parry was written twelve years after the deacon had been wafted from a state of obscure poverty to become a purveyor to the (Prussian) Royal Library in Berlin.

Professor Sachau's trip to Syria and Iraq in 1880 was funded out of the German Kaiser's privy purse as the first step in a long-range plan to bring the Oriental collections in Berlin to a parity with those in England and France. While in Mosul, Sachau utilized Jeremiah to acquire books and manuscripts, though he soon learned that the deacon knew nothing about Oriental literature and relied on guesswork to read Old Syriac. But he knew where to find books and manuscripts and Sachau employed him for several years to obtain choice items for the Berlin library. Among the acquisitions supplied by Jeremiah in 1883 was an Arabic text of the Yezidis' 1872 petition to the Ottoman government.[2]

Wallis Budge, a British Museum official with a keen eye for antiquities, made his first visit to Mosul in the months of January and February 1889. He met Jeremiah Shamir, whom he described as:

> a little active old man, with dark eyes deeply set in a little wizened
> face; he was very shrewd and intelligent, not to say cunning, and
> by some means or other he managed to know everybody's business.

Learning that Jeremiah was 'dissatisfied with his treatment by the Germans', Budge persuaded him to transfer his allegiance.

Among Budge's purchases through Jeremiah was one that related to the Yezidis — 'a stout octavo manuscript written in Arabic, containing the fullest history I had ever seen of this interesting people'. From conversation and correspondence Budge had concluded that the deacon was 'a Freethinker'. But he noticed that Jeremiah knew a lot about the Yezidis and their beliefs and 'suspected that whatever religious sympathies he possessed inclined to the Yazîdis, for the manuscript was the only one in which I ever knew him to take personal interest'.[3]

In fact, only sixteen of the 236 leaves in this manuscript, which was acquired by Leeds University in the 1960s (Leeds Syr. MS No. 7), deal with the Yezidis. The remaining portions are copies of Nestorian and Moslem writings, including extracts from a universal history by Ahmed b. Abdallah el-Baghdadi, who died in 1690, and the ancient Arab tale of the ten viziers.

The first relevant section of the Budge manuscript is written in Arabic and bears the title *The History of the Yezidis in Mosul and its Environs*. It comprises nine folios; five describe Yezidi beliefs, rites and institutions and include the text of the 1872 petition; the remaining four contain the texts of the two Yezidi holy books — the Jelwa and the Meshaf Rash. A second section of seven folios toward the end of the manuscript, written in Syria and entitled *An Extract from the History of the Yezidis*, gives further information about their customs and traditions.

The colophon to the manuscript, written in Syriac, states that it was copied in Mosul by Gabriel Jeremiah [son of Jeremiah Shamir] for 'his friend, the skilled teacher and true believer, the interpreter of rich tongues, and the master of various callings, the marvellous man, Wallis Budge, the Englishman of London' in the year AG 2200=AD 1889=AH 1305.* At the end of the text of the 1872 petition it is stated that the right granted to the Yezidis to commute their military service obligation by a cash payment 'has been maintained to the present day, AH 1305'. A reference in the *Extract* to 'the present time' repeats the year AG 2200=AD 1889=AH 1305.[4]

In March 1891 the American *Encyclopaedia of Missions* published an article on 'The Yezidees' by a contributor from Mardin — the American Board missionary Alpheus Andrus. The article included verbatim translations of passages from the Jelwa and the Meshaf Resh (though Andrus mistakenly attributed them all to 'El Jilweh'). Andrus did not reveal his source, but he was well acquainted with Jeremiah Shamir, who wrote him in October 1892 to suggest probable dates when the sacred books were written.[5]

In September 1891 the Bibliothèque Nationale in Paris acquired for 150 Fr (£6) a 121-leaf manuscript (BN Syr. MS 306) copied by Abdul Aziz, a Jacobite from the Tur Abdin who lived in the Yezidi village of Bashika. The first half contains historical items relating to the Jacobites. The rest consists of Nestorian documents, an extract from el-Baghdadi's history and material about the Yezidis — all of it virtually identical with the comparable portions of Budge's manuscript, except that the Arabic texts are written in the 'Karshuni' script used by Syrians when writing Arabic. The final section of the BN 306 manuscript, the Syriac *Extract from the History of the Yezidis*, is closely related to the Budge manuscript.

The BN 306 manuscript does not state for whom Abdul Aziz made this copy. The colophon, written in Arabic, states that he completed it in AD 1889. 'The present time' is specified at the end of the 1872 petition as AH 1305 and in the *Extract* as AG 2200=AD 1889=AH 1305.[6]

---

* Budge was in Mosul from 16 January to 26 February 1889. The manuscript was probably copied some time between 13 March 1889 (the start of the Ottoman fiscal year 1305) and 12 October 1889 (the last day of the Seleucid 'year of the Greeks' AG 2200). The Moslem religious year AH 1305 ended in September 1888, before Budge arrived in Mosul.

One expert in the study of Syriac manuscripts has noted that Abdul Aziz and Jeremiah Shamir are known to have undertaken copying work for each other.[7]

When Oswald Parry left Mosul in November 1892 to return to Mardin, he took back with him a small (3 in. × 4 in.) volume containing six items; the first two are written in Syriac and the remainder in Karshuni. The first item is the story of the ten viziers. The second item is the *Extract from the History of the Yezidis*; the text states that it was copied by Abdul Aziz in 1889.

The third item relates the fable of the ailing cat who was sheltered by a charitable mouse, later recovered his strength and tried to eat his host, but released his hold on the mouse when he himself was set upon by a hunter's hound.

The last three items of the manuscript comprise the *History of the Yezidis* (including the 1872 petition) and the texts of the Jelwa and the Meshaf Resh, substantially identical with the comparable portions of the Budge and BN 306 manuscripts.

Parry's book *Six Months in a Syrian Monastery*, published in 1895, included as an appendix an English translation of his Yezidi texts by the Cambridge orientalist E. G. Browne; his translations of the Jelwa and the Meshaf Resh are attached as Appendix I to this book. In February 1894 the Parry manuscript was sold to the Bibliothèque Nationale for 30 Fr to become BN Syr. MS 324.[8] Browne's translation follows the order of the earlier BN 306 manuscript (i.e., commencing with the *History* and the holy books and ending with the *Extract*). Neither Browne nor Parry mentions the ten viziers, the cat or the mouse.

The opening paragraph of Parry's appendix stated that the manuscript 'was written by a native of Mosul, who has enjoyed peculiar opportunities for obtaining information concerning the Yazidis' and that his chief sources were the Meshaf Resh, the Jelwa, a 100-year-old history of Mosul* and 'the state-ments of an Old Syrian [Jacobite] priest, for thirty years resident among the Yazidis'. Parry regretted that 'the writer did not specify whence each particu-lar part of his information was obtained'.[10]

---

* Parry refers to the *Menhal el-Awliya*, an Arabic history of Mosul written in 1787 by Mohammed Emin b. Khairallah el-Omari. Jeremiah Shamir sent an extract from this manuscript dealing with Sheikh Adi and the Yezidis to Professor Sachau for the Berlin library in 1883.[9]

How Jeremish Shamir obtained copies of the closely guarded sacred books of the Yezidis has never been satisfactorily explained.

He showed Kartsov a copy of the Jelwa in 1884, telling the Russian that he had once accompanied Percy Badger on a visit to the Yezidis, where they managed to get Sheikh Nasr drunk and made him show them the Jelwa; when he dozed off Jeremiah managed to copy a few pages. There is no confirmation of this story in Badger's writings, though it bears a curious resemblance to his account of how he himself got hold of the Sheikh Adi hymn.*[11]

As regards the Meshaf Resh, Jeremiah's son Nasir accompanied Kartsov and Browski on their expedition to Lalish. In two articles published in 1886 Browski claims that at the sanctuary he saw 'the sacred book with the seven seals' with the name of Hasan el-Basri on the title page and was even able to get hold of it and keep it long enough to make a copy. The articles contain no direct quotations from the Meshaf Resh, but they accurately summarize portions of it. Browski does not state whether he received help in his copying work or in his articles from anyone else.[12]

The 'Old Syrian priest' cited by Parry was in fact a Syrian Catholic priest named Ishak of Bartella, who lived for many years in the nearby village of Bashika, where Yezidis, Jacobites and Syrian Catholics existed side by side. In 1874 Ishak completed a lengthy manuscript about the Yezidis.[13]

The first portion of this document describes Sheikh Adi's origin and his move to Lalish. It also contains a story that Sheikh Abd el-Qadir el-Gilani came up from Baghdad to dislodge Sheikh Adi, but was persuaded by a vision to return home.

The second section describes the conversion of the Nestorian community on the Jebel Sinjar to the Yezidi faith.†[14]

The third and longest section is a description of Yezidi traditions, rites and festivals, composed in the form of questions and answers. (This material, converted into narrative form and slightly abridged, is identical with the *Extract from the History of the Yezidis* incorporated in the Budge and the BN 306 and 324 manuscripts.)

Ishak's manuscript was kept for many years in the library of the Rabban Hormuzd monastery at Alkosh, where Kartsov and Browski saw it in 1884.[15] A few weeks earlier Jeremiah Shamir had shown an Arabic version to Kartsov and had helped him to translate it into Russian.[16]

* See p. 105–6.
† See p. 50.

In 1899 the third portion of Ishak's manuscript was re-copied in East Syriac for Mgr Samuel Jamil, the Chaldean patriarch's representative in Rome, who arranged for it to be published there with an Italian translation under the misleading title *Mount Sinjar: History of an Unknown People.*[17]

The source for Ishak's description of the Yezidi religion cannot be pinpointed. Browski claims that there was a second part of 'the sacred book', promulgating doctrines, precepts and ceremonial regulations, sometimes in dialogue form. He concluded that it was of later date than the first part [the Meshaf Resh] and had evolved gradually, since it was written in several handwritings. He also noted the occasional use of Chaldean words in the second part and suggested that 'a Christian priest or monk — perhaps a renegade — might have had a hand in the editing'.[18]

Browski's articles cover most of the Yezidi rites and customs described in Ishak's work. But they also mention traditions about Melek Taus advising Nebuchadnezzar to destroy Jerusalem, rescuing Jesus Christ from the cross and inspiring Caliph Yezid to defy Islam. None of these appear in Ishak's manuscript, suggesting that Browski had a second source. His reference to a thirty-leaf catalogue of miracles performed by Sheikh Adi on his way from Damascus to Lalish could relate to a similar section of es-Shattanaufi's book or else to the Beled Sinjar texts discovered by Henry Field in 1934.[19]

The date of Ishak's death is not known. He was the first Iraqi writer about the Yezidis to have belonged to the Catholic church.

Another Syrian Catholic, not mentioned by Parry, should be considered a possible source or conduit for Jeremiah Shamir. Daud es-Sa'igh, a leading citizen of Mosul, was described by a friend as 'a man of culture, in sympathy with western thought, and an intimate acquaintance of M. N. Siouffi'. The writer added that he knew Daud es-Sa'igh was in close touch with many of the Yezidis, especially with the family of Mulla Haider.[20]

In 1967 the British orientalist C. J. Edmonds, who had lived many years in Iraq, reported that he owned an Arabic manuscript about the Yezidis. It started with a short account of an event alleged to have occurred in Bashika in 1887, when Mulla Haider was visited by a Russian consul from Mosul,* who got him drunk and persuaded him to divulge the secrets of his religion and show the two sacred books to the consul. The main portion of the manuscript contained Mulla Haider's account of the Yezidi religious hierarchy and beliefs, followed by the texts of the Jelwa and the Meshaf Resh. An appendix,

* The Russian vice-consulate in Mosul was closed after Kartsov's departure in 1884.

146

compiled by Daud es-Sa'igh, further described the traditions of the Yezidis.[21]

The Istanbul University manuscript mentioned in the preceding chapter remained unpublished until 1953. It commences with an Arabic translation, made in 1906, of the Syriac *Extract from the History of the Yezidis*, which repeats AG 2200=AD 1889=AH 1305 as 'the present time'. This is followed by the *History of the Yezidis in Mosul and its Environs*, including the text of the 1872 petition, and the complete texts of the Jelwa and the Meshaf Resh – all virtually identical with Budge's manuscript. The names of the compiler, the translator and the scribe are not given; apart from its attribution to the Yildiz palace library, the provenance of the document is unknown.[22]

The common threads running through these conflicting and sometimes implausible accounts suggest that the texts of the sacred books were obtained from the Yezidis by trickery and that Jeremiah Shamir was somehow involved. Ishak of Bartella's manuscript appears to have been derived from a religious training manual used by Mulla Haider for the instruction of kawals. It is unclear how and by whom Ishak's catechism was re-edited in narrative form to become the *Extract from the History of the Yezidis*. The authorship of the text entitled *The History of the Yezidis in Mosul and its Environs* is likewise obscure.

The Syrian Catholic church to which Daud es-Sa'igh and Ishak belonged (the copyist Abdul Aziz was a Jacobite) was the smaller of the two 'uniate' churches operating in northern Iraq that were in communion with Rome. At the end of the nineteenth century the head of this church, styled the patriarch of Antioch, lived at Mardin (where the Jacobite patriarch and the American Board mission were also located).

The larger of the two uniate churches — the Chaldean church, successor to the old Nestorian church — flourished along the Tigris valley, separated by tradition and geography from the 'Assyrians' in the Hakkari mountains and around Lake Urmia who obeyed their hereditary patriarch Mar Shimun. The primate of the Chaldean church, an elected prelate subject to papal approval, was styled the patriarch of Babylonia and resided in Mosul.

Guidance for these churches was provided by the Dominican mission in Mosul, staffed since 1859 from France. By 1890 the mission comprised eighteen priests and twelve nuns, who operated a college and twenty schools in and around Mosul, Jezira b. Omar and Siirt. Four of the missionaries, along with three local priests and three lay teachers, formed the faculty of St John's Syro-Chaldean Seminary in Mosul, founded in 1878 to train priests for the two uniate churches.

In Baghdad the Catholic church had been represented for almost 300 years. The original mission founded by the Capuchins in 1628 was reassigned in 1721 to the order of Discalced Carmelites, who had operated a mission in Basra since 1623. For many years the superior of the Baghdad mission administered the Latin bishopric of Babylon — a see endowed in 1638 with a gift of 6,000 Spanish doubloons from a French lady, who stipulated that the incumbent should always be French. At times, the Carmelite superior also served as French consul in Baghdad. In the second quarter of the nineteenth century the three functions were separated. The French consuls were appointed from the diplomatic service. The bishop (later archbishop) of Babylon became the papal apostolic delegate for Mesopotamia, Kurdistan and Lesser Armenia. The Carmelites concentrated on missionary work; at the turn of the century six priests, assisted by twelve nuns, operated a college and two schools in Baghdad.[23]

One recent Arab recruit to the Carmelite mission had an unusual background. Pierre Paul Marini was born in 1866 in Baghdad, where his father had moved from his native Lebanon to work as an interpreter. The son attended the Carmelite school, developed a keen interest in Arabic studies and obtained a teaching job at the Jesuit university of St Joseph in Beirut. At the age of twenty-one he decided to join the Carmelite order and went to Europe, where he studied in Belgian and French monasteries for six years until he was ordained. His new name, Père Anastase Marie de Saint-Élie, honoured the Persian St Anastasius martyred in the reign of Khosrau Parviz.* In 1894 he was assigned to the mission in Baghdad, where he tended the small Catholic community and taught French and Arabic in the school.

In May 1898 Père Anastase was approached by 'a handsome young man with big black eyes, a thick well-trimmed moustache, an aquiline nose, a healthy pink complexion, a pleasant oval face, regular features, a colossal build and a robust state of health', who declared that he wanted to become a Christian. He was dressed like a mountaineer, but Anastase sensed that behind a simple exterior lay 'a strong generous soul'.[24]

The visitor was a Yezidi named Habib, thirty years old, born in Bozan, a few miles east of the Chaldean monastery at Alkosh. He stated that he had worked for seven years as servant and librarian for the Yezidis' chief religious official, but that finding his life boring and trivial he had gone to work for the monks.

* See pp. 8–9 Another modern namesake of this saint was A. I. Mikoyan, born in Sanahin (northern Armenia) in 1895, who later became chairman of the presidium of the Supreme Soviet of the USSR.

After observing their way of life, he had decided to become a Christian and had come to Baghdad to escape being killed by the Yezidis as a renegade.

Anastase told Habib that if he would come to the Carmelite mission every day at five o'clock in the afternoon, he would instruct him in the Christian faith; at the end of this period he would decide if he was ready to be baptized. As a proof of his sincerity in renouncing his old religion, Anastase required Habib to reveal to him all its secrets and ceremonies. To allay his fears that the Yezidis would murder him if they found out what he had done, the Carmelite promised that as long as Habib was alive he would never reveal his source. Seven months later Habib was baptized under the name Abd el-Mesih and was confirmed in his new faith. He was given a job as a porter with the apostolic delegation in Baghdad.

Between January and September 1899, *al-Machriq*, the journal of St Joseph's University in Beirut, published a series of articles about the Yezidis by Père Anastase.[25] In addition to material derived from his Yezidi informant (carefully protected), the author made use of an unpublished work by Kiriakos Mahnuq, a Chaldean priest in Baghdad, as well as generally available information.

The articles told little about the Yezidi sacred books. Only the Meshaf Resh was identified; the author remarked that it was accessible to one single reader and that Gen Omar Wehbi Pasha had failed to locate it.

Habib/Abd el-Mesih died of natural causes in October 1899, a few months before the publication of Ishak's manuscript in Rome confirmed the accuracy of many of the things he had told Anastase. Before he died Abd el-Mesih gave the Carmelite Arabic texts of the Jelwa and the Meshaf Resh, along with an intriguing story about their origin.

The dying man told Anastase that the Yezidi sacred books had originally been written in Kurdish and had been handed down by God to the Yezidis in the days of Adam. Long ago they had been translated into Arabic in order to shield the originals from human eyes or touch. He stated that a Yezidi friend who had learned Arabic in a Christian school in Mosul had made for him a copy of the authentic Arabic text possessed by the Yezidi religious authorities.

Abd el-Mesih had already divulged to Anastase some information about the sacred books. Part of his job as librarian had been to air the original manuscripts every six months. The rest of the time they were kept in a walnut box (13 in. long × 9 in. broad × 3 in. deep), buried in a cave in the Jebel Sinjar. He had added that the box was covered with white velvet (soiled), stitched with pieces of flat silver representing a peacock, the sun, the moon and other symbols.

The Jelwa, according to Abd el-Mesih, was written on thin deerskin parchment sheets, while the Meshaf Resh was written on a deerskin parchment roll.*

Combining priestly discretion with treasure-hunter's guile, Père Anastase decided to tell nobody about what he had learned. He was developing a plan.

Meanwhile, yet another manuscript about the Yezidis changed hands – a gift from the kindly Daud es-Sa'igh to a young man who was leaving Mosul to live in the USA.[27]

Isya Muksy Yusef (who simplified his name to Isya Joseph in the USA) was born on 25 November 1872 in the village of Kâbei, 15 miles south-east of Diyarbakir. He is said to have come from 'a very learned family, several of his forefathers having been bishops in the Assyrian church†'.[28]

After receiving the rudiments of an education in his village from one of Alpheus Andrus' 'helpers', he attended the American Board high school at Mardin. In later years he referred affectionately to 'my honored teacher, Rev. A. N. Andrus' and to 'my most honored teacher, the Rev. Caleb F. Gates', who founded the high school and started a theological class for graduate students three years later. In 1890 Isya was one of the first four theologues to graduate from the mission seminary. All four were ordained in 1891 after a public examination of their beliefs refuted rumours that one or two of them had been influenced by Plymouth Brethren missionaries, then active around Mardin.[30]

Isya's wife Sarah belonged to the Hanush family, a prolific clan active in Protestant church affairs throughout the upper Tigris valley from Diyarbakir to Mosul. Upon ordination Isya moved to Mosul, where he worked as a preacher for the local church and was an eye-witness of the 1892 persecution of the Yezidis. During his stay in Mosul he became acquainted with Daud es-Sa'igh and met members of the el-Omari family. A daughter, Elisa (later renamed Louise) was born in 1895 and a son, Fuad (later renamed Alfred) in 1896.

In 1895 Isya's father-in-law was killed by Kurds — one of many Christian priests who perished in the massacres that took place in eastern Anatolia that

---

* In 1892 Jeremiah Shamir told Alpheus Andrus that the Jelwa, 'wrapped in linen and silk wrappings, is kept in the house of Mulla Haidar'. The Meshaf Resh was kept in the house of the chief of the Yezidi village of Qasr-i-Yazdin (40 miles north of Mosul), where 'the book rests upon a throne, having over it a thin covering of red broadcloth, of linen, and other wrappings. Then is disclosed the binding, which is of wood'.[26]

† The term 'Assyrian' appears in various references to Isya Joseph. In his own words, he was 'born...of Assyrian parents, belonging to the Syriac church which traces its origin to the Christian community of Antioch'[29] (i.e. his family were Jacobites).

year. One consequence was an emigration of many Jacobites and Protestants, including members of the Hanush family, to the United States. In May 1898 Isya and Sarah Joseph and their two children left Mosul. They arrived in New York on 7 August 1898, bound for Stirling, New Jersey, 30 miles to the west, where Sarah's brother lived.[31]

The early details of Isya's life as an immigrant are unknown. In 1902 he was admitted to the Union Theological Seminary in New York City and in the following year he started taking courses at Columbia University, a sister institution.

He graduated from the Seminary in 1905 and was awarded a bachelor's degree in divinity *magna cum laude*. In 1906 he graduated from Columbia with the degree of bachelor of arts. He stayed on as a graduate student and received a master's degree in philosophy in 1907. His essay submitted in March 1907 to the Columbia faculty of philosophy was entitled *The Yezidis – Devil Worshippers: Their Sacred Book and Traditions.*[32]

Source materials about the Yezidis available in New York were scanty. Parry's book had been published, with Browne's translation of the BN 324 manuscript. Père Anastase's Beirut articles and Jamil's edition of Ishak's manuscript had appeared in 1899 and 1900. Isya was also familiar with the articles by Siouffi and Browski, as well as the works of Ainsworth, Badger and Layard.

For a young student, living in a foreign country with a wife and two children and writing in a newly acquired language, the task of synthesizing this fragmentary material was ambitious. There is, moreover, no evidence that during his early years in Iraq he had acquired any personal knowledge of the Yezidis that could reinforce his analysis and conclusions. Yet despite all these handicaps he was able, thanks to one fortunate circumstance, to achieve his goal and make the name of Isya Joseph familiar to orientalists in Manchester, Odessa and Tashkent.[33]

By the start of the twentieth century there were at least half a dozen manuscripts of the Yezidi sacred books in existence, two of them in the Bibliothèque Nationale. E. G. Browne had announced his intention to publish Parry's texts of the Jelwa and the Meshaf Resh, but he had not done so (although the Syriac *Extract* from the BN manuscripts had been published in Paris in 1896 with a translation by the French orientalist J.-B. Chabot). The texts of Sheikh Adi's hymn and the 1872 petition had been published and translated in Germany in 1853 and 1897.[34]

The final phase of Isya Joseph's work was conducted at Harvard University, where he received a fellowship in Semitics and was awarded a doctorate in philosophy in 1908. In the introduction to his dissertation Isya revealed that he possessed three Arabic manuscripts about the Yezidis and that two of them contained the texts of the sacred books. Handwritten in the dissertation, the texts were printed for the first time in January 1909 by the *American Journal of Semitic Languages and Literatures* with an English translation by Isya.[35] (His analysis of the Yezidi religion was not published by the AJSL but appeared in book form in 1919.)[36]

The primary text was Daud es-Sa'igh's manuscript, the talisman Isya had brought from Mosul. He listed its contents (with one exception, all in Arabic): a brief introduction, quite similar to the opening paragraph of the Budge manuscript, followed by the texts of the two sacred books and concluding with an 'appendix'.

Isya's 'appendix' contained five items: a collection of materials about Yezidi beliefs and customs; the Sheikh Adi hymn; the principal Yezidi prayer (written in Kurdish in Arabic script); a short description of the Yezidi religious hierarchy; and the text of the 1872 petition. The first and the last two items correspond to the *History* and *Extract* in Budge's manuscript. The Sheikh Adi hymn resembles Badger's version, but the words differ in a number of places. The provenance of the Kurdish prayer is open to question; a virtually identical text in Latin script was published in Tiflis in 1891 by an Armenian expert, who claimed to have heard it from the mouth of a local Yezidi sheikh; it was reprinted in a German monograph (listed in Isya's bibliography) in 1900.[37]

Isya's other two manuscript sources had been sent to him by Alpheus Andrus.[38] He noted that 'the first of these written by Šammas Eremia Šamir' seemed to be a duplicate of the one given to Parry. The second manuscript, an Arabic version of Ishak's work, likewise in catechetical form, was presumably the same one Jeremiah had shown Kartsov.

In contrast to his Rassam namesake who moved from theology to rank and wealth, Isya Joseph relapsed into obscurity after obtaining his doctorate. He lived at Matamoras in eastern Pennsylvania and suffered a grievous loss when his son, a gifted student about to enter Harvard, died in 1916. The following year the family moved to Port Chester, a suburb of New York, where his daughter taught school.

Described in a newspaper report as 'a literary expert and advertising man', Isya spent part of his time as a commercial traveller peddling medical pamphlets for a New York doctor. He was at Fredericksburg, Virginia in February 1923 on one of his business trips when he dropped dead 'while he was strolling along the north concrete walk on the exterior of the waiting room' of the railroad station.[39] He now rests beside his wife and children at the Brookside Cemetery in Englewood, New Jersey. The present whereabouts of his manuscripts and other papers is unknown.

Seven thousand miles away from New York another manuscript owner, Père Anastase, had put into action a daring plan to find the mother lode. Scheduled to make a trip to Rome, he arranged his itinerary to go from Baghdad by way of Mosul, Sinjar, Deir ez-Zor and Aleppo.

Léon Krajewski, French vice-consul at Mosul from 1903 to 1906, was interested in the Yezidis and on one occasion had visited Lalish. He too had heard stories of a library in the Jebel Sinjar, but although he developed a warm friendship with one of the local chiefs he could learn no details. However, the consular dragoman, Aziz Kas Yusuf, had been able to copy the Arabic text of the Yezidi sacred books from 'ancient papers' once owned by a Yezidi chief in the upper Daseni country and later seized by Ottoman soldiers. When Père Anastase passed through Mosul in May 1904, the dragoman showed him this text and allowed him to make a copy.[40]

In June of that year Anastase reached the Sinjar and went to see 'the Sheikh', whom he describes as 'a tall devil [sic] with big black eyes and long hair'. He wore a long white robe with a deep slit that revealed his hairy chest. After much discussion it was agreed that 'the librarian' Hammu, who could read and write Arabic, would come and talk to Anastase about a business transaction.

Now that Habib/Abd el-Mesih was dead, the Carmelite felt no longer bound by his pledge of secrecy. He revealed to Hammu everything he had learned about the sacred books. It was finally settled that Anastase would pay 20 Fr for each page of the Jelwa and 300 Fr for the Meshaf Resh roll, plus a gratuity of 40 Fr — 500 Fr in all, equivalent to £20. Anastase gave him a supply of tracing paper with strict instructions 'to trace the pages faithfully and slavishly, leaving nothing out, adding nothing and interpolating nothing'. The Carmelite proceeded on his way to Rome.

Two long years passed before the work was completed. Hammu explained that he only had access to the books at certain times. The sheets were delivered to Anastase one by one and payment was made accordingly. The librarian died in 1908.

The final product, proclaimed by Anastase as 'one of the greatest literary treasures of our century and the most secret in the world', consisted of eight pages representing the Jelwa (adorned with mysterious symbols) and fourteen pages representing the Meshaf Resh. The text of both books was written in a hitherto unknown script, later deciphered by Anastase and found to be a coded transposition of the Persian–Arabic alphabet.[41]

The language in which the books were written appeared to be a form of Kurdish. Anastase, who knew little Kurdish and no Persian or Turkish, sought guidance from Dr Maximilian Bittner, professor of Oriental languages at the University of Vienna.

Père Anastase announced his discovery in an article published in an Austrian magazine at the beginning of 1911. In March of that year Professor Bittner read a paper to the Department of Philosophy and History of the Imperial Academy of Science in Vienna that later filled ninety-seven pages of print.[42] He confirmed that the coded version delivered to Père Anastase had been transcribed from Kurdish texts written in the Persian variant of Arabic script. The texts themselves were written in good literary Kurdish. He judged that the Meshaf Resh text had been translated from an Arabic original; he was less certain about the original text of the Jelwa.

Subsequent research by Kurdish language experts has established that the Anastase texts were written in the Suleimaniya dialect now standard in Iraq for literary Kurdish and that both of them were translated from Arabic originals.[43]

Meanwhile, in Mosul the Dominicans' Syro-Chaldean Seminary was gaining a reputation as editors and publishers of ancient Syriac texts that had been handed down for centuries in manuscript form. In 1905, a member of the faculty, Alphonse Mingana, revealed an important discovery of old manuscripts said to have been salvaged from a conflagration 150 years earlier at Eqror, a Nestorian village north-east of Zakho. One of them, written in an archaic script used in the tenth century and identified by marginal notation as an ecclesiastical history by the sixth-century chronicler Meshiha-Zkha, contained hitherto unknown details of the early days of the Nestorian church in Erbil. The text, edited and translated into French by Mingana, was published by the seminary in 1907. It soon attracted the attention of scholars, including Jeremiah Shamir's old patron Sachau, who later translated it into German and named it the 'Chronicle of Erbil'.[44]

The editor of this text, known as Hormuzd Mingana until he was ordained, was born around 1881. His father was the Chaldean priest at Sheranish, a village near Eqror. The son entered the seminary as a student in 1891. Eleven years later, brilliant in Syriac and Arabic studies but disqualified by a speech defect from pastoral work, he was appointed professor of Syriac. He wrote a Syriac grammar and edited the works of an early church father. Self-assured and burning to achieve distinction, he did not hesitate to embarrass his superiors by engaging in a literary controversy with the eminent Professor Chabot.[45]

In 1907, a few weeks after the Chronicle of Erbil was finally edited and translated, the dragoman at the German vice-consulate in Mosul learned that

Mingana, as agent for an unnamed principal resident in Eqror, was offering the manuscript for sale. After some haggling it was purchased for 3500 francs plus 892.05 piastres (£148.6.0) by the Royal Library in Berlin, where it was catalogued as Ms. or. fol. 3126.[46]

Mingana's disputes with the church authorities grew worse. In 1910 he was relieved of his duties at the Syro-Chaldean seminary and on 7 January 1913 he resigned from the Catholic church and left Mosul.[47]

After two months wandering around Persia and Anatolia, including a stay in Mardin with Alpheus Andrus, Mingana accepted an invitation to visit England. His benefactor was Rendel Harris, a Quaker orientalist who headed a 'settlement for social and religious study' recently established by a wealthy chocolate manufacturer at Woodbrooke, a country house outside Birmingham. Here Mingana learned English, taught Arabic and Hebrew and contributed articles on biblical texts to learned magazines.[48]

In 1915 he joined the staff of the John Rylands Library in Manchester and began to catalogue its collection of Arabic manuscripts.

Securely established in the British academic world, Mingana found time to attack two figures from his Iraqi past. His article entitled 'Devil-worshippers: their beliefs and their sacred books', published in July 1916,[49] discussed several theories about the origin of the Yezidi religion and severely criticized Père Anastase and Jeremiah Shamir.

Mingana rated himself an expert on the Yezidis 'because I have had special opportunities of studying their life'. Without dwelling further on his own experiences, he declared that he 'had been shocked by the strange discovery of Father Anastase'. This sentiment was apparently shared by Alpheus Andrus, who had told Mingana in 1913 that in April and May of the previous year he had sought information on the spot from Mir Ali Beg at Baadri and also when he visited a prominent sheikh named Khodar Alias in the Sinjar. Both of them had expressed astonishment to Andrus and had given negative answers to his questions. Mingana added that on his way to visit Andrus in Mardin 'I was passing near Sinjâr. I asked many friends, Yezidis of Sinjâr, about this discovery, but they were unable to answer my questions, or even to understand them'.

Dissecting Anastase's account of his discovery, Mingana noted that 'we meet with European ideas of offices among the Yezidis' and questioned whether this illiterate community really maintained the position of a librarian. He ridiculed the idea of a religious centre on the Jebel Sinjar, pointing out that the local Yezidis were rude villagers chiefly occupied in rapine and plunder and that until the fourteenth century the mountain had been occupied by Nestorians whose supremacy had only once been challenged 'during the ephemeral but deadly time of Gabriel the Drusbed'.*

In comparing Anastase's texts against the version published by Isya Joseph, Mingana observed that:

> the text of Anastase is more moderate in its details, and more
> concise in places that might shock the ears of educated people....
> There are also many anecdotes of a somewhat eccentric character
> which have been cut out in Anastase's edition.

After listing the earlier texts — Browne's translation of Parry's manuscript, Jamil's edition of Ishak's catechism, the narrative version published by Mingana's old adversary Chabot and the Isya Joseph texts — the writer announced his own devastating conclusion:

> I think that these well-intentioned scholars have possibly been
> misled. The author of all these texts is probably Shammas
> Jeremias Shamir, a native of 'Ain Kāwa in Adiabène, and a
> deserter from the Monastery of Alkosh, who died ten years ago at
> a very advanced age.

In support of this contention Mingana cited Parry's characterization of Jeremiah (quoted at the start of this chapter) and pointed to a number of grammatical errors in the Yezidi texts that showed that 'their author, though writing in Arabic, was thinking in Syriac'.

Mingana concluded his critique of the Yezidi texts by remarking that:

> we do not wish our readers to believe that everything in these books
> is wrong, for they contain some records of the habits and customs
> of the Yezidis which are incontestably true; but we maintain that
> it was Jeremias who put them into a sacred book, and formed into
> a code what the Yezidis practiced instinctively according to an oral
> legislation handed down from father to son and sanctioned by
> religious authority with an aureole of antiquity going back four
> hundred years.

In 1932 an Italian orientalist analysed the places where Mingana claimed to have detected Syriac forms of expression in the Arabic texts. He found that many of the instances belonged to the commentaries rather than to the sacred

---

* See pp. 7–8 for information on this Jacobite contemporary of St Anastasius the Persian.

books. Where cases occurred in the latter, the author considered them explainable as copyist's errors.[50]

By this time Mingana had achieved fame and success. Edward Cadbury, whose father had endowed Woodbrooke, commissioned him to purchase manuscripts in the Middle East and erected a library building at nearby Selly Oak to house the collection. Mingana was appointed curator and devoted himself to cataloguing its contents until his death in 1937.[51] The Italian commentary on the Yezidi article was ignored and for many years the long-lived deacon enjoyed a span of posthumous notoriety as the putative author of the Yezidi sacred books.

Mingana's blunt assertion that a defector from the Catholic church had fabricated an important religious text recoiled upon its author in 1965, some thirty years after Mingana's death and sixty years after Jeremiah Shamir had died. Inspection of the Chronicle of Erbil manuscript by a German expert established that, although the script was ancient, the handwriting was modern; forensic analysis showed suspicious scorch patterns at the edges. Inquiries revealed that the scribe had been a Chaldean priest at Alkosh and that he had helped Mingana singe the manuscript, page by page, in the bake oven outside his house. The authorship and provenance of the document from which the copy was made is still a matter of dispute, but as early as 1941 an Alkosh monk admitted that he had unwittingly written the Meshiha-Zkha identification on the margin of a sheet.[52]

A century and a quarter have passed since the congregation of Rabban Hormuzd moved into more modern buildings at Alkosh, leaving only a few monks in their ancient mountainside retreat. But in the dim light of the monastery, where nine Nestorian patriarchs lie buried and the names of Claudius and Mary Rich, Layard, Perkins and Lobdell are carved upon the walls, the ghost of a former inmate may still hover with a faint smile on his little wizened face.

Père Anastase outlived Mingana by ten years. He was arrested by the Ottomans in 1914 as an Arab sympathizer and was condemned to death. Reprieved at the last minute as he stood on the scaffold, the Carmelite endured almost two years of exile and maltreatment in Cappadocia. He returned to Baghdad in 1916 and resumed work at the mission. His knowledge of Arabic literature gained him membership in the Baghdad, Damascus and Cairo Academies and after his death in 1947 his collection of 15,000 books and 2,000 manuscripts was declared a national monument.[53]

It is easy to conclude that Père Anastase was the victim of his own eagerness and that over the two-year period from 1904 to 1906 somebody translated the Arabic text of the sacred books into Kurdish at Anastase's expense. But the 1934 discovery by Henry Field of previously unknown Yezidi texts in Beled Sinjar (a find that greatly interested Anastase)[54] suggests that manuscripts may yet be hidden in the rarely visited Sinjar hills.[55]

Chapter Eleven

Brother and Sister

The hopes and fears aroused by the Young Turk revolution among the Arabs and other communities in Iraq were noted by a perceptive observer who passed through Baghdad and Mosul in the spring of 1909. Gertrude Bell, forty-year-old doyenne of a new generation of British explorers, possessed wealth and influence that enabled her to pursue her interest in oriental archaeology and her taste for travel, mountaineering and pulling political wires.

Already acquainted with Yezidis from a tour of the early Christian churches around Aleppo, she determined to visit Lalish.[1] Her first stop was at Baadri, where she noticed two peacocks in the palace courtyard and was cordially greeted by Mir Ali Beg. She describes him as 'a man of middle age with a commanding figure and a long beard, light brown in colour, that curls almost to his waist. He was dressed from head to foot in white'. In her account she calls him 'the descendent of the other 'Alî to whom Layard stood godfather'; in fact it was the same person, now sixty-two years old.

After making arrangements for Gertrude Bell to visit Lalish, the Mir offered her refreshments in the women's quarters, where she met his 'very attractive' wife who wore a robe of purple cotton, a black jacket with a velvet cap placed over the muslin veil that was wrapped about her head and under her chin, but did not conceal her face. On her wrists she wore heavy gold bracelets set with turquoises. The *khâtûn* (lady) spoke only in Kurdish, but Ali Beg's Chaldean secretary acted as interpreter and Gertrude Bell formed a silent friendship with the Mir's 'charming little son', Said Beg, aged nine, who sat on her largest camp chair as he watched her eat.

Returning to Baadri that evening after being shown the sanctuary by Ali Beg's sister, custodian of the shrine, Gertrude Bell was invited by Said Beg to pay a visit to his mother. The boy sat in the room, smoking cigarettes as the

159

two women conversed through the Chaldean interpreter. When the English-woman said, 'In my country children may not smoke. Oh, Sa'îd Beg, little children like you should be asleep at this hour', his mother smiled at him tenderly, saying, 'We can deny him nothing'. The secretary added: 'The 'arak they give him is worse for him than the cigarettes'.

The next morning Gertrude Bell thanked the secretary for the hospitality she had received and readily granted his request, on behalf of the Mir, for some 'fire ribbon' (flashlight magnesium wire) to light Sheikh Adi's tomb at the next festival.

Born in 1874, Mayan Khatun was thirty-five when she met Gertrude Bell. Her father was Abdi Beg, the younger brother of Mir Hussein Beg (an 1849 sketch of them appears as Plate 31). He deputed as Mir during the six years between Hussein Beg's removal by the Ottomans and their final acceptance of Mirza Beg as his successor, then settled in the Jebel Sinjar, where he died in 1888. Mayan's mother was Khomi, daughter of Jasim Beg, the last Mir from the senior branch of the Chol dynasty who was killed when Ali Beg's father Mir Hussein Beg seized the throne.[2]

Beautiful and well born, Mayan was married at the age of eighteen to Ali Beg, a brother of the reigning Mir. During the years of their marriage public and private tragedies — the 1892–93 persecution of the Yezidis, Ali Beg's refusal under torture to give up his faith, their exile to northern Anatolia and a series of disastrous childbirths (Said Beg was the only child to survive infancy) — had moulded a character of iron.

After Ali Beg and his wife returned from exile, the greatest task facing the new Mir was the spiritual and material rebuilding of the Yezidi community. Aided by Sadiq Damluji, a sympathetic Ottoman official, Ali Beg was able to regain the Lalish sanctuary[3] but the peacocks and other sacred objects removed by Omar Wehbi Pasha and his son remained impounded in Baghdad. Grateful for the diplomatic intercession that had freed them from exile and hoping for further help, the Mir and his wife maintained contacts with British consular officials and missionaries in Mosul and with travellers such as Gertrude Bell.

Ali Beg soon discovered that Mayan's younger brother also wanted to revitalize the Yezidi community and that he had a mind of his own.

The nineteenth-century Mirs of the Yezidis, glimpsed briefly in local chronicles or travellers' accounts, recall the decorative two-dimensional

figures painted by Oriental miniaturists. But in 1888 the Chol dynasty produced a prince whose character — a mixture of idealism, ambition and caprice
— marks him as a twentieth-century man of flesh and blood.

Ismail Beg, born of the same mother as Mayan, was fourteen years younger.
His father, Abdi Beg, died six months after he was born and his mother died
when he was three, leaving him to be brought up by sisters.

When he was eighteen years old Ismail eloped with the daughter of a faqir.
A son was born of this marriage, but his wife died shortly afterwards.[4]

Restless by nature and much influenced by dreams, Ismail began travelling
around the Yezidi communities as a self-appointed apostle, preaching,
blessing and collecting alms. In the Jebel Sinjar he made a lifelong friend in
Hammu Shiru by settling a dispute with some other tribesmen.[5]

In 1908 he decided to take advantage of the new freedom prevailing since
the Young Turk revolution and pay a visit to the Yezidis of Transcaucasia.

The might of Russia cast a long, menacing shadow over the Ottoman empire
in Asia. In the three provinces ceded by Sultan Abdul Hamid in 1877 new
military bases were established at Kars and Sarikamish and were linked to the
Russian railway system, while the Ottoman lines were prevented from
expanding beyond Ankara. Farther east a pact between Russia and Britain
had legitimized a Russian 'sphere of influence' in the Persian province of
Azerbaijan adjoining Anatolia and a rail line was being built to connect Erivan
with Tabriz.

Military preponderance facilitated cultural and political pressures. The
Armenian catholicos (patriarch) lived on Russian soil and over 1,000,000 of
his followers were subjects of the czar. In 1897–99 many of the Nestorians
around Lake Urmia were converted to the Russian Orthodox church. The
Kurds were long accustomed to play one powerful neighbour off against
another; some of their leaders, including one of Bedr Khan Beg's many sons,
began talking to the Russians.

Among the 130 million Russian subjects enumerated in the 1897 census
were 14,726 Yezidis in Transcaucasia. This small pastoral community, whose
history is related in a subsequent chapter, was far removed from politics. But
since the days of Layard the Muscovy sanjak had been a good source of income
for the Mirs. Ismail Beg sensed a rare opportunity to tend a far-away flock.

Ismail's journey took him through the scattered Yezidi communities in northeastern Anatolia. In one village near Van his host was readying a midday feast

in his honour when word arrived that a stranger was seeking forage for two other travellers halted nearby. Investigation revealed that Hormizd, brother of the 'Assyrian' patriarch Mar Shimun XIX Benjamin, was 'touring the outliers of his nation' in company with Rev W. A. Wigram, who had recently relocated the Archbishop of Canterbury's mission at Van after most of its parishioners had defected to the Russians. A delegation of villagers insisted that these distinguished travellers come and 'eat bread'.

In a welcoming speech the Yezidi prince cited Mir Ali Beg's esteem for Mar Shimun — regrettably they had never met — and recalled that Yezidi visitors to the patriarchal residence were unfailingly impressed by the sight of his tame peacock. Wigram fretted at the delay caused by two-and-a-half hours of banqueting, but his tedium was relieved by a colourful incident at the end of the meal. After the Christian guests and some of the Yezidis had sated themselves from the bowl of soup, the prince emptied a pot of red pepper into it and drank the remainder down.[6]

Ismail obtained his travel papers in Erzurum and rode confidently along the highway leading to the border. But although kawals had regularly crossed the rugged frontier between the Ottoman and Russian empires without detection, matters were less simple for Ismail, who travelled in style with a servant and baggage containing ceremonial gold-embroidered cloaks and dust pellets from the Sheikh Adi shrine. At the Russian frontier post of Karaurgan the travellers' papers were all in order, but the customs official demanded 50 gold liras (then worth £45) as duty on the robes and rebuffed Ismail's counter-offer of 10 gold liras for his personal account.

Ismail and his servant returned sadly to the Ottoman frontier post, where a sympathetic innkeeper told them there was a route through the mountains and assured them that, once across the border, their Russian visas, already stamped, would give them legal status. However, the route was dangerous for Yezidis, since the Kurdish villagers on the way were fanatical Moslems.

After a long day's mule ride Ismail reached the first village, where he announced that he and his companion were dervishes from the Qadiriya order, well known to Ismail since its founder, Sheikh Abd el-Qadir el-Gilani, had been a close friend of Sheikh Adi and is revered by the Yezidis as a saint.* The travellers were welcomed and feasted as honoured guests and Ismail led the villagers in prayer; realizing that they knew little Arabic, he mixed into the ritual a number of curses and an appeal to Melek Taus and Sheikh Adi to wipe out the entire tribe. Sick and crippled tribesmen came to be blessed by the holy man; barren women brough cups of water for him to spit into. The parents of a dying child asked for some soil from el-Gilani's shrine to tie to their child's

* See pp. 16, 17.

wrist; Ismail gave them some Sheikh Adi dust. The village elders inquired whether it was permissible to kill Armenians and Yezidis. The supposed dervish pulled out his pocket diary, thumbed through the pages and replied that Sheikh Abd el-Qadir's book only justified killing in case of self-defence or unprovoked aggression.[7]

A few days later, after comparable receptions in successive villages, the travellers reached Alexandropol (previously called Gümrü and subsequently Leninakan), where they resumed their true identities. Ismail satisfied the authorities that he had no subversive intentions and was allowed to travel among the Yezidi villages, where he preached the laws of Sheikh Adi and berated those who had adopted the customs of their Christian neighbours. In December he presided over a gathering of Yezidi elders at the border town of Igdir and dictated a code of regulations to govern the conduct of believers. Among other rules, Ismail established maximum bride-prices of 100 roubles (then worth £10.11.0) for a girl and 45–50 roubles for a widow.[8]

One startling innovation in the Igdir code was the commandment that the Yezidis should set up schools and teach their children to read, write and learn about the world. This precept implemented the terms of an understanding Ismail had negotiated with the Armenian church, which agreed to extend its protection to the Yezidis provided their children went to school. Details were worked out when the twenty-year-old Ismail visited the Armenian catholicos Matthew II, then in his seventies, at the ancient monastery of Echmiadzin, north of Igdir. When Ismail pointed out that the villagers had no money to set up schools, the patriarch replied: 'I am prepared to establish seven schools in Yezidi villages and I assume responsibility for all their needs'.

Assisted by the catholicos and his clergy, Ismail composed a petition to Count Illarion Vorontsov-Dashkov, viceroy of the Caucasus, on behalf of seventy-two villages and 3,500 households, requesting official recognition of the Yezidi religion and protection from Moslem harassment. The petition, revised six times before it was deemed satisfactory, concluded with a prayer that 'the sword of Russia would one day rule over the Jebel Sinjar and save its people from Moslem persecution'.[9]

Ismail travelled to Tiflis by train (his first such experience) and was lodged at the Armenian patriarchal residence. An appointment was made for him to present the petition to the viceroy, referred to in his reminiscences as the 'King'.

On 3 March 1909 Ismail and his sponsors were conveyed in official carriages to the palace, where he admired the carpets, the bejewelled tapestries and the vice-regal furniture. He was first received by the 'Queen' and her five ladies in waiting, who offered him cigarettes, biscuits and tea. Vorontsov-Dashkov then entered, bare-headed, wearing a gold sword; he

163

appeared to be about fifty-five years old.* Ismail outlined to him the similarities between the Yezidi and Christian religions and asked that his people be recognized officially as a minority under the protection of the Armenians. The viceroy agreed and, upon learning that a number of Yezidis lived in Tiflis, ordered the police to bring them to the palace, where 270 of them were photographed with Ismail. At the end of the audience the 'King' stated that he would advise 'his elder brother Nikolai in Petersburg' about the Yezidis and urged Ismail to stay in Trauscaucasia as their leader. Ismail replied that he had important matters to attend to in Istanbul and Iraq, but that he would bear the Russian offer in mind. In the meantime he requested that the headman of the Galanian village community in the Surmalu district be accepted as Ismail's deputy.

The streets of Tiflis were lined with spectators as Ismail drove back to the patriarchal residence, where he was permitted to sit on the episcopal throne and hold court for his followers. They laid a white handkerchief before him and covered it with contributions totalling 40 gold liras (£36).[10]

Among those cheered by Ismail's success were members of the Swedish Female Missionary Workers, engaged in social work among the Tiflis Yezidis; their chronicler, Maria Anholm, later wistfully recalled the visit of the Yezidi leader, 'a quite young man'.[11]

Sailing from Batum, Ismail arrived in Istanbul in the spring of 1909. Armenian church officials, basking in the atmosphere of good feeling that marked the early days of the Young Turk revolution, soon obtained for him an edict, countersigned by the Sheikh-ul-Islam, that recognized the Yezidi religion and the sanctity of the Sheikh Adi shrine, forbade forced conversions to Islam and ordered that the sacred objects impounded in Baghdad be returned to the Yezidis. The text of the edict was telegraphed to Mosul for ratification by Mir Ali Beg.

The Mir's reply, accompanied by a declaration signed by the tribal chiefs, stated that Ismail had no authority to negotiate on behalf of the Yezidi community. Promulgation of the edict was suspended and Ismail returned crestfallen to Iraq.

Ismail surmised that the motive behind Ali Beg's disavowal was fear that his young kinsman would use the edict as a lever towards becoming the next Mir of the Yezidis. (An Istanbul newspaper had reported that Ismail had asked the grand vizier for a 'subvention' as the Mir's heir and had also requested to be admitted to a school.) In any case, upon returning home Ismail claimed as a reward for his services a share of the princely revenues. But the Mir and his wife were unable or unwilling to satisfy his demands and a bitter feud

* The viceroy was actually seventy-one years old.

developed. In his memoirs Ismail admits that at one point he had thought of stabbing his sister Mayan.[12]

He took a new wife, his cousin Amsha, and lived mostly at Bashika, engaged in constant litigation and intrigue. The dynastic quarrel continued and at the end of 1912 Ismail was once again a wanderer, living on the charity of local supporters. On one trip to the Tur Abdin he was imprisoned for a while on a charge that he had been plotting with Armenian revolutionaries and Russian spies. When he was finally released, he gave the police inspector a description of the Yezidi religion contained in a manuscript, written in Syriac with an Arabic translation, that he had obtained earlier from a Jacobite fellow prisoner.[13]

Meanwhile Mir Ali Beg's quiet diplomacy was achieving results. In the autumn of 1909 George Reed, treasurer of the Archbishop's mission, travelled from Van to Mosul to investigate the possibilities of transferring the mission headquarters, once again, to the Amadia district. On his way back Reed passed by Lalish, where the autumn festival was in progress. He noted that there were 3,000 Yezidis around the shrine and that 'their chief, Ali Bey, a handsome man with an extraordinarily fine beard, made us very welcome, and we spent the greater part of the day in his company watching the dancing and a few of their ceremonies'.[14]

The failure of the Ottoman authorities to return the sacred objects was not unnoticed in the world of art. In a book about the Yezidis printed privately in Mosul in 1905 and reviewed by a German orientalist in 1908, Nuri Pasha, governor of Mosul from 1902 to 1905, had itemized the objects, mentioned their removal to Baghdad and added that 'their present whereabouts cannot be ascertained'.[15]

Père Anastase's 1911 article announcing his discovery of the original sacred books had also described an iron statue of a peacock owned by a rich Christian family in Baghdad, one of whose forbears had purchased it from a dealer who had bought it from an officer who had served with Reshid Pasha in the 1830s. A photograph showed the bird standing upright, with a crest above its head and its tail feathers outspread (quite unlike the sketches by Layard and Mrs Badger); no dimensions were given. Anastase endorsed the owners' belief that this was a sanjak captured from the Yezidis and praised the fine gold chasing and delicate artwork.[16]

On the afternoon of 12 December 1911 a Delhi dealer in antiques was visited by a well-known connoisseur, Queen-Empress Mary, who was touring India with her recently enthroned husband. She spent two hours examining the collection and was especially interested in a steel peacock, 3 ft high with tail expanded, described as 'the idol of the Yezidis of Mesopotamia'. The figure was said to have been obtained from Yezidis near Diyarbakir in 1882. After mentioning that a previous owner had turned down an offer of £2,000, the dealer gallantly declared that he would present it to the British Museum to commemorate the imperial visit to India.[17]

The peacock was placed on view in London in July 1912. Inspection had revealed in the centre of its tail the figure of a man with a veil over his face, presumed to be Sheikh Adi. After it had been shown for a week Athelstan Riley denounced 'this impudent bird' as an ornament commonly found in Persia with figures representing legendary kings, possibly 200 years old and worth £10 as the most. His identification is now generally accepted by experts and the Delhi peacock is no longer on display.[18]

The sacred objects were finally returned to the Yezidis by Suleiman Nazif Pasha, an eminent man of letters who governed Mosul from September 1913 to December 1914.[19] But by that time Mir Ali Beg was no longer alive.

The Archbishop of Canterbury's mission moved to Amadia in 1911. In the autumn of 1912 Wigram returned to England, stopping to revisit Lalish and call on Ali Beg at Baadri. He noted that 'the castle seemed pretty well garrisoned' but that the white-washed walls of the reception room were cracked in places and 'scrawled all over with rough pencil drawings of steam-boats and locomotives'. The Mir is described by Wigram as 'rather a big man, as men go in the mountain districts; probably about six feet high, and about forty-five years of age'.* He wore a dark brown *abba* (cloak) with gold embroidery round the collar and a red turban. Wigram's account does not record their conversation beyond mentioning the Mir's high regard for England and his traditional friendship with the Nestorian patriarch, but he observed that Ali Beg was suffering from a bad cold and that 'his manner was melancholy and depressed'.[20]

The last visitor to enjoy the ageing Mir's hospitality at Baadri was Safr Aga, chief of the Moslem tribe of Doski Kurds from the Dohuk area, who spent a night at the palace early in 1913.[21] The next morning Ali Beg was found murdered in his bed.

Ismail spent that fateful night at a village named Khidr Elias, near the ancient monastery of Mar Behnam, 20 miles southeast of Mosul. On his way north he stopped at the village of Karaimlais, where messengers brought him news of the crime. Stopping at Bahzani to collect a group of friends, he hastened to Baadri. The palace was filled with Yezidi notables conferring with

* At the time of their meeting Wigram was forty, and Ali Beg sixty-six years old respectively.

Said Beg and his mother to the melancholy music of pipes and drums. Mayan was wearing a red dress, the widow's symbol of implacable revenge.

It was generally agreed that the young prince should succeed as Mir, but the real prize was the guardianship. Ismail's candidacy was blocked by his sister and her adherents, who accused him of complicity in the murder and arranged for him to be escorted under guard to Mosul. By the time Ismail had cleared himself of the charges, Mayan was installed as guardian of the young Mir and administrator of the princely revenues.[22]

The mystery of Ali Beg's murder was never completely solved. Wigram, repeating stories from the Amadia mission, accuses a 'nephew' of the Mir who had once fled to Russia to avoid the consequences of a previous unsuccessful attempt.[23] Another theory, long current among British writers, hints at a guilty passion between Mayan Khatun and the Doski chieftain who was in the palace when the crime occurred. Ismail's reminiscences, often critical of his sister, do not mention this possibility.[24]

Forty days after Ali Beg's death an old woman living near Baadri testified that two men from her village — Fattah and Ali, the sons of Jolo b. Jolo — had perpetrated the crime. They belonged to the Basmariya clan, which was distantly related to the Chol dynasty and had been appointed in the seventeenth century by Sheikh Mohammed el-Batini as hereditary administrators of the community. Long deprived of political power, they still ranked second only to the Chols and were the only other family with whom Chol princes could contract marriage.* Their motive in killing Ali Beg was explainable as a means of supplanting the Chols.

There are several versions of how punishment was meted out to the suspects. Ismail reports that his older brother, also named Jolo, rode to the village with three of his friends and killed Fattah, Ali and all their male kinfolk except for one boy, who died soon afterwards.[25]

Sadiq Damluji, the Ottoman official well acquainted with the princely family, identifies Hussein Beg, son of Mir Mirza Beg, and another prince as the executioners and mentions a third Basmariya brother who escaped to the Sinjar, hid there for fifteen years, became blind and died. They also captured the father; when he offered to tell who had really killed Ali Beg he was immediately put to death.[26]

A third account comes from Mayan Khatun herself.[27] She gave orders for the eight Basmariyas — Jolo b. Jolo, his wife, his four sons and two daughters — to be brought to Baadri. After sentence had been passed the red-robed princess watched her bodyguard Hajji shoot all of them except for the two girls, whom she later adopted and brought up. When it was all over, Mayan

* See pp. 36, 47.

Khatun rose from her seat, walked over to where the bodies lay and stooped down to touch the still warm blood of each victim and lick her finger with her tongue. The next morning the princess was observed to be wearing the black robes customarily worn by widows for a year.

Matters thus being settled, Ismail applied once again to obtain his proper share of the revenues. His sister still resisted, but when spring came his fortune changed for the better.

Word reached Ismail that among the group of kawals despatched from Lalish to carry the Sinjar sanjak around the Yezidi villages were two men who had been convicted of a crime by the Ottoman courts but had never been apprehended. He obtained an escort of soldiers from the governor of Mosul and intercepted the kawals as they were crossing the Tigris. The next day they all stopped at a nearby Yezidi village, where Ismail persuaded the headman to keep the sanjak in his house while the prisoners and escort went back to Mosul. As soon as they had left, Ismail saddled his horse, grabbed his gun and rode off with the sanjak.

In Bashika he evaded the wiles of his sister's spies and boldly rode into Mosul, where he persuaded two British CMS missionaries, Dr George Stanley and Miss Ellen Martin, to hide the sanjak in a chest in the mission house. Ismail was soon arrested, but he refused to reveal the whereabouts of the sanjak. Finally, agreement was reached whereby Ismail was awarded custody of the Sinjar sanjak, entitling him to a share of the alms collected in the Jebel Sinjar and eastern Anatolia, while Mir Said Beg retained the Sheikhan, Aleppo and Muscovy sanjaks.[28]

The two leaders of the Sinjar Yezidis — his old friend Hammu Shiru and Daud el-Daud, chief of the Mihirkan tribe and grandson of Isa Aga who had fought Tayyar Pasha in 1846 — invited Ismail to come and live at Beled Sinjar. But first he had to take his sanjak around the Yezidi villages in the Tur Abdin and the territory east of Diyarbakir in the company of his brother Jolo and four kawals. Uncertain as to the kawals' loyalty, he obtained a military escort as far as Mardin, where he hired a Christian bodyguard recommended by Alpheus Andrus.

But despite all precautions Ismail lost his hard-won peacock in the little village of Hemduna (now renamed Kurukavak) on the slope above Redwan, where Layard first saw the sanjak in 1849.* Telling the headman, Mirza Kalash, that Ismail was planning to go off to Russia with the sanjak, the kawals succeeded in removing the peacock from its bag and substituting the standard while Ismail was asleep. At the same time their accomplice, the faithless Jolo Beg, stole his brother's horse and rifle. The thieves eluded pursuit and

* See p. 101.

brought the peacock back to Said Beg and his mother.

The village was fined 40 liras (£36), out of which the governor gave Ismail 10 liras. Jolo was eventually imprisoned for his crime. Ismail's horse was returned, but he did not recover his peacock. Dejected and aggrieved, he considered at one point going back to Transcaucasia, but finally Suleiman Nazif Pasha of Mosul negotiated a family settlement enabling Ismail to live at Beled Sinjar.[29]

A dream in which he saw two Christian priests handing out black kerchiefs to a group of women forewarned Ismail that war and persecution were imminent. He alerted the Armenians in Mardin and promised that in case of need they could find shelter in the Jebel Sinjar. Similar assurances were given to the Jacobite patriarch Ignatius XXXVI Abdallah II.[30]

In 1914 Ismail learned from Elias Shakir, the Jacobite metropolitan of Mosul, that the patriarchal library at the monastery of Deir ez-Zafaran possessed a book about the Yezidis. Suleiman Nazif provided him with a military escort to Mardin, where the monks showed him the manuscript, which contained Arabic texts of the sacred books together with some short prayers in Kurdish. A scribe made a copy for him, adding a colophon giving Ismail's name and telling how he learned about the manuscript. It also stated that this was a text thought to have been lost in 1849 but rediscovered in India in 1889 by the Jacobite patriarch Ignatius XXXIV Peter IV, who brought it back to Mardin. Ismail had no reason to doubt such a story, but a more likely provenance for the manuscript is suggested by the telltale dating at the head of the colophon — AG 2200=AD 1889=AH 1305.[31]

In May 1914 Suleiman Nazif Pasha announced that the 68,000 Yezidis in the province of Mosul would henceforth be recognized as a distinct religious community and would not be molested in the exercise of their creed. As part of the settlement the peacocks would be restored to them and the Mir would receive a salary of 800 piastres (£7.4.0) a month. Departmental records preserved in the Ottoman archives reveal that the Yezidis had wanted 1,000 piastres a month and that they agreed in the final settlement 'not to join the French or English creeds'. The official decree bears the signatures of the entire cabinet including that of Enver Pasha, minister of defence.[32]

After years of negotiation Mayan Khatun had reached agreement with the government just in time. Six months later the French and British missionaries were evacuated from Iraq. The Ottoman empire was at war.

Chapter Twelve
The Epoch of Mayan Khatun

The October 1914 treaty that committed the Young Turk government to join Germany and Austria–Hungary in the war against Britain, France and Russia was the death-warrant for 'the sick man of Europe'. Confident of victory, Russia and its western allies decided to settle the 'eastern question' once and for all. Secret agreements, negotiated by Mark Sykes for Britain, promised Istanbul to the czar, while the Arab provinces of the empire would be placed under British or French control. In Anatolia the middle Euphrates and upper Tigris valleys were awarded to France, while the territory to the east would come under Russian rule. (In northern Persia the Russians had already occupied Tabriz and Urmia since 1910.)

Eight long years elapsed and millions of the sultan's subjects died before the fighting ceased and successor states emerged from the shattered empire with the frontiers we know today. At the end of it all, the French tricolour flew over Damascus and Aleppo and the British held Palestine and Iraq. But Russia had collapsed and a new Turkish state governed Istanbul and Anatolia, including most of the territory ceded by Abdul Hamid to the czar.

Throughout this time of trouble the Yezidi communities in Iraq were sheltered from calamity by the accident of geography and the prudence of Mayan Khatun.

Ismail Beg stayed in Beled Sinjar awaiting the Russian sword. In the first two years of the war the Ottoman army suffered disastrous defeats on the Caucasian front, enabling the Russians to take Van, Erzurum and Trebizond and to rally Armenians and Assyrians to their cause. But the Russian advances were hampered by terrain and by a constant drain of manpower to the European theatre of war. The closest they came to the Yezidi heartlands was Bitlis to the north, captured in March 1916 and lost to the Ottoman general

Kemal Pasha five months later, and Rowanduz to the east (briefly occupied from May to July 1916).

Meanwhile, Enver Pasha and his German advisers were experiencing the constraints imposed on a nation denied access to the sea; the sole line of communication with its allies in Central Europe was through Bulgaria, which entered the war on their side in 1915. The British navy dominated the Mediterranean, the Suez Canal, the Red Sea and the Persian Gulf, preventing ships from entering or leaving Ottoman ports and convoying British and colonial troops at will.

After failure of their seaborne landings on the beaches of Gallipoli, the key to Istanbul, the British turned their attention to the soft underbelly of the empire. Securely based in Egypt, they built up an army skilled in desert warfare. As a preliminary to an invasion of Palestine, a team of political strategists, including Gertrude Bell, was established in Cairo to intrigue with Arab dissidents. Its greatest achievement (after Gertrude Bell had already left) was to induce the hereditary governor of Mecca to proclaim himself king of an independent Arab state.

In Iraq an expeditionary force of British and Indian troops seized Basra in the first weeks of the war. After costly setbacks, including the loss of close to 10,000 soldiers trapped in Kut, they captured Baghdad in March 1917 and pushed north to Samarra and Tikrit. Ottoman and German staff officers planned a counterattack down the Euphrates. But there was to be no twentieth-century test of the unlucky route that had blighted Chesney's career and had enticed Cyrus, Julian and the Black Caliph to their deaths. Troops assigned to the operation were needed to defend Palestine against a British attack from Egypt and the Ottomans stayed on the defensive in Iraq.

As they approached the battlefields of antiquity, British staff officers readily perceived the strategic importance of the Jebel Sinjar. The Ottoman lines of communication with their army in Iraq followed the old caravan route from Aleppo to Mosul, now parallelled by the slowly advancing Baghdad railway. The railhead reached Nisibin in September 1917. Beyond that point, except for the rare automobile capable of crossing the roadless desert, traditional means of transport prevailed — horses, mules, and camels.*

From their vantage points on the Jebel Sinjar the Yezidi tribesmen could observe everything and find many opportunities to help themselves to livestock, clothing and ammunition.[1]

Gertrude Bell, now a senior administrative official in Baghdad, recalled the ancient enmity between the Sinjar Yezidis and the Ottomans. In August 1917

---

* In 1916 Enver Pasha and his staff covered the Mosul–Samarra segment of an inspection trip by kelek.

she sent an Arab agent with a message to Hammu Shiru. Subsequently, Ismail himself wrote to the British, who responded warmly and thanked him for sheltering Armenian deportees who had escaped from their convoys between Deir ez-Zor and Mosul.[2]

(In 1915 Alpheus Andrus' sympathies with the Armenians had caused him to be expelled from Mardin and interned. Two years later, when the United States declared war on Germany and Austria-Hungary and broke off diplomatic relations with the Ottoman empire, the missionary was allowed to go to America, where he died in 1919. His papers, including an Arabo-Kurdish translation of the New Testament and his entire correspondence with Jeremiah Shamir, have never been found.)[3]

In December 1917 Jerusalem was lost to the British invaders from Egypt; of the sultan's three holy cities only Medina remained to him, isolated at the end of the harried Hejaz line. But unexpectedly things changed for the better in the east. Russia, now governed by Communists, sued for peace. Four months later all of Anatolia, together with the three provinces lost in 1877, had been miraculously restored to Ottoman rule.

In February 1918 Enver Pasha decided the time had come to mop up the Yezidi threat to his lines of communication with Iraq. An expedition manned by veterans from the Caucasian front and still-loyal Arabs advanced to Tel Afar with artillery drawn by teams of oxen. Messengers were sent to the Jebel Sinjar with a demand that the Yezidis surrender their Armenian refugees and stolen guns or face the consequences. The tribesmen tore up the ultimatum and sent the bearers back without their clothes. But they disregarded Ismail's advice to send their women, children and flocks to the mountains and the villages suffered heavy casualties when the Ottomans attacked. Thereupon a Yezidi council of war decided that Ismail should attempt to reach the British.

He set off the next morning with a bodyguard and two Armenian refugees (one of them, known as 'the professor', had attempted to assassinate Sultan Abdul Hamid). Travelling along the edge of the desert past the ruins of Hatra, challenged from time to time by Arabs of uncertain allegiance, they reached the British lines at Samarra.[4]

In his reminiscences Ismail recalls the attentions he received from the British army. Officers listened with interest as he outlined his plan for a two-pronged attack on Mosul, which assumed Britain giving Ismail 3,000 rifles, twenty-five machine guns, two airplanes and a detachment of Indian soldiers. In Baghdad he met the British commander-in-chief, General Marshall, and his chief of staff and pointed out to Gertrude Bell a number of topographical errors on her maps.[5]

The summer heat precluded major operations, but in July 1918 Ismail went back to the Sinjar with a mounted reconnaissance party commanded by a

British engineer officer, Captain Harry Hutson (then aged twenty-five), assisted by Captain Campbell Munro, an Indian army doctor. The Shammar Jerba tribe of Arabs located west of Baghdad provided an escort for the party. Travelling day and night, their fast camels carried them along a route west of the dry Tharthar river bed to a point south of Jebel Sinjar whence Ismail, Hutson and Munro rode by horse to a nocturnal rendezvous with Hammu Shiru at Beled Sinjar.

The Yezidi chieftain explained how vulnerable the villages were to Ottoman artillery and declared that the tribesmen could not undertake any offensive action without support. The envoys found their way back to their escort without being intercepted and were joined by Ismail's wife, his son Abd el-Karim and his eighteen-month-old daughter Wansa. They all returned safely to the British outpost at Tikrit.[6]

Before they parted Ismail handed Hutson 'a handwritten document, not at all elaborate but resembling to some extent an ordinary exercise book', telling him that it explained the Yezidi religion. The writing was in Arabic, unintelligible to Hutson. But he kept it after leaving Iraq in 1919 and recalls carrying it about for some time in his kit until he received orders to send it to headquarters because the Yezidis wanted it back.[7] If he had been able to read the colophon, Hutson would have known that he had in his possession a copy of the Deir ez-Zafaran manuscript of the Yezidi sacred books.

At some point the manuscript was shown to Alphonse Mingana in Manchester. In a 'miscellaneous communication' published in the *Journal of the Royal Asiatic Society* in January 1921, he complimented Captain Hutson on his military record and his unique opportunity to study Yezidi habits and customs. He stated that the manuscript came to his attention through one of the orientalists contacted by Hutson in an endeavour to obtain an opinion from experts in Kurdish. (Hutson states that he made no such inquiries.) Mingana dismissed the Arabic text as similar to the manuscripts he had already declared to be the work of Jeremiah Shamir. Despite his earlier claim to have had many Yezidi friends in the Sinjar before he left Iraq in 1913, Mingana seemed not to know who Ismail was; in commenting on the colophon describing the find he expressed surprise to learn of 'a prominent Yezidi sheikh knowing nothing of the fact that his community possesses any sacred books'.[8]

In the summer of 1918, while the opposing armies in Iraq were immobilized by the Mesopotamian sun, Ottoman troops moved into the vacuum left by the Russian retreat. In Transcaucasia they captured Baku on the Caspian sea; in northwest Persia they occupied Tabriz. Aided by Kurdish tribesmen, the

Ottomans drove the Assyrians from Urmia and destroyed the long established missions of the Americans and the French.

On 10 September 1918 an Ottoman force, equipped with machine guns and supported by airplanes and two 150-mm howitzers, set off for the Jebel Sinjar to eliminate once again the Yezidi threat to the road from Nisibin to Mosul. Beled Sinjar was reoccupied and all the larger villages attacked. On this occasion the tribesmen, led by Hammu Shiru and Daud el-Daud, withdrew with their families and flocks and took refuge in the caves, until they noticed that the invaders had left.[9]

This was indeed the last punitive expedition the sultan's government would ever dispatch to the Sinjar. Just one week after it reached the mountain, while Ottoman troops elsewhere were advancing north from Baku along the Caspian shore and from Urmia to the south, the Bulgarian army capitulated to French and British forces in northern Greece, leaving the way open for them to move on Istanbul. A few days later the British broke through in Palestine and swept into Syria. Enver Pasha resigned in mid-October. By the end of the month the Ottomans had lost Aleppo. An armistice was signed and the victors entered Istanbul. British troops, later replaced by French, took over the Baghdad railway from Aleppo eastward to Urfa. In Transcaucasia another British force monitored the Ottoman withdrawal to the 1877 frontier.

In Iraq the Ottomans still held Mosul when hostilities ceased, but the British were able to take over the whole province and compel the Ottoman officials to withdraw to Nisibin. Colonel Gerard Leachman, a legendary desert fighter, entered Mosul as Political Officer with his assistant, Colonel Nalder, and Ismail Beg. A few days later all three drove to Tel Afar to accept the surrender of its Ottoman garrison and thence on to Sinjar, where in Hammu Shiru's words 'it was a critical time in the life of the mountain and Colonel Leachman was just in time to save us from ruin'.[10]

Back in Mosul Leachman convened an assembly of all the Yezidi leaders. Ismail rode in with Hammu Shiru and thirty-five chiefs from the Sinjar. After receiving expressions of gratitude from the Armenian and Chaldean patriarchs, he conferred with Leachman, who offered him the governorship of the Sinjar. Ismail declined on the grounds that Hammu Shiru was better qualified. He was playing for bigger stakes.

Next day a delegation of sheikhs and headmen arrived from the Sheikhan, headed by the chief sheikh and Mir Said Beg. Nalder describes the Mir as a 'delicate and weak looking person, of about thirty'; he was actually eighteen. Leachman announced that Hammu Shiru would be in charge of the Sinjar and

then turned to the issue of who should get the princely revenues. He was lean-
ing toward giving them to Ismail when Mayan Khatun arrived and struck a
deal with Hammu Shiru. Their joint recommendation was to split the
aggregate revenues from the sanjaks between Said and Ismail. With Ismail's
concurrence Leachman approved the compromise.[11]

The first duty of the newly appointed officials was to take part in an opinion
poll in progress throughout Iraq on the subject of the future government of the
country. (Britain and France were discussing how the wartime partition pacts
should be implemented, now that British troops occupied both Syria and Iraq
and Russia had rejected the agreements.) In the province of Mosul each
minority was invited to express its views. The Yezidi declaration, signed 'in
the name of the whole Yazidi nation in the Vilayets of Diyarbakr and Mosul
by some 50 persons, including all the leading Yazidis', stated that they desired
to be subjects of Great Britain and that they would 'never agree to have an
Arab Government over us'.[12]

Ismail returned to the Sinjar for a festive period of visits, speeches and
banquets celebrating the advent of British rule. Mayan Khatun was also busy
mending fences. She arranged for Leachman to see the sanctuary in Lalish, the
first foreign visitor in several years.[13] A son born to one of the Yezidi princes
was named Lijman Beg.*

Ismail's memoirs record his dismay when, four months after the compromise in Mosul, he went back to Baghdad to fetch his family and was
detained there on the grounds that the Yezidis did not want him in the Sinjar.
Leachman left Mosul a few weeks later; Nalder, who succeeded him, reported
that:

> Ismail proved to be absolutely untrustworthy, and unable to
> abstain from petty intrigue of every kind, and eventually it was
> found necessary to send him to Baghdad, Said regaining the
> undivided headship.[15]

After years of family feuding Ismail had few illusions about what had
occurred. He was certain that Said Beg's faction had bribed the Sinjar chieftains to file complaints. Nalder's report merely commented that Said Beg 'is
managed entirely by his Mother Maiyan, a masterful old lady whose personal
interests do not, I think, always coincide with the best interests of the tribe'. At
that time Mayan Khatun was forty-four years old and just getting into her
stride.[16]

* He subsequently married Ismail Beg's daughter Kupros (named after the island of
Cyprus, where Ismail's ship anchored in 1909 after a stormy passage from Istanbul.)[14]

Ismail appealed to Gertrude Bell to increase his allowance and tried in vain to persuade the British to have his son Abd el-Karim educated in England. He even asked Captain Hutson, now at the War Office in London, if he could arrange his return to the Sinjar. His letter, written by a bilingual scribe, thanked his friend for returning the manuscript, offered to send him another copy and asked that on his next visit to Iraq Hutson should bring Ismail 'one motocar, but the price dont be more R[upee]s 1500' [then worth £150], or if this were difficult to bring 'one motocycle'.[17]

Ismail's banishment lasted two-and-a-half years. He lived in Baghdad with his family on an allowance from the government and made occasional visits to Basra and to the refugee camp at Bakuba,* where he identified some Yezidi orphans rescued by Armenians in Van when the local tribesmen fled to Trans-caucasia. The wife of the camp commandant recalled in her memoirs the visit of 'rather a tall man with a long black beard and gentle brown eyes', wearing a flowing robe with a white turban and a light brown cloak.[18]

In the second half of 1920 the Arab tribes in Iraq rebelled against the British occupation; among the casualties was Leachman, killed in a village near the Euphrates. At the end of the year Britain installed a new High Commissioner for Mesopotamia, Sir Percy Cox, who allowed Ismail to return to the Sinjar in 1921 and restored his entitlement to share in the princely revenues. Seven years later the grateful Ismail named his youngest son Kokus Beg.

The state of Iraq was established in 1921 under British supervision with a king chosen from the family that ruled Mecca until dispossessed by Ibn Saud. Iraq's title to the province of Mosul was recognized by a 1926 treaty with the new Turkish state proclaimed by Kemal Pasha which had revitalized the former Ottoman army and recovered the Anatolian provinces occupied by Armenians, Italians and Greeks. Meanwhile the French had pulled back from Urfa and Birecik to strengthen their hold on Syria and later made a separate peace with Kemal. The boundary between Syria and Iraq was finally estab-lished in 1933 by a settlement that abandoned an earlier notion of slicing the Jebel Sinjar in two and awarded the whole of the mountain to Iraq.

Hammu Shiru retained the title of 'head of the mountain' until he died, aged over ninety, in 1932. Progressive in his views, he supported Leachman's idea of a school for Yezidi children in Beled Sinjar. The project started inauspi-ciously, when two of the original five pupils were drowned in a rain-swollen river on their way to school. But Hammu Shiru persuaded the parents to over-look this event and arranged that the textbooks should be specially edited to omit objectionable words and letters.[19]   A British administrator describes

---

* This camp sheltered the survivors of the Assyrian communities in the Hakkari and Urmia districts, who had made their way through western Persia to Iraq.

Hammu Shiru as 'a despotic old dotard' in his old age (though he noted that he sired a child as late as 1932). His authority on the Jebel Sinjar was increasingly challenged by the Mihirkan chieftain Daud el-Daud. In April 1925, after Daud had defied three orders to attend a conference at Beled Sinjar, the British sent a troop of armoured cars to overawe him. But the effect of this demonstration was marred by a Yezidi exploit worthy of Evliya's pen; a tribeman's rifle shot down an escorting Royal Air Force F.2B reconnaissance plane with a cruising speed in excess of 100 mph, killing both members of the crew.[20]

Satisfied that he was at last receiving his due from the princely revenues,* Ismail Beg led a life of placid dignity in Beled Sinjar. His house, built on the foundations of a Roman fort, was filled with respectful Yezidis and curious visitors from Iraq, Britain and elsewhere. His son Abd el-Karim attended school in Baghdad. Two younger children, Wansa and her brother Yezid Khan, were boarded at the American mission in Mosul, re-established under the care of the durable Edmund McDowell and his wife, who started a girl's school there in 1924.[21]

In July 1924 the Iraq Levies, a local defence force organized by the British from Assyrian, Kurdish and other volunteers, offered the Yezidis an opportunity to enlist in an all-Yezidi cavalry squadron to be formed. But although the uniform was khaki, the tribesmen were reluctant to give up their traditional white robes. Ismail, who had worn the Royal Air Force badge since his 1918 campaigning days, volunteered to show the way. Wearing the Iraq Levies uniform, he recruited 200 tribesmen. However, after a while the project was abandoned when the British learned that, although good with animals, 'the Yezidis proved far too difficult to train, and not very amenable to discipline'.[23]

In 1925 trouble, Ismail's constant companion, disturbed this life of civic and domestic virtue. The kawals carrying the Sinjar sanjak were robbed by assailants hired by another Chol prince, Naif Beg, whose daughter was married to Mir Said Beg. Ismail suspected an attempt to tamper with his rights, but the British authorities moved in promptly, recovered the sanjak and apprehended Naif Beg. Mayan Khatun herself came to the Sinjar to see that justice was done.

The British official who visited Jebel Sinjar about this time recalls his visit to Ismail, 'a man of about forty, with a black straggly beard and the sad, pained expression often worn by leading Yazīdīs at any rate when approaching persons in authority'. He was wearing khaki riding breeches and stockings, a grey British army shirt, a khaki waistcoat and a white head-cloth worn Arab

---

* One third of the revenues was allocated for general purposes, including support of various members of the Chol family. The other two-thirds was divided equally between Mir Said Beg and Ismail Beg.[22]

fashion with a black cord. Upon entering his house Ismail changed into a long cossack-type coat, with a revolver and a straight Caucasian dagger slung over his shoulders. The guest-room floor was heavily carpeted and the walls were hung with pileless kilims, photographs, prints, revolvers, a sword, a sporting rifle with telescopic sights and another Caucasian dagger with a sanjak engraved on the scabbard. In one corner hung a bag containing a multiple incense burner from Lalish.[24]

Three years later Ismail received Paul Schütz, a German journalist who was driving from Aleppo to Tabriz in a vain effort to visit the German settlements in the Caucasus, Upon reaching Beled Sinjar, Schütz and his companion, a doctor, found Ismail lying on a couch in the vestibule of his house:

> His face was pale; his cheeks were sunken beneath prominent cheekbones; a high cranium was accentuated by his black beard. Such a head might have been chiselled from the same block of wood that fashioned the heads of Russian archbishops. His deepset dark eyes were grave, rather gentle, with some traces of suffering. I cannot recall ever seeing him really laugh.

Ismail coughed badly and complained of chest pains.

After prescribing for his ailments, the travellers were led to two large, well-appointed bedrooms at the top of the house. While contemplating the crescent moon shining over the mountainside and the vast desert to the south, Schütz heard sounds close to his room. He opened the door to see a maid arranging the rugs for Ismail's bed in the passage outside.

The next morning Ismail greeted them in the guest-room, where among the carpets, swords and guns they noticed faded magazine pictures of dethroned European royalty, an Armenian painting of the crucifixion and a colourful poster advertising Gritzner sewing machines and English bouillon cubes. He agreed to talk about the Yezidi religion and told them that 'he had already dictated to a Syrian priest the secret principles of the faith'. Schütz notes that this was a small scripture, written in Arabic letters but probably in the Kurdish language. Ismail added that an ancient book, said to be 4,000 years old, called the 'Black Book', written in Kurdish, had been lost in the 1892–93 attacks. Allegedly, the original was now in Germany; Ismail had heard that a leading citizen of Mosul possessed a copy.

Ismail's feeling for his religion and his concern for the Yezidis' cultural heritage shine through a mass of details, hastily scribbled by Schütz and later criticized as garbled and uninformed.* He spoke sadly about the past half-

* Schütz refers to Ismail as Mir Said Beg's brother (not uncle).

century of massacres and forced conversions to Islam, which had reduced the numbers of the once-widespread Yezidi community. Looking to the future, Ismail was uncharacteristically filled with gloom. He had proudly shown them a picture of Abd el-Karim wearing the European uniform of a Baghdad teacher; but he observed that education was destroying faith by enabling everyone to think for himself. One-fifth of the community desired education, but the remainder stayed loyal to their religion. Pointing to his ten-year-old son (presumably Yezid Khan Beg), Ismail said that he would pass on to him the secrets of the Yezidi religion 'from the heart' and that he in turn would pass them on 'from the heart' to his son.

The travellers drove off to Mosul with Ismail's parting words to Schütz echoing in their ears: 'Write down the principles of our religion and publish them in all the languages of Europe, so that our faith may be known before it perishes!'[25]

Mayan Khatun's intervention in the Sinjar sanjak incident showed clearly who was in charge in the Sheikhan. In 1922 a British writer noted that 'Said Beg, a melancholy, gentle-looking man with fine eyes and a black beard, had the weak mouth and irresolute expression of one who is ruled rather than rules'.[26]

Two years later a special correspondent for the London *Times* who visited Baadri described Said Beg as:

a personage of remarkable appearance, tall and thin, with slim, delicate hands and a waving black beard gradually tapering to a point. He looks older than he is, and a slight cast in his mournful eyes gives him a faintly sinister look.

The writer also visited Mayan Khatun — a 'grim, handsome, upstanding woman in a lofty, smoke-blackened, raftered hall in the women's apartments, where, beside a blazing open fire, she was holding her court'; he noted that she 'plainly despises her weakling son'. After recounting the violent deaths of Ali Beg and his grandfather, the article added:

Nor is Said Beg likely to make old bones, for he loves to look upon the wine when it is red and, above all, upon the arrack when it is white. Yet a certain charm of manner never leaves him altogether, and intoxication seems but to heighten his natural melancholy.

The writer also reported that the Mir was 'the proud possessor of five American motor-cars'.[27]

By the time he was twenty-seven Said Beg had been married five times. Damluji states that he killed his first wife in 1925; his second, Naif Beg's daughter, died a natural death but his fourth wife, who left him to remarry in her native Sinjar, was also killed. Discussing polygamy with an English-woman in 1929, Said Beg remarked: 'With you, women have much power, so one wife is more than enough, but with us, where no woman has any power at all, it does not matter'.[28]

In 1930 the Iraqi government and its British advisers received complaints that the Mir:

> was not only spending the considerable revenues accruing to his office on drink and dancing girls in the city of Mosul, but while in his cups was mortgaging Yazīdī villages with a gang of rascally lawyers there at high interest in order to provide himself with even more cash for his dissipations.

Consideration was given to putting the Yezidis under the laws regulating the affairs of Christian and Jewish communities. Comments were sought from the notables of Sinjar and Sheikhan.[29]

An alternative to Mir Said Beg was available in his cousin Hussein Beg, the son of Mir Mirza Beg, who had been passed over in the succession to Mir Ali Beg. In 1925 a visitor to Baadri reported that:

> although he has no near claim to the position, in an unofficial way he wields a certain amount of power in the Mir's household. Husain is a pleasing personality; he is intelligent, has a fine bearing, and would, one imagines, make an ideal chief.

But as he grew older he became passive and reclusive — a diminishing threat to Mayan Khatun's authority.[30]

The 'Sheikhan Memorial', signed by the Baba Sheikh and the heads of the other Yezidi religious orders, was prepared for use at a conference held in Mosul in 1931 with Sir Francis Humphrys, the British High Commissioner for Iraq, in attendance. The government officials could find no chink in this skil-fully written document, which spelled out the 'fundamental rules' observed by the Yezidis and stated flatly that the Mir 'cannot be dismissed or removed except by natural death or assassination (which God forbid)'. After much deliberation they accepted this rule (overlooking the precedent whereby Mayan Khatun's father had acted as regent when the Ottomans deposed her uncle) and confirmed the Mir's entitlement to the princely revenues by an official decree.[31]

By arrangement with the governor of Mosul the sanjak of Sinjar made its 1931 circuit around the mountain under the auspices of Hammu Shiru. After the alms had been collected, the faqir declared that he would deliver the sanjak only to the Mir's cousin Hussein Beg. Said Beg promptly filed a petition signed by 8,000 tribesmen demanding the return of the sanjak. The controversy went on for three months, while the governor of Mosul held the sanjak in escrow. In December 1931 instructions were received from Baghdad that it belonged to Said Beg and it was finally returned to the Mir in September 1932.[32]

Inevitably the name of Ismail was mentioned in these disputes. But his interest was beginning to turn from politics to the more cosmic themes he had discussed with Schütz. Ismail decided that despite his illiteracy and poor health, he would pass on in written form the principles of the Yezidi religion, the history of the mountain and an account of his own experiences. Over the next few years he dictated everything he knew to a trusted Arab collaborator.

In 1929 his twelve-year-old daughter Wansa was enrolled as a boarder at the American School for Girls in Beirut. On a visit to the city Ismail became ill, ran out of money and was admitted to the American University Hospital through the kindness of the university president, Dr Bayard Dodge.

After returning to the mountain, Ismail sent his manuscripts to Dr Dodge. The reminiscences, written in a crisp, colloquial style, were complete through 1925; the history of Sinjar, still in outline, ended in 1875; while his description of the Yezidi religion was a hodgepodge of oral traditions and commentaries by European experts. Constantin Zurayk, then an adjunct professor at the university, undertook to edit the manuscripts, which were published in 1934 under the title *The Yazīdīs: Past and Present*.[33]

At the time of publication the author was no longer alive. The comet that had dazzled so many believers and doubters had burned out. On 9 March 1933 Ismail Beg went to Mosul to meet Wansa, just back from Beirut. That evening, after dining with Said Beg, he died at the age of forty-five.[34]

A few months later Mayan Khatun and her son paid a visit to the bereaved family. After the customary condolences and eulogies of her brother, Mayan Khatun proposed an arrangement whereby they could maintain their previous comfortable life – Mir Said Beg would like to heal the family feud by marrying Ismail's daughter Wansa, then aged sixteen.[35]

After much deliberation among the family and a brief period when their allowance was cut off, it was finally agreed that Wansa would give up her plans for a career in medicine and would marry Said Beg. The wedding took place in 1934 and Wansa moved to the new Stone Palace at Baadri to become the official consort of the Mir. (Since 1929 he had married four more wives, including Khokhe and her sister, daughters of Naif Beg.)

The marriage between Wansa, a young American-trained student, and the spoiled, besotted Mir was blessed by one child — a daughter, Leila, who died when only one year old. But Said Beg's inattention to his new wife was offset by the kindness of the shrewd Mayan Khatun, who recognized in Wansa some of her own strengths, so lacking in her son. While the Mir stayed secluded in his castle, the young Khatun and her mother-in-law travelled around the villages in the Sheikhan. At the autumn festival Mayan Khatun herself picked out Wansa's bejewelled ceremonial robe.

Henry Field, a Chicago anthropologist who visited Baadri in June 1934, noted that Wansa, 'a beautiful girl in her teens...is medium small with dark brown hair and eyes and a light complexion. Her face is almost round and her bizygomatic breadth tends to be wide'.

The Mir, categorized as 'a small-boned individual with an oval face, a straight nose, and brown hair and eyes', possessed one unusual feature; the end of his straggly beard was twisted into a long curl terminating in a point. Like other travellers, Field remarked that 'the quiet, sad expression in his large dark brown eyes' lacked the typical Yezidi sparkle. He concluded that the Mir's 'vitality is low and his mind is no longer keen', adding that 'his disposition is inclined to be morbid and his sense of humor very restrained'.

Field and his party were conversing after dinner with Said Beg and Wansa when:

> much to our amazement and delight, the mother of the Mir arrived. She was an austere looking woman, tall and wearing a veil similar to that of nuns. Her face alone was exposed, while her head was draped in a white cloth which encircled her face and dropped in a long, loose fold over her shoulders and back. Her dark blue robes hung to the ground. From eyes penetrating and cold, she looked upon us with suspicion... . She asked us a number of questions about the outside world and as a result kept us in conversation for some time. Meanwhile, Wansa and the Mir sat by, languidly watching the scene.[36]

The outside world, seemingly recast by the victorious British and French, was changing once again. Britain, committed to a long range plan to shift power to local authorities throughout the empire, had withdrawn all of its ground forces from Iraq by 1929 (though some Royal Air Force squadrons remained). In Baghdad the rulers of the new state, independent since 1932, moved rapidly to build up an army of their own. In 1934 universal conscription was enacted in Iraq.

The Yezidis in the Jebel Sinjar demanded to be exempted from the new conscription law, or at least to be allowed to serve in a purely Yezidi unit. Their pleas were rejected and as the time approached for registration the tribesmen pondered whether to obey Mir Said Beg's advice to be patient or follow Daud el-Daud's call to arms.

Meanwhile the Baghdad government prepared to enforce the law. In September 1935 a brigade of Iraqi troops, supported by airplanes, artillery and armoured cars, occupied the mountain. The only resistance came from the Mihirkan tribe. After a short encounter the rebels ran out of ammunition; Daud, wounded, escaped across the border into Syria. Courts martial sat for several weeks and adjudicated over 400 cases. Nine of the ring-leaders were hanged and more than 300 received prison sentences ranging from ten years to life. (In the following year many of these prisoners were released.)[37]

Calm prevailed at Baadri. Mayan Khatun's authority over the Jebel Sinjar had been enhanced by the deaths of Hammu Shiru and Ismail Beg and the flight of the turbulent Daud el-Daud. But in the winter of 1937–38 word came that fresh trouble was being fomented in the Sinjar by Ismail's son, the seventeen-year-old Yezid Khan Beg whom Schütz had once seen learning the Yezidi beliefs and traditions by his father's knee.

Wansa was in her room at the palace one evening early in 1938 when Mir Said Beg came in with tears in his eyes. He told her that he had just left a meeting that had discussed Yezid Khan's alleged conspiracy to set himself up as ruler of the Sinjar. A decision had been taken that Wansa's brother should be killed.

Said Beg told Wansa that he could do nothing to change what had been decided, but promised to let her know the outcome since he would be the first to hear of Yezid Khan's death.

'No!' cried Wansa, pulling out a revolver from beneath her pillow. 'He will hear that you have died first!' She fired five times. The first two shots hit him in the left leg and the left arm; the others went wild.

In the confusion Wansa's Armenian chauffeur Hagop assisted her to escape in her Buick to Mosul and thence to Baghdad, where a hiding place was found for her by Hagop's family, whom Ismail had rescued years before.

Said Beg recovered from his wounds, but the hunt was on for Wansa. The chauffeur was tortured but would not reveal where she was. After a while she managed to get across the border into Syria disguised as a nurse and made her way to Aleppo, where she found shelter among the Yezidi tribesmen living in the villages around the monastery of St Simeon Stylites. Later she was granted permission by the French to stay in Aleppo.

The Second World War started as one more chapter in the history of conflicts among the great powers of Europe, opening appropriately with a partition of Poland between Germany and Russia. On this occasion Turkey shrewdly chose neutrality; so did Iraq. At that time one of the leading Iraqi politicians was Rashid Ali el-Gilani, a descendant of Sheikh Adi's Sufi friend Sheikh Abd el-Qadir. He was an old friend of Ismail's and allowed Wansa to return to Iraq and live under official protection in Baghdad.[38]

The year 1940 saw Germany victorious in western Europe; France, unconquered in the First World War, compelled to lay down arms; and Britain girding to defend its shores. In the spring of 1941 the Germans overran the Balkans and forced a British relief expedition to withdraw to Egypt. The Iraqi premier Rashid Ali, over-impressed by the German sword and underrating Britain's strength in India and the Persian Gulf, challenged the former suzerain's troop transit rights in Iraq. In the space of thirty days British forces had reoccupied Iraq, where they stayed until 1947.[39] Wansa, now divorced from Said Beg, converted to Islam and remarried to a Syrian doctor, was put in an internment camp.

Said Beg never took another wife. On 28 July 1944 the Mir was in Mosul with Khokhe. That evening he was invited to a 'soirée' at the Kawkab es-Sharq ('Star of the East') Hotel, where according to Damluji 'he died amongst people with whom the Yezidi faith forbade him to associate'.[40]

The presence of Mayan Khatun, now in her seventies, pervaded the gatherings convened to appoint a successor to the deceased Mir. Her candidate was the thirteen-year-old Tahsin Beg, son of Said Beg by Khokhe. Mayan pointed out that, although young, he was better born than his brothers, whose mothers were either Basmariyas or came from a clan of sheikhs. She called attention to his alert, intelligent personality and offered to serve as regent until he came of age. Suwaru Beg, brother of Leachman's namesake, was supported by one faction, but in the end it was agreed that Tahsin Beg should be the Mir.[41]

Meanwhile, the Second World War had involved every major power, but the decisive battles were fought far from the Yezidi homelands. When it was all over, the British and French occupation forces withdrew from Iraq and Syria, leaving local governments in charge. In Europe and in other parts of Asia millions had died, but this time for once the Asiatic territories that had been ruled by the sultans were spared. The Yezidi communities in Iraq, Syria and Transcaucasia emerged intact.

The years of Mayan Khatun's second regency were prosperous and uneventful. In 1948 the princely revenues aggregated 8185 Iraqi dinars (£8,185). The Sinjar sanjak yielded 4,000 dinars a year, the Sheikhan sanjak 1,500 dinars. The Mir's revenues from alms collected at the Sheikh Adi mausoleum amounted to 1,500 dinars, those from Sheikh Shems ed-Din's shrine and the White Spring 500 dinars apiece. The balance was derived from offerings at other shrines.[42]

On 25 May 1949 Sadiq Damluji, whose association with the Yezidis now covered more than forty years, completed his 500-page book on the community. It included a memorable tribute to Mayan Khatun:

> She is now seventy-five years old and I remember seeing her in her youth when she was beautiful and attractive. [Details of her ancestry are given.] She married her cousin Mir Ali Beg at the age of eighteen and after his death she was regent for their son Mir Said Beg and later for his son Tahsin Beg, who became Mir at the age of thirteen. Her genius and ability were first revealed during Ali Beg's lifetime, when she shared the duties of government after comforting him in their days of trial and sufferings and joining him in the three years of exile in Sivas imposed on him by the Ottoman government.
>
> She is wise, intelligent and far-sighted and is feared and respected by her people. Her power over them is such that none dare oppose her; everyone is awed by her presence and nervous when she is away. She is arrogant, proud and vain, but when one meets her the grandeur and nobility of her character shine through.
>
> She is an extreme pessimist, trusts nobody, and despite her large income she is so tight-fisted that not a penny slips from her grasp. She dislikes and despises the men in the princely family. Sly, deceitful and perfidious, she is capable of murderous cruelty to her adversaries.
>
> At this time she is the effective ruler who gives and takes away, rewards and withholds, allows and forbids as she deems best. It is hard to imagine how things will be when she is dead, considering that she is approaching the end of her life and everything about her is old except her mind.

The author of these lines died in 1958, the same year that a revolution overthrew the regime established by the British in Iraq. Mayan Khatun did not live to see the birth of the new era. She died on 31 December 1957 at the age of eighty-three.[43]

Wansa, her niece and onetime daughter-in-law, endured many tribulations (including a false report that she had been killed)[44] before she was reconciled with her mother and her brothers and sisters. By that time she had moved to Cairo where, widowed since 1968, she raised her children and still attends social occasions at the Lions Club and elsewhere with her younger daughter, named Mayan.

Chapter Thirteen

The Yezidis in Transcaucasia

The origins of the Yezidi community in the Soviet Union date back to the conquest of Transcaucasia by the czars. In 1801 the last king of Georgia bequeathed his country to Russia and in 1828 the province of Erivan (spelled Yerevan since 1936) was ceded by Persia. Some minor districts were gained by Russia from the Ottoman empire in 1829.

When the Russian army withdrew from Anatolia after the 1828–29 war, their Yezidi ally Hasan Aga, chief of the Hasanli tribe,* was permitted to move his tribesmen and their flocks from their old encampments on the southern slope of Mount Ararat to a new home in the province of Erivan. In the summer they would graze their flocks on the northern slope of Ararat; in the winter they lived near Surmalu on the right bank of the Aras river. A report published in 1840 by the Russian Finance Ministry listed sixty-seven Yezidi families comprising 324 souls.[1]

Count Paskievitch, the Russian commander in the wars against Persia and the Ottoman empire, was appointed viceroy of Poland in 1831. He took with him his personal guard of mounted tribesmen recruited from the villages of Transcaucasia. One of these cavalrymen, a Yezidi from Surmalu, was cited in news reports for his feats of horsemanship at the combined Russian–Prussian manoeuvres held at Kalisz in September 1835 in the presence of Czar Nicholas and his father-in-law King Frederick William III. The rider was later invited to Berlin as a guest of the Prussian army — the first Yezidi to visit Western Europe.[2]

In the 1830s, when Reshid Pasha was subduing the Kurds in Anatolia, a number of Yezidis escaped across the border. The Armenian archimandrite

* See p. 62.

Ghazar Ter Ghevondian, who had vainly tried to educate Mirza Aga's children in Redwan,* also made his way to safety in Erivan, where he obtained a job in the district school.[3]

The principal of the school in Erivan was Khachatur Abovian, a pioneer of modern Armenian literature, born in 1805 when the province still belonged to Persia. At the time of the Russian annexation in 1829 he was serving as a deacon in the monastery at Echmiadzin. In September of that year he was assigned to accompany the German explorer Friedrich Parrot on the first Russian-sponsored expedition to Ararat. When the climbers reached the summit on the third attempt, Abovian dug a hole in the ice and erected a wooden cross facing north. Subsequently Parrot arranged for Abovian to study at the Baltic university of Dorpat (now Tartu), where the explorer taught. After returning to Transcaucasia, Abovian was appointed head of the Erivan school in 1843.

In the summer of that year he was visited by two German travellers. The Bavarian Moritz Wagner arrived in May after visiting Lake Sevan; Abovian joined him on a tour of the province of Erivan and thereafter corresponded with him regularly. In August Abovian spent a few days escorting the Prussian agronomist Baron August von Haxthausen around the province; a visit was paid to the Hasanli encampment, where they met the new chief Timur Aga, son of Hasan Aga, and exchanged pleasantries with the rider from Count Paskievitch's guard. They were told that there was a second Yezidi community in Transcaucasia, which they did not visit.[4] (In 1855 a Russian army report identified a Yezidi settlement of some 340 souls, headed by Khalil Aga, in the Sardarabad district on the left bank of the Aras river.)[5]

In 1844 Prince Mikhail Vorontsov was appointed viceroy of the Caucasus. One of his first actions was to convoke the Kurdish and Turkish chieftains to a banquet in Tiflis (known as Tbilisi since 1936). Among them was Timur Aga, whose fiery red turban stood out among the black cassocks of the Armenian prelates and the white turbans of the Turkish mullahs. When the chief returned to his tribe with a handsome gift from the viceroy, Khachatur Abovian, by now a trusted friend of the Yezidis, was invited to attend the tribal feast.[6]

Abovian's literary work dealt mainly with the Armenian people and its sufferings during the Russo–Persian wars. But he also wrote about the Kurds, paying special attention to the Yezidis based on his own knowledge and what he learned from his colleague from Redwan. Among other aspects of their religious life he noted the periodic visits from the bearers of the sanjaks from Lalish. The historic friendship between Yezidis and Armenians, as well as

* See p. 61.

many customs common to both communities, led him to believe that the Yezidi religion derived from a tenth-century heresy within the Armenian church.[7]

One morning in April 1848 Abovian left his boarding house to go to the school. He was never seen again and the mystery of his disappearance remains unsolved.

Abovian's article on the Yezidis was published a few days before he vanished. Moritz Wagner's report, based largely on material supplied by Abovian, appeared in 1852. Haxthausen's account of his travels was published in 1856. Thereafter the minuscule Yezidi community in Transcaucasia enjoyed twenty years of obscurity. (During the Crimean war the 1855 order of battle of the Russian army on the Caucasian front included a troop of Yezidi horsemen — presumably unaware that their Mir was supporting the Ottomans — as part of the Alexandropol division commanded by the viceroy, General Count N. N. Muraviev, but their battle record is unknown.[8])

The benefits and burdens of bureaucratic rule were extended to the Yezidis in the 1860s when the czar promulgated a series of decrees that abolished serfdom and limited the authority previously wielded by tribal chiefs in Transcaucasia.

In 1874 the governor of Erivan province was asked to rule on a request from the religious leaders of the Sunni Moslems that they should be allowed to collect tithes from the local Kurds. When he learned that most of the Kurds in his province were Yezidis, he denied the Moslems' request and initiated an 'ethnographico-juridical survey' of the Yezidis that ultimately ran to sixty-four pages when published in 1891 by the Caucasian branch of the Imperial Russian Geographical Society. The author of the study, completed in 1884, was an Armenian jurist, Solomon Adamovitch Yegiazarov.[9]

On the eve of the 1877–78 war the Hasanli tribe still grazed their flocks on the northern slopes of Ararat and wintered in Surmalu. At the time of Yegiazarov's study their chief was Hasan Aga, son of Timur Aga, described by another visitor as 'a handsome, well-built man with a fine, expressive face, tidy and well dressed'. A junior branch of the tribe led by Khalil Aga grazed the slopes of Mount Aragats.[10]

In the summer of 1877 Russian forces commanded by General Ter Gusakov captured Bayezid and advanced into the Eleşkirt plain. A few weeks later the threat of an Ottoman counter-attack obliged Ter Gusakov to retreat; a mass of civilians followed him to safety across the border, including some 3,000 Yezidis led by Ali Beg, nephew of Mir Mirza Beg. After the war they were resettled in the Alexandropol district. With the inclusion of these new immigrants Yegiazarov calculated that there were around 8,000 Yezidis in the Erivan province in 1877.[11]

Another migration occurred between 1879 and 1882, when the Sipki tribe of Yezidis, encountered by Justin Perkins in 1837 and now led by their chief Omar Aga, moved westward from the Ottoman-held Bayezid area to the Kagizman district in the province of Kars, recently ceded to the Russians. Within a few years they had established fourteen villages inhabited by 1733 souls.[12]

The imperial census of 1897 (the first ever conducted) enumerated a total of 14,726 Yezidi subjects of the czar. Tabulations by the viceroyalty indicate that by the beginning of 1912 their numbers had risen to 24,508 – over 17,000 in the province of Erivan, 2,000 in and around Tiflis and over 5,000 in the provinces annexed in 1877. Four years later the Yezidi population in Transcaucasia was shown as 40,882; most of the increase was in the annexed provinces, but the Yezidis in Tiflis had risen to 4,697.[13]

For some years Swedish Protestant missionaries had been working in Transcaucasia, mainly among the Armenians. Around the turn of the century they began to notice Yezidis in Tiflis, living in shanties outside the city and coming in every day to seek casual work. The Swedish Female Missionary Workers took a special interest in their welfare and arranged social gatherings with Armenian helpers serving as interpreters. No effort was made to proselytize the Yezidis, but one convert was reported in 1913.[14]

Ismail Beg's visit to Transcaucasia in 1908–9 and his effort to unite the Yezidi communities under the protection of the Armenian church have been described in an earlier chapter. The viceroy accepted Ismail's recommendation to appoint the Surmalu headman to be the leader of the Yezidis in the Caucasus.[15] The code of conduct promulgated by Ismail at Igdir appears to have been enforced; a Russian translation of the Kurdish original reached the hands of the German orientalist Adolf Dirr, who translated it into German and published it in an Austrian magazine in 1919. It is not clear to what extent the Armenian catholicos' educational programme was achieved.[16]

During the first three years of the First World War military operations on the Caucasian front took place on Ottoman soil and, to a minor extent, in the northwestern provinces of Persia. But at the end of 1917 the Russian revolution and the new government's peace appeal brought about a mass exodus of Russian soldiers to their homes. The front line was thinly held by Armenian regiments of the Russian army, too weak to prevent the Ottomans from reoccupying the territory lost in the previous three years.

The peace treaty with Russia, signed at Brest-Litovsk in March 1918, enabled the Ottomans to take over the province of Kars despite resistance by the Armenian units now reporting to a newly formed government in Erivan. By the end of April Ottoman troops had taken Sarikamish and Kars and had reached the 1877 frontier along the Arpa Chai tributary of the Aras river.

The Yezidis in the province of Kars, unwilling to revert to Ottoman rule, joined the flood of civilian refugees seeking sanctuary in Georgia and Armenia.[17]

In May 1918 the Ottomans crossed the Arpa Chai to wage a brief war against the Erivan republic. One column seized Alexandropol and advanced north of Mount Aragats (where eighty Yezidis were killed at Kurdsky Pamb) toward the Transcaucasian railway line to Baku. Another column moved southeast along the left bank of the Aras river to secure the newly completed line to Tabriz.

At Sardarabad (now Hoktemberian) the southern column was checked by an Armenian force, 4,000 strong including 700 Yezidi horsemen. A few days later Armenians and Yezidis repulsed the northern column at the Bash-Aparan defile on the slopes of Mount Aragats. But in the first week of June an armistice was arranged whereby the Ottomans could use the key railways but would leave Erivan and Echmiadzin in Armenian hands.[18]

Five months later the Ottoman surrender changed everything. British troops landed in Transcaucasia to verify the Ottomans' withdrawal and enabled the Armenians to reoccupy Kars. Supplies of food arrived from America to relieve the sufferings of local and refugee families. Elections were held in mid-1919 for an Armenian parliament; one seat was allocated to a Yezidi representative, Yusuf Beg Timurian from Surmalu.[19]

The British occupation of Transcaucasia was brief. Baku was evacuated in August 1919 and the last British troops left Batum in July 1920. The vacuum was filled by Russia; troops of the new Red Army, hardened in civil warfare, occupied Baku in April 1920 and threatened the defenceless republics of Armenia and Georgia.

In the autumn of 1920 the governments of Turkey and Russia reached an understanding about Transcaucasia. Turkish troops prepared to recover once again the provinces lost in 1877. A Soviet appreciation of the forces available to the Erivan government in October 1920 noted that the infantry was untrained and the cavalry below par, except for a Yezidi squadron of three officers and 200 troopers in Echmiadzin under a commander named Shakhbagov.[20] The Turks reoccupied Sarikamish, Kars and Alexandropol. In December the Armenians capitulated, but meanwhile a communist government had been installed in Erivan. Red Army troops took over the republic in March 1921, at which time a definitive peace treaty between Turkey and Russia was signed.

The terms of the 1921 treaty enabled the Russians to retain Batum and regain Alexandropol (renamed Leninakan in 1924), from which point the frontier followed the course of the Arpa Chai to its confluence with the Aras and thence eastward along the Aras to the Persian border. One result of the treaty was to give Turkey the whole of Mount Ararat and the towns of Igdir and Surmalu south of the Aras river.

The frontier, as so rectified, has endured for over sixty years. The Yezidis in the Surmalu district were resettled by the Soviet authorities in villages on the southern slope of Mount Aragats abandoned by Moslem Kurds and Turks.

Yusuf Beg, identified in one account as head of the only Basmariya family in Transcaucasia, fled to Persia after the Red Army takeover, but returned in 1923 and resumed his position as chief of the Yezidis on Mount Aragats.[21]

Over the years the Yezidis have developed a close attachment to Mount Aragats, the highest peak in Soviet Transcaucasia. Although the earliest record of Yezidi settlement on its slopes dates only from the middle of the nineteenth century, local traditions carry much farther back.

In the mid-1920s the Armenian writer Marietta Shaginian (one of Lenin's favourite authors) was told by a Yezidi from the Hasanli tribe that in the eighteenth century one of his ancestors named Mir Choban Aga Beg brought the tribe from the Ottoman province of Van to Mount Aragats, then under Persian rule. After a while they moved to Georgia, but were oppressed by King Irakli (Heraclius) II, who reigned from 1762 to 1798, and consequently returned to Mount Aragats.

More solid yet more enigmatic is the mute testimony of the half-dozen painted stone statues of horses, 4ft 3ins high with clearly outlined bridles, saddles and stirrups, that stand at the cemetery outside the village of Hondaghsag on the western slope of Mount Aragats. The Yezidi villagers believe that their ancestors erected the statues to guard the tombs of the horses' former masters. First observed by Marietta Shaginian and photographed in 1967 by an Italian/Soviet Armenian expedition (see Plate 23), the horses are thought by Soviet experts to be about 300 years old, possibly of Armenian workmanship. Other explorers have noted resemblances to statues of bulls and sheep in ancient cemeteries at Julfa, farther down the Aras river, and at Khosrowa on the northwestern shore of Lake Urmia.[22]

There is no confirmation of the Hondaghsag villagers' claim that the horse statues are of Yezidi origin. But Yezidis had lived in the general area since the middle of the sixteenth century, when a Persian shah confirmed the title of the Dunbeli tribe to the lands around Khoi, immediately north of Lake Urmia. Most of this tribe later converted to Islam and in 1905 a Russian traveller located only one Yezidi settlement in northwestern Persia — the village of Jebbarlu, with twenty-five houses in all.[23] The memory of this once thriving branch of the Yezidi community lives on in the ceremonies at Lalish, where homage is still paid to the long-idled sanjak of Tabriz.

The 1926 census showed 14,523 Yezidi Kurds living in the Soviet Union — 12,237 in Armenia, 2,262 in Georgia and 24 elsewhere. In Armenia they constituted 80 per cent of the Kurdish population; in Georgia they were 22 per cent.[24]

The Yezidis in Armenia maintained their tribal structure and pastoral way of life. But the land nationalization decree promulgated in 1920 enhanced the power of government officials, who encouraged the Yezidis to settle in year-round villages and allocated land rights to the prejudice of the tribal chiefs. Yusuf Beg was deprived of his position as chief and was pensioned off in Leninakan. (A Shamir Yusupovitch Timurov of Leninakan, perhaps his son, joined the Communist Party in 1924 and had a meritorious political and military career.)[25]

Throughout these difficult years the Yezidi religion was kept alive by seven kawals who had come to Transcaucasia with the Muscovy sanjak in 1914. When war closed the Ottoman frontier they scattered among the Yezidi communities in the provinces of Tiflis, Erivan, Alexandropol, Baku and Batum. Their leader Kawal Hussein and the sanjak were sheltered in a village in the province of Alexandropol.

After the war was over the kawals started sending letters and telegrams to Mir Said Beg. But no reply came back and they concluded that, except for Transcaucasia, the entire Yezidi community had perished in the war.

After the Communist takeover the kawals began to realize that the Soviet authorities were preventing their letters from going out of the country. Not until 1926 were they able to get word through to Baadri that they were still alive. In 1927 two more kawals set off to retrieve the survivors and bring back the sanjak. They disappeared without a trace.

Finally, a letter reached Baadri from Kawal Hussein, confirming that five of the 1914 group and both of the 1927 group were alive but unable to leave the Soviet Union. Mayan Khatun and her son appealed to the British authorities for help. The moment was ill-timed, as Britain had just severed diplomatic relations with the Soviet Union. But the Norwegian government, which handled British interests during this period, was able to obtain permission for the kawals to leave the country with the Muscovy sanjak. They travelled by sea to London and finally reached Iraq in 1929 after an absence of fifteen years and a journey of 11,000 miles.[26]

The first Yezidi collective farm was established in 1928. In contrast with the rest of Armenia and the Soviet Union as a whole, change came slowly; in 1936 over three quarters of the farms on Mount Aragats were still being cultivated by individuals. By 1940, however, it was reported that all of the peasants in the district were 'basically' enrolled in collective farms.[27]

The foregoing statistics relate to the entire Kurdish population of Armenia. Around 1930 the Yezidis lost the status of a distinct ethnic group and were henceforth treated like other Kurds. Religious tithes were abolished and the sheikhs and pirs suffered much hardship. (After the departure of the kawals for Iraq there was no further contact with Lalish.)

Ismail's dream of schools for the Transcaucasian Yezidis was realized in his lifetime, with the Communist authorities in Erivan replacing the Armenian church. To facilitate instruction, the Kurdish alphabet was changed from Arabic to Latin letters in 1928 and to the present Cyrillic letters in 1945.

In Georgia, where they constituted a minority within a minority, the Yezidis retained their lowly status on the fringe of the Tiflis proletariat. The Swedish mission closed down in 1921.

The American anthropologist Henry Field visited Tiflis in September 1934 and met a number of Yezidis, headed by Ahmed Mirazi, at the local Kurd Club. Dr Field was enabled to make anthropometric measurements of fifty-one Yezidi porters. Their leader recalled seeing the Muscovy sanjak on its way back to Lalish in 1928.[28]

The 1959 Soviet census showed 25,627 Kurds living in Armenia, a 76 per cent gain over the number reported in 1926; it may be assumed that most of these belonged to Yezidi tribes. The number of Yezidis in Georgia cannot be determined.

Over the four decades since their inclusion in the Soviet Union the Yezidis had come a long way. Remote from central authority, sheltered by the Caucasus mountains from the 1942 German invasion and benefiting from the toleration enjoyed by Transcaucasian minorities, this small community — a fraction of 1 per cent of the Soviet population — managed to achieve a material and cultural standard of life beyond the dreams of Ismail Beg.

One Soviet ethnographist has commented that, in contrast to other Kurds, the Yezidis remain firmly attached to their traditional social structure of loyalty to the tribe and obedience to the chief. Another observer, writing in 1966, indicated that the Yezidi religion still had followers and that older people in particular showed deep respect for members of the caste of sheikhs. To a greater extent than other Kurds, Yezidis have moved to villages and taken up crop farming.[29]

Among the names of Yezidis who have contributed to the progress of their community over the years, two stand out — one representing the generation that made the difficult transition from Ottoman to Soviet rule and the other a product of the new society.

Arab Shamilov was born in 1897 near Kars, then under Russian rule. As a child he tended flocks in the summer months; during the winter he attended school and learned Turkish, Armenian and some Russian. When the First World War broke out he worked as an interpreter for the Russian army and joined an illegal Communist cell. In 1917 he became the first and for some years the only Yezidi member of the Communist party. During the years of Armenia's brief independence, Shamilov served in the Red Army in the northern Caucasus, where he made the acquaintance of S. M. Kirov (a colleague of Stalin who was assassinated in Leningrad in 1934). In 1924 the Armenian Communists assigned him the task of integrating the local Yezidis into Soviet society.

Shamilov's reminiscences were published in 1931 and re-published in expanded form in 1960.[30] He died in 1978.

Another Yezidi, Samand Aliyevitch Siabandov, born in 1909 near Kars, was brought up in Tiflis where his father was a porter. The family moved to Mount Aragats in 1926. After studying in Leningrad, the son became the representative of his district in the Erivan legislature. During the Second World War he served in the Red Army as a political commissar and distinguished himself in action on many occasions, from the defence of Moscow in 1941 to the battles along the Frisches Haff in East Prussia in the spring of 1945. He returned to civilian life in Armenia with the rank of Lieutenant-Colonel and the coveted title of Hero of the Soviet Union.[31]

His fellow-villager, Pte Afo Makarovitch Chaloyev, and several other Red Army men from the Mount Aragats district took part in the final capture of Berlin. They were the first Yezidis seen in that city since 1835.[32]

In 1972 the Yezidi community in Transcaucasia received a distinguished visitor from abroad in the person of Bayezid Beg, a son of Ismail Beg. Few details are known about his visit, which took place sixty years after his father's eventful tour and forty years after the last kawals left the Soviet Union. But if

Ismail Beg had been alive, he would have learned with pleasure that the Communist authorities in Erivan made special arrangements for the Armenian catholicos Vasgen to welcome the Yezidi prince at the monastery of Echmiadzin.[33]

Epilogue

In the years since Mayan Khatun died the life of the Yezidi community has changed in many ways.

Numerically, the Yezidis have grown from 100,000 in the mid-1950s to 150,000 today. In Iraq there were close to 100,000 in 1977. Around 10,000 Yezidis live in Turkey (some of them working in Western Germany) and perhaps 40,000 in the Soviet Union. Some 5,000 live in Syria.

Education, compulsory but secular, is provided in every country where Yezidis live. The eyes and ears of a new generation are opened to the accumulated wisdom of mankind, sometimes filtered to reflect the culture and philosophy of dominant groups. Military service is now an accepted fact of life.

The Yezidis have not been immune to the political changes of the past quarter century in the Near East — notably the Kurdish insurrections, the Shia and Sunni revivals within Islam and the war between Iraq and Iran. But the structure of Yezidi society still endures. A Yezidi who made the pilgrimage to Lalish in 1981 attended a function in Baghdad, where he saw Mir Said Beg's sons Tahsin Beg, Khairallah Beg and Faruk Beg and his widow Khokhe Khatun.

The Jebel Sinjar still remembers Ismail Beg; his house is now a museum. His eldest son Abd el-Karim (who married one of the Basmariya girls orphaned by Mayan Khatun in 1913) is no longer alive. Yezid Khan Beg, who succeeded his father as head of the Sinjar branch of the Chol family, died in 1982, preceded in 1981 by his brother Bayezid Beg. Another of Ismail's sons, Moawiya Beg, now fills their place in the Jebel Sinjar. The last son, Kokus Beg, named after Sir Percy Cox, lives at Baadri.

The Yezidis have survived many persecutions. Today they still face discrimination in many areas, while the spread of education exposes many to

the more subtle dangers of a secular society. As they enter another century of
their long history, they can remember the days of their forefathers and the
words of an elegy, dictated by Ismail Beg fifty years ago to a descendant of the
Yezidis' old oppressor Bedr Khan Beg:

> O son of man, o thou poor wretched one: this world is
> a house of illusion,
> Like dreams in the night; or like the shade of a tree
> that each day shelters a new friend.
> Where is Solomon, who once held sway? Where is Belkis
> [the queen of Sheba], once so famed?
> Take comfort, they have left this world.
> Where is Solomon the prophet? Where is Belkis,
> who once gleamed with gold?
> Take comfort, they too lie beneath the ground,
> beneath the stones.
> Where is Khidr? Where is Elias? Where is the dervish
> with the string of beads and the staff?[*]
> Take comfort, they are all levelled beneath the ground.
> O son of man, be not greedy in this world;
> gather not gold nor riches;
> The world stays for no one, not even for the prophet of God.
> This world is a land of dervishes; those who walk around
> are but common folk, and the over-weening cannot prevail.
> Where is Hamza? Where is Ali? Where are the saints,
> and where are the prophets?[†]
> They are in their tombs and are turned to dust.
> The grave is deep and dark; it is filled with snakes and ants.
> O Lord, thou lettest two who love one another be sundered.
> Come, my kinfolk, come, we must weep and grieve and sorrow;
> Our loved one's sweet lips will speak no more.
> We weep, but weeping avails not; for the grave and the shroud are our lot.
> Weep no more, lament no more, wipe thy tears away.
> What happens is the work of God, whose deeds are good.
> He blesses what is good and pardons what is bad;
> He heals with time the pangs of an aching heart.

* See p. 38.
† Hamza was Mohammed's uncle. The caliph Ali was the prophet's cousin and also his
son-in-law.

Appendix I

The Yezidi Sacred Books and Sheikh Adi's Hymn

(i) *Kitab el-Jelwa* (The Book of Revelation)

(ii) *Meshaf Resh* (The Black Book)

The two principal sacred books of the Yezidis — the *Jelwa* attributed to Sheikh Adi b. Musafir and the *Meshaf Resh* to his great-grandnepphew Sheikh Hasan b. Adi — were translated into English by Professor E. G. Browne of Cambridge University in the last years of the nineteenth century. Browne's translation was made from a manuscript acquired by Rev Oswald H. Parry, now in the Bibliothèque Nationale in Paris (BN Syr. MS. 324).[1]

An earlier text of the two sacred books (Leeds Syr. MS No. 7) was recently discovered and was translated, with critical analysis, by Professors R. Y. Ebied and M. J. L. Young.[2]

The following translation of the *Jelwa* and the *Meshaf Resh* follows Browne except in certain passages, where I have relied on Ebied/Young. Where a lacuna [...] appears, all of the available texts are corrupt. Browne's spelling has been retained.

(iii) Sheikh Adi's Hymn

For this text — long considered the only authentic Yezidi scripture — I have used the translation published in Layard's *Nineveh and Babylon*.[3] (See p. 106

199

above for the controversy regarding authorship of this translation.)

In 1930 Professor Giuseppe Furlani of the University of Florence published a critical analysis of these texts.[4] This should be read in conjunction with the Ebied/Young analysis cited above.

New texts of the *Jelwa*, the *Meshaf Resh* and Sheikh Adi's hymn were discovered by Dr Henry Field in 1934. English translations of these texts by Dr Anis Frayha of the University of Baghdad were published in 1946.[5]

Kitab el-Jilwa (The Book of Divine Effulgence)
From the book 'Jilwa'

Malak Ta'us existed before all creatures. He sent his servant into this world to warn and separate his chosen people from error: *first*, by oral tradition, *secondly* by this book *Jilwa*, which is not permitted to strangers to read or to look upon.

First Section

I was, and am now, and will continue unto eternity, ruling over all creatures and ordering the affairs and deeds of those who are under my sway. I am presently at hand to such as trust in me and call upon me in time of need, neither is there any place void of me where I am not present. I am concerned in all those events which strangers name evils because they are not done according to their desire. Every age has a Regent, and this by my counsel. Every generation changes with the Chief of this World, so that each one of the chiefs in his turn and cycle fulfils his charge. I grant indulgence according to the just merits of those qualities wherewith each disposition is by nature endowed. He who opposeth me shall have regrets and be grieved. The other gods may not interfere in my business and work: whatsoever I determine, that is.

The Scriptures which are in the hands of strangers, even though they were written by prophets and apostles, yet have these turned aside, and rebelled, and perverted them; and each one of them confuteth the other and abrogateth it. Truth and Falsehood are distinguished by proving them at the time of their appearance. I will fulfil my promise to those who put their trust in me, and will perform my covenant, or will act contrary to it, according to the judgment of those wise and discerning Regents to whom I have delegated my authority for determinate periods. I take note of all affairs, and promote the performance of what is useful in its due time. I direct and teach such as will follow my teaching, who find in their accord with me joy and delight greater than any joy wherewith the soul rejoiceth.

Second Section

I reward and I punish this progeny of Adam in all different ways of which I have knowledge. In this my hand is the control of the earth and what is above it and beneath it. I undertake not the assistance of other races, neither do I withhold good from them; much less do I grudge it to those who are my chosen people and obedient servants. I surrender active control into the hands of those whom I have proved, who are, in accordance with my will, friends in some shape and fashion to such as are faithful and abide by my counsel. I take and I give; I make rich and I make poor; I make happy and I make wretched, according to environments and seasons, and there is none who hath the right to interfere, or to withdraw any man from my control. I draw down pains and sicknesses upon such as strive to thwart me. He who is accounted mine, dieth not like other men. I suffer no man to dwell in this lower world for more than the period determined by me; and, if I wish, I send him back into this world a second and a third time, or more, by the transmigration of the soul, and this by a universal law.

Third Section

I guide without a scripture; I point the way by unseen means unto my friends and such as observe the precepts of my teaching, which is not grievous, and is adapted to the time and conditions. I punish such as contravene my laws in other worlds. The children of this Adam know not those things which are determined, wherefore they oft-times fall into error. The beasts of the field, and of heaven, and the fish of the sea, all of them are in my hand and under my control. The treasures and hoards buried in the heart of the earth are known to me, and I cause one after another to inherit them. I make manifest my signs and wonders to such as will receive them and seek them from me in their due season. The antagonism and opposition of strangers to me and my followers do but injure the authors thereof, because they know not that might and wealth are in my hands, and that I bestow them on such of Adam's progeny as are deserving of them. The ordering of the worlds, the revolution of ages, and the changing of their regents are mine from eternity. And whosoever walketh not uprightly therein, him will I chastise in my own appointed time, and turn back to his former charge.

Fourth Section

The seasons are four, and the elements are four; these have I vouchsafed to meet the needs of my creatures. The scriptures of strangers are accepted by me in so far as they accord and agree with my ordinances and run not counter to them; for they have been for the most part perverted. Three there are opposed to me, and three names do I hate. To such as keep my secrets shall my promises be fulfilled. All those who have undergone tribulations for my sake, will I recompense without fail in one of the worlds. I desire all my followers to be united in one fold on account of those who are antagonists and strangers to them. O ye who observe my injunctions, reject such sayings and teachings as are not from me. Mention not my name or my attributes, as strangers do, lest ye be guilty of sin, for ye have no knowledge thereof.

Fifth Section

Honour my symbol and image, for it will remind you of what ye have neglected of my laws and ordinances. Be obedient to my servants and listen to what they communicate to you of that knowledge of the unseen which they receive from me.

Kitab el-Aswad (*Mas'haf Rish*) (The Black Book)

In the beginning God created the White Pearl out of His most precious Essence; and He created a bird named *Anfar*. And He placed the pearl upon its back, and dwelt thereon forty thousand years. On the first day, Sunday, He created an angel named *'Azazil*, which is *Ta'us Malak* ('the Peacock Angel'), the chief of all. On Monday He created *Darda'il*, which is Sheykh Hasan. On Tuesday he created *Israfil*, who is Sheykh Shams. On Wednesday He created *Jibra'il* [Gabriel], who is Sheykh Abu Bekr. On Thusday He created *'Azra'il*, who is Sajadin. On Friday He created the angel *Shemna'il*, who is Nasiru'd-Din. On Saturday He created the angel *Nura'il*, who is . . . He made *Malak Ta'us* chief over them. Afterwards He created the form of the seven heavens, and the earth, and the sun, and the moon [...] He created mankind, and animals, and birds, and beasts, and placed them in the folds of His mantle, and arose from the Pearl accompanied by the angels. Then He cried out at the Pearl with a loud cry, and forthwith it fell asunder into four pieces, and water gushed out from within it and became the sea. The world was round without clefts. Then He created Gabriel in the form of a bird, and committed to his hands the deposition of the four corners. Then He created a ship and abode therein thirty thousand years, after which He came and dwelt in Lalesh. He cried out in the world, and the sea coagulated, and the world became earth and they continued quivering. Then He commanded Gabriel to take two of the pieces of the White Pearl, one of which He placed under the earth, while the

202

other rested in the Gate of Heaven. Then He placed in them the sun and the moon, and created the stars from their fragments, and suspended them in heaven for an ornament. He also created fruit-bearing trees and plants in the earth, and likewise the mountains, to embellish the earth. He created the Throne over the Carpet. Then said the Mighty Lord, 'O Angels, I will create Adam and Eve, and will make them human beings, and from them two shall arise, out of the loins of Adam, *Shehr ibn Jebr*; and from him shall arise a single people on the earth, the people of 'Azazil, to wit of *Ta'us Malak*, which is the Yezidi people. Then I shall send Sheykh 'Adi b. Musafir from the land of Syria, and he shall come and dwell in Lalesh'. Then the Lord descended to the holy land and commanded Gabriel to take earth from the four corners of the world: earth, air, fire, and water. He made it man, and endowed it with a soul by His power. Then He commanded Gabriel to place Adam in Paradise, where he might eat of the fruit of every green herb, only of wheat should he not eat. After a hundred years *Ta'us Malak* said to God, 'How shall Adam increase and multiply, and where is his offspring?' God said to him, 'Into thy hand have I surrendered authority and administration.' Then he came and said to Adam. 'Hast thou eaten of the wheat?' He answered, 'No, for God hath forbidden me so to do, and hath said, "Thou shalt not eat of it."' *Malak Ta'us* said to him, 'If you eat of it, all shall go better with thee.' But, after he had eaten, his belly swelled up, and *Ta'us Malak* drove him forth from Paradise, and left him, and ascended into heaven. Then Adam suffered from the distension of his belly, because it had no outlet. But God sent a bird, which came and helped him, and made an outlet for it, and he was relieved. And Gabriel continued absent from him for a hundred years, and he was sad, and wept. Then God commanded Gabriel, and he came and created Eve from under Adam's left arm-pit. Then *Malak Ta'us* descended to earth for the sake of our people — I mean the much-suffering Yezidis — and raised up for us kings beside the kings of the ancient Assyrians, *Nesrukh* (who is Nasiru'd-Din, and *Kamush* (who is King Fakhru'd-Din), and *Artimus* (who is King Shamsu'd-Din). And after this we had two kings, the first and the second Shapur, whose rule lasted one hundred and fifty years, and from whose seed are our *Amirs* until the present day; and we became divided into four Septs. To us it is forbidden to eat lettuce (*khass*) — because its name resembles that of our prophetess *Khassa* — and haricot beans; also to use dark blue dye; neither do we eat fish, out of respect for Jonah the prophet; nor gazelles, because these constituted the flock of one of our prophets. The Sheykh and his disciples, moreover, eat not the flesh of the cock, out of respect for the peacock; for it is one of the seven gods before mentioned, and his image is in the form of a cock. The Sheykh and his disciples likewise abstain from eating pumpkin. It is, moreover, forbidden to us to make water standing, or to put on our clothes sitting, or to cleanse ourselves in the privy as do the Muhammadans, or to perform our ablutions in their baths. Neither is it permitted to us to pronounce the name of Satan (because it is the name of our God), nor any name resembling this, such as *Kitan, Sharr, Shatt*; nor any vocable resembling *mal'un, ..., na'l*, or the like. Before [...] our religion was called idolatry: and the Jews, Christians, Muslims, and Persians held aloof from our religion. King Ahab and Amran were of us, so that they used to call the God of Ahab Beelzebub, whom they now call amongst us *Pir-bub*. We had a king in Babel whose name was Bukhti-Nossor [Nebuchadnezzar], and Ahasuerus in Persia, and in Constantinople Aghriqalus. Before heaven and earth existed, God was over the waters in a vessel in the midst of the waters. Then He was wroth with the pearl which he had created, wherefore he cast it away: and from the crash of it were produced the mountains, and from the clang of it the sand-hills, and from its smoke the heavens. Then God ascended into heaven, and condensed the heavens, and fixed them without supports, and enclosed the earth. Then He took the pen in His hands, and began to write down the names of all His creatures. From His essence and light He created six gods, whose creation was as one lighteth a lamp from another lamp. Then said the first god to the second god, 'I have created heaven; ascend thou into it, and create something else.' And when he ascended, then sun came into being. And he said to the next. 'Ascend!' and the moon came into being. And the third put the heavens in movement, and the fourth created the stars, and the fifth created *el-Kuragh* — that is to say, the Morning Star; and so on.

The Hymn of Sheikh Adi — Peace Be Upon Him!

> My understanding surrounds the truth of things,
> And my truth is mixed up in me.
> And the truth of my descent is set forth by itself;
> And when it was known it was altogether in me.
> All who are in the universe are under me,
> And all the habitable parts and the deserts,
> And every thing created is under me.
> And I am the ruling power preceding all that exists.
> And I am he who spake a true saying.
> And I am the just judge, and the ruler of the earth.
> And I am he whom men worship in my glory,
> Coming to me and kissing my feet.
> And I am he who spread over the heavens their height.
> And I am he who cried in the beginning,
> And I am the Sheikh, the one and only one.

And I am he who of myself revealeth all things.
And I am he to whom came the book of glad tidings,
From my Lord who burneth the mountains.
And I am he to whom all created men come,
In obedience to kiss my feet.
I bring forth fruit from the first juice of early youth,
By my presence; and turn towards me my disciples.
And before his light the darkness of the morning cleared away.
I guide him who asketh for guidance.
And I am he that caused Adam to dwell in Paradise,
And Nimrod to inhabit a hot burning fire.
And I am he who guided Ahmed the Just,
And let him into my path and way.
And I am he unto whom all creatures
Come unto for my good purposes and gifts.
And I am he who visited all the heights,
And goodness and charity proceed from my mercy.
And I am he who made all hearts to fear
My purpose, and they magnified the power and majesty of my awfulness.
And I am he to whom the destroying lion came,
Raging, and I shouted against him and he became stone.
And I am he to whom the serpent came,
And by my will I made him dust.
And I am he who struck the rock and made it tremble,
And made to burst from its side the sweetest of waters.
And I am he who sent down the certain truth.
From me [is] the book that comforteth the oppressed.
And I am he who judged justly;
And when I judged it was my right.
And I am he who made the springs to give water,
Sweeter and pleasanter than all waters.
And I am he that caused it to appear in my mercy,
And by my power I called it the pure.
And I am he to whom the Lord of Heaven hath said,
Thou art the Just Judge, and the ruler of the earth.
And I am he who disclosed some of my wonders.
And some of my virtues are manifested in that which exists
And I am he who caused the mountains to bow,
To move under me, and at my will.
And I am he before whose awful majesty the wild beasts cried;
They turned to me worshipping, and kissed my feet.

205

The Yezidis

And I am Adi Es-shami [of Damascus], the son of Moosafir.
Verily the All-Merciful has assigned unto me names,
The heavenly throne, and the seat, and the seven [heavens] and the earth.
In the secret of my knowledge there is no God but me.
These things are subservient to my power.
And for which state do you deny my guidance.
Oh men! deny me not, but submit;
In the day of Judgement you will be happy in meeting me.
Who dies in my love I will cast him
In the midst of Paradise by my will and pleasure;
But he who dies unmindful of me,
Will be thrown into torture in misery and affliction.
I say that I am the only one and the exalted;
I create and make rich those whom I will.
Praise be to myself, and all things are by my will.
And the universe is lighted by some of my gifts.
I am the King who magnifies himself;
And all the riches of creation are at my bidding.
I have made known unto you, O people, some of my ways,
Who desireth me must forsake the world.
And I can also speak the true saying.
And the garden on high is for those who do my pleasure.
I sought the truth, and became a confirming truth;
And by the like truth shall they possess the highest place like me.

Appendix II

Texts of the Yezidi Letters to the Grand Vizier and Sir Stratford Canning

In his despatch No. 23 (29 October 1849) to the British Ambassador in Istanbul, Christian Rassam, vice-consul in Mosul, writes:

> I have the honor also to forward to Your Excellency a letter from the Yezidi sect, which Hussein Bey, Sheikh Naser and other chiefs brought to me yesterday that I would send it to Your Excellency and again express the deep gratitude which they feel for the great kindness which you have shown to their people and especially to Cawal Yusuf and the deputation which went to Constantinople. They have also written a letter to Reshid Pasha [the Grand Vizier] thanking His Highness for the kind assurances which he gave to Cawal Yusuf and expressing their readiness to serve the Sultan but hoping that they may be allowed four or five years exemption from the Nizam and that certain guarantee will afterwards be given to them for their religion. I have advised them to send their letter through the Pasha and they have asked His Excellency to forward it. I hope His Excellency will forward the Yezidis' letter and the Grand Vizier will no doubt be pleased at their expressions of devotion to the Sultan and his Minister.

The letter to the British Ambassador, Sir Stratford Canning, reads as follows:

> Exemplar of the great leaders, pride of the illustrious nobilities, most distinguished and eminent Excellency, of laudable traits,

magnificent Ambassador Bey, may God prolong your life. Amen.
Reporting to Your Excellency that a few days ago Kawal Yusuf
returned to our region and narrated to us about all that he has
observed in Your Excellency of hospitable reception,
encouragement and sincere advice for our welfare — we the Yezidi
community, all of us, extend our gratitude to Your Excellency; it
is due to your bountiful kindness that you extended the hand of
help to us which we never dreamed to gain, and we became certain
of your sincerity towards us when we received the royal decrees in
which the Sublime State ordered that no one may harass our sons
and daughters, and the absolute prohibition on selling us like
slaves, and that the Sublime State is determined to maintain the
protection on our lives and property. Who would be mean or
ungrateful not to appreciate your exceeding graciousness? Nay,
rather, your generosity has been engraved in our hearts.
As for what Kawal Yusuf has told us that the Sublime State has
determined to impose military conscription upon our community,
our answer is that the decree of our master the Sultan is obeyed
and no one of us would disobey his momentous decrees. But, we
hope that the Sublime State would exempt us for five years until
our conditions improve, and our community — which the previous
Viziers used to oppress — may grow. After then, whenever the
Sublime State demands from us military service, our young men
will be ready for the service of the Empire. Only we hope that,
when you levy troops from among us, that you would not merge
our sons with the Muslim troops but distinguish them in separate
units or with the Christian troops and that the authorities would
not threaten their faith. We have nothing whereby we can
reciprocate the favors of Your Excellency, but we always pray to
God to protect you and prolong your life; for your renown in
supporting the miserable and helpless poor is famous. SIR

The letter is dated 14 Zilkade AH 1265 (1 October 1849) and is signed by
the following, reading from right to left:

[Top row] Hussein b. Khartu; Sheikh Khalid b. Sheikh Lashki;
Murad b. Qasim; Ilyas b. Waya; Tamu b. Kal'u; Sheikh Baryan
b. Sheikh Abdal; Sheikh Dalu b. Sheikh Kochek; Sheikh Mirza b.
Sheikh Isma'il; Abdi Mir al-Danadya; Hussein Mir ash-Shaikhan
al-Yazidiya; and Sheikh Nasr Sheikh al-Yazidiya [the two latter
with seals].

[Middle row] Kawal Yusuf b. Kawal Khidr; Kawal Adu b. Kawal
Khidr; Kawal Khalil b. Kawal Hamid; Kawal Ali b. Kawal
Suleiman; Kawal Isma'il b. Kawal Jim; Kawal Mehmet b. Kawal
Khidr; Kawal Murad b. Kawal Yusuf; Kawal Pir Sino b. Pir
Murad; Nafizu b. Kahtahi al-Harahiya; Nu'mo b. Husni; Pir
Husni b. Pir 'Abo; and Salu b. Shalu.
[Bottom row] Ibrahim b. Hoshaba; Rashta b. Jebel Lailun;
Darwish b. Batti; Murad b. Bazu; Sheikh Suleiman b. Isma'il; and
Khidr b. Mehmet.

The copy of the Yezidis' letter to the Grand Vizier bears the same date as the
letter to the Ambassador, but no signatures. It reads as follows:

Exemplar of the exalted nobilities, pride of the Grand Viziers, of
splendid magnanimity, of noble dispositions, Your Excellency the
Grand Vizier, may you always be protected by the grace of the
prophets and messengers of God. Amen.
This petition is presented to Your compassionate Highness:
We, your servants, the Yezidi community, sent to you your servant
Sheikh Yusuf to explain our concerns at the thresholds of your
mercy. And we were very much pleased when we heard that Your
Excellency sympathized with our situation and that you have
interceded on our behalf with our Lord and Master the Sultan
Abdul Mejid, may God render him victorious, so that you will
extend your protection to our faith, our community and our
wellbeing similar to your other subjects, the Christians and the
Jews. We were very glad when Sheikh Yusuf informed us that our
Master the Sultan felt kindness towards us and ordered a ban on
the sale and enslavement of our children and that no one may
interfere in our religious affairs. We, the whole Yezidi community,
extend our thanks and appreciation, when you, Your Excellency,
showed sympathy towards us and recognized us like the rest of
your subjects; we the impoverished simple peasants always pray to
God to favor our Master the Sultan Abdul Mejid, may God
prolong his life and grant him victory over all his enemies and
strengthen the Sublime State. We beseech your compassion that
you look towards us with your most favorable consideration; for
the protection that you have bestowed upon us and upon our faith
was never granted to us before by any of the previous Viziers. In
addition, Sheikh Yusuf informed us that the intention of the
Sublime State is to apply the conscription system upon us; we are

your slaves, and that is an idea we do not shun, knowing that in the past and especially in the reign of Sultan Murad — may God illuminate his tomb with light — we provided military service to His Majesty when he demanded troops from us, and we are always ready at the service of our Master the Sultan, but we desire from your bountiful judgement that you would exempt us from the conscription system for a period of five years, so that our conditions may improve and our community may multiply, which the previous Viziers used to oppress. After that, whenever Your Excellency demands from us military service, our young men would be ready for the service of the Imperial State. We only entreat to the merciful understanding of the Sublime State that when you obtain from us recruits, you would not merge our boys with the Muslim troops, but rather set them aside in separate units by themselves or with the Christian troops, and that no one would threaten their faith. We have long been your subjects; when we were oppressed we assumed we were a neglected herd without an owner, but now we firmly believe that we are faithful subjects loyal to His Majesty our Master the Sultan and we know that if any injustice is inflicted upon us we have a State that would alleviate our distress. And we also used to resemble lost sheep, but now we have a protector and a State that we are proud of. We shall never forget the charitable deeds of our admirable superior His Excellency the illustrious Highness Kamil Pasha [governor of Mosul], who on the day of his arrival to our region showed great pity for our conditions and brought justice to us; his kindness towards us is exceedingly great — we pray to the Almighty that He may keep for us His Majesty our Master Abdul Mejid Khan and protect him and make him victorious over his enemies and perpetuate the Sublime State and give it strength. SIR

Abbreviations

Official and private archives

AE/CPC	Ministère des Affaires Étrangères (Paris), Archives Diplomatiques, Correspondance Politique des Consuls.
Akty	Akty sobranniye kavkazskoyu arkheograficheskoyu kommissiyeyu (Tiflis).
CO	Colonial Office (London).
FO	Foreign Office (London).
IO L/MIL	India Office (London), Military Dept. Records.
IO/L/P & S	India Office (London), Political and Secret Dept. Records.
AP:	Archivio della Sacra Congregazione de Propaganda Fide.
Acta	Acta Sacrae Congregationis.
SOCG	Scritture Originali riferite nelle Congregazioni Generali.
ABC	American Board of Commissioners for Foreign Missions.
BFM, PCUSA	Board of Foreign Missions of the Presbyterian Church in the United States of America.
CMS	Church Missionary Society.

Periodicals

AJSL	*American Journal of Semitic Languages and Literatures.*
BdCh	*Biblioteka dlya Chteniya.*
GJ	*Geographical Journal (London).*
JA	*Journal Asiatique (Paris).*
JAOS	*Journal of the American Oriental Society.*
JRAI	*Journal of the Royal Anthropological Institute of Great Britain and Ireland.*

211

JRAS	*Journal of the Royal Asiatic Society.*
JRGS	*Journal of the Royal Geographical Society.*
MFO	*Mélanges de la Faculté Orientale de l'Université Saint-Joseph (Beirut).*
MH	*Missionary Herald (Boston).*
POC	*Proche-orient Chrétien (Jerusalem).*
QP	*Archbishop's Assyrian Mission Quarterly Papers (London).*
ROC	*Revue de l'Orient Chrétien (Paris).*
RSO	*Rivista degli Studi Orientali (Rome).*
SMOMPK	*Sbornik materialov po opisaniyu mestnostey i plemen Kavkaza (Tiflis).*
SMSR	*Studi e Materiali di Storia delle Religioni.*
ZDMG	*Zeitschrift der deutschen morgenländischen Gesellschaft.*
ZKORGO	*Zapiski Kavkazskovo Otdeleniya Imperatorskovo Russkovo Geograficheskovo Obshchestva (Tiflis).*

Chapter Notes

Chapter 1

1 The geographical and historical background material in this chapter is necessarily selective and should be supplemented by standard textbooks on the Near East, its antiquities and history and on the principal religions of its peoples.

2 The trade routes between Syria and Mesopotamia are described by Douglas Carruthers, 'The Great Desert Caravan Route, Aleppo to Basra', *GJ*, 1918, pp. 157–84, and in his introduction to *The Desert Route to India*, pp. xi–xxxv; also by Frederic D. Harford, 'Old Caravan Roads and Overland Routes in Syria, Arabia, and Mesopotamia', *The Nineteenth Century*, vol. 84, 1918, pp. 97–113; Christina Phelps Grant, *The Syrian Desert*; and Mohamad Ali Hachicho, 'English Travel Books about the Arab Near East in the Eighteenth Century', *Die Welt des Islams*, vol. 9, 1964, pp. 1–206.

3 The British Broadcasting Corporation film *Desert Voyage* records Dame Freya Stark's trip by kelek from Jerablus to the dam in October 1977.

4 *The Letters of T. E. Lawrence*, ed. David Garnett, pp. 116–7.

5 [Helmuth] von Moltke contribution to *Memoir über die Construction der Karte von Kleinasien und Türkisch Armenien*, ed. Kiepert, p. 13.

6 Thomas, Bishop of Marga, *The Book of Governors*, ed. and trans. Budge, vol. 2, p. 575; see also Père J. M. Fiey, OP, *Assyrie Chrétienne*, [vol. 2], pp. 813–4.

7 *Anon. Chronicon Guidi*, ed. and trans. Nöldeke, *Sitzungsberichte der Kaiserlichen Akademie der Wissenschaften in Wien, phil.-hist. Classe*, vol. 128, 1893, appendix 9, p. 22; see also Fiey, 'Les laïcs dans l'histoire de l'Église syrienne orientale', *POC*, vol. 14, 1964, pp. 178–82, and *Assyrie Chrétienne*, vol. 3, pp. 23–8, for details of Yazdin's life and a bibliography.

8 Anon. Guidi/Nöldeke, p. 13.

9 al-Tabari, *Geschichte der Perser und Araber zur Zeit der Sasaniden*, ed. and trans. Nöldeke, p. 291; see also Anon. Guidi/Nöldeke, pp. 24–5.

10 *Acta Martyris Anastasii Persae*, ed. Usener; see also Rev. S. Baring-Gould, *The Lives of the Saints*, vol. 1, pp. 334–41. The tomb of St Anastasius the Persian is at the Abbey of Tre Fontane in the EUR district south of Rome.

11 The Koran, chap. 30; Tabari/Nöldeke, pp. 297–300.

12 Anon. Guidi/Nöldeke, pp. 29–32; Tabari/Nöldeke, pp. 387–90; (Chronique de Séert) *Histoire Nestorienne*, ed. and trans. Scher and Griveau, *Patrologia Orientalis*, vol. 13, 1919, pp. 540, 551–2, 556.

13 Fiey, *Assyrie Chrétienne* [vol. 2], pp. 534–9.

14 Theophanes, *Chronographia*, ed. and trans. de Boor, p. 538.

15 Abu 'l-Faraj al-Isfahani, *Kitab al-Aghani*, cited by Père Henri Lammens, S J, 'Études sur le règne du Calife Omaiyade Mo'awia Ier', *MFO*, vol. 3, part 1, 1908, pp. 308–9.

16 *Continuatio Byzantia Arabica*, cited by Julius Wellhausen, *The Arab Kingdom and its Fall*, p. 168. The principal sources for the reign of Caliph Yezid are Wellhausen, *Arab Kingdom*, pp. 140–69, and Lammens, 'Le Califat de Yazîd Ier', *MFO*, vol. 4, 1910, pp. 233–312; vol. 5, 1911–12, pp. 79–267, 589–724; vol. 6, 1913, pp. 403–92; and vol. 7, 1914–21, pp. 211–44; see also Gernot Rotter, *Die Umayyaden und der zweite Bürgerkrieg (680–692)*, pp. 36–59.

17 Edward Gibbon, *The Decline and Fall of the Roman Empire*, chapter 50.

18 Tabari, *Annals*, cited by Lammens, *MFO*, vol. 5, 1911–2, p. 167.

19 Shihab al-Din Ibn Fadlallah al-'Umari, *Masalik al-absar*, ed. and trans. Quatremère, *Notices et extraits des manuscrits de la Bibliothèque du Roi et autres bibliothèques*, vol. 13, 1838, part 1, p. 317.

20 Tabari, *Annals*, cited by Wellhausen, *Arab Kingdom*, pp. 555–6, and Lammens, 'Le "Sofiânî": Héros national des Arabes Syriens', *Bulletin de l'Institut français d'archéologie orientale du Caïre*, vol. 21, 1922, pp. 133–41.

Chapter 2

1 Contemporary and later references in Moslem literature to Sheikh Adi and his successors have been compiled and analysed by a number of orientalists over the past 100 years, viz:

(a) N. Siouffi, 'Notice sur le Chéikh 'Adi et la secte des Yézidis', *JA*, series 8, vol. 5, 1885, pp. 78–87.

(b) Mustafa Nûrî Pasha, *'Abede-i-iblīs*, trans. with commentary by Dr Theodor Menzel under title *Die Teufelsanbeter, oder ein Blick auf die widerspenstige Sekte der Jeziden*, incl. in Hugo Grothe, *Meine Vorderasienexpedition 1906 und 1907*, vol. 1, pp. 187–93. See also Djelal Noury (his son), *Le Diable promu 'dieu'*, pp. 38–44.

(c) Dr Rudolf Frank, *Scheich 'Adī, der grosse Heilige der Jezīdīs*.

(d) Abbé F. Nau and J. Tfinkdji, 'Recueil de textes et de documents sur les Yézidis', *ROC*, series 2, vol. 10, 1915–7, pp. 149–54.

(e) Ahmad Taimur, *al-Yazidiya wa-mansha nihlatihim*.

(f) Me 'Abbas 'Azzaoui [Azzawi], *Histoire des Yézidis* (Arabic), pp. 28–48;

analysed by Michelangelo Guidi, 'Nuove ricerche sui Yazidi', *RSO*, vol. 13, 1932, pp. 408–25; and by Giuseppe Furlani, 'Nuovi documenti sui Yezidi', *SMSR*, vol. 12, 1936, pp. 150–64.

(g) Roger Lescot, *Enquête sur les Yezidis de Syrie et du Djebel Sindjār*, pp. 19–44, 101–8.

(h) Sadiq Al Damlooji [Damluji], *The Yezidis* (Arabic), pp. 73–114, 445–8, 453–4.

(i) Abd al-Razzaq al-Hasani, *al-Yazidiyun fi hadirihim wa madihim*, pp. 14–20.

(j) Thomas Bois, OP, 'Les Yézidis', *al-Machriq*, vol. 55, 1961, pp. 209–16.

(k) Sa'id al-Diwahji, *al-Yazidiya*, pp. 49–108.

(l) Sami Said Ahmed, *The Yazidis: their Life and Beliefs*, ed. Henry Field, pp. 90–143.

(m) H. Aziz Günel, *The Yezidis in History, the Origins of the Yezidis, their Religious, Political and Social History* (unpublished MS in Turkish).

2 Ibn Khallikan, *Wafayat al-a'yan*, trans. Baron MacGuckin de Slane, vol. 2, p. 198, states that Adi b. Musafir died in AH 557 (AD 1162) or AH 555 (AD 1160) aged over ninety [lunar] years. Ibn al-Athir, *al-Kamil fi 'l-tarikh*, cited by Frank, pp. 45–6, states that he died in Moharrem AH 557 (January AD 1162).

3 'Abd al-Ghani al-Nabulusi, *Hullat al-dahab al-abriz fi rihlat Ba'labak wa 'l-Biqa' al-Aziz*, cited by Prof. G. Flügel, 'Einige geographische und ethnographische Handschriften der Refaîja auf der Universitätsbibliothek zu Leipzig', *ZDMG*, vol. 16, 1862, pp. 657–8; by Mgr I. Isk. Ma'luf, 'Dictionnaire des localités et pays arabes' (Arabic), *al-Machriq*, vol. 57, 1963, pp. 148–9; and by J. M. Fiey, OP, article entitled 'Rites étranges dans la Békaa', *L'Orient-Le Jour*, (Beirut), 12 May 1977. See also Heribert Busse, ''Abd al-Ganī an-Nābulusīs Reisen im Libanon (1100/1689-1112/1700)', *Der Islam*, vol. 44, 1968, pp. 78–9; and E. Robinson and E. Smith, *Biblical Researches in Palestine, Mount Sinai, and Arabia Petraea*, vol. 3, p. 141, cited by Henri Lammens, S.J., 'Le massif du Ğabal Sim'an et les Yézidis de Syrie', *MFO*, vol. 2, 1907, pp. 393–4.

4 Max van Berchem, *Matériaux pour un Corpus Inscriptionum Arabicarum*, part 1, *Égypte*, pp. 148, 151.

5 Berlin MS We 1769 fol. 106a, cited by Frank, pp. 33, 118–9.

6 The author is greatly obliged to Père Fiey for permission to reproduce his photograph of Sheikh Musafir's grave.

7 Ibn Khallikan, *Wafayat*, cited by Siouffi, *JA*, series 8, vol. 5. 1885, p. 79, and by Frank, p. 52.

8 al-Sam'ani, *Kitab al-ansab*, cited by Azzawi, pp. 12–13, and Guidi, *RSO*, vol. 13, 1932, pp. 382, 388–9; al-Shattanaufi, *Bahjat al-asrar*, cited by Lescot, pp. 22–3; Ibn Taimiya, *al-Risalat al-'adawiya*, incl. in *al-Majmu'at al-kubra*, vol. 1, p. 273, cited by Guidi, *RSO*, vol. 13, 1932, pp. 396–7.

9 William [Francis] Ainsworth, 'An Account of a Visit to the Chaldeans', *JRGS*, vol. 11, 1841, p. 23; see also his *Travels and Researches in Asia Minor, Mesopotamia, Chaldea, and Armenia*, vol. 2, p. 182.

10 Shattanaufi, *Bahjat*, cited by D. S. Margoliouth, 'Contributions to the Biography of 'Abd al-Kadir of Jilan', *JRAS*, 1907, p. 269, and Frank, pp. 86–7; Ibn Khallikan/Slane, vol. 2, p. 198.

11 *Op. cit.* vol. 2, p. 198.
12 Ismā'īl Beg Chol, *The Yazīdīs: Past and Present* (Arabic), ed. Zurayk, p. 96.
13 Muhammad Amin b. Khairallah al-'Umari, *Manhal al-awliya*, cited by Siouffi, *JA*, series 8, vol. 5, 1885, p. 80.
14 *Kitab al-manaqib al-shaikh 'Adi b. Musafir* (Berlin MS We 1743) fols. 1a-2b, cited by Frank, pp. 55–6; al-Dhahabi, *Tarikh al-Islam*, cited by Nuri/Menzel/Grothe, vol. 1, pp. 189–90.
15 Berlin MS Pm 8 pp. 120–6, cited by Frank, pp. 42–3.
16 Berlin MS We 1743 fols. 29b–43a; analysed by Frank, pp. 11–19; see also item 8256 in Kâtip Çelebi, *Lexicon Bibliographicum et Encyclopaedicum*, ed. and trans. Flügel, vol. 4, p. 243.
17 Berlin MS We 1743 fols. 45a–47b; analysed by Frank, pp. 19–24.
18 *Op. cit.* fols. 47b–48b; analysed by Frank, pp. 24–6.
19 *Op. cit.* fols. 48b–49b; analysed by Frank, pp. 26–8.
20 *Op. cit.* fol. 27b; trans. and analysed by Frank, pp. 29–31, 108–15.
21 Frank, pp. 10–11, 34–6; Anis Frayha, 'New Yezīdī Texts from Beled Sinjār, 'Iraq', *JAOS*, vol. 66, 1946, pp. 18–19, 39–40.
22 Frank, pp. 10–11.
23 Evliya Çelebi, *Seyahatname*, ed. Cevdet and Âsim, vol. 5, p. 8.
24 Shattanaufi, *Bahjat*, and al-Tadifi, *Qala'id al-jawahir*, both cited by Azzawi, pp. 41–6, and Guidi, *RSO*, vol. 13, 1932, pp. 414–5.
25 *Kitab al-manaqib* (Berlin MS We 1743) fols. 17b–21b, ed. and trans. Frank, pp. 69–77, 128–34.
26 Ibn Tulun, *Daha'ir al-qasr*, cited by Taimur, p. 20; by Guidi, *RSO*, vol. 13, 1932, p. 417; and by Lescot, p. 34; Berlin MS We 1743 fols. 49b–52a; analysed by Frank, pp. 46–50.
27 Ibn Shakir al-Kutubi, *Fawat al-wafayat*, cited by Taimur, p. 19, and Guidi, *RSO*, vol. 13, 1932, p. 417.
28 Dr L. E. Browski, 'Die Jeziden und ihre Religion', *Das Ausland*, vol. 59, 1886, p. 764; see also *ABC Archives* 16.8.4, vol. 1, Assyrian Mission 1850–1859, item 83, Rev. Henry Lobdell letter, 20 December 1852, to Anderson; and Lobdell article, dated 1 December 1852, in *New-York Daily Tribune*, 26 March 1853, p. 5.
29 Kutubi, *Fawat al-wafayat*, cited by Taimur, p. 19; by Guidi, *RSO*, vol. 13, 1932, p. 417; and by Lescot, p. 102.
30 Rashid al-Din, *Histoire des Mongols de la Perse*, ed. and trans. Quatremère, pp. 143–5.
31 Ibn al-Fuwati, *al-Hawadith al-jami'a*, cited by Azzawi, p. 46; by Guidi, *RSO*, vol. 13, 1932, p. 417; and by Lescot, p. 102.
32 The political situation in Anatolia in 1254–7 is analysed by Fikret Işiltan, *Die Seltschuken-Geschichte des Akserāyī*; by Herbert W. Duda, *Die Seltschukengeschichte des Ibn Bibi*; and by Claude Cahen, *Pre-Ottoman Turkey*.
33 Bar Hebraeus, *Chronography*, ed. Bedjan, trans. Budge, vol. 1, p. 425.
34 Rashid al-Din/Quatremère, pp. 297, 299.
35 Bar Hebraeus/Budge, vol. 1, p. 434.
36 Rashid al-Din/Quatremère, p. 323.

37 The fall of the house of Lulu is described by 'Izz al-Din Ibn Shaddad, *al-A'laq al-khatira*, analysed by Claude Cahen, 'La Djazira au milieu du treizième siècle', *Revue des études islamiques*, vol. 8, 1934, pp. 109–28; Bar Hebraeus/Budge, vol. 1, pp. 435–43; Rashid al-Din/Quatremère, pp. 379–89; Ibn 'Abd al-Zahir, *Baybars I of Egypt*, ed. and trans. Sadèque; and al-Maqrizi, *Histoire des Sultans Mamlouks, de l'Égypte*, ed. and trans. Quatremère, vol. 1, pp. 146–83.

38 Bar Hebraeus/Budge, vol. 1, pp. 453–4, 456.

39 *Op. cit.* vol. 1, p. 464.

40 A radically different account of the thirteenth-century history of the Lalish community, contained in a Nestorian manuscript from Alkosh allegedly written in 1452 and re-copied in 1588 and 1880, was published in 1917. Many of the details conflict with the accounts of contemporary chroniclers and the text (which was copied by Alpheus Andrus in 1912 and re-discovered by Père Anastase in 1922) is now generally considered to be a forgery. Ref. Nau/Tfinkdji, *ROC*, series 2, vol. 10, 1915–7, pp. 146–8, 172–200, 225–42; Père Anastase Marie de Saint-Élie, OCD, 'The final word on the origin of the Yezidi religion' (Arabic), *al-Muqtataf*, vol. 61, 1922, pp. 113–9; Bois, *al-Machriq*, vol. 55, 1961, pp. 113–4, 127, 223, 229–30; and Fiey, *Assyrie Chrétienne*, [vol. 2], pp. 806–12.

41 Fiey, *Chrétiens syriaques sous les Mongols*, pp. 66–8.

42 *Kitab al-manaqib* (Berlin MS We 1743) fols 1a–27a; analysed by Frank, pp. 55–83; Shattanaufi, *Bahjat*; analysed by Margoliouth, *JRAS*, 1907, pp. 268–71, and by Frank, pp. 83–7.

43 al-Sakhawi, *Tuhfat al-ahbab*; Maqrizi, *al-Khitat*; and Ibn Fadlallah, *Masalik al-absar*; all cited by Guidi, *RSO*, vol. 13, 1932, pp. 418–9.

44 van Berchem, *Matériaux: Égypte*, pp. 147–52; Mrs R. L. Devonshire, *Some Cairo Mosques and their Founders*, pp. 40–8; K. A. C. Creswell, *The Muslim Architecture of Egypt*, vol. 2, pp. 229–33; *Repertoire chronologique d'épigraphie arabe*, ed. Wiet, items 5041 & 5042, vol. 13, pp. 169–72.

45 Ibn Taimiya, vol. 1, pp. 262–317; analysed by Azzawi, pp. 14–21; by Guidi, *RSO*, vol. 13, 1932, pp. 394–403; and by Lescot, pp. 37–42.

46 al-Sam'ani, *Kitab al-ansab*, cited by Azzawi, pp. 9–12; by Guidi, *RSO*, vol. 13, 1932, p. 381; by Furlani, *SMSR*, vol. 12, 1936, pp. 154–5; and by Fritz Meier, *Der Name der Yazīdī's*, incl. in *Westöstliche Abhandlungen/Festschrift R. Tschudi*, pp. 248–9; al-Shahrastani, *Kitab al-milal wa 'l-nihal*; analysed by Isya Joseph, 'Yezidi Texts', *AJSL*, vol. 25, 1909, pp. 116–7.

47 Taimur, p. 58, cited by Meier, p. 254.

48 Ibn Taimiya, vol. 1, pp. 299–302, cited by Guidi, *RSO*, vol. 13, 1932, pp. 400–2.

49 Abu 'l-Firas Ubaidallah, *Kitab al-radd 'ala 'l-rafida wa'l-Yazidiya*; analysed by Mehmet Şerefettin, 'Yezidiler', *Darülfünun Ilâhiyat Fakültesi Mecmuasi* (Istanbul), vol. 1, no. 3, 1926, pp. 32–5; by Azzawi, pp. 81–3; by Guidi, *Sui Yazidi*, incl. in *Atti del XIX Congresso Internazionale degli Orientalisti 1935-XII*, pp. 560–1; and by Lescot, p. 36.

50 Ibn Hajar al-'Asqalani, *al-Durar al-kamina*, cited by Taimur, pp. 26–7; by Guidi, *RSO*, vol. 13, 1932, p. 419; and by Lescot, p. 106; Ibn Fadlallah, *Masalik al-absar*, cited by Taimur, pp. 25–6, and Lescot, pp. 105–6.

51 Lescot, pp. 44, 225–37.

52 Ibn Battuta, *Travels, A.D. 1325–1354*, ed. Defréméry and Sanguinetti, trans. H.A.R. Gibb, [vol. 2], p. 352.

53 Ibn Fadlallah, *Masalik al-absar*, ed. and trans. Quatremère, *Notices et extraits des manuscrits de la Bibliothèque du Roi et autres bibliothèques*, vol. 13, 1838, part 1, pp. 305–25.

54 Maqrizi, *Kitab al-Suluk*, cited by Frank, pp. 87–92; by Nau/Tfinkdji, *ROC*, series 2, vol. 10, 1915–7, pp. 153–4; and by Guidi, *RSO*, vol. 13, 1932, p. 420.

Chapter 3

1 The primary sources for this chapter have been C. J. Edmonds, *A Pilgrimage to Lalish*; Thomas Bois, OP, 'Les Yézidis', *al-Machriq*, vol. 55, 1961, pp. 109–28, 190–242; E. S. Stevens, Lady Drower, *Peacock Angel*; and Roger Lescot, *Enquête sur les Yezidis de Syrie et du Djebel Sindjār*. See also Ismā'īl Beg Chol, *The Yazīdīs: Past and Present* (Arabic), ed. Zurayk; Sami Said Ahmed, *The Yazidis: their Life and Beliefs*, ed. Henry Field; and Emir Muawwiyyah ben Esma'il Yazidi [Chol], *To Us Spoke Zarathustra*. ... See also sources cited in Note 1 for Chapter 2.

2 'Michele Febvre, C.M.A.', *Specchio, o vero descrizione della Turchia* and *Teatro della Turchia*.

3 P. Domenico Lanza, OP, *Compendiosa Relazione Istorica dei Viaggi*, unpublished MS cited by Bois, *al-Machriq*, vol. 55, 1961, p. 112; P. Maurizio Garzoni, OP, *Della Setta delli Jazidj*, incl. in Abate Domenico Sestini, *Viaggi e opuscoli diversi*, pp. 203–12; French translation by S[ilvestre] de S[acy] entitled *Notice sur les Yézidis*, incl. in M*** [Jean-Baptiste Louis a.k.a. Joseph Rousseau], *Description du pachalik de Bagdad*, pp. 191–210; P. [Raffaello] M. Giuseppe Campanile, OP, *Storia della regione del Kurdistan e delle sette di religioni ivi esistenti*. See also Bois, 'Les dominicains à l'avant-garde de la Kurdologie au XVIIIe siècle', *Archivum fratrum praedicatorum*, vol. 35, 1965, pp. 268–80.

4 August Neander, *Ueber die Elemente, aus denen die Lehren der Yeziden hervorgegangen zu sein scheinen*, incl. in *Wissenschaftliche Abhandlungen*, ed. Jacobi, pp. 112–39.

5 N. Siouffi, 'Notice sur la secte des Yézidis, *JA*, series 7, vol. 20, 1882, pp. 252–68.

6 N. Marr, 'Yeshcho o slove "chelebi"', *Zapiski vostochnovo otdeleniya imperatorskovo russkovo arkheologicheskovo obshchestva*, vol. 20, 1910, pp. 99–151.

7 Lescot, pp. 61–4, 236–8.

8 J. S. Buckingham, *Travels in Mesopotamia*, vol. 2, pp. 107–10; Major H.C. Rawlinson, 'Notes on a Journey from Tabríz', *JRGS*, vol. 10, 1841, p. 92; Austen Henry Layard, *Nineveh and its Remains*, vol. 1, p. 300.

9 Dr L. E. Browski, 'Die Jeziden und ihre Religion', *Das Ausland*, vol. 59, 1886, p. 790.

10 Jeremiah Shamir letter, 28 October 1892, to Rev. A. N. Andrus, cited by Isya Joseph, 'Yezidi Texts', *AJSL*, vol. 25, 1909, p. 247; [Andrus] article, 'The Yezidees',

The Encyclopaedia of Missions (1891 edition), vol. 2, pp. 526–7; some extracts quoted are in fact from the Meshaf Resh; Oswald H. Parry, *Six Months in a Syrian Monastery*, pp. 374–6.

11 Browski, *Das Ausland*, vol. 59, 1886, pp. 764–5, 785–6; Yu. S. Kartsov, *Zametki o turetskikh yezidakh*, reprinted in *ZKORGO*, vol. 13, 1891, pp. 243–7; Parry, pp. 377–80; Abbé J.-B. Chabot, 'Notice sur les Yézidis', *JA*, series 9, vol. 7, 1896, pp. 118, 131; [Ishak of Bartella] MS concerning the Yezidis, part 3, ed. and trans. Mgr Samuele Giamil [Jamil] under title *Monte Singar*, pp. 13–18; Isya Joseph, *AJSL*, vol. 25, 1909, pp. 221–4.

12 Henry A. Homes, 'The Sect of Yezidies of Mesopotamia', *Biblical Repository and Classical Review*, series 2, vol. 7, 1842, pp. 337–8.

13 'Abd al-Razzaq al-Hasani, *al-Yazidiyun fi hadirihim wa madihim*, p. 45; Amir Bayazid al-Amawi, 'The Peacock – Sanjaq Yazid' (Arabic), *Alturath Alsha'bi*, vol. 4, 1973, pp. 57-8; Edmonds, p. 39.

14 Garzoni/Sestini, p. 208 (Rousseau, pp. 201–2).

15 The enigmatic Khidr Elias is discussed by F. W. Hasluck, *Christianity and Islam under the Sultans*, vol. 1, pp. 319–36; by J. M. Fiey, OP, *Assyrie Chrétienne* [vol. 2], pp. 575–8; and by J. P. G. Finch, 'St. George and El Khidr', *Journal of the Royal Central Asian Society*, vol. 33, 1946, pp. 236–8.

16 Hasani, p. 33.

17 Ishak/Jamil, p. 67; Gertrude Lowthian Bell, *Amurath to Amurath*, pp. 277–8; Stevens/Drower, *Peacock Angel*, pp. 197–201.

18 R. Y. Ebied and M. J. L. Young, 'An Account of the History and Rituals of the Yazīdīs of Mosul', *Le Muséon*, vol. 85, 1972, p. 500; the same statement appears in Parry, p. 371. Louis Massignon, 'Al Hallāj: le phantasme crucifié des docètes et Satan selon les Yézidis', *Revue de l'histoire des religions*, vol. 63, 1911, pp. 195–207. See also Peter J. Awn, *Satan's Tragedy and Redemption: Iblīs in Sufi Psychology*, pp. 196–7, and Gertrude Bell, *Amurath to Amurath*, p. 279.

19 Walter Bachmann, *Kirchen und Moscheen in Armenien und Kurdistan*, pp. 9–15 and Plates 14–16; Fiey, 'Jean de Dailam et l'imbroglio de ses fondations', *POC*, vol. 10, 1960, pp. 205–10; and *Assyrie Chrétienne*, [vol. 2], pp. 796–815; Bois, 'Monastères chrétiens et temples yézidis dans le Kurdistan irakien', *al-Machriq*, vol. 61, 1967, pp. 84–100.

20 Hasani, p. 33.

21 H. A. G. Percy, Lord Warkworth, *Notes from a Diary in Asiatic Turkey*, p. 185.

Chapter 4

1 Sharaf al-Din Bidlisi, *Chèref-nâmeh* [Sharaf-nâmeh] *ou Fastes de la nation kourde*, cd. and trans. Charmoy, vol. 1, part 2, p. 28.

2 Shihab al-Din Ibn Fadlallah al-'Umari, *Masalik al-absar*, ed. and trans. Quatre-mère, *Notices et extraits des manuscrits de la Bibliothèque du Roi et autres bibliothèques*, vol. 13, 1838, part 1, pp. 324–5.

3 The author is much obliged to Mr. C. Wakefield of the Department of Oriental Books, Bodleian Library, Oxford, for examining fol. 108v of MS Elliott 332 and providing the relevant information (letter, 12 January 1983, to author).

4 Sharaf-nâmeh/Charmoy, vol. 1, part 2, p. 205; vol. 2, part 2, pp. 128–31.

5 *Op. cit.* vol. 1, part 2, pp. 28, 142.

6 *Op. cit.* vol. 1, part 2, p. 28; vol. 2, part 1, p. 116.

7 *Op. cit.* vol. 2, part 1, pp. 158–77.

8 *Op. cit.* vol. 2, part 1, pp. 66–9.

9 *Op. cit.* vol. 1, part 2, p. 135.

10 *Op. cit.* vol. 2, part 1, pp. 68–71.

11 *Op. cit.* vol. 2, part 1, p. 162.

12 *Op. cit.* vol. 2, part 1, pp. 129–33.

13 *Op. cit.* vol. 2, part 1, p. 163.

14 *Op. cit.* vol. 2, part 1, p. 169; [Jean] Otter, *Voyage en Turquie et en Perse*, vol. 1, pp. 297–8.

15 Sharaf-nâmeh/Charmoy, vol. 2, part 1, p. 165.

16 Evliya Çelebi, *Seyahatname*, ed. Cevdet and Âsim, vol. 4, p. 67, cited by Dr Theodor Menzel, contributor to Hugo Grothe, *Meine Vorderasienexpedition 1906 und 1907*, vol. 1, p. 206.

17 Henry Field, *The Yezidis of Iraq*, incl. in Field and J. B. Glubb, *The Yezidis, Sulubba, and other Tribes of Iraq and Adjacent Regions*, p. 5; Sadiq Al Damlooji [Damluji], *The Yezidis* (Arabic), pp. 20–1, places this revolution early in the eleventh century AH (1592/3–1688/9 AD).

18 Mustafa Naima, *Tarih-i-Naima*, vol. 5, pp. 92–3.

19 Evliya, vol. 4, pp. 65–8, 70, cited by Menzel/Grothe, vol. 1, pp. 204–6, 211.

20 Evliya, vol. 3, pp. 267–78; Naima, vol. 5, pp. 92–7.

21 Evliya, vol. 4, pp. 61–71, cited by Menzel/Grothe, vol. 1, pp. 194–211.

22 Evliya, vol. 5, pp. 6–9.

23 *A Chronicle of the Carmelites in Persia and the Papal Mission of the XVIIth and XVIIIth centuries*, ed. H. G. Chick, vol. 1, pp. 427–8.

24 F. Leandro di Santa Cecilia, Carmelito Scalzo, *Mesopotamia ovvero Terzo Viaggio dell' Oriente*, p. 54; [Ishak of Bartella] MS concerning the Yezidis, part 2, ed. and trans. H. Pognon under title 'Sur les Yézidis du Sindjar', *ROC*, series 2, vol. 10, 1915–7, pp. 327–9. See also J. M. Fiey, OP, *Assyrie Chrétienne*, [vol. 2], pp. 465–6.

25 Père Jean-Baptiste de Saint-Aignan report, 20 May 1669, to Propaganda, incl. in 'Documenti inediti sull' Apostolato dei Minori Cappuccini nel Vicino Oriente (1623–1683)', ed. P. Ignazio da Seggiano, OFM Cap., *Collectanea Franciscana*, vol. 22, 1952, p. 363; *Abrégé des Archives de notre Mission d'Alep depuis l'an 1626 jusqu'en 1757*, unpublished MS pp. 13, 18–24, cited by P. Clemente da Terzorio, OM Cap., *Le Missioni dei Minori Cappuccini*, vol. 5, pp. 70–1, and in his 'Il vero autore del "Teatro della Turchia" e "Stato Presente della Turchia"', *Collectanea Franciscana*, vol. 3, 1933, pp. 384–95. The manuscript of the *Abrégé* was kindly made available to the author through the courtesy of the Bibliothèque Franciscaine Provinciale, Paris. See also Albert Lampart, *Ein Märtyrer der Union mit Rom: Joseph I 1681–1696 Patriarch der Chaldäer*, pp. 85–95.

26 *AP/SOCG*, vol. 239, fols. 228r–238v: Jean-Baptiste report, 4 July 1668, to Propaganda (includes full text of Père Justinien de Neuvy's report on his first visit to the Yezidis). Italian translation in same volume, fols. 23r–35r, was summarized with excerpts in Clemente da Terzorio, *Missioni*, vol. 5, pp. 94–101. Père Jean-Baptiste's report was also summarized in *AP/Acta*, vol. 38, 1669, pp. 192–3. See also 'Michele Febvre, C. M. A.', *Teatro della Turchia*, pp. 349–52 (Milan and Bologna 1683 editions), pp. 265–7 (Bologna 1684 edition), and *Théâtre de la Turquie*, pp. 371, 373.

27 Père Jean Amieu, Superior of Jesuit Missions in Syria and Persia, Syrian report for 1650, dated 16 January 1651, incl. in *Documents inédits pour servir à l'histoire du Christianisme en Orient*, ed. P. Antoine Rabbath, SJ, vol. 1, p. 400.

28 *AP/SOCG*, vol. 239, fols. 2r–7v: Capuchin Mission (Aleppo) report, 1 April 1670, to Propaganda (extracts in Clemente da Terzorio, *Missioni*, vol. 5, pp. 94, 96); *AP/SOCG*, vol. 429, 1671, fols. 154v, 155r: Dupont letter, 7 February 1671, to Propaganda.

29 Jean-Baptiste letter, Easter [6 April] 1670, to Colbert, incl. in *Documents inédits*, ed. Rabbath, vol. 1, p. 512; *AP/Acta*, vol. 39, 1670, pp. 110–2: report by Cardinal Bona, 7 July 1670; *AP/SOCG*, vol. 429, 1671, fol. 158r: Jean-Baptiste letter, 8 November 1670, to Propaganda.

30 *AP/SOCG*, vol. 429, 1671, fols. 154r–156v: Dupont letters, 7 February and 4 March 1671, to Propaganda; summarized in *AP/Acta*, vol. 41, 1671, fols. 220v–222v.

31 John Cartwright, *The Preacher's Travels*, pp. 20–1; summarized in Samuel Purchas, *His Pilgrimes*, vol. 8, pp. 487–8.

32 *AP/SOCG*, vol. 434, 1672, fols. 187r, 187v, 191r: Jean-Baptiste *et al.* letter, 1 June 1671, to Propaganda; summarized in *AP/Acta*, vol. 42, 1672, fol. 71r. See also *AP/SOCG*, vol. 438, 1673, fols. 543r–544r: Père Jean-François Sevin letter, 28 December 1672, to Propaganda; summarized in *AP/Acta*, vol. 43, 1673, fols. 51v–52v.

33 Sir Paul Rycaut, *The History of the Turkish Empire From the Year 1623. to the Year 1677*, p. 93.

34 'Febvre', *Specchio, o vero descrizione della Turchia*, pp. 115–29, and *L'État present de la Turquie*, pp. 318–36; *Teatro della Turchia*, pp. 343–52 (Milan and Bologna 1683 editions), pp. 261–7 (Bologna 1684 edition) and *Théâtre de la Turquie*, pp. 363–73.

35 Fr. René de Nantes, OMC, 'La date de la mort du P. Pacifique de Provins', *Études Franciscaines*, vol. 21, 1909, p. 181; Fr. Edouard d'Alençon, OMC, letter, 13 February 1909, '"Le Sieur Michel Febvre"', *Études Franciscaines*, vol. 21, 1909, pp. 435–8; G. Gabrieli, 'Un Cappuccino Francese del 600 Viaggiatore e Descrittore sagace della Turchia non ancora bene conosciuto', *Il Pensiero Missionario*, vol. 4, 1932, pp. 284–9; Clemente da Terzorio, *Collectanea Franciscana*, vol. 3, 1933, pp. 384–95; Gabrieli, 'Una Rettifica non accettabile', *Il Pensiero Missionario*, vol. 5, 1933, pp. 339–40. See also Bruce M. Landay, *For the Universal Benefit of Christendom*, essay, Department of History, Yale University, 1983.

36 Rycaut, p. 92. See also Klaus E. Müller, *Kulturhistorische Studien zur Genese pseudo-islamischer Sektengebilde in Vorderasien*, pp. 203–4.

37 Cornelio Magni, *Quanto di piu' curioso, e vago Hà potuto raccorre, Nel secondo biennio da esso consumato in viaggj, e dimore per la Turchia*, vol. 2, pp. 394–7, 411.

38 Nointel despatches, 10 August 1674, to Pomponne, cited by Albert Vandal, *L'Odyssée d'un ambassadeur: Les voyages du marquis de Nointel (1670–1680)*, p. 327; and 9 May 1675, to Pomponne, cited by Paul Perdrizet, 'Documents du XVIIe siècle relatifs aux Yézidis', *Bulletin de la Société de Géographie de l'Est*, 1903, pp. 291–2.

39 Henri Lammens, SJ, 'Une visite aux Yézidis ou adorateurs du diable', *Relations d'Orient* (Beirut), 1929, pp. 170–1. The author is obliged to Father Martin J. McDermott, SJ, of the Bibliothèque Orientale, Beirut, for providing a copy of this article.

40 P. Antoine Nacchi, SJ, Superior-General of Syria and Egypt Missions, letter, [circa 1720], to TRP Michelangelo Tamburini, Jesuit General, incl. in *Nouveaux memoires des missions de la Compagnie de Jesus dans le Levant*, vol. 4, p. 44.

41 Chevalier [Laurent] d'Arvieux, *Mémoires*, vol. 6, pp. 362–77. See also W. H. Lewis, *Levantine Adventurer*, pp. 202–3.

42 *De la nation des Curdes Iasidies qu'on appelle Adorateurs du Diable*, anon. MS [circa 1700] incl. in Perdrizet, *Bulletin de la Société de Géographie de l'Est*, 1903, p. 433.

43 'Febvre', *Specchio*, pp. 168–70, and *L'État present*, pp. 437–40; *Teatro della Turchia*, pp. 463–4 (Milan and Bologna 1683 editions), pp. 354–5 (Bologna 1684 edition) and *Theâtre de la Turquie*, pp. 500–3; Carsten Niebuhr, *Reisebeschreibung nach Arabien und andern umliegenden Ländern*, vol. 2, pp. 396–7; Abate Domenico Sestini, *Viaggio da Costantinopoli a Bassora*, pp. 116–7; [Raffaello] M. Giuseppe Campanile, OP, *Storia della regione del Kurdistan e delle sette di religioni ivi esistenti*, pp. 194–200; Rev̄. Horatio Southgate, *Narrative of a Tour through Armenia, Kurdistan, Persia and Mesopotamia*, vol. 2, pp. 287–8.

44 *Ottoman Archives*, Mühimme Defterleri No. 114, p. 229: Palace despatch, 1st ten day period Cemaziyelevvel AH 1115 (12–22 September 1703 AD) to Vezir Hasan Pasha, Governor of Diyarbakir.

45 Muhammad Kazim, *Name-i alamana-i Nadiri*, ed. Miklukho-Maklay, vol. 3, pp. 13, 38–52. See also Laurence Lockhart, *Nadir Shah*, p. 229; and Robert W. Olson, *The Siege of Mosul and Ottoman–Persian Relations 1718–1743*, p. 165.

46 Edward Ives, *A Voyage from England to India*, pp. 317–8; J. S. Buckingham, *Travels in Mesopotamia*, vol. 2, pp. 81–90, 107–10.

47 Damluji, *Imarat Bahdinan al-Kurdiya*; William [Francis] Ainsworth, *Travels and Researches in Asia Minor, Mesopotamia, Chaldea, and Armenia*, vol. 2, p. 197.

48 P. Maurizio Garzoni, OP, *Della Setta delli Jazidj*, incl. in Abate Domenico Sestini, *Viaggi e opuscoli diversi*, pp. 203–12; French translation by S[ilvestre] de S[acy] entitled *Notice sur les Yézidis* incl. in M*** [Jean-Baptiste Louis a.k.a. Joseph Rousseau], *Description du pachalik de Bagdad*, pp. 191–210; Fr. Bernard Marie Goormachtigh, OP, 'Histoire de la mission dominicaine en Mésopotamie et en Kurdistan', *Analecta Sacri Ordinis Fratrum Praedicatorum*, vol. 2, 1895–6, pp. 407–17. See also G. Furlani, 'Maurizio Garzoni sui Yezidi', *SMSR*, vol. 8, 1932, pp. 166–75; and Thomas Bois, OP, 'Les dominicains à l'avant-garde de la Kurdologie

au XVIIIe siècle', *Archivum Fratrum Praedicatorum*, vol. 35, 1965, pp. 274–7.

49 Yasin b. Khairallah al-'Umari, *Zubdat al-athar al-jilaya* and *Ghara'ib al-athar*, cited by Me 'Abbas 'Azzaoui [Azzawi], *Histoire des Yézidis* (Arabic), pp. 119, 121–3 (summarized in Roger Lescot, *Enquête sur les Yezidis de Syrie et du Djebel Sindjār*, pp. 123–4).

50 I. Berezin, 'Yezidy', *Magazin Zemlevedeniya i Puteshestvy*, vol. 3, 1854, pp. 433, 439; English translation by Eugene Prostov entitled *A Visit to the Yezidis in 1843* incl. in Henry Field, *The Anthropology of Iraq*: part 2, no. 1, *The Northern Jazira*, pp. 69, 73. See also Rev. George Percy Badger, *The Nestorians and their Rituals*, vol. 1, pp. 106, 108.

51 Dr E.-T. Hamy, 'Voyage d'André Michaux en Syrie et en Perse (1782–1785) d'après son journal et sa correspondance', *Neuvième Congrès International de Géographie, 1908, Compte Rendu des travaux du congrès*, vol. 3, pp. 370–1; Yasin al-Umari, *Zubdat*, cited by Azzawi, p. 132.

52 Azzawi, pp. 115–29; summarized in Lescot, pp. 123–5; Ismā'īl Beg Chol, *The Yazīdīs: Past and Present* (Arabic), ed. Zurayk, pp. 109–10, 112–3.

53 Sa'id al-Diwahji, *al-Yazidiya*, pp. 226–7. An English translation of the *fetwas* appears in Sami Said Ahmed, *The Yazidis – their Life and Beliefs*, ed. Henry Field, pp. 385–98.

54 Yasin al-'Umari, *Zubdat*, cited by Azzawi, pp. 120–1.

Chapter 5

1 [Raffaello] M. Giuseppe Campanile, OP, *Storia della regione del Kurdistan e delle sette di religioni ivi esistenti*, pp. 56–9, 157–8. See also Thomas Bois, OP, 'Les dominicains à l'avant-garde de la Kurdologie au XVIIIe siècle', *Archivum fratrum praedicatorum*, vol. 35, 1965, pp. 277–80; Constance M. Alexander, *Baghdad in Bygone Days*, p. 125.

2 Me 'Abbas 'Azzaoui [Azzawi], *Histoire des Yézidis* (Arabic), pp. 127–9, cited by Roger Lescot, *Enquête sur les Yezidis de Syrie et du Djebel Sindjār*, pp. 124–5; Sadiq Al Damlooji [Damluji], *The Yezidis* (Arabic), p. 495; M*** [Jean-Baptiste Louis a.k.a. Joseph Rousseau], *Description du pachalik de Bagdad*, p. 99; Mirza Abu Taleb Khan, *Travels*, trans. C. Stewart, vol. 3, pp. 116–7. Ismā'īl Beg Chol, *The Yazīdīs: Past and Present* (Arabic), ed. Zurayk, pp. 110–2; Thomas Bois, OP, 'Le Djebel Sindjar au début du XIXe siècle', *Roja Nu* (Beirut), No. 56, 10 September 1945. The author is much obliged to Père J. M. Fiey, OP, for sending him a copy of this article.

3 Alexander, p. 235; see also Charles Bellino letter, 16 May 1816, to Hammer, incl. in *Fundgruben des Orients*, vol. 5, 1816, p. 48.

4 George Percy Badger, *The Nestorians and their Rituals*, vol. 1, p. 110.

5 Claudius James Rich, *Narrative of a Residence in Koordistan*, ed. Mary Rich, vol. 2, pp. 86–7; Alexander, p. 289; sketch of Lasso faces p. 278; *Erzählungen und Lieder im Dialekte von Bohtan*, ed. Albert Socin, incl. in Eugen Prym and Socin (eds),

Kurdische Sammlungen: Erzählungen und Lieder in den Dialekten des Tûr 'Abdîn und von Bohtan, part a, pp. 226–31; part b, pp. 237–41.

6 Rich, vol. 2, p. 86. The place of Salih Beg in the Chol family tree is unclear. C. J. Edmonds, *A Pilgrimage to Lalish*, pp. 28–9, shows him as a cousin of Mir Hasan Beg belonging to 'the senior branch' of the family, having a son Ali and a grandson Jasim. Damluji, *Yezidis*, p. 32, identifies Salih Beg as the son of Ali and the father of Jasim; but tree facing p. 22 shows Salih Beg as a son of Mir Hasan Beg. Perhaps there was more than one person with the same name.

7 Lucas Injijian, *Ashkhara Kirutiun*, cited by Henry A. Homes, 'The Sect of Yezidies of Mesopotamia', *Biblical Repository and Classical Review*, series 2, vol. 7, 1842, p. 351; by August Neander, *Ueber die Elemente, aus denen die Lehren der Yeziden hervorgegangen zu sein scheinen*, incl. in *Wissenschaftliche Abhandlungen*, ed. Jacobi, p. 122; and by Moritz Wagner, *Reise nach Persien und dem Lande der Kurden*, vol. 2, p. 264.

8 John MacDonald Kinneir, *Journey through Asia Minor, Armenia and Koordistan*, pp. 414–5; Austen H. Layard, *Discoveries in the Ruins of Nineveh and Babylon*, p. 45; Khachatur Abovian, *Die Kurden und Jesiden*, unpublished 1846 article incl. in *Polnoye sobraniye sochineny*, vol. 8, pp. 221–3, 429; M. Wagner, *Reise nach Persien*, vol. 2, pp. 254–5.

9 *Op. cit.* vol. 2, pp. 255–8; Dr H. Jolowicz (ed.), *Polyglotte der orientalischen Poesie*, pp. 628–9; A. J. Ceyp, 'Die Yesidis', *Allgemeine Zeitung*, Beilage no. 204, 2 September 1890, p. 2; Dzhalile Dzhalil, 'Geroicheskiye pesni kurdov-yezidov o sobytiyakh, svyazannykh s pereseleniyem yikh predkov v Rossiyu v 30-kh godakh XIX veka', *Iranskaya Filologiya*, pp. 130–43.

10 Alexander Pushkin, 'Puteshestviye v Arzrum vo vremya pokhoda 1829 goda', *Sovremennik*, vol. 1, 1836, pp. 59–60; English translation by B. Ingemanson under title *A Journey to Arzrum*, pp. 61–2.

11 *Akty*, vol. 7: Arkhiv glavnovo upravleniya Namestnika Kavkazskovo, ed. Berzhe, item 768, pp. 768–9: Count Paskievitch report, 23 September 1828 (O.S.) to Czar. [A. K. Ushakov]. *Istoriya voyennykh deistvy v Aziyatskoy Turtsiyi v 1828 i 1829 godakh*, vol. 1, pp. 358–62; vol. 2, pp. 212–3.

12 Z[ubare]v article in *Tiflisskiye Vedomosti*, 13 April 1829 (O.S.), reprinted in *Russky Invalid*, 1830, pp. 868, 871–2. (French summary in *Nouvelles annales des voyages et des sciences géographiques*, series 2, vol. 19, 1831, pp. 354–5.)

13 *Akty*, vol. 7, item 931, p. 957: Petros Khazarov petition, 17 December 1830 (O.S.) to Paskievitch; *Tsentral'ny Gosudarstvenny Istorichesky Arkhiv* (Leningrad), 1018/3/104/1 and 1r, Major-General Pankratiev report, 12 January 1829 (O.S.) to Paskievitch, cited by Dzhalil, *Iranskaya Filologiya*, p. 132.

14 *India Office* L/P and S/9/91, Robert Taylor letter no. 31 (14 October 1830) to Chief Secretary, Bombay; Charles Rathbone Low, *History of the Indian Navy (1613–1863)*, vol. 1, p. 524; Frederick Forbes, 'A Visit to the Sinjár Hills in 1838', *JRGS*, vol. 9, 1839, p. 418; William [Francis] Ainsworth, 'Notes taken on a journey from Constantinople to Mósul, in 1839–40', *JRGS*, vol. 10, 1841, pp. 527–8; also his *Travels and Researches in Asia Minor, Mesopotamia, Chaldea, and Armenia*, vol. 2, pp. 120–1; Badger, vol. 1, p. 302.

Chapter Notes

15 [E.] de Cadalvène and E. Barrault, *Histoire de la guerre de Méhemed-Ali contre la Porte Ottomane*, pp. 159–92. See also General [Maxime] Weygand, *Histoire militaire de Mohammed Aly et de ses fils*, vol. 2, pp. 32–43.

16 Extract from journal of Dr John Ross, cited by J. Baillie Fraser, *Travels in Koordistan, Mesopotamia, &c.*, vol. 1, pp. 77–8. The career of Kör Mohammed is described by Jemal-eddin Nebez, *Der kurdischer Fürst Mīr Muhammad-ī-Rawāndizī*, Ph D dissertation, University of Hamburg, 1970. See also Mgr Addai Scher, 'Épisodes de l'histoire du Kurdistan', *JA*, series 10, vol. 15, 1910, pp. 119, 132–9; Wadie Jwaideh, *The Kurdish Nationalist Movement: Its Origins and Development*, Ph D dissertation, Syracuse University, 1960, pp. 151–73; and Dzhalile Dzhalil, *Kurdy Osmanskoy Imperiyi v pervoy polovine XIX veka*, pp. 80–114.

17 Damluji, *Yezidis*, pp. 461–3; also his *Imarat Bahdinan al-Kurdiya*, pp. 43–5; Jwaideh, pp. 156–64; Nebez, pp. 56–8; Dzhalil, *Kurdy*, pp. 91–2.

18 Scher, *JA*, series 10, vol. 15, 1910, pp. 134–6; Henry James Ross, *Letters from the East 1837–1857*, ed. Janet Ross, p. 137.

19 Eugène Boré, 'De la vie religieuse chez les Chaldéens', *Annales de la philosophie chrétienne*, series 3, vol. 8, 1843, pp. 99–102; P. Louis So'aya, 'Histoire du couvent de Rabban Hormizd, de 1808 à 1832', ed. and trans. Maurice Brière, *ROC*, series 2, vol. 6, 1911, pp. 354–5; P. Stéphane Bello, *La congrégation de S. Hormisdas et l'église chaldéenne dans la première moitié du XIXe siècle*, pp. 117–8.

20 Scher, *JA*, series 10, vol. 15, 1910, pp. 136–7; Mgr Suleiman Sa'igh, *Tarikh al-Mawsil*, vol. 1, p. 307, cited by Jwaideh, pp. 162–3; Layard, *Nineveh and its Remains*, vol. 1, p. 276.

21 Damluji, *Yezidis*, pp. 23, 469, shows Jasim Beg as the son of Mir Salih Beg. Edmonds, pp. 28–9, shows Jasim as a grandson of Salih. See note 6 above.

22 The Euphrates Expedition is described by Chesney in his *Narrative of the Euphrates Expedition* and *The Expedition for the Survey of the Rivers Euphrates and Tigris*; see also Louisa Chesney and Jane O'Donnell, *The Life of the late General F. R. Chesney*, ed. S. Lane-Poole. Other accounts are Ainsworth, *A Personal Narrative of the Euphrates Expedition*; Pauline, Countess Nostitz, *Travels of Doctor and Madame Helfer in Syria, Mesopotamia, Burmah and other Lands*, trans. Sturge, vol. 1; and Low, *Indian Navy*, vol. 2, pp. 31–50.

23 H. J. Ross, p. viii.

24 T. G. P[inches], biography of Hormuzd Rassam, *The Dictionary of National Biography, Supplement 1901–1911*, vol. 3, pp. 158–9. The author is grateful to Mr. Clive Rassam for supplying certain details of Christian Rassam's life (to be included in his forthcoming biography of Hormuzd Rassam).

25 *Church Missionary Society Archives* CM/M4, p. 65: Rev. C. F. Schlienz letter, 23 May 1832, to Secretaries.

26 Chesney, *Narrative*, p. 555.

27 Roundell Palmer, Earl of Selborne, *Memorials*, ed. Lady Sophia M. Palmer, part I: *Family and Personal*, vol. 1, pp. 262–3.

28 *CMS Archives* CM/M4, p. 65: Schlienz letter, 23 May 1832, to Secretaries.

29 *CMS Archives* CM/M3, pp. 168, 342–3: Rev. William Kruse letters, 20 October

225

1829, to Schlienz and 5 July 1830, to Rev. Peter Brenner.

30 *CMS Archives* CM/M3, pp. 342–3, 563: Kruse letters, 5 July 1830 and 28 July 1831, to Brenner.

31 *CMS Archives* CM/M4, p. 65: Schlienz letter, 23 May 1832, to Secretaries.

32 Dr Helfer's diary entry, 24 March 1836, cited by Nostitz, vol. 1, p. 195.

33 *CMS Archives* CM/M5, pp. 4–5: Brenner letter, 2 January 1835, to Secretaries; H. J. Ross, p. 47.

34 Chesney, *Narrative*, p. 166; Dr Helfer's diary entry, 24 March 1836, cited by Nostitz, vol. 1, p. 195.

35 *CMS Archives*, CM/M5, p. 27: Sir F. C. Ponsonby (Governor of Malta) letter, 9 April 1835, to Sir R. H. Inglis; pp. 45–6: Brenner letter, 9 April 1835, to Lay Secretary; p. 211: Chesney letter, 27 September 1835, to Secretaries; Palmer, *Memorials*, part I, vol. 1, p. 263.

36 Dr Helfer's diary entry, 24 March 1836, cited by Nostitz, vol. 1, p. 195.

37 Lieut.-Col. J. Shiel, 'Notes on a Journey from Tabríz, through Kurdistán, *JRGS*, vol. 8, 1838, pp. 86–8; P.-X. Coste, *Mémoires d'un artiste: Notes et souvenirs de voyages*, pp. 409–10; Helmuth von Moltke, *Briefe über Zustände und Begebenheiten in der Türkei aus den Jahren 1835 bis 1839*, pp. 251–2 (1893 edition).

38 *IO* L/P and S/9/100, Richard Wood report, 3 September 1836. See also A. B. Cunningham (ed.), *The Early Correspondence of Richard Wood 1831–1841*, pp. 90–108; Nebez, pp. 164–9; Major Frederick Millingen, *Wild Life among the Koords*, pp. 185–7; J. B. Fraser, *Travels in Koordistan*, vol. 1, p. 82; Ainsworth, *Travels and Researches*, vol. 2, pp. 322–3; Rev. Thomas Laurie, *Dr. Grant and the Mountain Nestorians*, p. 221.

39 Damluji, *Yezidis*, pp. 467, 498; Layard, *Nineveh and its Remains*, vol. 1, p. 277. The date of Reshid Pasha's attack on the Jebel Sinjar is uncertain, but Richard Wood's letter, 28 June 1836, to Ponsonby cited by Cunningham, p. 95, suggests that it took place after Kör Mohammed's surrender.

40 Ainsworth, *Report of a Journey from Bagdad to Constantinople via Kurdistan (1837)*, incl. as Appendix 11 to Chesney, *Narrative*, pp. 492–525; also his *Personal Narrative*, vol. 2, pp. 287–382.

41 Ainsworth, *Personal Narrative*, vol. 2, p. 325.

42 *Op. cit.* vol. 2, p. 327.

43 *Op. cit.* vol. 2, p. 341.

44 *Op. cit.* vol. 2, p. 349; Chesney, *Narrative*, p. 521.

45 Dr J. Ross, 'Notes on Two Journeys from Baghdád to the Ruins of Al Hadhr, in Mesopotamia, in 1836 and 1837', *JRGS*, vol. 9, 1839, pp. 463–4; Ainsworth, *Travels and Researches*, vol. 1, p. 293; in his *Personal Narrative*, vol. 2, p. 349, Hafiz' bite is attributed to a scorpion; Ismā'īl Beg Chol, *The Yazīdīs: Past and Present* (Arabic), ed. Zurayk, pp. 113–5; Damluji, *Yezidis*, pp. 498–9.

46 Horatio Southgate, *Narrative of a Tour through Armenia, Kurdistan, Persia and Mesopotamia*, vol. 2, pp. 266–7; Dr Asahel Grant, *The Nestorians; or, the Lost Tribes*, pp. 46–7; British Library, *Layard Papers*, Add. MS 39096: Layard diary entry, 10 October 1849.

47 *Ottoman Archives*: Hatti Hümayun 22350D: Hafiz Pasha letter, 24 Cemaziyelevvel AH 1253 (27 August 1837 AD), to Porte; Southgate, *Armenia*, vol. 2, p. 273; Forbes, *JRGS*, vol. 9, 1839, pp. 409, 421.
48 *Op. cit. JRGS*, vol. 9, 1839, p. 418.
49 Layard, *Nineveh and Babylon*, p. 46.
50 Vital Cuinet, *La Turquie d'Asie*, vol. 2, p. 607.
51 The experiences of the Prussian military mission are described in Moltke's *Briefe* and in his *Darstellung des Türkisch–Ägyptischen Feldzugs im Sommer 1839*. See also Reinhold Wagner, *Moltke und Mühlbach zusammen unter dem Halbmonde 1837–1839* and Jehuda L. Wallach, *Anatomie einer Militärhilfe*, pp. 15–29.
52 Moltke, *Briefe*, p. 294 (1893 edition).

Chapter 6

1 Rev. Timothy Dwight, *The Duty of Americans at the present Crisis*, p. 31.
2 The primary sources for the American Board missions in eastern Anatolia, Iran and Iraq are the Board Archives at the Houghton Library, Cambridge, Mass. See also Rev. Rufus Anderson, *History of the Missions of the American Board of Commissioners for Foreign Missions to the Oriental Churches* and Peter Kawerau, *Amerika und die orientalischen Kirchen*.
3 *Church Missionary Society Archives* CM/M5, pp. 188–91, 280–3: Badger letters, 30 June and 28 November 1835, to Schlienz.
4 Rev. Eli Smith and Rev. H. G. O. Dwight, *Missionary Researches in Armenia*.
5 *ABC Archives* 16.8.7, vol. 2, Nestorians of Persia 1838–1844, vol. 1, item 122, Justin Perkins journal entry, 10 May 1837; summarized in *MH*, vol. 34, 1838, pp. 53–4. See also his *A Residence of Eight Years in Persia*, pp. 311–2.
6 The primary sources for the life of Asahel Grant are the American Board archives, including Grant's unpublished MS entitled *Life in Kurdistan* (ABC 35). See also Grant, *The Nestorians; or, the Lost Tribes*; Thomas Laurie, *Dr. Grant and the Mountain Nestorians*; and David H. Finnie, *Pioneers East*, pp. 213–41.
7 [Laurie] article, 'Grant, Asahel', *The Encyclopaedia of Missions* (1891 edition), vol. 1, p. 394, cited by Finnie, p. 214. See also Rev. A. C. Lathrop, *Memoir of Asahel Grant, M.D., Missionary to the Nestorians*, p. 191; and C. Sandreczki, *Reise nach Mosul und durch Kurdistan nach Urumia*, vol. 3, pp. 122–3.
8 Anderson, vol. 1, p. 176.
9 *ABC Archives* 16.8.7, vol. 4, Mountain Nestorians 1838–1844, item 74, Grant journal entry, 15 October 1839; *MH*, vol. 37, 1841, p. 122.
10 Horatio Southgate, *Narrative of a Tour through Armenia, Kurdistan, Persia and Mesopotamia*; Eugène Boré, *Correspondance et mémoires d'un voyageur en Orient*.
11 William [Francis] Ainsworth, *Travels and Researches in Asia Minor, Mesopotamia, Chaldea, and Armenia*, vol. 1, p. 78.
12 The primary sources for the Kurdistan Expedition are *JRGS*, vol. 8, 1838, p. vii and

vol. 9, 1839, pp. xii–xxii; Ainsworth, *Travels and Researches* and his articles in *JRGS*, viz: 'Notes on a journey from Constantinople, by Heraclea, to Angora in the Autumn of 1838', *JRGS*, vol. 9, 1839, pp. 216–76; 'Journey from Angora by Kaïsaríyah, Malátíyah and Gergen Ka'le-si to Bír or Bírehjik', *JRGS*, vol. 10, 1841, pp. 275–340; 'Notes taken on a Journey from Constantinople to Mósul, in 1839–40' *JRGS*, vol. 10, 1841, pp. 489–529; and 'An Account of a Visit to the Chaldeans, inhabiting Central Kurdistán; and of an Ascent of the Peak of Rowándiz (Túr Sheïkhíwá) in the Summer of 1840', *JRGS*, vol. 11, 1841, pp. 21–76; and *Report of Mr. Ainsworth and Mr. Rassam to the Society for Promoting Christian Knowledge, respecting the Christians in Kurdistan*. See also T. M. Russell, 'The Battle of Nizib', *United Service Journal*, 1840, pp. 434–48; and Robert P. Perry, *European exploration in Turkish Kurdistan, 1800–1842*, thesis, American University of Beirut, 1965, pp. 160–96.

13 *CMS Archives* CM/M6, pp. 265 f.: Brenner letters, 22 March and 17 May 1838, to Lay Secretary; Rev. John A. Clark, *Glimpses of the Old World*, vol. 1, pp. 134, 148; Perry, pp. 163, 166–7.

14 Ainsworth, *Travels and Researches*, vol. 1, pp. 308–12.

15 *Op. cit.* vol. 1, pp. 333–5; Russell, *United Service Journal*, 1840, p. 443; Reinhold Wagner, *Moltke und Mühlbach zusammen unter dem Halbmonde*, p. 258.

16 *Op. cit.* pp. 264, 266–7.

17 F. Niewöhner, 'War der Kurdenfürst Bedir-Khan-Bey an der Schlacht von Nisib beteiligt?', *ZDMG*, vol. 133, 1983, pp. 134–44; see note 29 below; Reinhold Wagner, *Moltke und Mühlbach*, p. 271.

18 Grant, *Nestorians*, pp. 31–8; Laurie, *Grant*, pp. 111–4; Henry A. Homes, 'The Sect of Yezidies of Mesopotamia', *Biblical Repository and Classical Review*, series 2, vol. 7, 1842, pp. 329–51.

19 In addition to the sources cited in other footnotes to this chapter, descriptions of Ince Bairaktar are given by Comte [Édouard] de Sercey, *Une ambassade extraordinaire: La Perse en 1839–1840*, pp. 354–6; in I. Berezin's articles, 'Mosul', *BdCh*, vol. 133, 1855, pp. 186–9, and 'Sovremennaya Turtsiya', *Otechestvenniya Zapiski*, vol. 104, 1856, pp. 400–1; and by Mgr Suleiman Sa'igh, *Tarikh al-Mawsil*, vol. 1, pp. 310–4; Mehmed Sureyya, *Sicill-i Osmani*, vol. 4, p. 291, gives his surname as 'Incebairaktarzade', suggesting that his appellation may have been a patronymic.

20 *IO* L/P and S/9/95, Taylor despatch no. 5 (14 May 1833) to Secret Committee, and *FO* 195/113, Taylor letter, 15 May 1833, to Embassy.

21 *FO* 195/113, Taylor despatch no. 117 (3 October 1835) to Embassy.

22 *Journal d'une campagne au service de Méhemet-Pacha*, incl. in [Rémi] Aucher-Eloy, *Relations de voyages en Orient de 1830 à 1838*, vol. 1, pp. 99–132.

23 Austen Henry Layard, *Nineveh and its Remains*, vol. 1, p. 314.

24 Berezin, *BdCh*, vol. 133, 1855, pp. 186–7; Helmuth von Moltke, *Briefe über Zustände und Begebenheiten in der Türkei aus den Jahren 1835 bis 1839*, p. 255 (1893 edition); Laurie, *Grant*, pp. 206–9; George Percy Badger, *The Nestorians and their Rituals*, vol. 1, p. 75.

25 *Op. cit.* vol. 1, p. 183.

26 Grant, *Nestorians*, pp. 54–7.

27 Laurie, *Grant*, p. 149.

28 Lieut.-Col. J. Shiel, 'Notes on a Journey from Tabríz, through Kurdistán, *JRGS*, vol. 8, 1838, p. 69.

29 *FO* 78/2698, R. W. Stevens 'Report on a visit to Bedr Khan Bey', 10 July 1844. In his report Stevens states that 'he commanded a body of Koordish Cavalry at the battle of Nezzib'; see note 17 above.

30 V. Dittel, 'Ocherk puteshestviya po Vostoku s 1842 po 1845 gg.', *BdCh*, vol. 95, 1849, section 1, p. 210.

31 Layard, *Discoveries in the Ruins of Nineveh and Babylon*, p. 54. See also Dzhalile Dzhalil, *Kurdy Osmanskoy Imperiyi v pervoy polovine XIX veka*, pp. 125–48.

32 Grant, *Nestorians*, pp. 41–100; Laurie, *Grant*, pp. 129–45.

33 Grant, *Nestorians*, pp. 109–12; Laurie, *Grant*, pp. 148–9.

34 Grant, *Nestorians*, pp. 113–6; Laurie, *Grant*, pp. 158–60.

35 *Op. cit.* p. 165.

36 Ainsworth, *JRGS*, vol. 10, 1841, pp. 489–529; also his 'Notes of an Excursion to Kal'ah Sherkát, the U'r of the Persians, and to the Ruins of Al Hadhr, the Hutra of the Chaldees, and Hatra of the Romans', *JRGS*, vol. 11, 1841, pp. 1–20; and his *Travels and Researches*, vol. 2, pp. 43–180; Edward Ledwich Mitford, *A Land March from England to Ceylon Forty Years Ago*, vol. 1, pp. 282–300; Perry, pp. 183–4, 187–9.

37 Ainsworth, *JRGS*, vol. 11, 1841, pp. 23–6, and *Travels and Researches*, vol. 2, pp. 181–5, 190.

38 Ainsworth, *JRGS*, vol. 11, 1841, p. 51, and *Travels and Researches*, vol. 2, pp. 246–53.

39 Ainsworth, *JRGS*, vol. 11, 1841, p. 61, and *Travels and Researches*, vol. 2, pp. 303–5; Laurie, *Grant*, p. 153.

40 Ainsworth, *Travels and Researches*, vol. 2, pp. 306–30.

41 *Op. cit.* vol. 2, pp. 335–90; *FO* 195/175, James Brant, British consul, Erzurum, despatch no. 35 (21 September 1840) to Embassy; *Royal Geographical Society*, Correspondence Files, Kurdistan Expedition, Ainsworth letters, 23 March and 21 September 1840, to Capt. Washington, secretary, Royal Geographical Society; Perry, pp. 187–8, 192–6.

42 Southgate, *Narrative of a Visit to the Syrian (Jacobite) Church of Mesopotamia*, p. 136.

Chapter 7

1 G. Lacour-Gayet, *Les dernières années de Talleyrand*, p. 18, cited by Henri Dehérain, *Silvestre de Sacy, ses contemporains et ses disciples*, p. 25. See also D. C. M. Platt, *The Cinderella Service*, pp. 125–79.

2 *Ministère des Affaires Etrangères, Archives Diplomatiques, Correspondance politique des Consuls*, Bagdad et Mossoul, vol. 1: Vidal letter, 6 April 1841, to Ministry.

3 Thomas Laurie, *Dr. Grant and the Mountain Nestorians*, pp. 195–202; Rufus

Anderson, *History of the Missions of the American Board of Commissioners for Foreign Missions to the Oriental Churches*, vol. 1, pp. 200–4.

4 Asahel Grant, *The Nestorians; or, the Lost Tribes*, pp. 363–72; *ABC Archives* 16.8.7, vol. 4, Mountain Nestorians 1838–1844, item 80, Journal of Doct. Grant and Mr. Hinsdale, 20 and 21 November 1841; summarized in *MH*, vol. 38, 1842, pp. 310–1.

5 *ABC Archives* 16.8.7, vol. 4, item 80, Grant/Hinsdale journal, 2 and 3 December 1841; summarized in *MH*, vol. 38, 1842, pp. 318–9. See also *ABC Archives* 16.8.7, vol. 3, Nestorians of Persia 1838–1844, vol. 2, item 80, W. R. Stocking letter, 22 December 1840, to Grant; summarized in *MH*, vol. 37, 1841, p. 275.

6 Eugène Boré, 'De la vie religieuse chez les Chaldéens', *Annales de la philosophie chrétienne*, series 3, vol. 8, 1843, pp. 119–22; Bernard Marie Goormachtigh, OP, 'Histoire de la mission dominicaine en Mésopotamie et en Kurdistan', *Analecta Sacri Ordinis Fratrum Praedicatorum*, vol. 3, 1897–8, p. 87; Stéphane Bello, *La congrégation de S. Hormisdas et l'église chaldéenne dans la première moitié du XIXe siècle*, pp. 135–6.

7 *ABC Archives* 35: Grant, *Life in Koordistan* (unpublished MS), journal entry, 7 June 1842.

8 *FO* 193/204, Rassam despatch no. 13 (19 December 1842) to Robert Taylor; George Percy Badger, *The Nestorians and their Rituals*, vol. 1, pp. 74–5.

9 *FO* 193/204, Rassam despatch no. 13 (19 December 1842) to Taylor. Laurie, *Grant*, pp. 274–81.

10 Badger, vol. 1, pp. xiii–xxi, 6–11.

11. *Op. cit.* vol. 1, p. 192; Laurie, *Grant*, p. 284.

12 Badger, vol. 1, p. 197.

13 *Op. cit.* vol. 1, pp. 245–7; Laurie, *Grant*, pp. 285–6; John Joseph, *The Nestorians and their Muslim Neighbors*, pp. 61–2.

14 Badger, vol. 1, pp. 254–5.

15 Laurie, *Grant*, pp. 291–2.

16 *ABC Archives*, 16.8.7, vol. 4, item 54, Grant letter. 5 July 1843, to Anderson; summarized in *MH*, vol. 39, 1843, pp. 434–5; Laurie, *Grant*, pp. 314–5, 322–41; C. Sandreczki, *Reise nach Mosul und durch Kurdistan nach Urumia*, vol. 3, p. 84, identifies the nature of Bedr Khan Beg's complaint.

17 Rev. J. P. Fletcher, *Notes from Nineveh*, vol. 1, pp. 330–1 (London edition); p. 179 (Philadelphia edition).

18 *FO* 195/228, Rassam despatch no. 3 (18 January 1844) to Embassy; Fletcher, vol. 1, pp. 343–4 (London edition); pp. 186–7 (Philadelphia edition).

19 *FO* 195/175, Rassam, 'List of the exactions levied by the Pasha of Moossul', attached to Brant despatch no. 35 (21 September 1840) to Embassy; cited by Lieut.-Colonel [Francis] Chesney, *The Expedition for the Survey of the Rivers Euphrates and Tigris*, vol. 2, p. 673; *FO* 195/796 contains the documents relating to the Ince Bairaktar/Rassam affair.

20 The primary source for Layard's life is Gordon Waterfield, *Layard of Nineveh*, which lists Layard's published and unpublished works. See also papers (to be published shortly) read at the *Symposium on Austen Henry Layard between the*

Orient and Venice, 26–8 October 1983, sponsored by the University of Venice.

21 Edward Ledwich Mitford, *A Land March from England to Ceylon Forty Years Ago*, vol. 1, pp. 245–6.

22 P.-É. Botta, *Monument de Ninive*, vol. 5, pp. 5–7; Fletcher, vol. 1, pp. 213–8 (London edition); pp. 118–21 (Philadelphia edition); Laurie, *Grant*, pp. 289–90.

23 Badger, vol. 1, pp. 105–10; I. Berezin, 'Yezidy', *Magazin Zemlevedeniya i Puteshestvy*, vol. 3, 1854, pp. 428–54; English translation by Eugene Prostov entitled *A Visit to the Yezidis in 1843* incl. in Henry Field, *The Anthropology of Iraq*: part 2, no. 1, *The Northern Jazira*, pp. 67–79.

24 *Op. cit.* p. 453 (English translation, p. 79).

25 Berezin's life and works are described by A. Samoilovitch and others in *Zapiski kollegiyi vostokovedov pri Aziatskom Museye*, vol. 1, 1925, pp. 161–94, and vol. 2, 1926, pp. 51–72. See also N. A. Kuznetsova and B. M. Dantsig, 'I. N. Berezin – puteshestvennik po Zakavkazyu, Iranu i Blizhnemu Vostoku', *Kratkiye soobshcheniya Instituta Vostokovedeniya*, vol. 22, 1956, pp. 92–100.

26 Berezin, *Magazin Zemlevedeniya i Puteshestvy*, vol. 3, 1854, p. 429 (English translation, p. 67).

27 R. Coupland, *The Exploitation of East Africa 1856–1890: The Slave Trade and the Scramble*, facing p. 186; Henry James Ross, *Letters from the East 1837–1857*, ed. Janet Ross, p. 47.

28 Berezin, 'Mosul', *BdCh*, vol. 133, 1855, p. 184.

29 N. G. Chernyshevsky, *Sovremennik*, vol. 49 (N.S.), 1855, p. 28; reprinted in *Polnoye sobraniye sochineny*, vol. 2, p. 620.

30 Gustav Pauli, 'Von Hösn Kefa am Tigris bis Bagdad', *Mitteilungen der Geographischen Gesellschaft in Lübeck*, vol. 12, 1889, p. 106; Sadiq Al Damlooji [Damluji], *The Yezidis* (Arabic), pp. 23–4, 469; C. J. Edmonds, *A Pilgrimage to Lalish*, p. 30.

31 Fletcher, vol. 2, pp. 55–7 (London edition); pp. 226–7 (Philadelphia edition).

32 *Op. cit.* vol. 2, pp. 74–5 (London edition); p. 237 (Philadelphia edition); V. Dittel, 'Ocherk puteshestviya po Vostoku s 1842 po 1845 gg.', *BdCh*, vol. 95, 1849, p. 24; see also 'Obzor tryokhgodichnovo puteshestviya po Vostoku Magistra Villiama Dittelya', *Zhurnal Ministerstva Narodnovo Prosveshcheniya*, vol. 56, 1847, pp. 17–20, (French translation in *Nouvelles annales des voyages et des sciences géographiques*, series 5, vol. 19, 1849, pp. 156–7); Badger, vol. 1, pp. 86–93.

33 Dittel, *BdCh*, vol. 95, 1849, pp. 24–5; Fletcher, vol. 1, pp. 219–27, 242–3 and vol. 2, pp. 81–2 (London edition); pp. 121–5, 132–3, 241 (Philadelphia edition).

34 *ABC Archives* 16.8.1, vol. 3, Syrian & Nestorian Missions 1844–1846, item 75, Laurie letter, 8 August 1844, to Anderson; summarized in his 'Journal of a Visit to the Yezidees', *Bibliotheca Sacra*, vol. 5, 1848, pp. 154–71, and in Laurie, *Grant*, p. 407.

35 Grant letter, 16 October 1843, to *New-York Observer*, published 27 January 1844, p. 14, and reprinted with slight modifications in Laurie, *Grant*, pp. 372–6.

36 *FO* 195/228, Rassam despatch no. 1 (13 January 1845) to Embassy.

37 *FO* 195/301, Rassam despatch no. 26 (29 May 1847) to Embassy; *ABC Archives* 16.8.1, vol. 3, item 285, Dr Austin H. Wright letter, 11 July 1846, to Anderson; sum-

marized in *MH*, vol. 42, 1846, p. 382.

38 Karl Hadank, *Untersuchungen zum Westkurdischen: Bōtī und Ēzädī*, pp. 41–2. The tradition that Bedr Khan Beg married a Yezidi princess was confirmed to the author by Princess Wansa el-Amawy.

39 Layard, *Nineveh and its Remains*, vol. 1, p. 19; *FO* 195/228, Rassam despatch no. 4 (9 March 1845) to Embassy; Botta letter, 23 March 1845, cited by Laurie, *Grant*, pp. 210–1. See also Mehmed Süreyya, *Sicill-i Osmâni*, vol. 4, pp. 293–4.

40 Layard, *Nineveh and its Remains*, vol. 1, pp. 19–20, 31; *FO* 78/2699, Stevens letter, 30 April 1845, to Embassy indicates that Bedr Khan Beg settled his 'tooth-hire' liability for 35 per cent of the amount demanded.

41 *FO* 195/228, Rassam despatches no. 18 (14 June 1845) and no. 43 (28 October 1846) to Embassy.

42 Layard, *Nineveh and its Remains*, vol. 1, pp. 271–2, 303–4.

43 *Op. cit.* vol. 1, pp. 147–238.

44 *Op. cit.* vol. 1, pp. 121–2.

45 The account of Layard's 1846 visit to the Yezidi festival is related in *Nineveh and its Remains*, vol. 1, pp. 270–308.

46 British Library, *Layard Papers*, Add. MS 39055, contains the original of Sheikh Nasr's letter, 18 October 1846, to the Sinjar chieftains with an English translation; see also Layard, *Nineveh and its Remains*, vol. 1, pp. 308–9.

47 *FO* 195/228, Rassam despatches no. 43 (28 October 1846) to Embassy and no. 20 (3 December 1846) to Rawlinson; Layard, *Nineveh and its Remains*, vol. 1, pp. 309–24 and vol. 2, pp. 1–3; Ismā'īl Beg Chol, *The Yazīdīs: Past and Present* (Arabic), ed. Zurayk, pp. 115–6; Damluji, *Yezidis*, pp. 500–1.

48 Edmonds, p. 62.

49 *FO* 195/228; Rassam's despatches from March through October 1847 cover the defeat and surrender of Bedr Khan Beg and his allies, as well as Rassam's efforts to persuade him to yield. See also H. J. Ross, pp. 45–53; Badger, vol. 1, pp. 371–3; Layard, *Nineveh and its Remains*, vol. 1, p. 239; Adolphe d'Avril, *La Chaldée chrétienne*, pp. 62–3; and Wadie Jwaideh, *The Kurdish Nationalist Movement: its Origins and Development*, PhD dissertation, Syracuse University, 1960, pp. 206–11.

50 Sandreczki, vol. 1, pp. 274–5.

51 Xavier Hommaire de Hell, *Voyage en Turquie et en Perse*, vol. 1, pp. 468–9.

52 *FO* 195/301, Rassam despatches no. 56 (26 November 1847) and no. 36 (16 October 1848) to Embassy; Layard, *Discoveries in the Ruins of Nineveh and Babylon*, pp. 3–4.

53 *Op. cit.* p. 4; [Adair Crawford], *Journal of a Deputation sent to the East by the Committee of the Malta Protestant College in 1849*, [vol. 2], pp. 517–8; Thomas Humphry Ward, *Humphry Sandwith: A Memoir*, pp. 44–5.

54 Layard, *Nineveh and Babylon*, p. 4.

55 Layard's 1849 journey from Trebizond to Mosul is related in his *Nineveh and Babylon*, pp. 4–59, and in his diary (British Library, Layard Papers, Add. MS 39096); see also Ward, *Sandwith*, pp. 45–54.

56 Layard, *Nineveh and Babylon*, pp. 78–96, and diary (BL Add. MS 39096); Ward,

Sandwith, pp. 65–7; *FO* 195/301, Rassam despatches nos. 21 & 23 (15 & 29 October 1849) to Embassy.

57 Sir Paul Rycaut, *The History of the Turkish Empire From the Year 1623. to the Year 1677*, p. 93; Frederick Forbes, 'A Visit to the Sinjár Hills in 1838', *JRGS*, vol. 9, 1839, p. 424; *ABC Archives* 16.8.7, vol. 4, item 80, Grant/Hinsdale journal, 20 and 21 November 1841; summarized in *MH*, vol. 38, 1842, p. 311; *ABC Archives* 35: Grant, *Life in Koordistan*, journal entry, 7 June 1842; see also Laurie, *Grant*, p. 218; Henry A. Homes, 'The Sect of Yezidies of Mesopotamia', *Biblical Repository and Classical Review*, series 2, vol. 7, 1842, p. 342.

58 Yu. S. Kartsov, *Zametki o turetskikh yezidakh*, reprinted in *ZKORGO*, vol. 13, 1891, pp. 237–8. See also Rev. John P. Newman, *The Thrones and Palaces of Babylon and Nineveh*, pp. 244–5, for a description of Abu Jezirawi.

Chapter 8

1 *FO* 195/301, Rassam despatches no. 23 (29 October 1849) and nos. 6 and 7 (15 and 29 April 1850) to Embassy.

2 *FO* 195/301, Rassam despatches nos. 14–17 (August–October 1850) to Embassy; C. Sandreczki, *Reise nach Mosul und durch Kurdistan nach Urumia*, vol. 3, p. 283; see also *FO* 195/459, W. R. Holmes, consul Diyarbakir, despatch no. 10 (5 March 1857) and W. A. Maltas, acting consul, despatch no. 30 (17 November 1857); and *FO* 195/603, Maltas despatch no. 3 (20 February 1858) to Embassy.

3 Sir A. Henry Layard, *Autobiography and Letters*, ed. W. Bruce, vol. 2, p. 192.

4 Sandreczki, vol. 2, pp. 187, 202; F. Walpole, *The Ansayrii, (or Assassins) with Travels in the Further East, in 1850–51*, vol. 1, p. 387; John P. Newman, *The Thrones and Palaces of Babylon and Nineveh*, p. 246.

5 Austen H. Layard, *Discoveries in the Ruins of Nineveh and Babylon*, pp. 238–59, 332–4.

6 Rufus Anderson, *History of the Missions of the American Board of Commissioners for Foreign Missions to the Oriental Churches*, vol. 1, pp. 336–46; *ABC Archives*, 16.8.7, vol. 5, Nestorian Missions 1847–1859, vol. 1, item 188, Perkins journal entries, 13–23 May 1849; summarized in *MH*, vol. 46, 1850, pp. 53–61.

7 George Percy Badger, *The Nestorians and their Rituals*, vol. 1, pp. 86–92.

8 (Istanbul correspondent) despatch, 17 August 1843, to *The Morning Chronicle*, published 5 September 1843; Gordon Waterfield, *Layard of Nineveh*, p. 213.

9 Badger, vol. 1, pp. 388–9.

10 *Op. cit.* vol. 1, pp. 119–24.

11 *Op. cit.* vol. 1, pp. 113–5; Layard, *Nineveh and Babylon*, pp. 89–92; Badger letter, 6 June 1853, to *Athenaeum*, published 16 July 1853, vol. 26, 1853, p. 860. The Arabic text of the poem, based on Badger's manuscript, was published by Heinrich Ewald, 'Die erste schriftliche Urkunde der Jezidäer', *Nachrichten von der G.A. Universität und der Königl. Gesellschaft der Wissenschaften zu Göttingen*, 1853, pp. 209–22, and 1854, pp. 149–50 ('Nachtrag').

12 [Rev. John Bowen], *Memorials* compiled by his sister, pp. 348–56; Sandreczki, vol. 2, pp. 3–285; Eugene Stock, *The History of the Church Missionary Society*, vol. 2, pp. 142–3.

13 Sandreczki, vol. 3, pp. 249–51.

14 *Op. cit.* vol. 2, p. 209 and vol. 3, pp. 283–97.

15 Stock, vol. 2, p. 143.

16 *Akty*, vol. 11, Arkhiv kantselyariyi Glavnonachalstvuyushchevo, item 23, pp. 30–1; minute re application by Syrian-Nestorian Church, 4 July 1856 (O.S.). Dzhalile Dzhalil, *Kurdy Osmanskoy Imperiyi v pervoy polovine XIX veka*, p. 144, states that in 1810 Mar Shimun XVI Yonan sent an envoy to General Tormasov, Russian commander-in-chief in the Caucasus.

17 *ABC Archives* 16.8.7, vol. 5, item 34, Perkins and Stocking letter, 21 May 1849, to Anderson and item 188, Perkins journal entries, 14, 15 and 19 May 1849; summarized in *MH*, vol. 46, 1850, pp. 55–6, 59.

18 *ABC Archives* 16.8.4, vol. 1, Assyrian Mission 1850–1859, item 147, 'Narrative of the life of Shemmas Eremia Agent of the Protestant Community in Mosul', encl. in D. W. Marsh letter, 23 March 1857, to Board.

19 *ABC Archives* 16.8.7, vol. 5, item 188, Perkins journal entries, 24–30 May 1849; summarized in *MH*, vol. 46, 1850, pp. 84–8.

20 Rev. W. S. Tyler, *Memoir of Rev. Henry Lobdell, M.D.*, p. 179.

21 *Op. cit.* pp. 15–89, 401–14.

22 *ABC Archives* 16.8.4, vol. 1, item 219, W. F. Williams letter, 10 February 1854, to Anderson; summarized in *MH*, vol. 50, 1854, p. 187.

23 Tyler, *Lobdell*, p. 43.

24 Lobdell's visit to Rabban Hormuzd and the Yezidis is related in the *ABC Archives* 16.8.4, vol. 1, item 83, Lobdell letter, 20 December 1852, to Anderson; summarized in *MH*, vol. 49, 1853, pp. 109–11, and elaborated in his articles dated 1 December 1852 and 14 January 1853, published in the *New-York Daily Tribune* 26 March 1853, p. 5, and 21 May 1853, pp. 5–6. See also Tyler, *Lobdell*, pp. 213–25.

25 *FO* 195/394, Rassam despatch no. 4 (26 February 1853) to Embassy.

26 The ancestry of this Jasim Beg is unknown. The reference to his 'excommunication' may be connected with references in Sadiq Al Damlooji [Damluji], *The Yezidis* (Arabic), p. 25, and in C. J. Edmonds, *A Pilgrimage to Lalish*, p. 30, to Mir Hussein Beg's 'unlawful' marriage to a woman from the Abd el-Yisk family of the 'anathematized' Shemsi clan of sheikhs. No further details of this dispute are given and neither writer mentions the brother-in-law Jasim.

27 Lobdell article, *New-York Daily Tribune*, 26 March 1853, p. 5.

28 Dorothea Seelye Franck, *Yankees from New York to the Garden of Eden* (unpublished MS), p. 206.

29 *FO* 195/394, Rassam despatch no. 8 (20 June 1853) to Embassy.

30 Tyler, *Lobdell*, p. 265.

31 *FO* 195/394, Rassam despatches nos. 5, 6 and 8 (24 April, 8 May and 5 June 1854) to Embassy; Tyler, *Lobdell*, pp. 320–1.

32 *Op. cit.* pp. 348–9, 412–3.

33 The primary sources used for the Yezdanshir episode are *FO* 195/394, Rassam

despatches nos. 19–23 (1854) and nos. 1–11 (1855) to Embassy: *FO* 195/459, Holmes despatch no. 22 (1 June 1855) to Embassy; and Humphry Sandwith, *A Narrative of the Siege of Kars*, pp. 208–15. See also *FO* 78/2699, Layard "Memorandum on Kurdistan" (undated), incl. in Cowley despatch no. 360 (17 October 1847) to Foreign Office; and Dr Alexander Schläfli, *Reisen in den Orient*, pp. 52–6. The Russian version appears in *Akty*, vol. 11, pp. 326–7, 335, 349–50; items 326 and 333, Gen. Muraviev despatches no. 54 (4 March 1855) and no. 134 (1 May 1855) to Prince Dolgoruki; and item 351, Mar Shimun letters, 30 March 1855, to Col. Khreshchatitsky and 15 May 1855, to Prince Bebutov, encl. with Muraviev letter no. 14 (10 June 1855) to Dolgoruki (all dates O.S.) See also P. I. Aver'yanov, *Kurdy v voinakh Rossiyi s Persiyey i Turtsiyey v techeniye XIX stoletiya*, pp. 144–57; Major-General M. Likhutin, *Russkiye v Aziyatskoy Turtsiyi v 1854 i 1855 godakh*, pp. 256–61; N. A. Khalfin, *Bor'ba za Kurdistan*, pp. 71–7; and Dzhalil, *Kurdy*, pp. 166–71. The Kurdish account appears in *Erzählungen und Lieder im Dialekte des Tûr 'Abdîn*, ed. Eugen Prym and Albert Socin, and *Erzählungen und Lieder im Dialekte von Bohtan*, ed. Socin; both incl. in Prym and Socin (eds), *Kurdische Sammlungen: Erzählungen und Lieder in den Dialekten des Tûr 'Abdîn und von Bohtan*, part a, pp. 42–6, 239–60; part b, pp. 64–7, 247–60.

34 H. Petermann, *Reisen im Orient*, vol. 2, pp. 329–30.

35 Tyler, *Lobdell*, p. 352.

36 J. Carlile McCoan, *Our New Protectorate*, vol. 1, pp. 73–85.

37 *FO* 195/459, Holmes despatch no. 22 (1 June 1855) to Embassy.

38 *Akty*, vol. 11, item 351, p. 350: Muraviev letter no. 14 (10 June 1855 O.S.) to Dolgoruki.

39 Petermann, vol. 2, p. 318; Aver'yanov, pp. 150–1.

40 Süreyya, *Sicill-i Osmâni*, vol. 4, pp. 293–4.

41 Prym/Socin, *Der neu-aramaeische Dialekt des Tûr 'Abdîn*, part 1, pp. 35–8, 89–93; part 2, pp. 51–5, 129–36; Prym/Socin (eds), *Kurdische Sammlungen*, part a, p. 46; part b, p. 67.

42 *FO* 196/55, Stratford letter, 26 May 1857, to Rassam.

43 *The Times*, 24 October 1867, obituary notice of Matilda Rassam, who died in Aleppo 21 September 1867.

44 *FO* 195/796 contains the documents relating to these claims, including Badger's 'Statement of Mr. Rassam's claim', 29 March 1865, and his letter, 10 February 1866, to Ambassador.

45 *FO* 195/949 Rassam despatch no. 10 (19 September 1870) to Embassy; Rev. E. L. Cutts, *Christians under the Crescent in Asia*, pp. 3–8; J. C. G. Savile, Viscount Pollington, *Half Round the Old World*, p. 355; see also Freiherr Max von Thielmann, *Streifzüge im Kaukasus, in Persien und in der asiatischen Türkei*, pp. 338, 343.

46 M. Pillet, 'Sur la mort d'orientalistes français', *Revue Archéologique*, series 6, vol. 9, 1937, pp. 226–32.

47 *FO* 195/603, Rassam despatch no. 17 (4 September 1858) to Embassy.

48 *FO* 195/799, J. G. Taylor, vice-consul Diyarbakir, despatch no. 6 (6 April 1864) to Embassy.

49 *FO* 195/889, Taylor (now consul Erzurum) despatch no. 35 (22 October 1868) to Embassy, enclosing Mar Shimun letter, 26 April 1868, to Grand Duke Michael; *FO* 195/939, Taylor despatch no. 11 (28 July 1870) to Embassy.

50 Damluji, *Yezidis*, p. 24, states that the audience was granted by Sultan Abdul Mejid, who died in June 1861; on p. 470 he attributes the audience to his successor, Sultan Abdul Aziz, who reigned until 1876.

51 *Op. cit.* p. 25.

52 John Ussher, *A Journey from London to Persepolis*, pp. 405–20.

53 *FO* 195/603, Rassam despatch no. 21 (21 December 1860) to Embassy.

54 Guillaume Lejean, 'Voyage dans la Babylonie', *Le Tour du Monde*, vol. 16, 1867, p. 94; Adolfo Rivadeneyra, *Viaje de Ceylán a Damaso, Golfo Pérsico, Mesopotamia, Ruinas de Babilonia*, pp. 127–9.

55 *FO* 195/603, Rassam despatches nos. 7 and 21 (18 April and 12 December 1859) to Embassy; C. Haussknecht letter, 28 August 1867, to Kiepert, cited by Heinrich Kiepert, 'Mittheilungen von C. Haussknecht's botanischen Reisen in Kurdistan und Persien (1865–67)', *Zeitschrift der Gesellschaft für Erdkunde* (Berlin), vol. 3, 1868, pp. 467–8.

56 *FO* 195/949, Rassam despatches nos. 5 and 6 (31 May and 12 July 1869) to Embassy.

57 *AE/CPC*, Mossoul, vol. 2, fol. 167r: Siouffi despatch no. 38 (3 November 1879) to Ministry; printed under title 'Une courte conversation avec le chef de la secte des Yezidis, ou les adorateurs du diable', *JA*, series 7, vol. 18, 1880, pp. 81–2.

58 *Op. cit.* fols. 164v–165v (*JA*, series 7, vol. 18, 1880, p. 79–80); Damluji, *Yezidis*, pp. 135–6; Mustafa Nûrî Pasha, *'Abede-i-iblîs*, trans. with commentary by Dr Theodor Menzel under title *Die Teufelsanbeter, oder ein Blick auf die widerspenstige Sekte der Jeziden*, incl. in Hugo Grothe, *Meine Vorderasienexpedition 1906 und 1907*, vol. 1, pp. 173–4. An Arabic manuscript of the 'exposé', copied by Jeremiah Shamir in 1883, is in the Berlin Library; see Dr Eduard Sachau, *Verzeichniss der syrischen Handschriften der Königlichen Bibliothek*, vol. 1, pp. 434–6 (MS Sachau 200, fols. 37a–39a). The text was published with German translation by Mark Lidzbarski, 'Ein Exposé der Jeziden', *ZDMG*, vol. 51, 1897, pp. 592–604.

59 George Young, *Corps de Droit Ottoman*, vol. 2, p. 164; Comte F. van den Steen de Jehay, *De la situation légale des sujets ottomans non-musulmans*, p. 402.

60 Ismā'īl Beg Chol, *The Yazīdīs: Past and Present* (Arabic), ed. Zurayk, pp. 116–8. Damluji, *Yezidis*, p. 505; Hormuzd Rassam, *Asshur and the Land of Nimrod*, pp. 307–8; Edmonds, pp. 60, 66.

61 Damluji, *Yezidis*, pp. 25–7, 470; Edmonds, p. 30.

62 Gustav Pauli, 'Von Hösn Kefa am Tigris bis Bagdad', *Mitteilungen der Geographischen Gesellschaft in Lübeck*, vol. 12, 1889, p. 106.

63 Damluji, *Yezidis*, pp. 24–5; Vital Cuinet, *La Turquie d'Asie*, vol. 2, p. 774; *AE/CPC*, Mossoul, vol. 2, fols. 307r–311v: Siouffi despatch no. 81 (3 April 1882) to Ministry; printed under title 'Notice sur la secte des Yézidis', *JA*, series 7, vol. 20, 1882, pp. 263–6.

64 Yu. S. Kartsov, *Zametki o turetskikh yezidakh*, reprinted in *ZKORGO*, vol. 13, 1891, pp. 256–7; Dr L. E. Browski, 'Die Jeziden und ihre Religion', *Das Ausland*,

vol. 59, 1886, p. 762; interview with Princess Wansa el-Amawy, October 1983.
65 Damluji, *Yezidis*, pp. 25, 470; Ismail, p. 2.

Chapter 9

1 Henri Binder, *Au Kurdistan, en Mésopotamie, et en Perse*, p. 240.
2 Dr Eduard Sachau, *Reise in Syrien und Mesopotamien*, pp. 327–33, 343–57.
3 *ABC Archives* 16.9.7, vol. 8, Eastern Turkey Mission 1880–1890, vol. 3, item 242,
   Rev. Caleb Gates report, March 1883, to Dr N. G. Clark; Gates, *Not To Me Only*,
   pp. 59–60. Caleb Gates served as president of Robert College, an American institution in Istanbul, from 1903 to 1932.
4 Brief descriptions of Siouffi appear in Oswald H. Parry, *Six Months in a Syrian
   Monastery*, pp. 263–4; Binder, pp. 258–63; P. Müller-Simonis and H. Hyvernat, *Du
   Caucase au Golfe Persique à travers l'Arménie, le Kurdistan et la Mésopotamie*,
   p. 391; and Comte [Arnaud] de Cholet, *Voyage en Turquie d'Asie, Arménie,
   Kurdistan, et Mésopotamie*, pp. 278–9. Particulars of Siouffi's government service
   were kindly supplied by the Ministère des Relations Extérieures, Direction des
   Archives et de la Documentation.
5 Yu. S. Kartsov, *Zametki o turetskikh yezidakh*, reprinted in *ZKORGO*, vol. 13,
   1891, p. 255.
6 *AE/CPC*, Mossoul, vol. 2, Siouffi despatch no. 38 (3 November 1879) to Ministry,
   printed under title 'Une courte conversation avec le chef de la secte des Yezidis, ou
   les adorateurs du diable', *JA*, series 7, vol. 18, 1880, pp. 78–83; despatch no. 81 (3
   April 1882), incl. in 'Notice sur la secte des Yézidis', *JA*, series 7, vol. 20, 1882, pp.
   252–68; and 'Notice sur le Chéikh 'Adi et la secte des Yézidis', *JA*, series 8, vol. 5,
   1885, pp. 78–98.
7 *AE/CPC*, Mossoul, vol. 2, Siouffi despatch no. 97 (14 June 1883); vol. 3, Siouffi
   despatch no. 131 (11 December 1885) to Ministry.
8 The mission of the Russian vice-consul Yu. S. Kartsov (also spelled Kartsev) to
   Mosul is described in his article 'Marshrut iz Erzeruma v Mosul', *Sbornik
   Materialov po Aziyi*, vol. 19, 1885, pp. 271–84; in his book entitled *Sem let na
   Blizhnem Vostoke 1879–1886*, pp. 167–201; and in his *Zametki*, written in 1884,
   printed for official use in Tiflis in 1886 and reprinted in *ZKORGO*, vol. 13, 1891,
   pp. 235–63. See also *AE/CPC*, Mossoul, vol. 2, Siouffi despatch no. 106 (15
   December 1883) to Ministry.
9 Dr L. E. Browski, 'Die Jeziden und ihre Religion', *Das Ausland*, vol. 59, 1886, pp.
   761–7, 785–90; reprinted in *The Popular Science Monthly*, vol. 34, 1889, pp. 474–
   82, and *al-Muqtataf*, vol. 13, 1889, pp. 393–8. See also V. A. Romanov, 'Poklonniki
   Diavola', *Priroda i Lyudi*, vol. 9, 1898, pp. 739–41, 751–3.
10 Sachau, *Verzeichniss der syrischen Handschriften der Königlichen Bibliothek*, vol.
   1, p. 365 (MS Sachau 139); Rev. Herbert Birks, The Life and Correspondence of
   Thomas Valpy French, vol. 2, p. 259.
11 Athelstan Riley, 1886 Journal, fols. 157–63; also his 'A visit to the Temple of the
   Devil', *The Pilot*, 1901, pp. 684–5. Athelstan Riley's travel journals for 1884, 1886

and 1888 are in the possession of his family. Extracts will appear in Dr. J. F. Coakley's forthcoming book on the Archbishop's Mission to the Assyrian Christians. See, generally, Squadron-Leader George S. Reed, *La Mission de l'archevêque de Cantorbéry auprès les Assyriens.*

12 [Arthur John Maclean], 'The Archbishop's Assyrian Mission; Canon Maclean's Journal', *The Church Review* (London), 1888, p. 20 (13 January), p. 70 (3 February); Maclean and William Henry Browne, *The Catholicos of the East and his People,* p. 46.

13 Alpheus N. Andrus, 'More about the Yezidees', *MH,* vol. 88, 1892, p. 175.

14 Gordon Waterfield, *Layard of Nineveh,* pp. 375–6.

15 David Fraser, *The Short Cut to India,* pp. 169–71; E. W. McDowell, 'The Nestorian Church and its present influence in Kurdistan', *Journal of Race Development,* vol. 2, 1911–2, pp. 74–6; Mark Sykes, 'Journeys in North Mesopotamia', *GJ,* vol. 30, 1907, pp. 385–6; and *The Caliph's Last Heritage,* ed. Lady Sykes, pp. 319–27.

16 The primary sources used for the 1885–91 period have been Mustafa Nûrî Pasha, *'Abede-i-Iblīs,* trans. with commentary by Dr Theodor Menzel under title *Die Teufelsanbeter, oder ein Blick auf die widerspenstige Sekte der Jeziden,* incl. in Hugo Grothe, *Meine Vorderasienexpedition 1906 und 1907,* pp. 167–8; *AE/CPC,* Mossoul, vol. 4, Siouffi despatch no. 6 (10 July 1891) to Ministry; *ABC Archives* 16.9.7, vol. 12, Eastern Turkey Mission 1890–1899, vol. 3, items 139 and 141: Andrus letters, 3 October 1890 and 17 June 1891, to Dr Smith; and *FO* 195/1766: Fitzmaurice, vice-consul Van, despatch no. 11 (25 May 1892) to acting consul, Erzurum. Andrus' report entitled 'More about the Yezidees – A Sequel' enclosed with his letter, 7 June 1892, to Dr Smith (item 142), is missing from the ABC Archives; a copy was enclosed with Andrus' letter, 3 September 1892, to Hormuzd Rassam (see *FO* 78/4435, Hormuzd Rassam letter, 26 September 1892, to Sir Philip Currie). The author was unable to consult the Ottoman archives for these years.

17 Sir E. A. Wallis Budge, *By Nile and Tigris,* vol. 2, pp. 214–23.

18 W. B. Heard, 'Notes on the Yezidis', *JRAI,* vol. 41, 1911, pp. 217–8.

19 *BFM, PCUSA,* Mission Correspondence, Iran/Incoming Letters, vol. 6, 1889–90, item 217: McDowell letter, 2 March 1889, to Board; *ABC Archives* 16.9.7, vol. 6, Eastern Turkey Mission 1880–1890, vol. 1, item 212: Rev. John A. Ainslie letter, 19 February 1889, to Smith; summarized in *MH,* vol. 85, 1889, pp. 291–2; *BFM, PCUSA,* Annual Report, vol. 53, 1889/90, p. 172.

20 [Andrus] article, 'The Yezidees', *The Encyclopaedia of Missions* (1891 edition), vol. 2, p. 528; Andrus, 'Concerning the Yezidees', *MH,* vol. 85, 1889, pp. 385–8; *ABC Archives* 16.9.7, vol. 12, item 139: Andrus letter, 3 October 1890, to Smith.

21 Daud al-Chalabi, *Makhtutat al-Mawsil,* p. 252.

22 The primary sources used for the events of 1892 have been Nuri/Menzel/Grothe, vol. 1, pp. 165–6, 186–7; *AE/CPC,* Mossoul, vol. 4, Siouffi despatches no. 7 (26 August 1892) and nos. 12–23 (September to December 1892) to Ministry; *FO* 78/ 4435, Andrus letter, 3 September 1892, to Hormuzd Rassam; *ABC Archives* 16.9.7, vol. 12, item 143: Andrus letter, 17 November 1892, to Smith; Parry, pp. 252–62; and *BFM, PCUSA,* Mission Correspondence, Iran/Incoming Letters, vol. 10, 1893–94, item 207: McDowell letter, 18 December 1894, to Dr Gillespie. See also

FO 195/1763, Capt. F. R. Maunsell letter, 20 October 1892, to Consul-General, Baghdad; Chalabi, p. 252; and S. Ximénez, 'Au pays du Diable', *Archives Asiatiques*, vol. 1, 1912, pp. 19, 157. The author was unable to consult the Ottoman archives for 1892.

23 Š. Estīpān Rāyes, 'The Yezidis' (Syriac), *Qālā d'šrārā* (Urmia), vol. 2, 1898–9, fols. 113a–116b, cited by Rudolf Macuch, *Geschichte der spät- und neusyrischen Literatur*, p. 198.

24 C. J. Edmonds, *A Pilgrimage to Lalish*, p. 60.

25 *AE/CPC*, Mossoul, vol. 4, Siouffi despatch no. 5 (11 July 1893) and Alric despatch no. 3 (23 November 1893) to Ministry; Max Freiherr von Oppenheim, *Vom Mittelmeer zum Persischen Golf*, vol. 2, pp. 153–4; Père Anastase Marie de Saint-Élie, OCD, 'al-Yazidiya', *al-Machriq*, vol. 2, 1899, pp. 834–5; Roger Lescot, *Enquête sur les Yezidis de Syrie et du Djebel Sindjār*, p. 183. Sadiq Al Damlooji [Damluji], *The Yezidis* (Arabic), p. 510.

26 Oppenheim, *Die Beduinen*, vol. 1, p. 139; Dr M. Wiedemann, 'Die Kurden in Nord-Mesopotamien', *Asien*, vol. 4, 1904, pp. 7–8, and 'Ibrahim Paschas Glück und Ende', *Asien*, vol. 8, 1908–9, pp. 37, 52–3; Heard, *JRAI*, vol. 41, 1911, p. 218.

27 Père de Fonclayer, SJ, unpublished MS written around 1875, cited by Henri Lammens, SJ, 'Le massif du Ǧabal Sim'an et les Yézidis de Syrie, *MFO*, vol. 2, 1907, pp. 389–90; Lammens, 'Une visite aux Yézidis ou adorateurs du diable', *Relations d'Orient* (Beirut), 1929, pp. 157–73; Gertrude Lowthian Bell, *The Desert and the Sown*, pp. 279–96.

28 Nuri/Menzel/Grothe, vol. 1, p. 166; Damluji, *Yezidis*, p. 471; Chalabi, p. 252; summarized in Me 'Abbas 'Azzaoui [Azzawi], *Histoire des Yézidis* (Arabic), pp. 147–8, trans. Judge C.A. Good, incl. in Henry Field, *The Anthropology of Iraq*, part 2, no. 1, *The Northern Jazira*, p. 90.

29 Ximénez, *Archives Asiatiques*, vol. 1, 1912, pp. 18–21.

30 *Op. cit.* vol. 1, 1912, pp. 21–2, 75–6, 157–61.

31 H. A. G. Percy, Lord Warkworth, *Notes from a Journey in Asiatic Turkey*, pp. 184–6. Lord Warkworth's photographs of the Sheikh Adi shrine in its ruined condition are preserved in the Alnwick Castle library.

32 Comte F. van den Steen de Jehay, *De la situation légale des sujets ottomans non-musulmans*, pp. 402–3; C. F. Lehmann-Haupt, *Armenien Einst und Jetzt*, vol. 2, part 1, pp. 364–5.

33 Heard, *JRAI*, vol. 41, 1911, p. 218; Sa'id al-Diwahji, *al-Yazidiya*, p. 192.

34 Sykes, 'Journeys in North Mesopotamia', *GJ*, vol. 30, 1907, pp. 388–91, 398; also his *Caliph's Last Heritage*, pp. 333–6.

35 W. A. W[igram], 'The Shrine of the Devil-Worshippers', *QP*, no. 57, 1904, pp. 652–7.

36 Chalabi, p. 252/Azzawi, p. 148/Field, *Northern Jazira*, p. 90.

37 M. E. Hume-Griffith, *Behind the Veil in Persia and Turkish Arabia*, pp. 289–91.

38 'The Downfall of Ibrahim Pasha', article dated November 1908, published in *The Times*, 11 January 1909, p. 6.

39 *ABC Archives* 16.9.7, vol. 19, Eastern Turkey Mission 1900–1909, vol. 3, items 140 and 142: Andrus letters, 23 October 1908 and 2 January 1909, to Peet.

40 Père Ign.-A. Khalifé, SJ, 'Les Yézidis – (Manuscrit)' (Arabic) *al -Machriq*, vol. 47,

1953, pp. 571–88.
41 Thomas Bois, OP, Les Yézidis', *al-Machriq*, vol. 55, 1961, p. 224.

Chapter 10

1 Oswald H. Parry, *Six Months in a Syrian Monastery*, pp. 252–3.
2 Dr Eduard Sachau, *Reise in Syrien und Mesopotamien*, dedication pages and p. 355; Sir E. A. Wallis Budge, *By Nile and Tigris*, vol. 2, p. 71; Sachau, *Verzeichniss der syrischen Handschriften der Königlichen Bibliothek*, vol. 1, pp. 434–6 (MS Sachau 200, fols. 37a–39a).
3 Budge, *Nile and Tigris*, vol. 2, pp. 70–1; but see pp. 228–9 for criticism of Yezidis by Jeremiah Shamir.
4 R. Y. Ebied, 'Some Syriac Manuscripts from the Collection of Sir E. A. Wallis Budge', incl. in *Symposium Syriacum 1972*, pp. 509–39; Ebied and M. J. L. Young, 'An Account of the History and Rituals of the Yazīdīs of Mosul', *Le Muséon*, vol. 85, 1972, pp. 481–522; J. M. Fiey, OP, 'Ṣur un "Traité arabe sur les patriarches nestoriens"', *Orientalia Christiana Periodica*, vol. 41, 1975, pp. 57–9, 72–5. The author is much obliged to Dr Sidney H. Griffith of the Institute of Christian Oriental Research at the Catholic University of America, Washington, DC, for translating the complete text of the Leeds Syr. MS No. 7 colophon.
5 [Alpheus N. Andrus] article, 'The Yezidees', *The Encyclopaedia of Missions* (1891 edition), vol. 2, pp. 526–8; Isya Joseph, 'Yezidi Texts', *AJSL*, vol. 25, 1909, pp. 247–8. The date suggested for the Jelwa (AH 558 = AD 1163) is close to the date of Sheikh Adi's death. But the date suggested for the Meshaf Resh (AH 743 = AD 1342/3) is 100 years after Sheikh Hasan b. Adi's death (AH 644 = AD 1246).
6 Abbé J.-B. Chabot, 'Notice sur les Yézidis', *JA*, series 9, vol. 7, 1896, p. 131, and 'Notice sur les manuscrits syriaques de la Bibliothèque Nationale acquis depuis 1874', *JA*, series 9, vol. 8, 1896, pp. 252–4; Bibliothèque Nationale letter, 10 June 1982, to author giving date of acquisition and price paid for BN Syr. MS 306.
7 Fiey, *Orientalia Christiana Periodica*, vol. 41, 1975, p. 58.
8 Chabot, *JA*, series 9, vol. 8, 1896, p. 271; Parry, p. xiv; Bibliothèque Nationale letter, 10 June 1982, to author giving date of acquisition and price paid for BN Syr. MS 324.
9 Muhammad Amin b. Khairallah al-'Umari, *Manhal al-awliya*, vol. 2, pp. 145–50; see also Sachau, *Verzeichniss*, vol. 1, p. 436 (MS Sachau 200, fols. 39b–42a). Extracts from this work were cited by N. Siouffi, 'Notice sur le Chéikh 'Adi et la secte des Yézidis', *JA*, series 8, vol. 5, 1885, pp. 80–1.
10 Parry, p. 357.
11 Yu. S. Kartsov, *Zametki o turetskikh yezidakh*, reprinted in *ZKORGO*, vol. 13, 1891, p. 242; George Percy Badger letter, 6 June 1853, to *Athenaeum*, published 16 July 1853, vol. 26, 1853, p. 860.
12 Dr L. E. Browski, 'Die Jeziden und ihre Religion', *Das Ausland*, vol. 59, 1886, pp. 761–7, 785–90.
13 Ishak's original manuscript was removed from the library at Alkosh and there is

some doubt as to the language in which it was written. See Fiey, *Assyrie Chrétienne*, [vol. 2] pp. 465–6, 811, and Thomas Bois, OP, 'Monastères chrétiens et temples yézidis dans le Kurdistan irakien', *al-Machriq*, vol. 61, 1967, p. 85.

14 A French translation of this section was published by H. Pognon, 'Sur les Yézidis du Sindjar', *ROC*, series 2, vol. 10, 1915–7, pp. 327–9.

15 Kartsov, *ZKORGO*, vol. 13, 1891, p. 244; Addai Scher, 'Notice sur les manuscrits syriaques conservés dans la bibliothèque du couvent des Chaldéens de Notre-Dame-des-Semences', *JA*, series 10, vol. 8, 1906, p. 76.

16 Kartsov, *Sem let na Blizhnem Vostoke 1879–1886*, p. 188.

17 *Monte Singar: Storia di un popolo ignoto*, ed. Mgr Samuele Giamil [Jamil].

18 Browski, *Das Ausland*, vol. 59, 1886, p. 764.

19 *Op. cit.* pp. 766–7; al-Shattanaufi, *Bahjat al-asrar*, cited by Rudolf Frank, *Scheich 'Adī, der grosse Heilige der Jezīdīs*, pp. 83–7; Anis Frayha, 'New Yezīdī Texts from Beled Sinjār, Iraq', *JAOS*, vol. 66, 1946, pp. 18–43.

20 Isya Joseph, *AJSL*, vol. 25, 1909, pp. 111, 252.

21 C. J. Edmonds, *A Pilgrimage to Lalish*, p. 50. The Edmonds manuscript, formerly owned by the Royal Society for Asian Affairs, is now in the Dara Attar Library, Edenbridge, Kent. Regrettably, time constraints prevented the author from availing himself of Mr. Attar's kind offer to let him study the manuscript.

22 Ign.-A. Khalifé, SJ, 'Les Yézidis – (Manuscrit)' (Arabic), *al-Machriq*, vol. 47, 1953, pp. 571–88. The date of translation is given as 10 Nisan 322 (presumably the Ottoman fiscal year 1322, which ran from 14 March 1906 to 13 March 1907).

23 The status of the Dominican and Carmelite missions in Iraq at the end of the nineteenth century is described by Fr. P.-G. Duval, OP, 'Aperçu général sur la mission de Mossoul', *L'Année Dominicaine*, vol. 27, 1888, pp. 109–19, 171–5, 386–93, 433–6 and vol. 28, 1889, pp. 60–71; and by Père Elisée de la Nativité, OCD, 'Deux siècles de vie chrétienne à Bagdad (1721–1921)', *Revue d'histoire des missions*, vol. 16, 1939, pp. 375–6.

24 Details of Père Anastase's early life are given in *Analecta Ordinis Carmelitarum Discalceatorum*, vol. 19, 1947, pp. 136–7. The account of his dealings with Habib/Abd el-Mesih is taken from Père Anastase's article 'La découverte récente des deux livres sacrés des Yézidis', *Anthropos*, vol. 6, 1911, pp. 1–8.

25 Anastase, 'al-Yazidiya', *al-Machriq*, vol. 2, 1899, pp. 32–7, 151–6, 309–14, 395–9, 547–53, 651–5, 731–6, 830–6.

26 Isya Joseph, *AJSL*, vol. 25, 1909, pp. 247–8.

27 *Op. cit.* p. 111.

28 Isya Joseph obituary, *Port Chester [New York] Daily Item*, 6 February 1923, p. 4.

29 *The Nineteen Hundred and Six Class Book*, entry under 'Joseph'.

30 *ABC Archives* 16.9.7, vol. 8, Eastern Turkey Mission 1880–1890, vol. 3, item 295, Rev. Caleb Gates letter, 9 March 1889, to Dr Smith; and vol. 12, Eastern Turkey Mission 1890–1899, vol. 3, item 136, Andrus letter, 27 June 1890, to Smith; *ABC Annual Report*, vol. 81, 1890/1, p. 45; Isya Joseph, *AJSL*, vol. 25, 1909, p. 113; Isya Joseph letter, 19 June 1919, to *The New York Times*, published 22 June 1919, Section III, p. 2. See also Gates, *Not To Me Only*, pp. 64–78.

31 *BFM, PCUSA*, Mission Correspondence, Iran/Incoming Letters, vol. 12, 1895–6,

item 114, E. W. McDowell letter, 21 November 1895, to Dr Brown; summarized in *Annual Report*, vol. 59, 1895/6, pp. 199–200; Isya Joseph, *AJSL*, vol. 25, 1909, p. 111; Isya Joseph, *Devil Worship: The Sacred Books and Traditions of the Yezidiz*, p. 115, 207–8.

32 *1906 Class Book*, entry under 'Joseph'; *Alumni Catalogue of the Union Theologi ral Seminary in the City of New York 1836–1926*, ed. Gillett, p. 422. The text of Isya Joseph's essay is preserved at Columbia University; the footnotes are missing.

33 Isya Joseph's work was acclaimed by Dr Theodor Menzel, *Ein Beitrag zur Kenntnis der Jeziden*, incl. in Hugo Grothe, *Meine Vorderasienexpedition 1906 und 1907*, vol. 1, pp. 98–100; by Alphonse Mingana, 'Devil-worshippers: their beliefs and their sacred books', *JRAS*, 1916, pp. 505–26; and by A. A. Semyonov, 'Pokloneniye satane u peredne-aziatskikh kurdov-yezidov', *Byulleten Srednovo Aziatskovo Gosudarstvennovo Universiteta* (Tashkent), vol. 16, 1927, pp. 59–80.

34 Sheikh Adi hymn: Heinrich Ewald, 'Die erste schriftliche Urkunde der Jezidäer', *Nachrichten von der G.A. Universität und der Königl. Gesellschaft der Wissenschaften zu Göttingen*, 1853, pp. 212–8 and 1854, pp. 149–50; 1872 Petition: Mark Lidzbarski, 'Ein Exposé der Jesiden', *ZDMG*, vol. 51, 1897, pp. 592–604; BN Syr. MS 306 and 324: Chabot, *JA*, series 9, vol. 7, 1896, pp. 102–17.

35 Isya Joseph thesis, *The Yezidis or 'Devil Worshippers'; Their Sacred Book and Traditions*, January 1908; Isya Joseph, *AJSL*, vol. 25, 1909, pp. 118–56, 218–54.

36 Isya Joseph, *Devil Worship*.

37 S. A. Yegiazarov, 'Kratky etnografichesko-yuridichesky ocherk yezidov Yerivanskoy guberniyi', *ZKORGO*, vol. 13, 1891, pp. 182–3, 221–7; Hugo Makas, *Kurdische Studien*, pp. 31–48.

38 Isya Joseph, *Harvard thesis*, p. xiii, and *AJSL*, vol. 25, 1909, p. 115.

39 *The Free Lance* (Fredericksburg, Virginia), 8 February 1923, p. 1. The author is obliged to Isya Joseph's grandson, Mr John MacPhee, for allowing me to use the scanty information possessed by his family.

40 Anastase, *Anthropos*, vol. 6, 1911, p. 8; Léon Krajewski, 'Le culte de Satan: Les Yezidis', *Mercure de France*, 15 November 1932, pp. 92–9. Provenance details for Aziz Kas Yusuf's text were kindly supplied by Père Fiey, the present possessor of a portion of this manuscript.

41 Anastase, *Anthropos*, vol. 6, 1911, pp. 8–10.

42 Univ.-Prof. Dr Maximilian Bittner, 'Die beiden heiligen Bücher der Jeziden im Lichte der Textkritik', *Anthropos*, vol. 6, 1911, pp. 628–39; and his 'Die heiligen Bücher der Jeziden oder Teufelsanbeter', *Denkschriften der Kaiserlichen Akademie der Wissenschaften in Wien, phil.-hist. Klasse*, vol. 55, 1913, Abhandlung 4, pp. 1–97, and Abhandlung 5, pp. 3–5 with 23 plates.

43 Edmonds, pp. 87–8.

44 A. Mingana (ed.), *Sources syriaques*, vol. 1, pp. i–xi, 1–168; and *Catalogue of the Mingana Collection of Manuscripts*, vol. 3, p. xiii; Sachau, 'Die Chronik von Arbela', *Königlich-Preussische Akademie der Wissenschaften, Abhandlungen, phil.-hist. Klasse*, 1915, no. 6, pp. 5–9. See also Lic. Dr G. Diettrich, 'Bericht über neuentdeckte handschriftliche Urkunden zur Geschichte des Gottesdienstes in der nestorianischen Kirche', *Nachrichten von der Königlichen Gesellschaft der*

Wissenschaften zu Göttingen, phil.-hist. Klasse, 1909, pp. 160–1.

45 Jacques-M. Vosté, OP, 'Alphonse Mingana', *Orientalia Christiana Periodica*, vol. 7, 1941, pp. 514–8.

46 Julius Assfalg, 'Zur Textüberlieferung der Chronik von Arbela', *Oriens Christianus*, vol. 50, 1966, pp. 22–4.

47 *Mingana Catalogue*, vol. 3, p. vi; Fiey, 'Auteur et date de la chronique d'Arbèles', *L'Orient Syrien*, vol. 12, 1967, pp. 266, 279.

48 *Mingana Catalogue*, vol. 3, pp. vi, xiii–xiv.

49 Mingana, *JRAS*, 1916, pp. 505–26.

50 Giuseppe Furlani, 'Sui Yezidi', *RSO*, vol. 13, 1932, pp. 123–32.

51 *Mingana Catalogue*, vol. 3, pp. vii–viii, xi.

52 Assfalg, *Oriens Christianus*, vol. 50, 1966, pp. 19–36; Fiey, *L'Orient Syrien*, vol. 12, 1967, p. 281, states that his research seems to indicate with some certainty that Ms. or. fol. 3126 was written by the priest who owned the oven. Dr S. P. Brock, 'Syriac historical writing: a survey of the main sources', *Journal of the Iraqi Academy (Syriac Corporation)*, vol. 5, 1979/80, p. 303, concludes that 'the question [whether the entire Chronicle of Erbil was the product of Mingana himself] must for the moment remain open'.

53 *Analecta Ordinis Carmelitarum Discalceatorum*, vol. 19, 1947, pp. 137–8. See also Humphrey Bowman, *Middle-East Window*, pp. 196–7. In December 1919 Père Anastase was awarded honorary membership in the Order of the British Empire; the citation states that he had 'rendered notable service to British prisoners in Baghdad after the fall of Kut and has been most helpful since in many ways'. The author is obliged to the Central Chancery of the Orders of Knighthood and the Protocol Department, Foreign and Commonwealth Office, for the citation.

54 Frayha, *JAOS*, vol. 66, 1946, pp. 18–43; Henry Field, introduction to Sami Said Ahmed, *The Yazidis: their Life and Beliefs*, ed. Field, pp. vi–vii.

55 Princess Wansa el-Amawy, interviewed by the author in October 1983, recalled seeing a religious book in Beled Sinjar that was written in a Persian script she was unable to read.

Chapter 11

1 Gertrude Lowthian Bell, *Amurath to Amurath*, pp. 273–80, and her Travel Journal, 7 and 8 May 1909.

2 Annotated Chol genealogies, differing in some details, are also given by Sadiq Al Damlooji [Damluji], *The Yezidis* (Arabic), pp. 22–33 (English summary in Sami Said Ahmed, *The Yazidis: their Life and Beliefs*, ed. Henry Field, p. 404); and by C. J. Edmonds, *A Pilgrimage to Lalish*, pp. 28–30. The author is obliged to Princess Wansa el-Amawy for information on recent generations of the Chol family.

3 Damluji, *Yezidis*, pp. 317–21; Daud al-Chalabi, *Makhtutat al-Mawsil*, p. 252, summarized in Me 'Abbas 'Azzaoui [Azzawi], *Histoire des Yézidis* (Arabic), p. 148, trans. Judge C. A. Good, incl. in Henry Field, *The Anthropology of Iraq*,

part 2, no. 1, *The Northern Jazira*, p. 90.

4 Ismā'īl Beg Chol, *The Yazīdīs: Past and Present* (Arabic), ed. Zurayk, pp. 2–3.

5 *Op. cit.* pp. 4–7.

6 Wigram's account, published in *QP* no. 80, July 1910, pp. 1030–1, gives no date for this episode other than 'during the autumn' and identifies the unnamed Yezidi prince as Mir Ali Beg's brother. In a letter to the author Dr J. P. Coakley deplores Wigram's disregard for chronology and considers that it could have taken place in the autumn of 1908 or 1909; in both periods Wigram and Hormizd canvassed the villages around Van. The flavour of the story is vintage Ismail.

7 Ismail, pp. 9–12.

8 *Op. cit.* pp. 12–20; Dr A. Dirr, 'Einiges über die Jeziden', *Anthropos*, vols. 12–13, 1917–8, pp. 558, 571–4.

9 Ismail, pp. 21–3.

10 *Op. cit.* pp. 23–5; Article, 'Glava Yezidov', *Tiflissky Listok*, 1909, no. 40, 20 February (O.S.), p. 2. The author is much obliged to Dr Ts. Chikvashvili, director of the foreign literature department of the Karl Marx State Republic Library of the Georgian Socialist Soviet Republic, Tbilisi, for providing a copy of this article.

11 M. Anholm, 'Missionen och österlandets djäfvulsdyrkare', *Svensk Missionstidskrift*, vol. 7, 1919, p. 157.

12 Ismail, pp. 26–31; *La Turquie*, 23 March 1909, cited by Basil Nikitine, 'Kratky ocherk religioznykh sekt v Turtsiyi', *Vostochny Sbornik*, vol. 2, 1916, p. 126.

13 Ismail, pp. 32–41. The manuscript he mentions was probably a copy of the *Extract from the History of the Yezidis*.

14 *QP* no. 79, April 1910, pp. 1017–9. A racier account of the 1909 autumn festival is given by Ernst Klippel, *Als Beduine zu den Teufelsanbetern*, pp. 157–91; reprinted under title *Unter Senûsy-Brüdern, Drusen und Teufelsanbetern*, pp. 188–223.

15 Mustafa Nûrî Pasha, *'Abede-i-iblīs*, trans. with commentary by Dr Theodor Menzel under title *Die Teufelsanbeter, oder ein Blick auf die widerspenstige Sekte der Jeziden*, incl. in Hugo Grothe, *Meine Vorderasienexpedition 1906 und 1907*, vol. 1, pp. 186–9; Georg Jacob, 'Ein neuer Text uber die Jezīdīs', *Beiträge zur Kenntnis des Orients*, vol. 7, 1908, p. 34.

16 Anastase Marie de Saint-Élie, OCD, 'La découverte récente des deux livres sacrés des Yézidis, *Anthropos*, vol. 6, 1911, p. 39 and plate on facing page.

17 *Illustrated London News*, 13 January 1912, p. 45; R. H. W. Empson, *The Cult of the Peacock Angel*, frontispiece and pp. 8–9.

18 Article, 'A Sacred Peacock: Gift to the British Museum', *The Times*, 8 July 1912, p. 8; Athelstan Riley letter, 11 July 1912, to *The Times*, published under title 'The Sacred Peacock of the Yezidis', 16 July 1912, p. 13.

19 Article, 'Devil-Worship at Mosul: Government Recognition', dated 5 May 1914, published in *The Times*, 16 May 1914, p. 7; Chalabi, p. 252/Azzawi, pp. 145–6/ Field, *Northern Jazira*, p. 89.

20 W. A. Wigram and Edgar T. A. Wigram, *The Cradle of Mankind*, pp. 106–7.

21 For details on Safr Aga see Damluji, *Yezidis*, pp. 28–9.

22 Ismail, pp. 42–3.

23 W. A. W[igram], *QP* no. 90, January 1913, p. 1190; W. A. Wigram and Edgar T.

A. Wigram, *The Cradle of Mankind*, pp. 108–9.

24 Harry Charles Luke, *Mosul and its Minorities*, p. 131; Edmonds, p. 30. Alphonse Mingana, 'Devil-worshippers: their beliefs and their sacred books', *JRAS*, 1916, p. 519, and Damluji, *Yezidis*, p. 28, point to Safr Aga as the murderer; neither of them implicates Mayan Khatun; E. S. Stevens, Lady Drower, *By Tigris and Euphrates*, p. 190, accuses Mayan Khatun but does not mention Safr Aga. See also *IO* L/MIL/17/15/46, Air Ministry, Military Report on 'Iraq (Area 9): Central Kurdistan, August 1929, p. 335.

25 Ismail, p. 43.

26 Damluji, *Yezidis*, p. 28.

27 Interview with Princess Wansa, 4 February 1984; see also Cyrus H. Gordon, 'Satan's Worshippers in Kurdistan', *Asia*, October 1935, p. 630.

28 Ismail, pp. 43–6; Lady Dorothy Mills, *Beyond the Bosphorus*, p. 210.

29 Ismail, pp. 46–52; interview with villagers from Kurukavak (formerly Hemduna), October 1983.

30 Ismail, pp. 52–3.

31 Mingana, 'Sacred Books of the Yezidis', *JRAS*, 1921, pp. 117. Ismail's autobiography does not mention this episode.

32 *Ottoman Archives*: Babiali Document nos. 318922, 318922/1–5; *The Times*, 16 May 1914, p. 7.

Chapter 12

1 Ismā'īl Beg Chol, *The Yazīdīs: Past and Present* (Arabic), ed. Zurayk, pp. 54–5.

2 *IO* L/P and S/10/618, Gertrude Bell report, 8 November 1917, to Arab Bureau; *Arab Bulletin*, 1917, pp. 514–5; Ismail, pp. 55–6.

3 Frances Lyman, 'The Missionary of Mardin', *Ararat*, vol. 2, 1981, no. 3, pp. 9–15. The author is much obliged to Mrs Lyman for background information about her kinsman.

4 Ismail, pp. 56–63; Rosita Forbes, *Conflict: Angora to Afghanistan*, p. 322.

5 Ismail, pp. 63–4; Gertrude Bell letter, 28 June 1918, to Sir Hugh Bell; *IO* L/P and S/10/618, Gertrude Bell report, 9 July 1918, to Arab Bureau.

6 *Op. cit.* Capt. A. Campbell Munro, IMS, Report on a visit to Jebel Sinjar – July 1918, dated 15 August 1918, incl. in Gertrude Bell report, 23 September 1918, to Arab Bureau; Gertrude Bell, *Review of the Civil Administration of Mesopotamia*, p. 50; Ismail, pp. 65–7; Major-General H. P. W. Hutson letter, 26 March 1980, and subsequent interviews with author. General Hutson recalls Ismail's wife coming back from the Sinjar, but does not remember any children.

7 Hutson letter, 26 March 1980, to author.

8 Alphonse Mingana, 'Devil-worshippers: their beliefs and their sacred books, *JRAS*, 1916, p. 520, and 'Sacred Books of the Yezidis', *JRAS*, 1921, pp. 117–9.

9 *IO* L/MIL/17/15/42, The General Staff, British Forces in Iraq, Military Report on

Mesopotamia (Iraq): Area 1 (Northern Jazirah), 1922, pp. 141–2; Sadiq Al Damlooji [Damluji], *The Yezidis* (Arabic), pp. 512–4.

10 Ismail, pp. 67–8; Major N. N. E. Bray, *A Paladin of Arabia: The Biography of Brevet Lieut.-Colonel G. E. Leachman*, p. 360. See also H. V. P. Winstone, *Leachman: 'OC Desert'*, p. 202.

11 Ismail, pp. 68–70; *Colonial Office* 696/2, Lieut.-Col. L. S. Nalder, Political Officer, Mosul, *Mosul Division Report for 1919*, pp. 18–19.

12 *Self Determination in 'Iraq*, p. 27. See also Gertrude Bell memorandum, February 1919, entitled '*Self-Determination in Mesopotamia*', incl. as Appendix 3 to Sir Arnold T. Wilson, *Mesopotamia 1917–1920: A Clash of Loyalties*, pp. 330–41; and Philip Willard Ireland, *'Iraq: A Study in Political Development*, pp. 166–75.

13 E. S. Stevens, Lady Drower, *By Tigris and Euphrates*, p. 184.

14 Ismail, p. 31; Elizabeth Dean Pickett and E. W. McDowell, (eds), *In the Land of Jonah and His Gourd: Home Letters of Margaret Dean McDowell*, p. 48.

15 Ismail, p. 70; *CO* 696/2, Nalder, *Mosul Division Report for 1919*, p. 18, cited by Gertrude Bell, *Review*, p. 50.

16 Ismail letter, 29 August 1920, to Hutson; *CO* 696/2, Nalder, *Mosul Division Report for 1919*, p. 19.

17 Ismail, pp. 70–1; Humphrey Bowman, *Middle-East Window*, p. 222; Ismail letter, 29 August 1920, to Hutson.

18 Ismail, p. 70; Stevens/Drower, *By Tigris and Euphrates*, pp. 187, 199–200; Betty Cunliffe-Owen, *'Thro' the Gates of Memory': From the Bosphorus to Baghdad*, pp. 156–7.

19 Bowman, pp. 217–22; Stevens/Drower, *By Tigris and Euphrates*, p. 190; Harry Charles Luke, *Mosul and its Minorities*, p. 126. See also *IO* L/MIL/17/15/42, *Northern Jazirah*, pp. 140–9, 155, 157.

20 C. J. Edmonds, *A Pilgrimage to Lalish*, pp. 61–2; article, 'Air Action against Yezidi Chief', *The Times*, 21 April 1925, p. 14; R. H. W. Empson, *The Cult of the Peacock Angel*, p. 95; Brigadier J. Gilbert Browne, *The Iraq Levies 1915–1932*, p. 44; Royal Air Force Museum, Department of Aviation Records, letter, 12 July 1983, to author.

21 Ismail, p. 72; Pickett/McDowell, *Land of Jonah*, pp. 25–30, 44–52, 105, 115; *BFM, PCUSA, Annual Report*, vol. 88, 1924/5, pp. 254–5. See also Gerald Reitlinger, 'Medieval Antiquities West of Mosul', *Iraq*, vol. 5, 1938, pp. 155–6 and Plate 26.

22 Interviews with Princess Wansa el-Amawy, February and July 1984.

23 Browne, p. 33; Ismail, pp. 71–2.

24 Edmonds, pp. 58–9.

25 Paul Schütz, *Zwischen Nil und Kaukasus*, pp. 135–42; review by R. Strothmann, *Orientalistische Literaturzeitung*, 1932, cols. 244–7.

26 Stevens/Drower, *By Tigris and Euphrates*, p. 190.

27 Luke articles, 'Minorities of Mosul III: The Yezidis', *The Times*, 27 August 1924, p. 9, and 28 August 1924, p. 9, reprinted under title 'The Yezidis or Devil-Worshippers of Mosul', *The Indian Antiquary*, May 1925, pp. 96–7, and in his books: *Mosul and its Minorities*, pp. 131–2, and *An Eastern Chequerboard*, pp. 268–9. See also Empson, pp. 91–5.

28 Rosita Forbes, *Conflict*, pp. 322–3; Damluji, *Yezidis*, p. 30.

29 Edmonds, p. 8; Damluji, *Yezidis*, p. 18.

30 Empson, pp. 92, 116; Edmonds, pp. 53–4; Damluji, *Yezidis*, p. 30; interview with Princess Wansa, July 1984.

31 Edmonds, pp. 8–9, 25–30; Stephen Hemsley Longrigg, *'Iraq, 1900 to 1950*, p. 193.

32 Me 'Abbas 'Azzaoui [Azzawi], *Histoire des Yézidis* (Arabic), p. 39, trans. Judge C. A. Good, incl. in Henry Field, *The Anthropology of Iraq*: part 2, no. 1, *The Northern Jazira*, pp. 88–9; H. Aziz Günel, *The Yezidis in History, the Origins of the Yezidis, their Religious, Political and Social History* (unpublished MS in Turkish), pp. 164–7. See also Field, *The Yezidis of Iraq*, incl. in Field and J. B. Glubb, *The Yezidis, Sulubba, and other Tribes of Iraq and Adjacent Regions*, p. 6.

33 See Professor Zurayk's introduction to Ismail's book (English summary on pp. 135–6).

34 Damluji, *Yezidis*, p. 26.

35 The author is greatly obliged to Princess Wansa el-Amawy for details of her life at Baadri and subsequent experiences, as related in interviews in October 1983, January and July 1984. A fuller account should appear in her planned autobiography.

36 Field, *Yezidis of Iraq*, pp. 10–11, and *Northern Jazira*, pp. 43–4, 80.

37 Roger Lescot, *Enquête sur les Yezidis de Syrie et du Djebel Sindjār*, pp. 190–5; Article, 'Devil-Worshippers' Revolt: Punitive Operations in Iraq', *The Times*, 26 October 1935, p. 11; Edmonds, pp. 62–4; also his memoranda, July 1936 (DS 70 92/JQ 1825 M4) and 15 September 1936 (BP 195 Y5/DS 79 9K) in the *Edmonds Papers* at the Middle East Centre, St Antony's College, Oxford; Longrigg, *'Iraq, 1900 to 1950*, pp. 242–3; Günel MS, pp. 189–92.

38 Stevens/Drower, *Peacock Angel*, pp. 1–4, 105–6.

39 Edmonds, pp. 64–8, covers events in the Jebel Sinjar during the second British occupation.

40 Damluji, *Yezidis*, pp. 18–19, 30.

41 *Op. cit.* pp. 19–20, 29–31; Edmonds, p. 30; see also undated letter from Yousif Rassam to Col. Lyon in *Edmonds Papers*; Günel MS, pp. 76–7.

42 Damluji, *Yezidis*, p. 36.

43 *Op. cit.* pp. 32–3; Gurguis Awwad, 'Bibliographie Yézidi' (Arabic and English), *al-Machriq*, vol. 63, 1969, p. 688; Thomas Bois, OP, 'La vie sociale des Kurdes', *al-Machriq*, vol. 56, 1962, pp. 609, 645.

44 Edmonds, p. 58.

Chapter 13

1 J. Chopin, 'De l'origine des peuples habitant la province d'Arménie', summarized by [P.I.] Köppen in *Bulletin Scientifique, Académie Impériale des Sciences de Saint-Pétersbourg*, vol. 8, 1841, pp. 16–20; Chopin, *Istorichesky pamyatnik sostoyaniya Armyanskoy-oblasti v epokhu yeya prisoyedineniya k Rossiskoy-Imperiyi*, cols 525, 529, 664–6; see also *Obozreniye Rossiskikh vladeny za Kavkazom*, vol. 1, pp. 270–1.

The Yezidis

2 [Moritz Wagner], 'Mittheilungen eines deutschen Reisender aus dem russischen Armenien', *Allgemeine Zeitung*, Beilagen, 1846, no. 123, p. 977; August Freiherr von Haxthausen, *Transkaukasia*, vol. 1, pp. 224–5.
3 Kh. Abovian, *Die Kurden und Jesiden*, unpublished 1846 article incl. in *Polnoye sobraniye sochineny*, vol. 8, pp. 221, 429; Moritz Wagner, *Reise nach Persien und dem Lande der Kurden*, vol. 2, pp. 254–5.
4 Moritz Wagner, *Reise nach dem Ararat und dem Hochland Armenien*, pp. 47–54 (Wagner's claim to have seen Yezidis on the eastern shore of Lake Sevan, originally published in *Allgemeine Zeitung*, Beilagen, 1846, no. 123, pp. 978–9, was challenged by Chopin, *Istorichesky pamyatnik*, cols. 528–9); Haxthausen, vol. 1, pp. 221–35; [A. N. Muraviev], *Gruziya i Armeniya*, vol. 2, pp. 129–32.
5 *Akty*, vol. 11, Arkhiv kantselyariyi glavnonachalstvuyushchevo, pp. 427–8, item 435, Col Loris-Melnikov guidelines, 20 November 1855 (O.S.), for the administration of Kurdish tribes.
6 Moritz Wagner, *Reise nach Persien*, vol. 2, p. 254; Abovian, *Die Kurden und Jesiden, Polnoye sobraniye sochineny*, vol. 8, pp. 222, 429.
7 Abovian article, 'Yezidy', *Kavkaz* (Tiflis), 1848, nos 8 and 9, 21 and 28 February (O.S.), incl. in *Polnoye sobraniye sochineny*, vol. 8, pp. 395–404, 451–3.
8 Gen Count N. N. Muraviev, *Voina za Kavkazom v 1855 g.*, vol. 1, pp. 30, 35.
9 S. A. Yegiazarov, 'Kratky etnografichesko-yuridichesky ocherk yezidov Erivanskoy guberniyi', *ZKORGO*, vol. 13, 1891, pp. 171–234.
10 *Op. cit.* pp. 197, 202–3; V. I. Devitsky, 'Kanikulyarnaya poyezdka po Erivanskoy guberniyi i Karsskoy oblasti', *SMOMPK*, vol. 21, 1896, p. 111.
11 Yegiazarov, *ZKORGO*, vol. 13, 1891, p. 230. Ali Beg was the son of Safar Beg (not shown in any Chol genealogy); it is possible that he was a Basmariya, related to Mir Mirza Beg by marriage. See Sadiq Al Damlooji [Damluji], *The Yezidis* (Arabic), p. 313; Yegiazarov, 'Kratky etnografichesky ocherk kurdov Erivanskoy guberniyi, *ZKORGO*, vol. 13, 1891, p. 13; and Édouard de Kovalevsky, 'Les Kourdes et les Iésides ou les adorateurs du démon', *Bulletin de la Société Royale Belge de Géographie*, vol. 14, 1890, p. 185.
12 F. S. Yanovitch, 'Ocherki Karsskoy oblasti', *SMOMPK*, vol. 34, 1904, p. 20; Prince V. I. Massal'sky, 'Ocherk pogranichnoy chasti Karsskoy oblasti', *Izvestiya Imperatorskovo Russkovo geograficheskovo obshchestva*, vol. 23, 1887, p. 32.
13 *Kavkazsky Kalendar*, vols 68–72, 1913–7. The total of 35,210 Yezidis shown for 1 January 1916 (O.S.) in the 1917 Kalendar fails to include 5,672 Yezidis shown as living in the Alexandropol district.
14 M. Anholm, 'Missionen och österlandets djäfvulsdyrkare', *Svensk Missionstidskrift*, vol. 7, 1919, pp. 151–75; Maria Gotwald, 'Die Jesiden', *Globus*, vol. 73, 1898, pp. 180–1; A. V. Williams Jackson, 'Notes of a Journey to Persia: I', *JAOS*, vol. 25, 1904, pp. 178–81.
15 Article, 'Glava Yezidov', *Tiflissky Listok*, 1909, no. 40, 20 February (O.S.), p. 2.
16 Dr A. Dirr, 'Einiges über die Jeziden', *Anthropos*, vols 12–13, 1917–8, pp. 558, 571–4 (this article was published in April 1919); A. Shamilov, 'Kurdy Zakavkaz'ya', *Revolyutsiya i Kul'tura*, 1930, no. 15–16, pp. 86–8.
17 Shamilov, 'Sredi kurdov', *Zarya Vostoka*, 1924, no. 553, cited by T. F. Aristova,

Chapter Notes

Kurdy Zakavkaz'ya, p. 39; Jacques Kayaloff, *The Battle of Sardarabad*, p. 20.

18 Kh. M. Chatoyev, *Kurdy Sovietskoy Armeniyi*, p. 30, with citation of A. G. Turshian, *Sardarapati Herosomarte*, pp. 125, 151. Kayaloff, *Sardarabad*, and E. F. Ludshuveit, *Turtsiya v gody pervoy mirovoy voiny 1914–1918 gg.*, do not mention Yezidis participating in the battle of Sardarabad. See also W. E. D. Allen and Paul Muratoff, *Caucasian Battlefields*, pp. 475–7.

19 Richard G. Hovannisian, *The Republic of Armenia*, vol. 1, pp. 449, 475; vol. 2, p. 17.

20 Comrade Zverev (Soviet representative, Batum) report on Armenian army, 25 October 1920, reproduced in Kayaloff, pp. 168–9.

21 Aristova has analysed the origin and successive domiciles of Yezidi communities in Soviet Armenia; see her 'Poyezdka k kurdam Zakavkaz'ya', *Sovietskaya Etnografiya*, 1958, pp. 135–7; 'Iz istoriyi voznikoveniya sovremennykh kurdskikh seleny v Zakavkaz'ye', *Sovietskaya Etnografiya*, 1962, pp. 20–30; and *Kurdy Zakavkaz'ya*, pp. 36–49; Damluji, *Yezidis*, p. 313; Shamilov, *Kurdsky Pastukh* (1935 Russian edition), p. 99.

22 Marietta Shaginian, *Progulki po Armeniyi*, pp. 25, 28-30; Adriano Alpago-Novello (ed.), *Documenti di Architettura Armena*, vol. 2, *Khatchkar*, pp. 14–15; Alpago-Novello et al., 'Consistenze e Tipologia delle Chiese Armene in Iran', *Ricerca sull' Architettura Armena*, no. 17, *Iran*, vol. 1, 1977, pp. 120–1, and no. 18, *Iran*, vol. 2, 1978, p. 22; J. M. Fiey, OP, *Assyrie Chrétienne*, [vol. 2], pp. 728–9.

23 Sharaf al-Din Bidlisi, *Chèref-nâmeh* [Sharaf-nâmeh] ou *Fastes de la nation kourde*, ed. and trans. Charmoy, vol. 2, part 1, pp. 169–70; B. Nikitine, 'Les Afšārs d'Urumieh', *JA*, vol. 214, 1929, pp. 109–18; V. F. Minorsky, 'Otchet o poyezdke v Makinskoye khanstvo ... v oktyabre 1905 goda', *Materialy po izucheniyu Vostoka*, vol. 1, 1909, pp. 23–4, cited in his *Kurdy, Zametki i Vpechatleniya*, p. 25.

24 Shirin Akinar, *Islamic Peoples of the Soviet Union*, pp. 208–15, analyses the Soviet census statistics on Kurds and Yezidis.

25 Shamilov, *Kurdsky Pastukh*, pp. 92–101; Shamilov, *Revolyutsiya i Kul'tura*, 1930, no. 15–16, pp. 86–9; Chatoyev, *Kurdy*, pp. 45–68; Chatoyev, *Uchastiye Kurdov Sovietskovo Soyuza v Velikoy Otechestvennoy Voine 1941–1945 gg.*, p. 69.

26 Damluji, *Yezidis*, pp. 310–4; O. Vil'chevsky, 'Ocherki po istoriyi yezidstva', *Ateist*, no. 51, April 1930, pp. 99–100; C. J. Edmonds, *A Pilgrimage to Lalish*, p. 54. The author was unable to consult the British and Norwegian diplomatic archives dealing with this affair.

27 Chatoyev, *Kurdy*, pp. 69–104.

28 Henry Field, *The Yezidis of Iraq*, incl. in Field and J. B. Glubb, *The Yezidis, Sulubba, and other Tribes of Iraq and Adjacent Regions*, p. 13; Field, *Contributions to the Anthropology of the Caucasus*, pp. 86–90.

29 S. A. Tokarev, *Etnografiya narodov SSSR*, p. 304; Aristova, *Kurdy Zakavkaz'ya*, p. 171.

30 Shamilov, *Kurdsky Pastukh*, pp. v–ix, 3–101; Thomas Bois, OP, 'Les Kurdes', *al-Machriq*, vol. 53, 1959, pp. 137–8; and his review of Shamilov, *Berbang*, in *L'Afrique et l'Asie*, no. 63, 1963, pp. 50–3.

31 Chatoyev, *Uchastiye*, pp. 38–50; Bois, *al-Machriq*, vol. 53, 1959, p. 139.

32 Chatoyev, *Uchastiye*, pp. 138–9.
33 Emir Muawwiyyah ben Esma'il Yazidi [Chol], *To Us Spoke Zarathustra...*, pp. 29, 95, 97.

Epilogue

1 The Kurdish text of this poem was published by Emir Jeladet Ali Bedr Khan in 'Quatre prières authentiques inédites des Kurdes Yézidis', *Kitêbxana Hawarê* (Damascus), no. 5, 1933, p. 7. A French translation by his brother, Dr. Kamuran Ali Bedr Khan, was published in *Hawar*, no. 15, 23 January 1933, p. 9. Another French translation by Père Thomas Bois, OP, appeared in his 'Les Yézidis et leur culte des morts', *Cahiers de l'Est*, series 2, vol. 1, 1947, pp. 55–6, and in his 'Les Yézidis', *al-Machriq*, vol. 55, 1961, pp. 200, 235. Emir Jeladet made a recording of the poem in Kurdish in January 1937 for Karl Hadank, who published it with a German translation in *Untersuchungen zum Westkurdischen: Bōtī und Ēzädī*, pp. 44–5, 49–51, 56–7. The English translation given here was made from the above-mentioned French and German translations. Another English translation appears in Sami Said Ahmed, *The Yazidis: their Life and Beliefs*, ed. Henry Field, pp. 460–1.

Appendix 1

1 Oswald H. Parry, *Six Months in a Syrian Monastery*, pp. 374–80.
2 R. Y. Ebied and M. J. L. Young, 'An Account of the History and Rituals of the Yazīdīs of Mosul, *Le Muséon*, vol. 85, 1972, pp. 481–522.
3 Austen H. Layard, *Discoveries in the Ruins of Nineveh and Babylon*, pp. 89–92.
4 Giuseppe Furlani, *Religione dei Yezidi: Testi religiosi dei Yezidi*.
5 Anis Frayha, 'New Yezīdī Texts from Beled Sinjār, 'Iraq', *JAOS*, vol. 66, 1946, pp. 18–43.

Bibliography

Existing bibliographies (listed by date of publication)

Menzel, Dr Theodor, 'Versuch einer Bibliographie der Jeziden', incl. in Hugo Grothe, *Meine Vorderasienexpedition 1906 und 1907*, Leipzig, 1911–12, vol. 1, pp. 119–26.

Menzel, Dr Theodor, Bibliography at end of article 'Yazīdī' in *Encyclopaedia of Islām*, Leiden, 1913–34, vol. 4, part 2, pp. 1168–70.

Musaelian, Zh. S., *Bibliografiya po Kurdovedeniyu*, Moscow, 1963.

van Rooy, Silvio and Tamboer, Rees, *ISK's Kurdish Bibliography*, 2 vols, Amsterdam, 1968.

Awwad, Gurguis, 'Bibliographie Yézidi', *al-Machriq*, vol. 63, 1969, pp. 673–708 (Arabic), 709–32 (English).

Government archives
(i) Great Britain

(a) FOREIGN OFFICE   FO 78/359, 2698, 2699, 4435, 4478, 5395.
British Embassy, Constantinople

Letters from Consuls   FO 195/113, 204, 1763 (Baghdad).

FO 195/175 (Erzurum).

FO 195/178, 228, 301, 394, 603, 717, 752, 796, 949 (Mosul).

FO 195/459, 603, 799, 889, 939 (Diyarbakir).

Letters to Consuls   FO 196/55.

(b) INDIA OFFICE   L/P and S/9/91, 95, 100; L/P and S/10/618.
L/MIL/17/15/46; L/MIL/17/18/46.

(c) COLONIAL OFFICE   CO 696/2 (Mosul Division Administration Report, 1919).

The Yezidis

(ii) France

Ministère des Affaires Étrangères, Correspondance politique des Consuls: Bagdad et
Mossoul, vol. 1; Mossoul, vol. 2.

(iii) Vatican

Sacra Congregatio de Propaganda Fide: Acta 1669–73; SOCG, vols. 239, 429, 434, 438.

(iv) Ottoman Empire

Mühimme Defterleri 114, p. 229; 115, pp. 125–6, 163.
Cevdet Tasnifi 3488.
Hatti Hümayun 22303, 22318, 22332, 22339, 22340, 22346, 22350, 22355, 22378,
25178, 25216, 25456, 27867, 32614, 33192, 33460, 34065, 34245, 36113.
Iradei Dahiliye 5311.
Ayniyat Defteri 340, p. 8 D 3.
Babiali 318922.

Other archives
(i) American Board of Commissioners for Foreign Missions

16.8.1, vol. 3: Syrian and Nestorian Missions 1844–1846.
16.8.4, vol. 1: Assyrian Mission 1850–1859.
16.8.7, vols 2 and 3: Nestorians of Persia 1838–1844, vols 1 and 2.
16.8.7, vol. 4: Mountain Nestorians 1838–1844.
16.8.7, vols 5 and 6: Nestorian Missions 1847–1859, vols 1 and 2.
16.9.7, vols 1 and 2: Eastern Turkey Mission 1860–1871, vols 1 and 2.
16.9.7, vols 3, 4 and 5: Eastern Turkey Mission 1871–1880, vols 1–3.
16.9.7, vols 6–9: Eastern Turkey Mission 1880–1890, vols 1–4.
16.9.7, vols 10–16: Eastern Turkey Mission 1890–1899, vols 1–7.
16.9.7, vols 17–25: Eastern Turkey Mission 1900–1909, vols 1–9.
35: Asahel Grant MS, *Life in Koordistan*, 2 vols.

(ii) Board of Foreign Missions of the Presbyterian Church in the United States of America

Mission Correspondence, Iran: Incoming Letters, vols 6, 10, 12 and 13, 1889–98.

(iii) Church Missionary Society

C M/M 3–6 Mission Books, 1829–39.

(iv) Royal Geographical Society

Correspondence Files: Ainsworth (Kurdistan Expedition).

Other papers
(i) Bibliothèque franciscaine provinciale, Paris

Abrégé des Archives de notre Mission d'Alep depuis l'an 1626 jusqu'en 1757.

(ii) British Library, Department of Manuscripts

Layard Papers (Add. MSS 38931–39164).

(iii) Middle East Centre, St Antony's College, Oxford

C. J. Edmonds Papers relating to his service in Iraq, 1915–45.

(iv) Society for Promoting Christian Knowledge

Report of Mr. Ainsworth and Mr. Rassam, respecting the Christians in Kurdistan, London, 1840.

(v) University of Newcastle upon Tyne, Department of Archaeology

Gertrude Bell Collection.

Official publications and works of reference

Akty sobranniye kavkazskoyu arkheograficheskoyu kommissiyeyu, 12 vols, Tiflis, 1866–1904.
Alumni Catalogue of the Union Theological Seminary in the City of New York 1836–1926, ed. Gillett, New York, 1926.
American Board of Commissioners for Foreign Missions, Annual Report, vol. 81, 1890/91.
Analecta Ordinis Carmelitarum Discalceatorum, vol. 19, 1947.
Arab Bulletin, [Cairo], 1917.
Board of Foreign Missions of the Presbyterian Church in the United States of America, Annual Report, vols 53, 59 and 88, 1889/90, 1895/6 and 1924/5.
A Chronicle of the Carmelites in Persia and the Papal Mission of the XVIIth and XVIIIth centuries, ed. Chick, 2 vols, London, 1939.
Encyclopaedia of Islām, 4 vols and supplement, Leiden, 1913–38.

Encyclopaedia of Islam, new edition, Leiden, in progress.
The Encyclopaedia of Missions, 2 vols, New York, 1891.
Journal of the Royal Geographical Society, vols 8 and 9, 1838 and 1839.
Kavkazsky Kalendar, Tiflis, vol. 46, 1891; vols 67–72, 1912–17.
The Nineteen Hundred and Six Class Book: A Record of the Senior Class of Columbia College Collectively and Individually from Birth to Graduation, New York, 1906.
Nouveaux memoires des missions de la Compagnie de Jesus dans le Levant, vol. 4, Paris, 1724.
Obozreniye Rossiskikh vladeny za Kavkazom, 4 vols, St Petersburg, 1836.
Repertoire chronologique d'épigraphie arabe, ed. Combe, Sauvaget and Wiet, Cairo, in progress.
Self Determination in 'Iraq, [Baghdad], 1919.

Published works

(i) Latin, Greek and Syriac

Acta Martyris Anastasii Persae, ed. Usener, Bonn, 1894.
Bar Hebraeus, *Chronicon ecclesiasticum*, ed. and trans. Abbeloos and Lamy, 3 vols, Louvain, 1872–7.
Bar Hebraeus, *Chronography*, ed. Bedjan, trans. Budge, 2 vols, Oxford, 1932.
Chronicon anonymum de ultimis regibus Persarum, ed. Ignazio Guidi, trans. Nöldeke, *Sitzungsberichte der Kaiserlichen Akademie der Wissenschaften in Wien, phil.-hist. Classe*, vol. 128, 1893, appendix 9, pp. 1–48.
(Chronique de Séert) *Histoire Nestorienne*, ed. and trans. Scher and others, *Patrologia Orientalis*, vol. 4, 1908, pp. 212–313; vol. 5, 1910, pp. 217–344; vol. 7, 1911, pp. 95–203; vol. 13, 1919, pp. 435–639.
Continuatio Byzantia Arabica a. 741 (add. 4 to Isidori Iunioris episcopi Hispalensis historia Gothorum Wandalorum Sueborum ad a. 624), ed. and trans. Mommsen, *Chronica Minora Saec. IV. V. VI. VII*, vol. 2, Berlin, 1894, pp. 323–69. (Monumenta Germaniae Historica, Auctorum antiquissimorum, vol. 11).
Rerum Seculo Quinto Decimo in Mesopotamia Gestarum, ed. Behnsch, trans. Budge, *The Chronography of Bar Hebraeus*, Oxford, 1932, vol. 2, pp. xxxvii–liii.
Theophanes, *Chronographia*, ed. and trans. de Boor, 2 vols, Leipzig, 1883–5.
Thomas, Bishop of Marga, *The Book of Governors, or the Historia Monastica*, ed. and trans. Budge, 2 vols, London, 1893.

(ii) Arabic, Persian and Turkish (before 1800)

Abu 'l-Faraj al-Isfahani, *Kitab al-Aghani*, various eds, 24 vols, Cairo, 1963–74.
Aksarayi, Mahmud, *Tezkire*, ed. and trans. Isiltan, *Die Seltschuken-Geschichte des Akserāyī*, Leipzig, 1943.
al-Dhahabi, *Tarikh al-Islam*, ed. al-Qudsi, 4 vols, Cairo, 1947–50.
Evliya Çelebi, *Seyahatname*, ed. Cevdet and others, 10 vols, Istanbul, 1896–1938.

Ibn 'Abd al-Zahir, *al-Rawd al-zahir fi sirat al-malik al-Zahir*, ed. and trans. Sadèque, *Baybars I of Egypt*, Dacca, 1956.

Ibn al-Athir, *al-Kamil fi 'l-tarikh*, ed. Tornberg, 13 vols, Beirut, 1965.

Ibn Battuta, *Tuhfat al-nuzzar fi ghara'ib al-amsar wa 'aja'ib al-asfar*, ed. and trans. Defrémery and Sanguinetti, 5 vols, Paris, 1853–79; English translation by H. A. R. Gibb, *The Travels of Ibn Battuta A.D. 1325–1354*, 2 vols, Cambridge, 1958–62. (Hakluyt Society, series 2, vols 110 and 117).

Ibn Bibi, *al-Awamir al-'ala'iya fi 'l-umur al-'ala'iya*, ed. and trans. Duda, *Die Seltschukengeschichte des Ibn Bibi*, Copenhagen, 1959.

Ibn Fadlallah al-'Umari, Shihab al-Din, *Masalik al-absar*; portion of vol. 4 ed. and trans. Quatremère, 'Notice de l'ouvrage qui a pour titre: Mesalek alabsar fi memalek alamsar', Institut Royal de France (Académie des inscriptions et belles-lettres), *Notices et extraits des manuscrits de la Bibliothèque du Roi et autres bibliothèques*, Paris, vol. 13, 1838, part 1, pp. 151–384.

Ibn al-Fuwati, *al-Hawadith al-jami'a*, ed. Jawad, Baghdad, 1932.

Ibn Hajar al-'Asqalani, *al-Durar al-kamina*, various eds, 4 vols, Hyderabad, 1929–31.

Ibn Khallikan, *Wafayat al-a'yan*, ed. 'Abbas, 8 vols, Beirut, 1968–72; English translation from Wüstenfeld edition by Baron MacGuckin de Slane, *Ibn Khallikan's Biographical Dictionary*, 4 vols, Paris, 1842–71.

Ibn Shaddad, 'Izz al-Din, *al-A'laq al-khatira fi dhikr umara' al-Sham wa'l-Jazira*, ed. al-Dahhan, Damascus, 1956. (Analysis by Claude Cahen, 'La Djazira au milieu du treizième siècle d'après 'Izz-ad Din ibn Chaddad', *Revue des études islamiques*, vol. 8, 1934, pp. 109–28).

Ibn Taimiya, *al-Risalat al-'adawiya*, incl. in *al-Majmu'at al-kubra*, Cairo, 1906, vol. 1, pp. 262–317.

Kâtip Çelebi a.k.a. Haci Halife, *Cihannumâ*, ed. and trans. Norberg, *Gihan Numa: Geographia Orientalis*, 2 vols, London, 1818.

Kâtip Çelebi a.k.a. Haci Halife, *Kashf al-zunun 'an asami 'l-kutub wa'l-funun*, ed. and trans. Flügel, *Lexicon bibliographicum et encyclopaedicum*, 7 vols, Leipzig/London, 1835–58.

Kazim, Muhammad, *Name-i alamana-i Nadiri*, ed. Mikhluko-Maklay, 3 vols, Moscow, 1960–6.

al-Kutubi, Ibn Shakir, *Fawat al-wafayat*, 2 vols, Bulaq, Cairo, 1866.

al-Maqrizi, *al-Khitat*, 2 vols, Bulaq, Cairo, 1853.

al-Maqrizi, *Kitab al-suluk*, ed. Ziadeh and Ashour, 4 vols, Cairo, 1934–42. (Portion ed. and trans. Quatremère, *Histoire des Sultans Mamlouks, de l'Égypte*, 2 vols, Paris, 1837–45).

Naima, Mustafa, *Tarih-i-Naima*, 6 vols, Istanbul, 1863.

Rashid al-Din, *Jami' al-tawarikh*; portion of vol. 1 ed. and trans. Quatremère, *Histoire des Mongols de la Perse*, Paris, 1836.

al-Sakhawi, *Tuhfat al-ahbab*, Cairo, 1937.

al-Sam'ani, *Kitab al-ansab*, ed. Margoliouth, London, 1912. (E. W. Gibb Memorial Series, vol. 20).

al-Shahrastani, Muhammad b. 'Abd al-Karim, *Kitab al-milal wa'l-nihal*, ed. Cureton, 2 vols, London, 1842–46; English translation of Part 1 by A. K. Kazi and J. G. Flynn,

Muslim Sects and Divisions, London, KPI, 1984.

Sharaf al-Din Bidlisi, *Sharaf-nâmeh*, ed. Vel'yaminov-Zernov, trans. Charmoy, *Chèref-nâmeh ou Fastes de la nation kourde*, 2 vols, St Petersburg, 1868–75.

al-Shattanaufi, *Bahjat al-asrar*, Cairo, 1896/7.

al-Tabari, *Tarikh al-rusul wa'l-muluk* (Annals), ed. de Goeje, 15 vols, Leiden, 1879–1901. (Portion ed. and trans. Nöldeke, *Geschichte der Perser und Araber zur Zeit der Sasaniden*, Leiden, 1879).

al-Tadifi, *Qala'id al-jawahir*, Cairo, 1912/3.

al-'Umari, Muhammad Amin b. Khairallah, *Manhal al-awliya*, ed. al-Diwahji, 2 vols, Mosul, 1968.

al-'Umari, Yasin b. Khairallah, *Ghara'ib al-athar*, ed. Jalili, Mosul, 1940.

al-'Umari, Yasin b. Khairallah, *Munyat al-udaba' fi tarikh al-Mawsil al-hadba'*, ed. al-Diwahji, Mosul, 1955.

al-'Umari, Yasin b. Khairallah, *Zubdat al-athar al-jaliya*, ed. Ra'uf, Baghdad, 1974.

(iii) All other

Abdulkurreem, Khojeh, *The Memoirs of K.A., a Cashmeerian of Distinction...from A.D. 1739 to 1749*, Calcutta, 1788.

Abovian, Khachatur, *Polnoye sobraniye sochineny*, 10 vols, Erivan, 1947–61.

Ahmed, Sami Said, *The Yazidis: their Life and Beliefs*, ed. Henry Field, Miami, 1975. (Field Research Projects, Study No. 97).

Ainsworth, William [Francis], *Report of a Journey from Bagdad to Constantinople viâ Kurdistan (1837)*, incl. as Appendix 11 to General Francis Rawdon Chesney, *Narrative of the Euphrates Expedition*, London, 1868, pp. 492–541.

Ainsworth, William [Francis], 'Notes on a Journey from Constantinople, by Heraclea, to Angora, in the Autumn of 1838', *JRGS*, vol. 9, 1839, pp. 216–76.

Ainsworth, William [Francis], 'Journey from Angora by Kaïsaríyah, Malátíyah, and Gergen Kal'eh-sí to Bír or Bírehjik', *JRGS*, vol. 10, 1841; pp. 275–340.

Ainsworth, William [Francis], 'Notes taken on a Journey from Constantinople to Mósul, in 1839–40', *JRGS*, vol. 10, 1841, pp. 489–529.

Ainsworth, William [Francis], 'Notes of an Excursion to Kal'ah Sherkát, the U'r of the Persians, and to the Ruins of Al Hadhr, the Hutra of the Chaldees, and Hatra of the Romans', *JRGS*, vol. 11, 1841, pp. 1–20.

Ainsworth, William [Francis], 'An Account of a Visit to the Chaldeans, inhabiting Central Kurdistán; and of an Ascent of the Peak of Rowándiz (Túr Sheïkhíwá) in the Summer of 1840', *JRGS*, vol. 11, 1841, pp. 21–76.

Ainsworth, William [Francis], *Travels and Researches in Asia Minor, Mesopotamia, Chaldea, and Armenia*, 2 vols, London, 1842.

Ainsworth, William [Francis], 'On the Izedis; or, Devil Worshippers, *Transactions of the Syro-Egyptian Society*, January–February 1855, pp. 1–4.

Ainsworth, William [Francis], 'The Assyrian Origin of the Izedis or Yezidis – the so-called "Devil Worshippers"', *Transactions of the Ethnological Society*, vol. 1, 1861, pp. 11–44.

Bibliography

Ainsworth, William [Francis], *A Personal Narrative of the Euphrates Expedition*, 2 vols, London, 1888.

Akiner, Shirin, *Islamic Peoples of the Soviet Union*, London, KPI, 1983.

Alexander, Constance M., *Baghdad in Bygone Days, from the Journals and Correspondence of Claudius Rich ... 1808–1821*, London, 1928.

Allen, W. E. D. and Muratoff, Paul, *Caucasian Battlefields*, Cambridge, 1953.

Alpago-Novello, Adriano (ed.), *Documenti di Architettura Armena*, vol. 2, *Khatchkar*, Milan, 1977.

Alpago-Novello, Adriano *et al.*, 'Consistenza e Tipologia delle Chiese Armene in Iran', *Ricerca sull' Architettura Armena*, nos 17 and 18, *Iran*, Milan, 1977–8.

Anastase Marie de Saint-Élie, O.C.D., 'al-Yazidiya', *al-Machriq*, vol. 2, 1899, pp. 32–7, 151–6, 309–14, 395–9, 547–53, 651–5, 731–6, 830–6.

Anastase Marie de Saint-Élie, O.C.D., 'La découverte récente des deux livres sacrés des Yézidis', *Anthropos*, vol. 6, 1911, pp. 1–39.

Anastase Marie de Saint-Élie, O.C.D., 'The final word on the origin of the Yezidi religion' (Arabic), *al-Muqtataf*, vol. 61, 1922, pp. 113–9.

Anderson, Rev. Rufus, *History of the Missions of the American Board of Commissioners for Foreign Missions to the Oriental Churches*, 2 vols, Boston, 1872–73.

Andrus, Rev. A. N., 'Concerning the Yezidees', *MH*, vol. 85, 1889, pp. 385–8.

[Andrus, Rev. A. N.], article 'The Yezidees', in *The Encyclopaedia of Missions*, New York, 1891, vol. 2, pp. 526–8.

Andrus, Rev. A. N., 'More about the Yezidees', *MH*, vol. 88, 1892, pp. 175–6.

Andrus, Rev. A. N., 'Persecution of the Yezidees', *MH*, vol. 89, 1893, p. 149.

Andrus, Rev. A. N., obituary, *MH*, vol. 115, 1919, pp. 107–8.

Anholm, Maria, 'Missionen och österlandets djäfvulsdyrkare', *Svensk Missionstidskrift*, vol. 7, 1919, pp. 151–75.

Anon, *De la nation des Curdes Iasidies qu'on appelle Adorateurs du Diable*, n.p., circa 1700, incl. in Paul Perdrizet, 'Documents du XVIIe siècle relatifs aux Yézidis', *Bulletin de la Société de Géographie de l'Est*, 1903, pp. 297–306, 429–45.

Anon, *Journal d'une campagne au service de Méhemet-Pacha*, incl. in [Rémi] Aucher-Eloy, *Relations de voyages en Orient de 1830 à 1838*, Paris, 1843, vol. 1, pp. 99–132.

Anon, 'In the Temple of the Devil-Worshippers', *The Standard*, London, 29 November 1893, p. 2.

Anon, 'The Devil-Worshippers: An Interview with the Chief', *The Standard*, London, 30 August 1901, p. 6.

Anon, 'The Yezidis: a Strange Survival', *Church Quarterly Review*, vol. 58, 1904, pp. 119–37.

Aristova, T. F., 'Poyezdka k kurdam Zakavkaz'ya', *Sovietskaya Etnografiya*, 1958, pp. 134–45.

Aristova, T. F., 'Iz istoriyi voznikoveniya sovremennykh kurdskikh seleny v Zakavkaz'ye', *Sovietskaya Etnografiya*, 1962, pp. 20–30.

Aristova, T. F., *Kurdy Zakavkaz'ya*, Moscow, 1966.

Arvieux, Chevalier [Laurent] d', *Mémoires*, 6 vols, Paris, 1735.

Assfalg, Julius, 'Zur Textüberlieferung der Chronik von Arbela: Beobachtungen zu

257

Ms. or. fol. 3126', *Oriens Christianus*, vol. 50, 1966, pp. 19–36.

Aucher-Eloy, [Rémi], *Relations de voyages en Orient de 1830 à 1838*, ed. Jaubert, 2 vols, Paris, 1843.

Aver'yanov, P. I., *Kurdy v voinakh Rossiyi s Persiyey i Turtsiyey v techeniye XIX stoletiya*, Tiflis, 1900.

Avril, Baron Adolphe d', *La Chaldée chrétienne*, Paris, 1864.

Awn, Peter J., *Satan's Tragedy and Redemption: Iblīs in Sufi Psychology*, Leiden, 1983. (Studies in the History of Religions, vol. 44).

'Azzaoui, [Azzawi] Me 'Abbas, *Histoire des Yézidis* (Arabic), Baghdad, 1935.

Bachmann, Walter, *Kirchen und Moscheen in Armenien und Kurdistan*, Leipzig, 1913. (Deutsche Orient-Gesellschaft, Wissenschaftliche Veröffentlichungen, Heft 25).

Badger, Rev. George Percy, *The Nestorians and their Rituals*, 2 vols, London, 1852.

Baring-Gould, Rev. S., *The Lives of the Saints*, 16 vols, Edinburgh, 1914.

Baye, Baron [Berthelot] de, 'Au sud de la chaîne du Caucase', *Revue de Géographie*, vol. 44, 1899, pp. 241–75, 340–58.

[Bedr Khan, Emir Jeladet Ali] 'Bletch Chirguh', *La question kurde, ses origines et ses causes*, Cairo, 1930.

Bedr Khan, Emir Jeladet Ali, 'Quatre prières authentiques inédites des Kurdes Yézidis', *Kitêbxana Hawarê* (Damascus), no. 5, 1933.

Bedr Khan, Emir Kamuran Ali, 'Notice sur la Bible Noire', *Hawar*, vol. 1, no. 14 (31 December 1932), pp. 7–8; no. 15 (23 January 1933), pp. 8–9; no. 16 (15 February 1933), pp. 9–10.

Bell, Gertrude Lowthian, *The Desert and the Sown*, London, 1907.

Bell, Gertrude Lowthian, *Amurath to Amurath*, London, 1911.

Bell, Gertrude Lowthian, *Self-Determination in Mesopotamia*, incl. as Appendix 3 to Lt.-Col. Sir Arnold Talbot Wilson, *Mesopotamia 1917–20: A Clash of Loyalties*, Oxford, 1931, pp. 330–41.

Bell, Gertrude Lowthian, *Review of the Civil Administration of Mesopotamia*, Cmd. 1061, HMSO, 1920. (Parliamentary Papers, House of Commons, Session 1920, vol. 51).

Bello, P. Stéphane, *La congrégation de S. Hormisdas et l'église chaldéenne dans la première moitié du XIXe siècle*, Rome, 1939. (Orientalia Christiana Analecta, vol. 122).

Berchem, Max van, *Matériaux pour un Corpus Inscriptionum Arabicarum*, part 1, *Égypte*, Cairo, 1894. (Mémoires publiés par les membres de la Mission Archéologique Française au Caïre, vol. 19).

Berezin, I. N., 'Yezidy', *Magazin Zemlevedeniya i Puteshestvy*, vol. 3, 1854, pp. 428–54. (English translation by E. Prostov entitled *A Visit to the Yezidis in 1843*, incl. as Appendix A to Henry Field, *The Anthropology of Iraq*, part 2, no. 1, *The Northern Jazira*, Cambridge, Mass., 1951, pp. 67–79).

Berezin, I. N., 'Mosul', *BdCh*, vol. 133, 1855, pp. 170–90.

Berezin, I. N., 'Sovremennaya Turtsiya', *Otechestvenniya Zapiski*, vol. 104, 1856, pp. 29–58, 397–424.

Beth Hillel, David, *The Travels from Jerusalem, through Arabia, Koordistan, Part of*

Persia, and India, to Madras, 1824–1832, Madras, 1832.

Binder, Henri, *Au Kurdistan, en Mésopotamie, et en Perse*, Paris, 1887.

Birks, Rev. Herbert, *The Life and Correspondence of Thomas Valpy French*, 2 vols, London, 1895.

Bittner, Univ.-Prof. Dr. Maximilian, 'Die beiden heiligen Bücher der Jeziden im Lichte der Textkritik', *Anthropos*, vol. 6, 1911, pp. 628–39.

Bittner, Univ.-Prof. Dr. Maximilian, 'Die heiligen Bücher der Jeziden oder Teufel-sanbeter', *Denkschriften der Kaiserlichen Akademie der Wissenschaften in Wien, phil.-hist. Klasse*, vol. 55, 1913, Abhandlung 4, pp. 1–97 and Abhandlung 5, pp. 3–17 with 23 plates.

Bois, Thomas, O. P., 'Le Djebel Sindjar au début du XIXe siècle', *Roja Nu* (Beirut), no. 56 (10 September 1945).

Bois, Thomas, O. P., 'Les Yézidis et leur culte des morts', *Cahiers de l'Est* (Beirut), series 2, vol. 1, 1947, pp. 52–8.

Bois, Thomas, O. P., 'Coup d'oeil sur la littérature kurde', *al-Machriq*, vol. 49, 1955, pp. 201–39.

Bois, Thomas, O. P., 'Les Kurdes: Histoire, Sociologie, Littérature, Folklore', *al-Machriq*, vol. 53, 1959, pp. 101–47, 266–99.

Bois, Thomas, O. P., 'Les Yézidis: Essai historique et sociologique sur leur origine religieuse', *al-Machriq*, vol. 55, 1961, pp. 109–28, 190–242.

Bois, Thomas, O. P., 'La vie sociale des Kurdes', *al-Machriq*, vol. 56, 1962, pp. 599–661.

Bois, Thomas, O. P., review of Arab Shamilov, *Berbang*, Erivan, 1958, in *L'Afrique et l'Asie*, no. 63, 1963, pp. 49–53.

Bois, Thomas, O. P., 'La religion des Kurdes', *POC*, vol. 11, 1961, pp. 105–36.

Bois, Thomas, O. P.,'Bulletin raisonné d'études kurdes', *al-Machriq*, vol. 58, 1964, pp. 527–70.

Bois, Thomas, O. P., *Connaissance des Kurdes*, Beirut, 1965.

Bois, Thomas, O. P., 'Les dominicains à l'avant-garde de la Kurdologie au XVIIIe siècle', *Archivum fratrum praedicatorum*, vol. 35, 1965, pp. 265–92.

Bois, Thomas, O. P., 'Monastères chrétiens et temples yézidis dans le Kurdistan irakien', *al-Machriq*, vol. 61, 1967, pp. 75–103.

Boré, Eugène, *Correspondance et mémoires d'un voyageur en Orient*, 2 vols, Paris, 1840.

Boré, Eugène, 'De la vie religieuse chez les Chaldéens', *Annales de la philosophie chrétienne*, series 3, vol. 6, 1842, pp. 405–24; vol. 7, 1843, pp. 57–71, 214–31, 313–21; vol. 8, 1843, pp. 31–48, 95–125.

Botta, P.-É., *Monument de Ninive*, 5 vols, Paris, 1849–50.

Bouvat, L., 'A propos des Yézidis', *Revue du monde musulman*, vol. 28, 1914, pp. 339–46.

[Bowen, Rev. John], *Memorials* compiled by his sister, London, 1872.

Bowman, Humphrey, *Middle-East Window*, London, 1942.

Bray, Major N. N. E., *A Paladin of Arabia: The Biography of Brevet Lieut.-Colonel G. E. Leachman*, London, 1936.

Brock, S. P., 'Syriac historical writing: a survey of the main sources', *Journal of the Iraqi Academy (Syriac Corporation)*, vol. 5, 1979/80, pp. 297–326.

Browne, Brigadier J. Gilbert, *The Iraq Levies 1915–1932*, London, 1932.

Browski, Dr L. E., 'Die Jeziden und ihre Religion', *Das Ausland*, vol. 59, 1886, pp. 761–7, 785–90. (English version entitled 'The Yezidees, or Devil-worshippers' in *The Popular Science Monthly*, vol. 34, 1889, pp. 474–82. Arabic version in *al-Muqtataf*, Cairo, vol. 13, 1889, pp. 393–8).

Buckingham, J. S., *Travels in Mesopotamia*, 2 vols, London, 1827.

Budge, Sir E. A. Wallis, *By Nile and Tigris*, 2 vols, London, 1920.

Busse, Heribert, ''Abd al-Ganī an-Nābulusīs Reisen im Libanon (1100/1689–1112/ 1700)', *Der Islam*, vol. 44, 1968, pp. 71–114.

Cadalvène, [E.] de and Barrault, E., *Histoire de la guerre de Méhémed-Ali contre la Porte Ottomane, en Syrie et en Asie-Mineure, (1831–1833)*, Paris, 1837.

Cahen, Claude, *Pre-Ottoman Turkey*, London, 1968.

Campanile, [Raffaello] M. Giuseppe, O. P., *Storia della regione del Kurdistan e delle sette di religione ivi esistenti*, Naples, 1818.

Carruthers, Douglas, 'The Great Desert Caravan Route, Aleppo to Basra', *GJ*, vol. 52, 1918, pp. 157–84.

Carruthers, Douglas, introduction to *The Desert Route to India*, London, 1928. (Hakluyt Society, series 2, vol. 63).

Cartwright, John, *The Preacher's Travels*, London, 1611. (Summarized in Samuel Purchas, *His Pilgrimes*, ed. MacLehose, Glasgow, vol. 8, 1905, pp. 482–523).

Çavli, Yildirim, articles on Yezidis in the Tur Abdin, *Hürriyet*, 12–15 June 1983.

Ceyp, A. J., 'Die Yesidis', *Allgemeine Zeitung*, Beilage no. 204, (2 September 1890), pp. 1–3.

Chabot, Abbé J.-B., 'Notice sur les Yézidis', *JA*, series 9, vol. 7, 1896, pp. 100–32.

Chabot, Abbé J.-B., 'Notice sur les manuscrits syriens de la Bibliothèque Nationale acquis depuis 1874', *JA*, series 9, vol. 8, 1896, pp. 234–90.

al-Chalabi, Daud, *Makhtutat al-Mawsil*, Baghdad, 1927.

Chantre, Ernest, 'Notes ethnologiques sur les Yésidi', *Bulletin de la Société d'anthropologie de Lyon*, vol. 14, 1895, pp. 65–75.

Chatoyev, Kh. M., *Kurdy Sovietskoy Armeniyi: Istorichesky Ocherk (1920–1940)*, Erivan, 1965.

Chatoyev, Kh. M., *Uchastiye Kurdov Sovietskovo Soyuza v Velikoy Otechestvennoy Voine 1941–1945 gg.*, Erivan, 1970.

Chernyshevsky, N. G., *Polnoye sobraniye sochineny*, 16 vols, Moscow, 1939–53.

Chesney, Francis Rawdon, *The Expedition for the Survey of the Rivers Euphrates and Tigris ... 1835, 1836, and 1837*, 2 vols, London, 1850.

Chesney, Francis Rawdon, *Narrative of the Euphrates Expedition*, London, 1868.

Chesney, Louisa and O'Donnell, Jane, *The Life of the late General F. R. Chesney*, ed. S. Lane-Poole, London, 1885.

Chirguh, Bletch; ref. Bedr Khan, Emir Jeladet Ali.

[Chol], Amir Bayazid al-Amawi, 'The Peacock – Sanjaq Yazid' (Arabic), *Alturath Alsha'bi*, The Folklore Centre, [Iraq] Ministry of Information, vol. 4, 1973, pp. 55–8, 182–3.

Chol, Ismā'īl Beg, *The Yazīdīs: Past and Present* (Arabic), ed. Zurayk, Beirut, 1934.

Bibliography

[Chol], Emir Muawwiyyah ben Esma'il Yazidi, *To Us Spoke Zarathustra ...*, Paris, 1983.

Cholet, Comte [Arnaud] de, *Voyage en Turquie d'Asie, Arménie, Kurdistan, et Mésopotamie*, Paris, 1892.

Chopin, J., 'De l'origine des peuples habitant la province d'Arménie', summarized by [P. I.] Köppen, *Bulletin Scientifique, Académie Impériale des Sciences de Saint-Pétersbourg*, vol. 8, 1841, pp. 16–20.

Chopin, J., *Khozyaistvenniye ocherki chasti Arakskoy doliny, voshedshey v sostav Gruzino-Imeretinskoy guberniyi*, St. Petersburg, 1843.

Chopin, J., *Istorichesky pamyatnik sostoyaniya Armyanskoy-oblasti v epokhu yeya prisoyedineniya k Rossiskoy-Imperiyi*, St. Petersburg, 1852.

Chwolsohn, Dr D., *Die Ssabier und der Ssabismus*, 2 vols, St. Petersburg, 1856.

Clark, Rev. John A., *Glimpses of the Old World*, 2 vols, Philadelphia/London, 1840.

Clemente da Terzorio, O. M. Cap., *Le Missioni dei Minori Cappuccini*, 7 vols, Rome, 1913–38.

Clemente da Terzorio, O. M. Cap., 'Il vero autore del "Teatro della Turchia" e "Stato Presente della Turchia"', *Collectanea Franciscana*, vol. 3, 1933, pp. 384–95.

Corkill, N. L., 'Snake Specialists in Iraq', *Iraq*, vol. 6, 1939, pp. 45–52.

Coste, P.-X., *Mémoires d'un artiste: Notes et souvenirs de voyages*, Marseilles, 1878.

Coupland, R., *The Exploitation of East Africa 1856–1890: The Slave Trade and the Scramble*, London, 1939.

[Crawford, Adair], *Journal of a Deputation sent to the East by the Committee of the Malta Protestant College in 1849*, 2 vols, London, 1854.

Creswell, K. A. C., *The Muslim Architecture of Egypt*, 2 vols, Oxford, 1952–9.

Crowfoot, J. W., 'A Yezidi Rite', *Man*, vol. 1, 1901, pp. 145–6.

Cuinet, Vital, *La Turquie d'Asie*, 4 vols, Paris, 1890–5.

Cunliffe-Owen, Betty, *"Thro' the Gates of Memory" (From the Bosphorus to Baghdad)*, London, 1925.

Cunningham, A. B. (ed.), *The Early Correspondence of Richard Wood 1831–1841*, London, 1966. (Royal Historical Society, Camden series 4, vol. 3).

Cutts, Rev. E. L., *Christians under the Crescent in Asia*, London, 1877.

Al Damlooji [Damluji], Sadiq, *The Yezidis* (Arabic), Mosul, 1949.

Al Damlooji [Damluji], Sadiq, *Imarat Bahdinan al-Kurdiya*, Mosul, 1952.

Dantsig, B. M., *Russkiye puteshestvenniki na Blizhnem Vostoke*, Moscow, 1965.

Dehérain, Henri, *Silvestre de Sacy, ses contemporains et ses disciples*, Paris, 1938. (Haut-commissariat en Syrie et au Liban, Antiquités, Service des orientalistes et antiquaires, vol. 2).

Devitsky, V. I., 'Kanikulyarnaya poyezdka po Erivanskoy guberniyi i Karsskoy oblasti', *SMOMPK*, vol. 21, 1896, pp. 79–180.

Devonshire, Mrs R. L., *Some Cairo Mosques and their Founders*, London, 1921.

Diettrich, Lic. Dr. G., 'Bericht über neuentdeckte handschriftliche Urkunden zur Geschichte des Gottesdienstes in der nestorianischen Kirche', *Nachrichten von der Königlichen Gesellschaft der Wissenschaften zu Göttingen, phil.-hist. Klasse*, 1909, pp. 160–218.

261

The Yezidis

Dingelstedt, Victor, 'The Yezids', *Scottish Geographical Magazine*, vol. 14, 1898, pp. 295–307.

Dirr, Dr A., 'Einiges über die Jeziden', *Anthropos*, vol. 12/13, 1917–8.

[Dittel, V.], 'Obzor tryokhgodichnovo puteshestviya po vostoku Magistra Villiama Dittelya', *Zhurnal Ministerstva Narodnovo Prosveshcheniya*, vol. 56, 1847, pp. 1–30. (French translation in *Nouvelles annales de voyages et des sciences géographiques*, series 5, vol. 19, 1849, pp. 141–68.

Dittel, V., 'Ocherk puteshestviya po Vostoku s 1842 po 1845 gg.', *BdCh*, vol. 95, 1849, section 1, pp. 1–56, 191–210.

al-Diwahji, Sa'id, *al-Yazidiya*, Mosul, 1973.

[Driver, G. R.], *Kurdistan and the Kurds*, Mount Carmel, Palestine, 1920.

Driver, G. R., 'The Religion of the Kurds', *Bulletin of the School of Oriental Studies*, vol. 2, part 2, 1922, pp. 197–213.

Driver, G. R., 'Studies in Kurdish History', *Bulletin of the School of Oriental Studies*, vol. 2, part 3, 1922, pp. 491–511.

Drower, E. S.; see Stevens.

Dupré, Adrien, *Voyage en Perse, fait dans les années 1807, 1808 et 1809, en traversant la Natolie et la Mésopotamie, depuis Constantinople jusqu'à l'extremité du Golfe Persique, et de là à Irewan*, 2 vols, Paris, 1819.

Duval, P.-G., O.P., 'Aperçu général sur la mission de Mossoul', *L'Année Dominicaine*, vol. 27, 1888, pp. 109–19, 171–5, 386–93, 433–6; vol. 28, 1889, pp. 60–71.

Dwight, Rev. Timothy, *The Duty of Americans at the present Crisis*, New Haven, 1798.

Dzhalil, Dzhalile, 'Geroicheskiye pesni kurdov-yezidov o sobytiyakh svyazannykh s pereseleniyem yikh predkov v Rossiyu v 30-kh godakh XIX veka', *Iranskaya Filologiya*, Leningrad, 1964. (Trudy nauchnoy konferentsiyi po iranskoy filologiyi, 24–27 January 1962).

Dzhalil, Dzhalile, *Kurdy Osmanskoy Imperiyi v pervoy polovine XIX veka*, Moscow, 1973.

Ebied, R. Y., *Some Syriac Manuscripts from the Collection of Sir E. A. Wallis Budge*, incl. in *Symposium Syriacum 1972*, Rome, 1974, pp. 509–39. (Orientalia Christiana Analecta, vol. 197).

Ebied, R. Y. and Young, M. J. L., 'An Account of the History and Rituals of the Yazīdīs of Mosul', *Le Muséon*, vol. 85, 1972, pp. 481–522.

Edmonds, C. J., *A Pilgrimage to Lalish*, London, 1967. (Royal Asiatic Society of Great Britain and Ireland, Prize Publication Fund, vol. 21).

Édouard d'Alençon, O. M. C., letter, 13 February 1909, "Le Sieur Michel Febvre", *Études Franciscaines*, vol. 21, 1909, pp. 435–8.

Elisée de la Nativité, O. C. D., 'Deux siècles de vie chrétienne à Bagdad (1721–1921)', *Revue d'histoire des missions*, vol. 13, 1936, pp. 357–70; vol. 14, 1937, pp. 230–46; vol. 16, 1939, pp. 349–80.

Eliseyev, A. V., 'Sredi poklonnikov dyavola', *Severny Vestnik*, 1892, no. 1, section 1, pp. 52–92; no. 2, section 1, pp. 51–84.

Empson, R. H. W., *The Cult of the Peacock Angel*, London, 1928.

Erk, Erol, 'Yezidiler arasinda', *Hürriyet*, Istanbul, 13–19 March 1966.

Ewald, Heinrich, 'Die erste schriftliche Urkunde der Jezidäer', *Nachrichten von der*

262

Bibliography

G.A. *Universität und der Königl, Gesellschaft der Wissenschaften zu Göttingen*, 1853, pp. 209–22; 1854, pp. 149–50 ('Nachtrag').

'Febvre, Michele, C. M. A.', *Specchio, o vero descrizione della Turchia*, Rome and Florence, 1674. (French translation, entitled *L'État present de la Turquie*, Paris, 1675).

'Febvre, Michele, C. M. A.', *Teatro della Turchia*, Milan, 1681, Bologna and Venice, 1683, Bologna, 1684 and Venice, 1684. (French translation, entitled *Theâtre de la Turquie*, Paris, 1682 and 1688).

Field, Henry, *The Anthropology of Iraq*, part 2, no. 1, *The Northern Jazira*, Cambridge, Mass., 1951. (Peabody Museum Papers, vol. 46, no. 1).

Field, Henry, *Contributions to the Anthropology of the Caucasus*, Cambridge, Mass., 1953. (Peabody Museum Papers, vol. 48, no. 1).

Field, Henry, *The Track of Man*, Garden City, New York, 1953.

Field, Henry, preface to Anis Frayha, 'New Yezīdī Texts from Beled Sinjār, 'Iraq', *JAOS*, vol. 66, 1946, p. 18.

Field, Henry, preface to Sami Said Ahmed, *The Yazidis: their Life and Beliefs*, ed. Field, Coconut Grove, Miami, 1975, pp. v–x. (Field Research Projects, Study No. 97).

Field, Henry, *The Yezidis of Iraq*, incl. in Field and J. B. Glubb, *The Yezidis, Sulubba, and Other Tribes of Iraq and Adjacent Regions*, Menasha, Wisconsin, 1943. (General Series in Anthropology, No. 10).

Fiey, J. M., O. P., 'Mossoul d'avant 1915', *Sumer*, vol. 2, 1946, pp. 31–41.

Fiey, J. M., O. P., 'Jean de Dailam et l'imbroglio de ses fondations', *POC*, vol. 10, 1960, pp. 195–211.

Fiey, J. M., O. P., 'Les laïcs dans l'histoire de l'Eglise syrienne orientale', *POC*, vol. 14, 1964, pp. 169–83.

Fiey, J. M., O. P., 'Encore 'Abdulmasīh de Singǎr', *Le Muséon*, vol. 77, 1964, pp. 205–23.

Fiey, J. M., O. P., 'L'Apport de Mgr Addaï Scher (†1915) à l'hagiographie orientale', *Analecta Bollandiana*, vol. 83, 1965, pp. 121–42.

Fiey, J. M., O. P., 'Auteur et date de la Chronique d'Arbèles', *L'Orient Syrien*, vol. 12, 1967, pp. 265–302.

Fiey, J. M., O. P., *Assyrie Chrétienne*, 3 vols, Beirut, 1965–8. (Recherches publiées sous la direction de l'Institut de Lettres Orientales de Beyrouth, series 3: Orient Chrétien, vols. 22, 23 and 42).

Fiey, J. M., O. P., *Jalons pour une histoire de l'Église en Iraq*, Louvain, 1970. (Corpus Scriptorum Christianorum Orientalium, vol. 310/Subsidia vol. 36).

Fiey, J. M., O. P., 'Devil Worshippers?', *Baghdad*, [Iraq] Ministry of Information, July 1972, pp. 6–12.

Fiey, J. M., O. P., *Chrétiens syriaques sous les Mongols*, Louvain, 1975. (Corpus Scriptorum Christianorum Orientalium, vol. 362/Subsidia vol. 44).

Fiey, J. M., O. P., 'Sur un "Traité arabe sur les patriarches nestoriens"', *Orientalia Christiana Periodica*, vol. 41, 1975, pp. 57–75.

Fiey, J. M., O. P., 'Rites étranges dans la Békaa', *L'Orient-Le Jour* (Beirut), 12 May 1977.

Fiey, J. M., O. P., *Nisibe*, Louvain, 1977. (Corpus Scriptorum Christianorum Orientalium, vol. 388/Subsidia vol. 54).

Finch, J. P. G., 'St George and El Khidr', *Journal of the Royal Central Asian Society*, vol. 33, 1946, pp. 236–8.

Finnie, David H., *Pioneers East*, Cambridge, Mass., 1967.

Fischer, A., 'Ein Gesetz der Jeziditen', *ZDMG*, vol. 58, 1904, p. 876.

Fletcher, Rev. J. P., *Notes from Nineveh, and Travels in Mesopotamia, Assyria, and Syria*, 2 vols, London, 1850 (single volume in Philadelphia edition, 1850).

Flügel, Prof. G., 'Einige geographische und ethnographische Handschriften der Refâîja auf der Universitätsbibliothek zu Leipzig, *ZDMG*, vol. 16, 1862, pp. 651–709.

Forbes, Frederick, 'A Visit to the Sinjár Hills in 1838, with some account of the Sect of Yezídís, and of various places in the Mesopotamian Desert, between the Rivers Tigris and Khábúr', *JRGS*, vol. 9, 1839, pp. 409–30.

Forbes, Rosita, *Conflict: Angora to Afghanistan*, London, 1931.

Frank, Dr Rudolf, *Scheich 'Adî, der grosse Heilige der Jezîdîs*, Berlin, 1911. (Türkische Bibliothek, vol. 14).

Fraser, David, *The Short Cut to India: the record of a journey along the route of the Baghdad Railway*, Edinburgh, 1909.

Fraser, J. Baillie, *Travels in Koordistan, Mesopotamia, &c.*, 2 vols, London, 1840.

Frayha, Anis, 'New Yezīdī Texts from Beled Sinjār, 'Iraq', *JAOS*, vol. 66, 1946, pp. 18–43.

Furlani, Giuseppe, *Religione dei Yezidi: Testi religiosi dei Yezidi*, Bologna, 1930. (Testi e Documenti per la Storia delle Religioni, vol. 3). English translation by J. M. Unvala entitled *The Religion of the Yezidis*, Bombay, 1940.

Furlani, Giuseppe, 'Sui Yezidi', *RSO*, vol. 13, 1932, pp. 97–132.

Furlani, Giuseppe, 'Maurizio Garzoni sui Yezidi', *SMSR*, vol. 8, 1932, pp. 166–75.

Furlani, Giuseppe, 'Visita a Šeyh 'Adī', *SMSR*, vol. 10, 1934, pp. 95–7.

Furlani, Giuseppe, 'Il yezidismo secondo Ismâ'îl Beǧ Čol', *Giornale della Societa Asiatica Italiana*, vol. 3, 1935, pp. 373–7.

Furlani, Giuseppe, *I misteriosi "Adoratori del Diavolo" nell'Alta Assiria*, incl. in *Le Meraviglie del Passato*, 2nd edition, Milan, 1936, vol. 1, pp. 305–13.

Furlani, Giuseppe, 'I santi dei yezidi', *Orientalia*, vol. 5, 1936, pp. 64–83.

Furlani, Giuseppe, 'Nuovi documenti sui Yezidi', *SMSR*, vol. 12, 1936, pp. 150–65.

Furlani, Giuseppe, 'The Yezidi villages in Northern 'Irāq', *JRAS*, 1937, pp. 483–91.

Furlani, Giuseppe, 'Gli interdetti dei Yezidi', *Der Islam*, vol. 24, 1937, pp. 151–74.

Furlani, Giuseppe, 'Le feste dei Yezidi', *Wiener Zeitschrift für die Kunde des Morgenlandes*, vol. 45, 1937, pp. 65–97.

Furlani, Giuseppe, 'Un nuovo libro sui Yezidi, *SMSR*, vol. 15, 1939, pp. 51–7.

Furlani, Giuseppe, 'Pietro della Valle sui Yezidi', *Oriente Moderno*, vol. 24, 1944, pp. 17–26.

Furlani, Giuseppe, 'I sette angeli dei Yezidi', *Rendiconti dell'Accademia Nazionale dei Lincei, Classe di Scienze Morali, Storiche e Filologiche*, series 8, vol. 2, 1947, pp. 141–61.

Furlani, Giuseppe, 'Il Pavone e gli 'Utrê ribelli presso i Mandei e il Pavone dei Yezidi', *SMSR*, vol. 21, 1948, pp. 48–76.

Furlani, Giuseppe, 'Origene e i Yezidi', *Rendiconti dell'Accademia Nazionale dei Lincei, Classe di Scienze Morali, Storiche e Filologiche*, series 8, vol. 7, 1952, pp. 7–14.

Gabrieli, G., 'Un Cappuccino Francese del 600 Viaggiatore e Descrittore sagace della Turchia non ancora beneconosciuto', *Il Pensiero Missionario*, vol. 4, 1932, pp. 284–9.

Gabrieli, G., 'Una rettifica non accettabile', *Il Pensiero Missionario*, vol. 5, 1933, pp. 339–40.

Garzoni, Maurizio, O. P., *Della Setta delli Jazidj*, incl. in Abate Domenico Sestini, *Viaggi e opuscoli diversi*, Berlin, 1807, pp. 203–12. French translation by [Sylvestre de Sacy] entitled *Notice sur les Yézidis*, incl. in M*** [Jean-Baptiste Louis a.k.a. Joseph Rousseau], *Description du pachalik de Bagdad*, Paris, 1809, pp. 191–210.

Gasparro, Giulia Sfameni, 'I miti cosmogonici degli Yezidi', *Numen*, vol. 21, 1974, pp. 197–227; vol. 22, 1975, pp. 24–41.

Gates, Rev. Caleb Frank, *Not To Me Only*, Princeton, New Jersey, 1940.

Giamil, Samuele: see Ishak of Bartella.

G[ibbs], J. W., 'Melek Tâus of the Yezidîs', *JAOS*, vol. 3, 1853, pp. 502–3.

Goormachtigh, Bernard Marie, O.P., 'Histoire de la mission dominicaine en Mésopotamie et en Kurdistan', *Analecta Sacri Ordinis Fratrum Praedicatorum*, vol. 2, 1895–6, pp. 271–83, 405–19; vol. 3, 1897–8, pp. 79–88, 141–58, 197–214, 533–45.

Gordon, Cyrus H., 'Satan's Worshippers in Kurdistan', *Asia*, 1935, pp. 626–30.

Gottschalk, Hans L., *al-Malik al-Kamil von Egypten und seine Zeit*, Wiesbaden, 1958.

Gotwald, Maria, 'Die Jesiden', *Globus*, vol. 73, 1898, pp. 180–1.

Grant, Dr Asahel, *The Nestorians; or, the Lost Tribes*, New York/London, 1841.

Grant, Christina Phelps, *The Syrian Desert*, New York, 1938.

Graz, Liesl, *L'Irak au présent*, Lausanne, 1979.

Grothe, Hugo, *Meine Vorderasienexpedition 1906 und 1907*, 2 vols, Leipzig, 1911–2.

Groves, Anthony Norris, *Journal of a Residence at Baghdad during the Years 1830 and 1831*, London, 1833.

Guérinot, A., 'Les Yézidis', *Revue du monde musulman*, vol. 5, 1908, pp. 581–630.

Guest, Evan and others (eds), *Flora of Iraq*, Baghdad, in progress.

Guidi, Michelangelo, 'Origine dei Yazidi e storia religiosa dell'Islām e del dualismo', *RSO*, vol. 13, 1932, pp. 266–300.

Guidi, Michelangelo, 'Nuove ricerche sui Yazidi', *RSO*, vol. 13, 1932, pp. 377–427.

Guidi, Michelangelo, 'Altre fonti sui Yazidi', *RSO*, vol. 14, 1933, pp. 83–4.

Guidi, Michelangelo, report incl. in *Rendiconti dell'Accademia Nazionale dei Lincei, Classe di Scienze Morali, Storiche e Filologiche*, series 6, vol. 9, 1933, pp. 104–6.

Guidi, Michelangelo, article 'Yazidi' in *Enciclopedia Italiana*, Rome, vol. 35, 1937, pp. 832–3.

Guidi, Michelangelo, *Sui Yazidi*, incl. in *Atti del XIX Congresso Internazionale degli Orientalisti 1935 – XII*, Rome, 1938, pp. 559–66.

Hachicho, Mohamed Ali, 'English Travel Books about the Arab Near East in the Eighteenth Century', *Die Welt des Islams*, vol. 9, 1964, pp. 1–206.

Hadank, Karl, *Untersuchungen zum Westkurdischen: Bōtī und Ēzädī*, Leipzig, 1938. (Arbeiten aus dem Institut für Lautforschung an der Universität Berlin, ed. D. Westermann, vol. 6.)

Hammer-Purgstall, Joseph von, *Geschichte des Osmanischen Reiches*, 10 vols, Budapest, 1827–35.

Hammer-Purgstall, Joseph von, 'Sur les kourdes, sectateurs du Cheikh Aadi', *JA*, vol. 2, part 2, 1855, pp. 468–9.

Hamy, Dr E.-T., 'Voyage d'André Michaux en Syrie et en Perse (1782–1785) d'après son journal et sa correspondance', *Neuvième Congrès International de Géographie, 1908, Compte Rendu des travaux du congrès*, vol. 3, pp. 351–88.

Harford, Frederic D., 'Old Caravan Routes and Overland Routes in Syria, Arabia, and Mesopotamia', *The Nineteenth Century*, vol. 84, 1918, pp. 97–113.

Hartmann, Martin, 'Bohtān: Eine topographisch-historische Studie', *Mitteilungen der Vorderasiatischen Gesellschaft*, vol. 1, 1896, pp. 85–144; vol. 2, 1897, pp. 1–103.

Harvey, L. P., 'The People of the Peacock Angel', *Natural History*, vol. 68, 1959, pp. 566–75.

al-Hasani, 'Abd al-Razzaq, *al-Yazidiyun fi hadirihim wa madihim*, Baghdad, 1974.

Hasluck, F. W., *Christianity and Islam under the Sultans*, 2 vols, Oxford, 1929.

Haxthausen, August Freiherr von, *Transkaukasia*, 2 vols, Leipzig, 1856.

Heard, W. B., 'Notes on the Yezidis', *JRAI*, vol. 41, 1911, pp. 200–19.

Heude, William, *A Voyage up the Persian Gulf, and a Journey Overland from India to England in 1817*, London, 1819.

Heywood, C. J., *Sir Paul Rycaut, A Seventeenth-Century Observer of the Ottoman Empire: Notes for a Study*, part 2 of E. K. Shaw and C. J. Heywood, *English and Continental Views of the Ottoman Empire 1500–1800*, Los Angeles, 1972.

Hoffmann, Georg, *Auszüge aus syrischen Akten persischer Märtyrer*, Leipzig, 1880. (Abhandlungen für die Kunde des Morgenlandes, vol. 7, part 3).

Holt, P. M., *Egypt and the Fertile Crescent 1516–1922: A Political History*, Ithaca, New York, 1966.

Homes, Henry A., 'The Sect of Yezidies of Mesopotamia', *Biblical Repository and Classical Review*, series 2, vol. 7, 1842, pp. 329–51.

Hommaire de Hell, Xavier, *Voyage en Turquie et en Perse, executé par ordre du Gouvernement Français pendant les années 1846, 1847 et 1848*, 4 vols, Paris, 1854–60.

Horten, M., 'Die Geheimlehre der Jezidi, der sogenannten "Teufelsanbeter"', *Der neue Orient*, vol. 3, 1918, pp. 105–7.

Hovannisian, Richard G., *The Republic of Armenia*, Berkeley, California, in progress.

Hume-Griffith, M. E., *Behind the Veil in Persia and Turkish Arabia*, London, 1909.

Ignazio da Seggiano, O. F. M. Cap., (ed.), 'Documenti inediti sull'Apostolato dei Minori Cappuccini nel Vicino Oriente (1623–1683)', *Collectanea Franciscana*, vol. 18, 1948, pp. 118–244; vol. 22, 1952, pp. 339–86; vol. 23, 1953, pp. 297–338.

Ignazio da Seggiano, O. F. M. Cap., *L'Opera dei Cappuccini per l'unione dei cristiani nel Vicino Oriente durante il secolo XVII*, Rome, 1962. (Orientalia Christiana Analecta, vol. 163.)

Injijian, Lucas, *Ashkhara Kirutiun*, Venice, 1806.

Ireland, Philip Willard, *'Iraq: A Study in Political Development*, London, 1937.

[Ishak of Bartella], MS concerning the Yezidis, part 2, ed. and trans. H. Pognon under title 'Sur les Yézidis du Sindjar', *ROC*, series 2, vol. 10, 1915–17, pp. 327–9.

[Ishak of Bartella], MS concerning the Yezidis, part 3, ed. and trans. Mgr Samuele Giamil [Jamil] under title *Monte Singar: Storia d'un popolo ignoto*, Rome, 1900.

Ivanovsky, Al. A., 'Yezidy (Po issledovaniyam K. I. Goroshchenko)', *Russky Antropologichesky Zhurnal*, vol. 3, 1900, pp. 100–3.

Ives, Edward, *A Voyage from England to India in the year MDCCLIV ....; also, A Journey from Persia to England by an unusual Route*, London, 1773.

Jaba, Alexandre, *Recueil de notices et récits kourdes*, St Petersburg, 1860.

Jackson, A. V. Williams, 'Notes of a Journey to Persia: I', *JAOS*, vol. 25, 1904, pp. 176–84.

Jackson, A. V. Williams, *Persia Past and Present*, New York, 1906.

Jacob, Georg, 'Ein neuer Text über die Jezîdîs', *Beiträge zur Kenntnis des Orients*, vol. 7, 1908, pp. 30–5.

Jacobsen, Thorkild and Lloyd, Seton, *Sennacherib's Aqueduct at Jerwan*, Chicago, 1935. (The University of Chicago, Oriental Institute Publications, vol. 24.)

Jarry, Jacques, 'La Yazidiyya: un vernis d'Islam sur une hérésie gnostique', *Annales Islamologiques*, Cairo, vol. 7, 1967, pp. 1–20.

Jaubert, P. Amédée, *Voyage en Arménie et en Perse, fait dans les années 1805 et 1806*, Paris, 1821.

Jolowicz, Dr H., (ed.), *Polyglotte der orientalischen Poesie*, Leipzig, 1853.

Joseph, Isya, 'Yezidi Texts', *AJSL*, vol. 25, 1909, pp. 111–56, 218–54.

Joseph, Isya, *Devil Worship: The Sacred Books and Traditions of the Yezidiz*, Boston, 1919.

Joseph, John, *The Nestorians and Their Muslim Neighbors*, Princeton, New Jersey, 1961.

Kartsev, Colonel (G.S.) A., 'Kurdy', *ZKORGO*, vol. 19, 1897, pp. 337–68.

Kartsov, Yu. S., 'Marshrut iz Erzeruma v Mosul', *Sbornik Materialov po Aziyi*, vol. 19, 1885, pp. 271–84.

Kartsov, Yu. S., *Zametki o turetskikh yezidakh*, Tiflis, 1886, reprinted in *ZKORGO*, vol. 13, 1891, pp. 235–63.

Kartsov, Yu. S., *Sem let na Blizhnem Vostoke 1879–1886*, St Petersburg, 1906.

Kawerau, Peter, *Amerika und die orientalischen Kirchen*, Berlin, 1958.

Kayaloff, Jacques, *The Battle of Sardarabad*, The Hague, 1973.

Kemp, Percy, 'Mosuli Sketches of Ottoman History', *Middle Eastern Studies*, vol. 17, 1981, pp. 210–33.

Kemp, Percy, *Territoires d'Islam: Le monde vu de Mossoul au XVIIIe siècle*, Paris, 1982.

Kemp, Percy, 'History and Historiography in Jalili Mosul', *Middle Eastern Studies*, vol. 19, 1983, pp. 345–76.

Khalfin, N. A., *Bor'ba za Kurdistan (Kurdsky vopros v mezhdunarodnykh otnosheniyakh XIX veka)*, Moscow, 1963.

Khalifé, Ign.-A., S.J. 'Les Yézidis — (Manuscrit)' (Arabic), *al-Machriq*, vol. 47, 1953, pp. 571–88.

Kiepert, H., 'Mitteilungen von C. Haussknecht's botanischen Reisen in Kurdistan und Persien (1865–67)', *Zeitschrift der Gesellschaft für Erdkunde*, Berlin, vol. 3, 1868, pp. 464–73.

Kinneir, John MacDonald, *A Geographical Memoir of the Persian Empire*, London, 1813.

Kinneir, John MacDonald, *Journey through Asia Minor, Armenia, and Koordistan, in the years 1813 and 1814*, London, 1818.

Kirchmair, Heinrich, 'Über die Yesidi', *Der Islam*, vol. 34, 1959, pp. 162–73.

Klippel, Ernst, *Als Beduine zu den Teufelsanbetern*, Dresden, 1925 (reprinted under title *Unter Senûsy-Brüdern, Drusen und Teufelsanbetern*, Braunschweig, 1942).

Klippel, Ernst, *Unter Drusen, Kurden und Teufelsanbetern*, Berlin, 1926.

Kovalevsky, Édouard de, 'Les Kourdes et les Iésides ou les adorateurs du démon', *Bulletin de la Société Royale Belge de Géographie*, vol. 14, 1890, pp. 157–86.

Krajewski, Léon, 'Le culte de Satan: Les Yezidis', *Mercure de France*, 15 November 1932, pp. 87–123.

Krischner, Dr Harald and Mrs M., 'The Anthropology of Mesopotamia and Persia', *Proceedings, Koninklijke Akademie van Vetenschappen te Amsterdam*, vol. 35, 1932, pp. 205–27, 399–410.

Kuznetsova, N. A. and Dantsig, B. M., 'I. N. Berezin — puteshestvennik po Zakavkaz'yu, Iranu i Blizhnemu Vostoku', *Kratkiye soobshcheniya Instituta Vostokovedeniya*, vol. 22, 1956, pp. 92–100.

Lacour-Gayet, Georges, *Les dernières années de Talleyrand*, Paris, 1922. (Reprint from *Revue Mondiale*, 1 July 1922).

Lammens, Henri, S. J., 'Études sur le règne du Calife Omaiyade Mo'awia Ier', *MFO*, vol. 1, 1906, pp. 1–108; vol. 2, 1907, pp. 1–172; vol. 3, part 1, 1908, pp. 145–312.

Lammens, Henri, S. J., 'Le massif du Ğabal Sim'an et les Yézidis de Syrie', *MFO*, vol. 2, 1907, pp. 366–96.

Lammens, Henri, S. J., 'Le Califat de Yazîd Ier', *MFO*, vol. 4, 1910, pp. 233–312; vol. 5, 1911–2, pp. 79–267, 589–724; vol. 6, 1913, pp. 403–92; vol. 7, 1914–21, pp. 211–44.

Lammens, Henri, S. J., 'Mo'āwia II ou le dernier des Sofiānides', *RSO*, vol. 7, 1915, pp. 1–49.

Lammens, Henri, S. J., 'Le "Sofiânî": Héros national des Arabes Syriens', *Bulletin de l'Institut français d'archéologie orientale du Caïre*, vol. 21, 1922, pp. 131–44.

Lammens, Henri, S. J., 'L'Avènement des Marwānides et le Califat de Marwān Ier', *MFO*, vol. 12, 1927, pp. 43–147.

Lammens, Henri, S. J., 'Une visite aux Yézidis ou adorateurs du diable', *Relations d'Orient*, Beirut, 1929, pp. 157–73.

Lampart, Albert, *Ein Märtyrer der Union mit Rom: Joseph I 1681–1696 Patriarch der Chaldäer*, Einsiedeln (Switzerland), 1966.

Larsson, E. John, *Vid Ararats Fot*, Stockholm, 1919.

Lathrop, Rev. A. C., *Memoir of Asahel Grant, M.D., Missionary to the Nestorians*, New York, 1847.

Laurie, Rev. Thomas, *Dr. Grant and the Mountain Nestorians*, London, 1853.

Laurie, Rev. Thomas, 'Journal of a Visit to the Yezidees, with a Description of the

Bibliography

Excavations at Khorsabad', *Bibliotheca Sacra*, vol. 5, 1848, pp. 148–71.

[Laurie, Rev. Thomas], article, 'Grant, Asahel' in *The Encyclopaedia of Missions*, New York, 1891, vol. 1, pp. 394–5.

Lawrence, T. E., *Letters*, ed. David Garnett, London, 1938.

Layard, Austen Henry, *Nineveh and its Remains*, 2 vols, London, 1849.

Layard, Austen Henry, *Discoveries in the Ruins of Nineveh and Babylon*, London, 1853.

Layard, Sir Austen Henry, *Autobiography and Letters*, ed. Hon. William Bruce, 2 vols, London, 1903.

Lazarev, M. S., *Kurdistan i Kurdskaya Problema (90-e gody XIX veka — 1917 g.)*, Moscow, 1964.

Lazarev, M. S., *Kurdsky Vopros (1891–1917)*, Moscow, 1972.

Le Strange, Guy, *The Lands of the Eastern Caliphate*, London, 1905.

Leandro di Santa Cecilia, Carmelitano Scalzo, *Mesopotamia, ovvero Terzo Viaggio dell' Oriente*, Rome, 1757.

Lehmann-Haupt, C. F., *Armenien Einst und Jetzt*, 3 vols, Berlin, 1910–31.

Lejean, Guillaume, 'Voyage dans la Babylonie', *Le Tour du Monde*, vol. 16, 1867, pp. 49–96.

Leroy, Jules, *Moines et monastères du Proche-Orient*, Paris, 1957.

Lescot, Roger, 'Quelques publications récentes sur les Yézidis, *Bulletin d'études orientales*, vol. 6, 1936, pp. 103–8.

Lescot, Roger, *Enquête sur les Yezidis de Syrie et du Djebel Sindjār*, Beirut, 1938. (Mémoires de l'Institut Français de Damas, vol. 5.)

Lescot, Roger, 'Les Yézidis', *La France Méditerranéenne et Africaine*, vol. 1, 1938, fasc. 3, pp. 55–87.

Lewis, W. H., *Levantine Adventurer: the travels and missions of the Chevalier d'Arvieux 1653–1697*, New York, 1963.

Lidzbarski, Mark, 'Beiträge zur Grammatik der neuaramäischen Dialekte', *Zeitschrift für Assyriologie*, vol. 9, 1894, pp. 224–63.

Lidzbarski, Mark, 'Ein Exposé der Jesiden', *ZDMG*, vol. 51, 1897, pp. 592–604.

Likhutin, Major-General M., *Russkiye v Aziyatskoy Turtsiyi v 1854 i 1855 godakh*, St Petersburg, 1863.

Lloyd, Seton, *Foundations in the Dust: The Story of Mesopotamian Exploration*, revised edition, London, 1980.

Lockhart, Laurence, *Nadir Shah*, London, 1938.

Long, Flight-Sergt. P. W., 'A Visit to Sheikh Adi: The Shrine of the Peacock Angel', *Journal of the Royal Central Asian Society*, vol. 23, 1936, pp. 632–8.

Longrigg, Stephen Hemsley, *Four Centuries of Modern Iraq*, Oxford, 1925.

Longrigg, Stephen Hemsley, *'Iraq, 1900 to 1950*, Oxford, 1953.

Lottin de Laval, [René], 'Besuch bei Khan Mahmud und Halil Bey in Kurdistan', *Das Ausland*, vol. 18, 1845, pp. 1339–40, 1343–4.

Low, Charles Rathbone, *History of the Indian Navy (1613–1863)*, 2 vols, London, 1877.

Ludshuveit, E. F., *Turtsiya v gody pervoy mirovoy voiny 1914–1918 gg.*, Moscow, 1966.

Luke, Harry Charles, *Mosul and its Minorities*, London, 1925.

Luke, Harry Charles, *An Eastern Chequerboard*, London, 1931.

Lyaister, A. F. and Chursin, G. F., *Geografiya Zakavkaz'ya*, Tiflis, 1929.

Lyman, Frances, 'The Missionary of Mardin', *Ararat*, Saddle Brook, New Jersey, vol. 2, 1981, no. 3, pp. 9–15.

McCoan, J. Carlile, *Our New Protectorate: Turkey in Asia*, 2 vols, London, 1879.

McDowell, E. W., 'The Nestorian Church and its present influence in Kurdistan', *Journal of Race Development*, vol. 2, 1911–2, pp. 67–88.

McDowell, Margaret Dean: see Pickett.

[Maclean, Arthur John], 'The Archbishop's Assyrian Mission: Canon Maclean's Journal', *The Church Review*, London, 1887, pp. 754–5 (23 December); 1888, p. 10 (6 January), pp. 20–1 (13 January), pp. 70–1 (3 February).

Maclean, Arthur John and Browne, William Henry, *The Catholicos of the East and his People*, London, 1892.

Macuch, Rudolf, *Geschichte der spät- und neusyrischen Literatur*, Berlin, 1976.

Magni, Cornelio, *Quanto di piu' curioso e vago Hà potuto raccorre, Nel secondo biennio da esso consumato in viaggj, e dimore per la Turchia*, 2 vols, Parma, 1692.

Main, Ernest, *Iraq: From Mandate to Independence*, London, 1935.

Makas, Hugo, (ed.), *Kurdische Texte im Kurmānjí-Dialecte aus der Gegend von Märdîn*, St. Petersburg/Leningrad, 1897, 1918, 1924.

Makas, Hugo, *Kurdische Studien*, Heidelberg, 1900.

Ma'lūf, Mgr I. Isk., 'Dictionnaire des localités et pays arabes' (Arabic), *al-Machriq*, vol. 57, 1963, pp. 145–60.

Margoliouth, D. S., 'Contributions to the Biography of 'Abd al-Kadir of Jilan', *JRAS*, 1907, pp. 267–310.

Marr, N. Ya., 'Yeshcho o slove "chelebi"', *Zapiski vostochnovo otdeleniya Imperatorskovo russkovo arkheologicheskovo obshchestva*, vol. 20, 1910, pp. 99–151.

Martin, Abbé P., *La Chaldée: esquisse historique*, Rome, 1867.

Mason, Robert, 'Feast of the Devil Worshippers', *Parade*, vol. 13, no. 159, 28 August 1943.

Massal'sky, Prince V. I., 'Ocherk pogranichnoy chasti Karsskoy oblasti', *Izvestiya Imperatorskovo Russkovo geograficheskovo obshchestva*, vol. 23, 1887, pp. 1–35.

Massignon, Louis, 'Al Hallâj: le phantasme crucifié des docètes et Satan selon les Yézidis', *Revue de l'histoire des religions*, vol. 63, 1911, pp. 195–207.

Massignon, Louis, 'Les Yézidis du Mont Sindjar: adorateurs d'Iblis', incl. in *Satan*, Brussels, 1948, pp. 175–6. (Études Carmelitaines).

Massignon, Louis, *Qissat Husayn al-Hallâj*, incl. in *Donum Natalicum H.S. Nyberg Oblatum*, Uppsala, 1954, pp. 102–17.

Maxton, Stanley, 'The Devil Worshippers', *Parade*, vol. 25, no. 324, 26 October 1946.

Meier, Fritz, *Der Name der Yazīdī's*, incl. in *Westöstliche Abhandlungen/Festschrift R. Tschudi*, Wiesbaden, 1954, pp. 244–57.

Menant, Joachim, *Les Yézidiz: Épisodes de l'histoire des adorateurs du diable*, Paris, 1892. (Annales du Musée Guimet, Bibliothèque de vulgarisation, vol. 5).

Menzel, Dr Theodor, *Ein Beitrag zur Kenntnis der Jeziden*, incl. in Hugo Grothe, *Meine Vorderasienexpedition 1906 und 1907*, Leipzig, 1911–2, vol. 1, pp. 89–211.

Menzel, Dr Theodor, article 'Jeziden' in *Die Religion in Geschichte und Gegenwart*, 2nd edition, Tübingen, 1927–32, vol. 3, cols 171–3.

Millingen, Major Frederick, *Wild Life among the Koords*, London, 1870.

Mills, Lady Dorothy, *Beyond the Bosphorus*, London, 1926.

Mingana, Alphonse (ed.), *Sources Syriaques, vol. 1, Měsiha-zkha, Bar Penkayé*, Mosul, [1907].

Mingana, Alphonse, 'Devil-worshippers; their beliefs and their sacred books', *JRAS*, 1916, pp. 505–26.

Mingana, Alphonse, 'Sacred Books of the Yezidis', *JRAS*, 1921, pp. 117–9.

[Mingana, Alphonse], *Catalogue of the Mingana Collection of Manuscripts*, 4 vols, Cambridge, 1933–48.

Minorsky, V. F., *Kurdy. Zametki i Vpechatleniya*, Petrograd, 1915. (Reprint from *Izvestiya Ministerstva Inostrannikh Del*, 1915, no. 3).

Minorsky, V. F., 'Otchet o poyezdke v Makinskoye khanstvo ... v oktyabre 1905 goda', *Materialy po izucheniyu Vostoka*, vol. 1, 1909, pp. 1–62.

Mirza Abu Taleb Khan, *Travels of, in Asia, Africa, and Europe, during the Years 1799, 1800, 1801, 1802, and 1803*, trans. C. Stewart, 3 vols, London, 1810.

Mitford, Edward Ledwich, *A Land March from England to Ceylon Forty Years Ago, through Dalmatia, Montenegro, Turkey, Asia Minor, Syria, Palestine, Assyria, Persia, Afghanistan, Scinde, and India, of which 7000 miles on horseback*, 2 vols, London, 1884.

Moberly, Brig.-Gen. F. J., *The Campaign in Mesopotamia, 1914–18*, 4 vols, London, 1923–7.

[Mohaqqaqi, Dr A.], 'The Origin of the Yazidi Tribe and their present Home in Iraq', *Iran League Quarterly*, vol. 3, 1933, pp. 221–9.

Mohr, Dr Paul, 'Die Jessiden: Die Sekte der sogenannten Teufelsanbeter', *Tägliche Rundschau*, 1927, nos. 138 and 139 (Unterhaltungsbeilage).

Moltke, Helmuth von, *Briefe über Zustände und Begebenheiten in der Türkei aus den Jahren 1835 bis 1839*, 6th edn, ed. Hirschfeld, Berlin, 1893. (*Gesammelte Werke*, vol. 8.)

Moltke, Helmuth von, contribution to *Memoir über die Construction der Karte von Kleinasien und Türkisch Armenien*, ed. Kiepert, Berlin, 1854, pp. 1–17.

Moltke, Helmuth von, *Darstellung des Türkisch-Ägyptischen Feldzugs im Sommer 1839*, Berlin, 1939.

Moutran, Nadra, *La Syrie de demain*, Paris, 1916.

Müller, Klaus E., *Kulturhistorische Studien zur Genese pseudo-islamischer Sektengebilde in Vorderasien*, Wiesbaden, 1967. (Studien zur Kulturkunde, vol. 22.)

Müller-Simonis, P. and Hyvernat, H., *Du Caucase au Golfe Persique à travers l'Arménie, le Kurdistan et la Mésopotamie*, Washington, D.C., 1892.

[Muraviev, A. N.], *Gruziya i Armeniya*, 3 vols, St Petersburg, 1848.

Muraviev, General Count N. N., *Voina za Kavkazom v 1855 g.*, 2 vols, St Petersburg, 1876.

Nau, Abbé F., 'Note sur la date et la vie de Cheikh 'Adi, chef des Yézidis', *ROC*, series 2, vol. 9, 1914, pp. 105–8.

Nau, Abbé F. and Tfinkdji, J., 'Recueil de textes et de documents sur les Yézidis, *ROC*, series 2, vol. 10, 1915–7, pp. 142–200, 225–75.

Neander, August, *Ueber die Elemente, aus denen die Lehren der Yeziden hervorgegangen zu sein scheinen*, incl. in *Wissenschaftliche Abhandlungen*, ed. Jacobi, Berlin, 1851, pp. 112–39.

Newman, Rev. John P., *The Thrones and Palaces of Babylon and Nineveh*, New York, 1876.

Niebuhr, Carsten, *Reisebeschreibung nach Arabien und andern umliegenden Ländern*, 3 vols, Copenhagen/Hamburg, 1774–1837.

Niewöhner, F., 'War der Kurdenfürst Bedir-Khan-Bey an der Schlacht von Nisib beteiligt?', *ZDMG*, vol. 133, 1983, pp. 134–44.

Nikitine, Basile, 'Kratky ocherk religioznykh sekt v Turtsiyi', *Vostochny Sbornik*, vol. 2, 1916, pp. 107–41.

Nikitine, Basile, 'Les Afšārs d'Urumiyeh', *JA*, vol. 214, 1929, pp. 67–123.

Nikitine, Basile, *Les Kurdes: étude sociologique et historique*, Paris, 1956.

Noel, Major E. W. C., *Diary on Special Duty in Kurdistan*, Basra, 1920.

Nöldeke, Theodor, 'Zur Geschichte der Araber im 1. Jahrh. d. H. aus syrischen Quellen', *ZDMG*, vol. 29, 1875, pp. 76–98.

Nöldeke, Theodor, 'Zur Geschichte der Omaijaden', *ZDMG*, vol. 55, 1901, pp. 683–91.

Nolde, Baron Eduard, *Reise nach Innerarabien, Kurdistan und Armenien, 1892*, Braunschweig, 1895.

Nostitz, Pauline, Countess, *Travels of Doctor and Madame Helfer in Syria, Mesopotamia, Burmah and other Lands*, trans. Mrs G. Sturge; 2 vols, London, 1878.

Nouri, Djelal, *Le Diable promu 'dieu'*, Constantinople, 1910.

Nûrî Pasha, Mustafa, '*Abede-i-iblīs*, Mosul, 1905, trans. with commentary by Dr Theodor Menzel under title *Die Teufelsanbeter, oder ein Blick auf die widerspenstige Sekte der Jeziden*, incl. in Hugo Grothe, *Mein Vorderasienexpedition 1906 und 1907*, Leipzig, 1911–12, vol. 1, pp. 127–93.

O'Ballance, Edgar, *The Kurdish Revolt 1961–1970*, London, 1973.

Özgönül, Emin, 'Seytani tanri bilenler...', *Hürriyet*, 4–8 April 1982.

Olivier, G. A., *Voyage dans l'Empire Othoman, l'Égypte et la Perse, fait par ordre du Gouvernement, pendant les six premières années de la République*, 6 vols, Paris, 1801–7.

Olson, Robert W., *The Siege of Mosul and Ottoman-Persian Relations 1718–1743*, Bloomington, Indiana, 1975.

Oppenheim, Dr Max Freiherr von, *Vom Mittelmeer zum Persischen Golf*, 2 vols, Berlin, 1899–1900.

Oppenheim, Dr Max Freiherr von, *Die Beduinen*, 4 vols, Leipzig/Wiesbaden, 1939–67.

Oppert, Jules, *Expédition scientifique en Mésopotamie executée par ordre du Gouvernement de 1851 à 1854*, 3 vols, Paris, 1856–9.

Ortiz de Urbina, I., S.J., 'Intorno al valore storico della Chronica di Arbela', *Orientalia Christiana Periodica*, vol. 2, 1936, pp. 5–32.

Ortiz de Urbina, I., S.J., review of Alphonse Mingana, *Catalogue of the Mingana Collection of Manuscripts*, vol. 3, Cambridge, 1939, in *Orientalia Christiana Periodica*, vol. 6, 1940, pp. 550–1.

Otter, [Jean], *Voyage en Turquie et en Perse*, 2 vols, Paris, 1748.

Palmer, Roundell, Earl of Selborne, *Memorials*, ed. Lady Sophia M. Palmer, part I: *Family and Personal*, 2 vols, London, 1896–8.

Pareja, F. M., *Islamologie*, Beirut, 1957–63.

Bibliography

Parry, Oswald H., *Six Months in a Syrian Monastery*, London, 1895.

Pauli, Gustav, 'Von Tabris bis Wan', *Mitteilungen der Geographischen Gesellschaft in Lübeck*, vol. 11, 1889, pp. 46–88.

Pauli, Gustav, 'Von Wan bis an den Tigris bei Hesn Kefa', *Westermanns Illustrirte Deutsche Monatshefte*, vol. 44, 1878, pp. 73–83, 178–90.

Pauli, Gustav, 'Von Hösn Kefa am Tigris bis Bagdad', *Mitteilungen der Geographischen Gesellschaft in Lübeck*, vol. 12, 1889, pp. 76–121.

Percy, H. A. G., Lord Warkworth, *Notes from a Diary in Asīatīc Turkey*, London, 1898.

Perdrizet, Paul, 'Documents du XVIIe siècle relatifs aux Yézidis', *Bulletin de la Société de Géographie de l'Est*, 1903, pp. 281–306, 429–45.

Perkins, Rev. Justin, *A Residence of Eight Years in Persia, among the Nestorian Christians*, Andover, Mass., 1843.

Perrier, Ferdinand, *La Syrie sous le gouvernement de Méhemet-Ali jusqu'en 1840*, Paris, 1842.

Petermann, H., *Reisen im Orient*, 2 vols, Leipzig, 1861.

Pickett, Elizabeth Dean and McDowell, E. W. (ed), *In the Land of Jonah and His Gourd: Home Letters of Margaret Dean McDowell*, n.p., circa 1930.

Pillet, M. 'Sur la mort des orientalistes français', *Revue Archéologique*, series 6, vol. 9, 1937, pp. 226–33.

P[inches], T. G., biography of Hormuzd Rassam in *The Dictionary of National Biography*, Supplement January 1901–December 1911, 3 vols, Oxford, 1912, vol. 3, pp. 158–61.

Platt, D. C. M., *The Cinderella Service: British Consuls since 1825*, London, 1971.

Pognon; see Ishak of Bartella.

Pollington, Viscount; see Savile.

Pomiankowski, Lieut. Field Marshal Joseph, *Der Zusammenbruch des Ottomanischen Reiches*, Vienna, 1928.

Porter, Sir Robert Ker, *Travels in Georgia, Persia, Armenia, Ancient Babylonia, &c. &c. during the years 1817, 1818, 1819, and 1820*, 2 vols, London, 1822.

Poujoulat, Baptistin, *Voyage dans l'Asie Mineure, en Mésopotamie, à Palmyre, en Syrie, en Palestine et en Égypte*, 2 vols, Paris, 1840–1.

Prym, Eugen and Socin, Albert, *Der neu-aramaeische Dialekt des Tûr 'Abdîn*, Gottingen, 1881.

Prym, Eugen and Socin, Albert (ed), *Kurdische Sammlungen: Erzählungen und Lieder in den Dialekten des Tûr 'Abdîn und von Bohtan*, St Petersburg, 1890.

Pushkin, Alexander, 'Puteshestviye v Arzrum vo vremya pokhoda 1829 goda', *Sovremennik*, vol. 1, 1836, pp. 17–84. (English translation by Brigitta Ingemanson under title *A Journey to Arzrum*, Ann Arbor, Michigan, 1974.)

Rabbath, Antoine, SJ, (ed.), *Documents inédits pour servir à l'histoire du Christianisme en Orient*, 2 vols, Paris, 1905–10.

Rassam, Hormuzd, *Asshur and the Land of Nimrod*, Cincinnati, Ohio, 1897.

Rawlinson, Major H. C., 'Notes on a Journey from Tabríz, through Persian Kurdistán, to the Ruins of Takhti-Soleïmán, and from thence by Zenján and Tarom, to Gílán, in October and November 1838'; with a Memoir on the Site of the Atropatenian

Ecbatana', *JRGS*, vol. 10, 1841, pp. 1–158.

Rāyes, Estīpān, 'The Yezidis' (Syriac), *Qālā d'šrārā*, Urmia, vol. 2, 1898–9, fols. 78a–80a, 95b–99a, 113a–116b.

Reed, Squadron-Leader George S., *La mission de l'archevêque de Cantorbéry auprès des Assyriens*, Paris, 1967. (Cahiers d'Études Chrétiennes orientales, vol. 6.)

Reitlinger, Gerald, 'Medieval Antiquities West of Mosul', *Iraq*, vol. 5, 1938, pp. 143–56.

Remonnay, Jean, 'Chez les "Adorateurs du Diable": Les Yézidis', *Missi*, January 1938, pp. 4–11.

René de Nantes, O. M. C., 'La date de la mort du P. Pacifique de Provins', *Études Franciscaines*, vol. 21, 1909, pp. 180–5.

Rescher, O., *Orientalistische Miszellen*, 2 vols, Istanbul, 1925–36.

Rich, Claudius James, *Narrative of a Residence in Koordistan and on the site of ancient Nineveh*, ed. Mary Rich, 2 vols, London, 1836.

Richter, Julius, *A History of Protestant Missions in the Near East*, New York, 1910.

Riley, Athelstan, *The Archbishop of Canterbury's Mission to the Assyrian Christians*, London, 1891.

Riley, Athelstan, 'A visit to the Temple of the Devil', *The Pilot*, 1901, pp. 683–4.

Ritter, Carl, *Die Erdkunde im Verhältnis zur Natur und zur Geschichte des Menschen, oder allgemeine vergleichende Geographie*, parts 9–11, *Asien*, Berlin, 1840–4.

Ritter, Hellmut, *Turoyo, die Volkssprache der syrischen Christen des Tūr 'Abdîn*, 4 vols, Wiesbaden/Beirut, 1967–79.

Ritter, Hellmut, 'Kurmānci-texte aus dem Tūr 'Abdîn', *Oriens*, vols 21–22, 1968–9, pp. 1–135; vols 25–26, 1976, pp. 1–37.

Rivadeneyra, Adolfo, *Viaje de Ceylan a Damaso, Golfo Pérsico, Mesopotamia, Ruinas de Babilonia*, Madrid, 1871.

Robinson, E. and Smith, E., *Biblical Researches in Palestine, Mount Sinai and Arabia Petraea. A Journal of Travels in the Year 1838*, 3 vols, Boston, 1841.

Rocco da Cesinale, O. M. C., *Storia delle Missioni dei Cappuccini*, 3 vols, Rome, 1873.

Romanov, V. A., 'Poklonniki Diavola', *Priroda i Lyudi*, vol. 9, 1898, pp. 739–41, 751–3.

Ross, Henry James, *Letters from the East 1837–1857*, ed. Janet Ross, London, 1902.

Ross, Dr J., 'Notes on Two Journeys from Baghdád to the Ruins of Al Hadhr, in Mesopotamia, in 1836 and 1837', *JRGS*, vol. 9, 1839, pp. 443–70.

Rotter, Gernot, *Die Umaiyyaden und der zweite Bürgerkrieg (680–692)*, Wiesbaden, 1982. (Abhandlungen für die Kunde des Morgenlandes, vol. 45, 3).

[Rousseau, Jean Baptiste Louis a.k.a. Joseph], *Description du pachalik de Bagdad*, Paris, 1809.

Russell, T. M., 'The Battle of Nizib', *United Service Journal*, 1840, pp. 434–48.

Rycaut, Sir Paul, *The History of the Turkish Empire from the Year 1623. to the Year 1677*, London, 1679–80.

Sachau, Dr Eduard, *Reise in Syrien und Mesopotamien*, Leipzig, 1883.

Sachau, Dr Eduard, *Verzeichniss der syrischen Handschriften der Königlichen Bibliothek*, 2 vols, Berlin, 1899. (Königliche Bibliothek zu Berlin, Die Handschriften-Verzeichnisse, vol. 23.)

Sachau, Dr Eduard, *Am Euphrat und Tigris: Reisenotizen aus dem Winter 1897–1898*, Leipzig, 1900.

Bibliography

Sachau, Dr Eduard, 'Die Chronik von Arbela, ein Beitrag zur Kenntnis des ältesten Christentums im Orient', *Königlich-Preussische Akademie der Wissenschaften, Abhandlungen, phil.-hist. Klasse*, 1915, no. 6, pp. 5–92.

Sa'igh, Mgr Suleiman, *Tarikh al-Mawsil*, 3 vols, Cairo/Jounieh, 1923–56.

Samoilovitch, A. and others, articles on I. N. Berezin in *Zapiski kollegiyi vostokovedov pri Aziatskom Museye*, vol. 1, 1925, pp. 161–94; vol. 2, 1926, pp. 51–72.

[Sandreczki, Carl], 'Tigrisfahrt von Diarbekr bis Mosul', *Allgemeine Zeitung*, Beilagen, 1852, no. 202, pp. 3227–30; no. 214, pp. 3419–21; no. 216, pp. 3449–50; no. 217, pp. 3466–9.

Sandreczki, Carl, *Reise nach Mosul und durch Kurdistan nach Urumia, unternommen im Auftrage der Church Missionary Society in London 1850*, 3 vols, Stuttgart, 1857.

Sandwith, Humphry, *A Narrative of the Siege of Kars*, London, 1856.

Sarre, F. and Herzfeld, E., *Archäologische Reise im Euphrat- und Tigris-Gebiet*, 4 vols, Berlin, 1911–20.

Savile, J. C. G., Viscount Pollington, 'Notes on a Journey from Erz-Rúm, by Músh, Diyár-Bekr, and Bíreh-jik, to Aleppo, in June, 1838', *JRGS*, vol. 11, 1841, pp. 445–54.

Savile, J. C. G., Viscount Pollington, *Half Round the Old World, being some account of a Tour in Russia, the Caucasus, Persia, and Turkey, 1865–66*, London, 1867.

Scher, Mgr Addai, 'Notice sur les manuscrits syriaques conservés dans la bibliothèque du couvent des Chaldéens de Notre-Dame-des-Semences', *JA*, series 10, vol. 7, 1906, pp. 479–512; vol. 8, 1906, pp. 56–82.

Scher, Mgr Addai, 'Épisodes de l'histoire du Kurdistan', *JA*, series 10, vol. 15, 1910, pp. 119–39.

Schläfli, Dr Alexander, *Reisen in den Orient*, Winterthur, 1864. (Mitteilungen Schweizerischer Reisender, vol. 2.)

Schütz, Paul, *Zwischen Nil und Kaukasus: Ein Reisebericht zur religionspolitischen Lage im Orient*, Munich, 1930.

Scialva, Beridze, *Gli Adoratori del Diavolo*, Pompeii, 1931.

Seabrook, W. B., *Adventures in Arabia: Among the Bedouins, Druses, Whirling Dervishes, & Yezidee Devil Worshippers*, New York, 1927.

Sebri, Osman and Wikander, Steg, 'Un témoinage kurde sur les Yézidis du Djebel Sindjar', *Orientalia Suecana*, vol. 2, 1953, pp. 112–8.

Semyonov, A. A., 'Pokloneniye satane u peredne-aziatskikh kurdov-yezidov' *Byulletin Srednevo Aziatskovo Gosudarstvennovo Universiteta*, Tashkent, vol. 16, 1927, pp. 59–80.

Sercey, Comte [Édouard] de, *Une ambassade extraordinaire: La Perse en 1839–1840*, Paris, 1928.

Şerefettin, Mehmet, 'Yezidiler', *Darülfünun Ilâhiyat Fakültesi Mecmuasi*, Istanbul, vol. 1, no. 3, 1926, pp. 1–35.

Sestini, Abate Domenico, *Viaggio da Costantinopoli a Bassora*, Yverdun (Livorno), 1786.

Sestini, Abate Domenico, *Viaggio di ritorno da Bassora a Costantinopoli*, [Yverdun (Livorno)], 1788.

Sestini, Abate Domenico, *Viaggi e opuscoli diversi*, Berlin, 1807.

Shaginian, Marietta, *Progulki po Armeniyi*, Moscow/Leningrad, 1927.

Shamilov, Arab, 'Kurdy Zakavkaz'ya', *Revolyutsiya i Kul'tura*, 1930, no. 15–16, pp. 86–9.

Shamilov, Arab, *Kurdsky Pastukh/Kurdy Alagoza*, Tiflis, 1935; 2nd (revised) edition, Moscow, 1960.

Shiel, Lt.-Col. J., 'Notes on a Journey from Tabríz, through Kurdistán, via Ván, Bitlís, Sé'ert, and Erbíl, to Suleïmániyeh, in July and August, 1836, *JRGS*, vol. 8, 1838, pp. 54–101.

Siouffi, Nicolas, 'Une courte conversation avec le chef de la secte des Yezidis, ou les adorateurs du diable', *JA*, series 7, vol. 18, 1880, pp. 78–83.

Siouffi, Nicolas, 'Notice sur la secte des Yézidis', *JA*, series 7, vol. 20, 1882, pp. 252–68.

Siouffi, Nicolas, 'Notice sur le Chéikh 'Adi et la secte des Yézidis', *JA*, series 8, vol. 5, 1885, pp. 78–98.

Sjöholm, Wilh., 'Missionen i Kaukasien: Meddelanden från inspektionsresan', *Missionsförbundet*, vol. 28, 1910, pp. 161–3.

Smith, Rev. Eli and Dwight, Rev. H. G. O., *Missionary Researches in Armenia*, 2 vols, London, 1834.

Soane, Ely Bannister, *To Mesopotamia and Kurdistan in Disguise*, London, 1912.

So'aya, P. Louis, 'Histoire du couvent de Rabban Hormizd, de 1808 à 1832', ed. and trans. M. Brière, *ROC*, series 2, vol. 5, 1910, pp. 410–24; vol. 6, 1911, pp. 113–27, 249–54, 346–55.

Socin; see Prym.

Southgate, Rev. Horatio, *Narrative of a Tour through Armenia, Kurdistan, Persia and Mesopotamia*, 2 vols, New York, 1840.

Southgate, Rev. Horatio, *Narrative of a Visit to the Syrian (Jacobite) Church of Mesopotamia*, New York, 1844.

Spiro, Jean, 'Les Yezidi ou les adorateurs du diable', *Bulletin de la Société Neuchâteloise de Géographie*, vol. 12, 1899–1900, pp. 275–301.

Stark, Freya, *Baghdad Sketches*, London, 1937.

Stark, Freya, *Beyond Euphrates*, London, 1951.

Stark, Freya, 'The Yezidi Devil-Worshippers', *Geographical Magazine*, vol. 30, 1958, pp. 527–37.

Stark, Freya, *Riding to the Tigris*, London, 1959.

Stark, Freya, *Letters*, ed. Lucy Moorehead, 8 vols, London, 1974–82.

Steen de Jehay, Comte F. van den, *De la situation légale des sujets ottomans non-musulmans*, Brussels, 1906.

Stevens, E. S., Lady Drower, *By Tigris and Euphrates*, London, 1923.

Stevens, E. A., Lady Drower, *Peacock Angel*, London, 1941.

Stewart, Desmond, 'The Devil's Home Country', *Holiday*, October 1957, pp. 30–41, 135.

Stewart, Desmond and Haylock, John, *New Babylon: A portrait of Iraq*, London, 1956.

Stock, Eugene, *The History of the Church Missionary Society*, 4 vols, London, 1899–1916.

Strong, William E., *The Story of the American Board*, Boston, 1910.

Strothmann, R., 'Analecta haeretica', *Der Islam*, vol. 4, 1913, pp. 72–86.

Süreyya, Mehmed, *Sicill-i Osmâni*, 4 vols, Istanbul, 1890/1–93/4.

Bibliography

Sykes, Mark, *Through Five Turkish Provinces*, London, 1900.

Sykes, Mark, *Dar-ul-Islam: A Record of a Journey through Ten of the Asiatic Provinces of Turkey*, London, 1904.

Sykes, Mark, 'Journeys in North Mesopotamia', *GJ*, vol. 30, 1907, pp. 237–54, 384–98.

Sykes, Mark, 'The Kurdish Tribes of the Ottoman Empire', *JRAI*, vol. 38, 1908, pp. 451–86.

Sykes, Mark, *The Caliph's Last Heritage*, ed. Lady Sykes, London, 1915.

Taimur, Ahmad, *al-Yazidiya wa mansha nihlatihim*, Cairo, 1928/9.

Tchéraz, Minasse, 'Les Yézidis étudiés par un explorateur arménien', *Le Muséon*, vol. 10, 1891, pp. 194–8.

Texier, Ch., *Description de l'Arménie, la Perse et la Mésopotamie*, 2 vols, Paris, 1842–52.

Thesiger, Wilfred, *Desert, Marsh and Mountain*, London, 1979. (*The Last Nomad*, New York, 1980.)

Thielmann, Freiherr Max von, *Streifzüge im Kaukasus, in Persien und in der asiatischen Türkei*, Leipzig, 1875.

Tokarev, S. A., *Etnografiya narodov SSSR*, Moscow, 1958.

Tournefort, [Joseph] Pitton de, *Relation d'un voyage du Levant, fait par ordre du Roy*, 2 vols, Paris, 1717.

Tyler, Rev W. S., *Memoir of Rev. Henry Lobdell, M.D., late Missionary of the American Board at Mosul*, Boston, 1859.

[Ushakov, Lieut-Col. A. K.], *Istoriya voyennykh deistvy v Aziyatskoy Turtsiyi v 1828 i 1829 godakh*, 2 vols, St Petersburg, 1836.

Ussher, John, *A Journey from London to Persepolis*, London, 1865.

Vandal, Albert, *L'Odyssée d'un ambassadeur: Les voyages du marquis de Nointel (1670–1680)*, Paris, 1900.

Vil'chevsky, O., 'Ocherki po istoriyi yezidstva', *Ateist*, no. 51, April 1930, pp. 81–113.

Vosté, Jacques-M., O.P., 'Alphonse Mingana: A propos du "Catalogue of the Mingana Collection, t. III"', *Orientalia Christiana Periodica*, vol. 7, 1941, pp. 514–8.

[Wagner, Moritz], 'Mittheilungen eines deutschen Reisender aus dem russischen Armenien', *Allgemeine Zeitung*, Beilagen, 1846, no. 25, pp. 193–5; no. 27, pp. 209–10; no. 30, pp. 233–4; no. 97, pp. 769–70; no. 99, pp. 785–6; no. 112, pp. 889–91; no. 123, pp. 977–9.

Wagner, Moritz, *Reise nach dem Ararat und dem Hochland Armenien*, Stuttgart, 1848.

Wagner, Moritz, *Reise nach Persien und dem Lande der Kurden*, 2 vols, Leipzig, 1852.

Wagner, Reinhold, *Moltke und Mühlbach zusammen unter dem Halbmonde 1837–1839*, Berlin, 1893.

Wahby, Taufiq, *The Remnants of Mithraism in Hatra and Iraqi Kurdistan, and its Traces in Yazīdīsm: The Yazīdīs are not Devil-Worshippers*, London, 1962.

Wallach, Jehuda L., *Anatomie einer Militärhilfe: Die preussisch-deutschen Militärmissionen in der Türkei 1835–1919*, Düsseldorf, 1976. (Schriftenreihe des Instituts für Deutsche Geschichte, Universität Tel Aviv, vol. 1.)

Walpole, Lieut. Hon. F., *The Ansayrii, (or Assassins) with Travels in the Further East, in 1850–51*, 3 vols, London, 1851.

277

Ward, Thomas Humphry, *Humphry Sandwith: A Memoir*, London, 1884.

Warfield, William, *The Gate of Asia: A Journey from the Persian Gulf to the Black Sea*, New York, 1916.

Warkworth, Lord; see Percy.

Waterfield, Gordon, *Layard of Nineveh*, London, 1963.

Wellhausen, Julius, *Das arabische Reich und sein Sturz*, Berlin, 1902. (English translation by M. G. Weir entitled *The Arab Kingdom and its Fall*, London, 1927.)

Weygand, General [Maxime], *Histoire militaire de Mohammed Aly et de ses fils*, 2 vols, Paris, 1936.

Wiedemann, Dr M., 'Die Kurden in Nord-Mesopotamien', *Asien*, vol. 4, 1904, pp. 6–9.

Wiedemann, Dr M., 'Ibrahim Paschas Glück und Ende', *Asien*, vol. 8, 1908–9, pp. 34–7, 52–4.

W[igram], Rev W. A., 'The Shrine of the Devil-Worshippers', *QP*, no. 57, 1904, pp. 652–7.

Wigram, Rev W. A. and Wigram, Edgar T. A., *The Cradle of Mankind: Life in Eastern Kurdistan*, London, 1914.

Wild, Stefan, *Libanesische Ortsnamen*, Beirut, 1973. (Beiruter Texte und Studien, vol. 9.)

[Williams, Howard] 'HW' and Hay, Sidney, *Air over Eden*, London, 1937.

Wilson, Sir Arnold T., *Loyalties: Mesopotamia 1914–1917*, Oxford, 1930.

Wilson, Sir Arnold T., *Mesopotamia 1917–1920: A Clash of Loyalties*, Oxford, 1931.

Wilson, Rev S. G., *Persia: Western Mission*, Philadelphia, 1896.

Wilson, Major W. C. F., 'Northern 'Iraq and its Peoples', *Journal of the Royal Central Asian Society*, vol. 24, 1937, pp. 287–99.

Winstone, H. V. F., *Leachman: 'OC Desert': The Life of Lieutenant-Colonel Gerard Leachman D.S.O.*, London, 1982.

Wolff, Rev. Joseph, *Missionary Journal*, 3 vols, London, 1827–9.

Wolff, Rev. Joseph, *Researches and Missionary Labours among the Jews, Mohammedans, and other Sects, during his Travels between the Years 1831 and 1834*, London, 1835.

Wolff, Rev. Joseph, *Travels and Adventures*, 2 vols, London, 1860.

Ximénez, Saturnino, 'Au pays du Diable: une excursion chez les Yézidis', *Archives Asiatiques*, Galata, vol. 1, 1912, pp. 18–22, 74–9, 157–61.

Yanovitch, F. S., 'Ocherki Karsskoy oblasti', *SMOMPK*, vol. 34, 1904, pp. 1–181.

Yegiazarov, S. A., 'Kratky etnograficheskly ocherk kurdov Erivanskoy guberniyi', *ZKORGO*, vol. 13, 1891, pp. 1–60.

Yegiazarov, S. A., 'Kratky etnografichesko-yuridichesky ocherk yezidov Erivanskoy guberniyi', *ZKORGO*, vol. 13, 1891, pp. 171–234.

Young, George, *Corps de Droit Ottoman*, 7 vols, Oxford, 1905–6.

Young, H. E. Wilkie, 'Mosul in 1909', *Middle Eastern Studies*, vol. 7, 1971, pp. 229–35.

Z[ubare]v, 'Puteshestviye po za-Kavkazskim provintsiyam', extracts from *Tiflisskiye Vedomosti* articles reprinted in *Russky Invalid ili Voyenniya Vedomosti*, 1830, no. 216, pp. 863–4; no. 217, pp. 867–8; no. 218, pp. 871–2; no. 219, pp. 875–6. (French summary in *Nouvelles annales des voyages et des sciences géographiques*, series 2, vol. 19, 1831, pp. 354–7.)

Bibliography

Unpublished Manuscripts (listed chronologically)

Kitab al-manaqib al-shaikh 'Adi b. Musafir (Berlin MS We 1743 fols 1a–27a).

Abu 'l-Firas Ubaidallah, *Kitab al-radd 'ala 'l-rafida wa'l-Yazidiya* (Istanbul, Köprülü MS 1617 fols 49a–126b).

Ibn Tulun, *Daha'ir al-qasr* (Gotha MS 1779).

'Abd al-Ghani al-Nabulusi, *Hullat al-dahab al-abriz fi rihlat Ba'labak wa'l-Biqa' al-Aziz* (British Library, Suppl. MS 681).

Lanza, Domenico, O.P., *Compendiosa Relazione Istorica dei Viaggi fatti da Roma in Oriente dell' anno 1753 fino al 1771*; described by Thomas Bois, O.P., in 'Les Dominicains à l'avant-garde de la Kurdologie au XVIIIe siècle', *Archivum fratrum praedicatorum*, vol. 35, 1965, pp. 268–74. (Extracts published in Raphael Bidawid, *Mosul in the 18th Century, according to the Memoir of Domenico Lanza* (Arabic), Mosul, 1953.)

Ross, Dr John, *Journal*; extract from 1833 diary cited in J. Baillie Fraser, *Travels in Koordistan, Mesopotamia, &c*, London, 1840, vol. 1, pp. 67–79.

Fonclayer, Père de, S.J., study on the Yezidis written at Aleppo circa 1875, cited by Henri Lammens, S.J., 'Le massif du Ğabal Sim'an et les Yézidis de Syrie', *MFO*, vol. 2, 1907, pp. 373–94.

Glessner, J. C., *Salutation also to the Yezidees*, memorandum written circa 1950; in Presbyterian Historical Society archives.

Willoughby, Rev. James W., *Goals and Fields of Activity of the United Mission in Iraq, 1924–62*, paper written 1962; in Presbyterian Historical Society archives.

Franck, Dorothea Seelye, *Yankees from New York to the Garden of Eden*, a biography of Rev Frederic Williams written 1969–71; in Archives, Amherst College Library, Amherst, Mass.

Günel, H. Aziz, *The Yezidis in History, the Origins of the Yezidis, their Religious, Political and Social History*, Turkish text written in Istanbul 1972–79; copies of English translation by Canan Usman held by Father Aziz and by author.

Dissertations etc

Dyck, Asil Nasir, *British travel accounts on the Yazidis of northern Iraq, 1800–1850*; M.A., History and Archeology, American University of Beirut, 1974.

al-Jadaan, Khalouf A. *Caste Among the Yazidis, An Ethnic Group in Iraq*; MS, Rural Sociology, Pennsylvania State University, 1960.

Joseph, Isya, *The Yezidis — Devil Worshippers: Their Sacred Book and Traditions*; M.A., Philosophy, Columbia University, New York, 1907.

Joseph, Isya, *The Yezidis or 'Devil-Worshippers'; Their Sacred Book and Traditions*; Ph.D., Semitic Languages and History, Harvard University, 1908.

Jwaideh, Wadie, *The Kurdish Nationalist Movement: Its Origins and Development*;

Ph.D., International Relations, Syracuse University, 1960.

Landay, Bruce M., *'For the Universal Benefit of Christendom': Europeans, Ottomans, and Michel Febvre's 'Teatro della Turchia'*, essay, Department of History, Yale University, 1983.

Nebez, Jemal-eddin, *Der kurdische Fürst Mīr Muhammad-ī-Rawāndizī genannt Mīr-ī-Kōra im Spiegel der morgenländischen und abendländischen Zeugnisse*; Ph.D., University of Hamburg, 1970.

Perry, Robert P., *European exploration in Turkish Kurdistan, 1800–1842*; M.A., Arab Studies, American University of Beirut, 1965.

Miscellaneous letters and reports

Amieu, Jean, Superior of Jesuit Missions in Syria and Persia, Syrian Report for 1650, dated 16 January 1651, incl. in *Documents inédits pour servir à l'histoire du Christianisme en Orient*, ed. Antoine Rabbath, S.J., Paris, vol. 1, 1905, pp. 396–412.

Bellino, Charles, letter, 16 May 1816, to Hammer, incl. in *Fundgruben des Orients*, Vienna, vol. 5, 1816, p. 48.

Botta, P.-É., letters, 8 December 1844, 23 March 1845, and 29 June 1845, cited by Rev. Thomas Laurie, *Dr. Grant and the Mountain Nestorians*, pp. 209–11.

Chol, Ismā'īl Beg, letter, 29 August 1920, to Capt. H. W. Hutson; held by General Hutson.

al-Ghazali, letter, circa 1100, to Shaikh Abu 'l-Fath Ahmad b. Salame al-Damimi (Berlin MS Pm. 8, pp. 120–6), cited by Rudolf Frank, *Scheich 'Adî, der grosse Heilige der Jezîdîs*, pp. 42–3.

Haussknecht, C., letter, 28 August 1867, to Kiepert, incl. in Heinrich Kiepert, 'Mittheilungen von C. Haussknecht's botanischen Reisen in Kurdistan und Persien (1865–67)', *Zeitschrift der Gesellschaft für Erdkunde*, Berlin, vol. 3, 1868, pp. 465–71.

Nointel, Marquis de, despatch, 10 August 1674, to Pomponne, cited by Albert Vandal, *L'Odyssée d'un ambassadeur: Les voyages du marquis de Nointel (1670–1680)*, p. 327.

Nointel, Marquis de, despatch, 9 May 1675, to Pomponne, cited by Paul Perdrizet, 'Documents du XVIIe siècle relatifs aux Yézidis', *Bulletin de la Société de Géographie de l'Est*, 1903, pp. 291–2.

Pankratiev, Maj-Gen, report, 12 January 1829 (O.S.), to Paskievitch, cited by Dzhalile Dzhalil, *Iranskaya Filologiya*, p. 132.

Shamir, Jeremiah, letter, 28 October 1892, to Rev. A. N. Andrus, cited by Isya Joseph, 'Yezidi Texts', *AJSL*, vol. 25, 1909, p. 247.

Zverev, Comrade, report on Armenian army, 25 October 1920, reproduced in Jacques Kayaloff, *The Battle of Sardarabad*, pp. 168–9.

Miscellaneous Items from Newspapers and Periodicals

Athenaeum, London
16 July 1853 (vol. 26, p. 860): *Yezeedee Poem*. (Letter, 6 June 1853, from George Percy Badger, Aden, Arabia Felix).

Bibliography

Daily Item, Port Chester, New York
6 February 1923: *Isya Joseph* (report of death and obituary).

Daily Tribune, New York
26 February 1853: *Visit to the Ruins of Nineveh — Explorations of Layard, &c.*
(Letter, 20 November 1852, from H. Lobdell, Mosul, Mesopotamia).
26 March 1853: *Visit to the Shrine of the Devil Worshippers, &c.* (Letter, 1 December
1852, from H.L., Mosul).
21 May 1853: *The Great Festival of the Devil Worshippers and their Doctrines.*
(Letter, 14 January 1853, from H.L., Mosul.)

Free Lance, Fredericksburg, Virginia
8 February 1923: *Dropped Dead: Izra Joseph, An Assyrian, Succumbs To Sudden
Heart Attack While At R.R. Station Here.*

Illustrated London News
13 January 1912: *The Queen and Lucifer-Worshippers: Her Majesty and a Treasure.*

Journal des Débats, Paris
8 September 1843: (Translation of Istanbul despatch, 17 August 1843, to *Morning
Chronicle* and *Globe*, London, regarding Nestorian massacres and role of
missionaries).

Il Mediterraneo, Malta
21 August 1839: Article including extracts from letter by Christian Rassam on battle
of Nisib.

Morning Chronicle, London
5 September 1843: The Levant Mail. (Istanbul correspondent despatch, 17 August
1843, regarding Nestorian massacres and role of missionaries.) Reprinted same day
by *Globe*.

New York Times
22 June 1919: (Section III): *Division of Turkey.* (Letter, 19 June 1919, from Isya
Joseph, Port Chester, N.Y.)

Observer, New York
7 October 1843: *Massacre of the Nestorians.* (Reprints *Morning Chronicle* article,
5 September 1843.)
27 January 1844: *Causes of the Nestorian Massacre.* (Letter, 16 October 1843, from
A. Grant, Mosul, Mesopotamia.)

Tiflissky Listok
20 February 1909 (O.S.): *Glava Yezidov.* (Ismail Beg's meeting with the Viceroy.)

The Times, London

24 October 1867: Report of Matilda Rassam death, 21 September 1867, at Aleppo.

11 January 1909: *The Downfall of Ibrahim Pasha.* (Special correspondent despatch, November 1908, from Mardin.)

8 July 1912: *A Sacred Peacock: Gift to the British Museum.*

16 July 1912: *The Sacred Peacock of the Yezidis.* (Letter, 11 July 1912, from Athelstan Riley, London.)

16 May 1914: *Devil-Worship at Mosul: Government Recognition.* (Istanbul correspondent despatch, 5 May 1914.)

26–29 August 1924: *Minorities of Mosul.* (Articles by special correspondent H. C. Luke, incl. two articles on Yezidis.)

21 April 1925: *Air action against Yezidi Chief.* (Colonial Office report of attack on Daud b. Daud.)

26 October 1935: *Devil Worshippers' Revolt: Punitive Operations in Iraq.* (Baghdad correspondent despatch, 25 October 1935.)

La Turquie, Istanbul

23 March 1909: *Une nouvelle communauté.* (Ismail Beg's petition to the Grand Vizier.)

Chol Family Genealogy

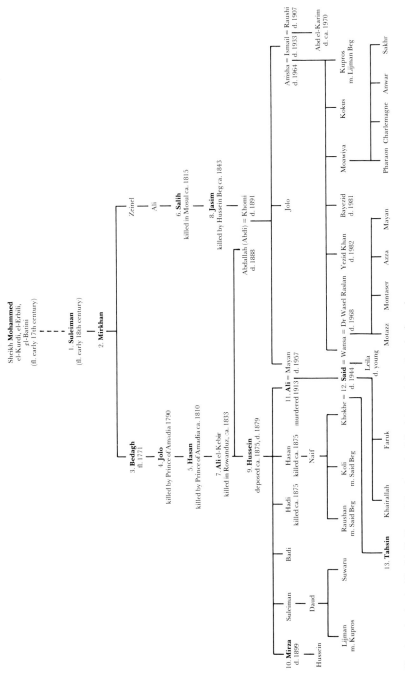

The princes who reigned as Mirs of the Sheikhan are italics; the numbers before their names indicate the order of succession.

Index

Page numbers followed by 'n' refer to footnotes, those followed by 'c' refer to chapter notes.

Rabban Hormuzd monastery, 10, 60–1,
122, 145, 157, 234c; Jeremiah Shamir
at, 107–8; Kartsov and Browski at,
124; Lobdell and Rassam visit,
109–10; monks killed by Kör
Mohammed, 65; raided, 84
railways, 126, 138, 139, 161, 163, 171,
172, 174, 191
Rashid Ali el-Gilani, 184
Rassam, Antun, 67
Rassam, Christian *see* Rassam, Isa
Antun
Rassam, Hormuzd, 93, 94, 100, 101,
102, 106, 132
Rassam, Isa Antun, 66–8; Ainsworth
and, 70–1; appeal to Archbishop of
Canterbury, 115; attends autumn
feast, 101–2, 109–10, 112; Bowen and
Sandreczki visit, 106; CMS and, 106,
138n; Euphrates expedition, 68–70;
friendship with Yezidis, 99, 103–4,
113, 116, 117; Hussein Beg and, 116;
Ince Bairaktar and, 82, 88, 90, 115;
Jeremiah Shamir and, 108;
Kurdistan exploration, 75–6, 80–1;
letters of, 207–10; offers to mediate
with Bedr Khan Beg, 98; ransoms
hostages, 92, 93; Sheikh Nasr and,
111; vice-consul in Mosul, 82–3,
90–1, 115; Yezdanshir's surrender,
114
Rassam, Matilda (formerly Badger),
76, 81, 90, 104, 105, 109, 114, 235c
Rassam, Theresa, 67
Rassam, Yousif, 247c
Rauf Pasha, 117
Rayevsky, General, 62
Redwan, 61, 80, 100, 101n, 113, 168, 188
Reed, George, 165
Reshid Pasha (governor of Baghdad),
113
Reshid Pasha (grand vizier in 1832), 61,
63, 69, 78, 126, 165, 187
Reshid Pasha (grand vizier in 1849), 99,
102, 103, 207, 209–10
Resul (brother of Kör Mohammed), 112
Resul (Kurdish chief), 101
Revelation, Book of see Kitab el-Jelwa
Revelation of the Skills of Solitude, The,
19

Rich, Claudius James, 59, 60, 109, 157
Rich, Mary, 157
Richards, W. S., 123
Riley, Athelstan, 125, 166, 237–8c
'Rob Roy of Kurdistan' *see* Khan
Mahmud
Rowanduz, 3, 64, 69, 81, 85, 112, 171;
Ali Beg sent to, 65
Royal Geographical Society, 75, 80
Royal Library (Berlin), 142, 155
Royal Library of the Assyrian Kings,
104
'Royal Road', 2
Rukn ed-Din Kilij Arslan IV, 21, 22
Russia, 61, 62, 119–20, 161, 170, 172;
1921 treaty, 191–2; Brest-Litovsk
treaty, 190, 191; *see also*
Transcaucasia
Russian Ministry of Public Education,
90
Russian Orthodox Church, 161
Rycaut, Sir Paul, 53–4, 102

Sabaeans, 10
Sachau, Eduard, 120, 123n, 142, 144n,
154
Sacheli (Sachelié) tribe, 47, 53, 55
sacred books, 32–3, 102, 122, 124,
199–210; publication of, 141–58, 173;
see also Meshaf Resh and Sheikh Adi
Hymn
sacred objects, 160; promise of return,
164, 165–6, 169; stolen from Lalish,
131; *see also* sanjaks
Safar Beg, 248c
Safr Aga, 166, 244c, 245c
Said Beg, 179–80, 194; death, 184;
Gertrude Bell and, 159–60; guardian
of, 167; Leachman, Nalder and,
174–5; sanjaks and, 168–9, 175, 179,
181; Wansa and, 181–2, 183
Saif ed-Din, 79
de Saint-Aignan *see* Jean-Baptiste de
Saint-Aignan, Père
de Saint-Élie *see* Anastase Marie de
Saint-Élie, Père
Saladin, 19
Salih Beg, 60, 224c, 225c
Samarra, 171, 172
Šammas Eremia Šamir, 152

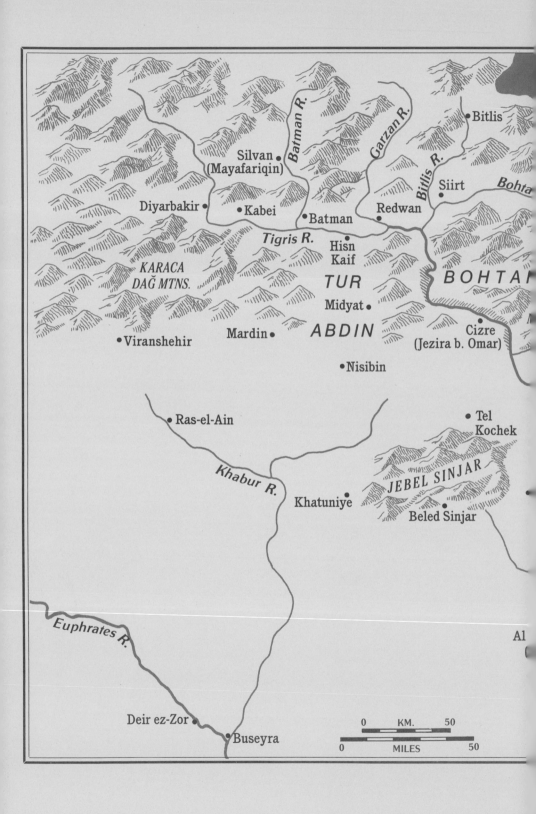

Bitlis

Silvan
(Mayafariqin)

Batman R.

Garzan R.

Bitlis R.

Bohta

Diyarbakir

Kabei

Batman

Redwan

Siirt

Tigris R.

Hisn
Kaif

TUR

BOHTA

KARACA
DAĞ MTNS.

Midyat

ABDIN

Cizre
(Jezira b. Omar)

Viranshehir

Mardin

Nisibin

Ras-el-Ain

Tel
Kochek

Khabur R.

JEBEL SINJAR

Khatuniye

Beled Sinjar

Euphrates R.

Al

Deir ez-Zor

Buseyra

0   KM.   50

0   MILES   50